T0326334

PEOPLE, MARKETS, GOODS:
ECONOMIES AND SOCIETIES IN HISTORY
Volume 20

Family Firms in Postwar Britain and Germany

People, Markets, Goods:
Economies and Societies in History

ISSN: 2051-7467

The interactions of economy and society, people and goods, transactions and actions are at the root of most human behaviours. Economic and social historians are participants in the same conversation about how markets have developed historically and how they have been constituted by economic actors and agencies in various social, institutional and geographical contexts. New debates now underpin much research in economic and social, cultural, demographic, urban and political history. Their themes have enduring resonance – financial stability and instability, the costs of health and welfare, the implications of poverty and riches, flows of trade and the centrality of communications. This paperback series aims to attract historians interested in economics and economists with an interest in history by publishing high quality, cutting edge academic research in the broad field of economic and social history from the late medieval/early modern period to the present day. It encourages the interaction of qualitative and quantitative methods through both excellent monographs and collections offering path-breaking overviews of key research concerns. Taking as its benchmark international relevance and excellence it is open to scholars and subjects of any geographical areas from the case study to the multi-nation comparison.

PREVIOUSLY PUBLISHED TITLES IN THE SERIES
ARE LISTED AT THE BACK OF THIS VOLUME

Family Firms in Postwar Britain and Germany

Competing Approaches to Business

David Paulson

THE BOYDELL PRESS

First published 2023
The Boydell Press, Woodbridge

ISBN 978-1-78327-758-2

The Boydell Press is an imprint of Boydell & Brewer Ltd
PO Box 9, Woodbridge, Suffolk IP12 3DF, UK
and of Boydell & Brewer Inc.
668 Mt Hope Avenue, Rochester, NY 14620–2731, USA
website: www.boydellandbrewer.com

A catalogue record for this book is available
from the British Library

Pour Joëlle
Qui fait briller le soleil

Contents

List of Figures   ix

Acknowledgements   xi

List of Abbreviations and Note on Translations   xiii

1. Introduction   I

PART ONE: OPERATING CONTEXTS

Prologue   21

2. Culture, Community, and Continuity   28

3. Banking   38

4. Recruitment and Training   63

PART TWO: COMPANY CASE STUDIES

Prologue   III

5. Chr. Wandel KG, Reutlingen   115

6. Kenrick & Jefferson Ltd., West Bromwich   142

7. Julius Schneider GmbH & Co. KG, Ludwigsburg   169

8. Braithwaite & Co. (Engineers) Ltd., West Bromwich   199

9. RECARO GmbH & Co., Stuttgart   232

10. Jensen Motors Ltd., West Bromwich   264

11. Conclusion – A Better Way of Doing Business?   290

Bibliography   303

Index   332

Figures

1	Apprenticeships, Britain and West Germany, 1950–88	66
2	Sketch for *Industriemeister* Training Programme, 1950	84
3	*Meister* Kurt Wagenknecht with his Karosserie Reutter Work Team	88
4	Enrolments at Baden-Württemberg Institutions and the University of Birmingham	99
5	Extract from Study Plan – Civil Engineering, Technische Hochschule Stuttgart, 1910–11	101
6	Extract from Schedule of Lectures and Exercises – Mechanical Engineering, Technische Hochschule Stuttgart, 1948	103
7	Career Destinations, 1950 Science and Engineering Graduates, the University of Birmingham	104–05
8	Chr. Wandel KG, Sales Performance 1949–70	126–27
9	Chr. Wandel KG, Sales Performance 1975–83	137
10	Kenrick & Jefferson Ltd., Nominal vs. Real Growth, 1949–79	167
11	Julius Schneider KG, Output and Sales, 1949–67	180
12	Julius Schneider KG, Output and Sales, 1967–75	189
13	Julius Schneider KG, Progression of Turnover, Personnel Costs, Materials, Overheads, 1966–75	191
14	Julius Schneider KG, Sales Turnover, 1910–18, 1931–75	192
15	Julius Schneider KG, Production Output, 1929–75	192
16	Braithwaite & Co. Engineers Ltd., Workforce Composition	212
17	Rates of Wage Increase, Britain, 1968–70	213
18	State Steel Price Increases, 1967–70	218
19	Braithwaite & Co. Engineers Ltd., Financial Performance in Nominal Terms, 1972–81	226
20	Advertisement for RECARO Sports Seats, 1964	250

21   Passenger Vehicle Production and Annual GDP Growth, West
     Germany, 1955–73   258
22   Jensen Motors Ltd., Key Production Data, 1957–58   267

Full credit details are provided in the captions to the images in the text. The author and publisher are grateful to all the institutions and individuals for permission to reproduce the materials in which they hold copyright. Every effort has been made to trace the copyright holders; apologies are offered for any omission, and the publisher will be pleased to add any necessary acknowledgement in subsequent editions.

Acknowledgements

During the course of my research I have incurred many obligations. I have been particularly aided by the staff of the following archives, to whom I offer my thanks: Frau Christina Hackl, Statistisches Landesamt Baden-Württemberg; Frau Regina Witzman at Stadtarchiv Ludwigsburg; Frau Sigrid Bratzke at Landesarchiv Baden_Württemberg in Ludwigsburg; Frau Andrea Daeuwel-Bernd at Stadtbibliothek Reutlingen; and most especially Herr Thorsten Maentel and colleagues at Wirtschaftsarchiv Baden-Württemberg, Stuttgart-Hohenheim. In the UK, I am indebted to the staff of Coventry History Centre; the staff of the Modern Records Centre at the University of Warwick; Helen Fisher at the Cadbury Research Library, University of Birmingham; Cori Dales at Teesside Archives, Middlesbrough; Frances Pond at Birmingham City University Archives; Dawn Southgate at the Chartered Institute of Marketing; Anne Archer and Karen Sampson at Lloyds Banking Group Archives; Sarah Kinsey and Jemma Lee at HSBC Group Archives; the staff of Cambridge University Library; Jayne Ringrose of Pembroke College, Cambridge; the archivist of Harrow School, and most particularly to Maureen Waldron and colleagues at Sandwell Archives in Smethwick.

Among the business community, I received help from Hugh Jefferson, Ivan Walker, and Jeremy Plimmer, who all kindly gave their time to be interviewed about Kenrick & Jefferson Ltd. Herr Martin Putsch, owner of RECARO Holding GmbH, graciously gave me permission to meet his staff and consult documents in the company's archives, and talked to me about his business, as did Dr. Mark Hiller, CEO of RECARO Aircraft Seating. Herr Frank Jung, former Head of Tradition at RECARO Holding GmbH and now Head of the Historic Archive at Porsche AG, has been extraordinarily helpful and supportive. Professor Heinz-Theo Wagner of the German Graduate School of Management and Law (GGS), Heilbronn, kindly met me to discuss RECARO and the Mittelstand. John Saynor was very supportive in allowing me to interview him about his career at Lloyds Bank and sharing his personal archive. I also acknowledge with thanks and respect the many former business colleagues, suppliers, customers and competitors whose example made me keep trying to be a better manager.

Within the academic community, I have received tremendously kind support from lots of people. Professor Alan Cassels of McMaster University taught me history and supported my doctoral plans, as did the late, great Robert Johnston. I began my first Ph.D. study at Harvard University a long time ago. Charles Maier of Harvard very kindly offered me his support on restarting it at Cambridge, as did fellow Harvard doctoral student Frank Trentmann. Kevin Cramer has been an inspiration since we started together there. At Cambridge, William Brown of Darwin College responded to my first email enquiry with a helpful meeting, and an introduction to Paul Ryan, who was a huge help in getting started. I was also assisted by Adrian Williamson, Adrian Leonard, Tae-Hoon Kim, Colin Chamberlain and especially by Duncan Needham. Alessa Witt of Edinburgh University aided me on my Mittelstand thinking, as did Jeff Fear, Hartmut Berghoff and Lutz Raphael. Lucy Newton and Peter Scott of Reading, and John Wilson, now of Northumbria, and Anna Tilba, now of Durham, kindly offered me teaching experience and general support. At Queen's University Belfast John Turner has been constantly supportive, as have many other great colleagues. At Boydell & Brewer, Michael Middeke and Elizabeth Howard have been patient guides, and I thank them and their anonymous readers for all their help. Particular thanks have to go to Martin Daunton, who has been the most supportive, patient, and inspirational mentor imaginable; I cannot thank him and Claire enough.

Within my family Claude Cossette has provided ongoing academic inspiration for forty years. Dennis Whittaker has offered me contemporary recollections and commented on various drafts. My parents have been a constant source of support, as have our children Emanuelle, Gabriel, Lily and William. But I owe most to my wife Joëlle. This work, like everything else, is for her.

Abbreviations and Note on Translations

A	*Akte* / file
AG	*Aktiengesellschaft* / Public Limited Company
B	*Bestand* / archival group
Bü	*Büschel* / bundle (e.g. *WABW B79/Bü198* indicates a document from Bundle 198 in archive 79, that of Chr. Wandel KG, in the Wirtschaftsarchiv Baden-Württemberg).
GmbH	*Gesellschaft mit beschränkter Haftung* / Limited Liability Company
KG	*Kommanditgeschellschaft* / Limited Partnership
Ltd.	Limited Liability Company
MRC	Modern Records Centre, Warwick University.
nd	No date.
Sandwell	Sandwell Community History and Archive Service, Smethwick.
TNA	The National Archives, Kew.
WABW	Wirtschaftsarchiv Baden-Württemberg, Hohenheim.

Translations are my own unless otherwise stated.

Introduction

Why Study the German Mittelstand?

This book began not as an academic study but as a personal investigation into a vexing business issue: why was it so difficult for me, the managing director of a small British manufacturing business, to compete against my German counterparts? Was the problem largely to do with my capabilities as a business leader, or were the differences between companies like mine and our German competitors more fundamental and wide-reaching? Could we make rapid changes that would make us more competitive, or were we battling against strengths that had deep historical roots? I set out to find the answers to these questions through an investigation, started while I was still leading the manufacturing company, of German and British approaches to business in the decades following the end of the Second World War. By reconstructing the histories of six companies, three in each country, and the environments in which they operated, I wanted to understand how small and medium-sized, family-controlled manufacturing companies in specific industries in each country had approached the challenge of achieving sustainable business growth. In Germany, these were companies which defined themselves as part of the so-called *Mittelstand*, family-owned firms with strong ties to the communities in which they originated and remain anchored, all long-term in their thinking and each specialising in high-value niche products for global markets. Throughout Germany's postwar history, their experienced leaders have supposedly sustained their commitment to *Made In Germany* quality (a commitment so ubiquitous that it has created a national brand) by continual investment in workforce skills and product design excellence: theirs was, and continues to be, a long-term, socially responsible approach to business. In contrast, British companies' managers, supposedly more short-lived and with less technical expertise, are assumed to have concentrated on maximising short-term profits rather than on making long-term investments to deliver superior products. Were these stereotypes true? And if they were, what was it that made the *Mittelstand*'s approach so distinctive?

Since Germany's post-unification economic challenges of the 1990s, doubts have sometimes been expressed about the continuing relevance of the

Mittelstand model.[1] Some sceptics have seen it as "an endangered species",[2] a potential weakness in the German economy because of firms' succession worries[3] and their inability to agree to cooperate with each other in the face of strengthening external competition[4] even while they are facing "the Grim Reaper".[5] Historian Hartmut Berghoff argued in 2006 that recent decades had shown that "the classic Mittelstand was suffering from a number of limitations that are often drowned out by the chorus of praise to its achievements."[6] Markets had been changing, as had social norms, affecting traditional family and career patterns. Companies faced internal and external challenges: involving non-family managers, changing financing, increasing international engagements, managing family succession. Mittelstand values remained fundamentally important, but adaptation was required to effect the transition from "classic to modern Mittelstand".[7]

Other commentators have been more positive, they would say with good reason. The Mittelstand's ongoing contribution has been critical to Germany's postwar economic success. In 2019 it accounted for 99.6% of all German companies, 82.2% of trainees, 59.4% of jobs and 36.8% of total corporate turnover,[8] justifying its identification as the "Mighty *Mittelstand*"[9] as a "booming" powerhouse growing faster than China's economy,[10] or as "the

1   See for example Herbert Giersch, Karl-Heinz Paqué, and Holger Schmiedling, *The Fading Miracle: Four Decades of Market Economy in Germany* (Cambridge, 1992); Stephen Broadberry and Mary O'Mahony, 'Britain's Productivity Gap with the United States and Europe: A Historical Perspective', *National Institute Economic Review*, 189 (2004), p. 80.
2   Deutsche Bank Research, *Germany's Mittelstand – an endangered species?* (2007).
3   Deutsche Bank Research, *Germany's Mittelstand – an endangered species?* (2007).
4   Philip Cooke, Kevin Morgan and Adam Price, *The Future of the Mittelstand: Collaboration versus Competition* (Cardiff, 1993), p. 2.
5   *The Economist* (16 December 1995), 57–58, cited in Harmut Berghoff, 'The End of Family Business? The Mittelstand and German Capitalism in Transition, 1949–2000', *Business History Review*, 80.2 (June 2006), 264.
6   Berghoff, 'The End of Family Business?', p. 282.
7   Berghoff, 'The End of Family Business?', pp. 285–95.
8   Federal Ministry for Economics Affairs and Energy, 'The German Mittelstand: Facts and Figures about German SMEs' (2019) <https://www.bmwi.de/Redaktion/EN/Publikationen/wirtschaftsmotor-mittelstand-zahlen-und-fakten-zu-den-deutschen-kmu.pdf?__blob=publicationFile&v=4> [accessed 20 February 2019]. Data refers to companies with fewer than 500 employees.
9   Brian Blackstone and Vanessa Fuhrmans, 'The Engines of Growth: Forget the Familiar Big Global Brands. Germany's Economy Is Powered by a Legion of Smaller Companies.', *Wall Street Journal*, 27 June (2011).
10   'Germany's Mittelstand – Beating China', *The Economist* (30 July 2011) [accessed 4 December 2011].

Wunder in Germany's post-war *Wirtschaftswunder*".[11] In a celebrated *Harvard Business Review* article, Hermann Simon brought lessons from the Mittelstand's "hidden champions", little-known German SMEs that held dominant positions in multiple world markets, to a wider audience.[12] Simon analysed thirty-nine Mittelstand companies, which he said shared five common practices: strategic focus combined with geographic diversity; an emphasis on customer value; a reliance on their own technical competence; blending technology with closeness to customers; and creating mutual interdependence between the company and its employees.[13] He demonstrated that their commitment to product quality, innovation and investment in staff capability had made it possible for almost all of the thirty-nine firms to achieve first place in world rankings in their own niche industry. The Mittelstand could therefore justifiably be seen, Simon and other commentators suggested, as an economic model which other countries should emulate if they too wanted to become the "hidden champions" of world markets.[14] Their enthusiasm for the German approach seemed warranted: in 2012, Mittelstand firms led 1 307 world niche markets. British firms, in contrast, led 67.[15]

British politicians searching for improved national productivity have been fascinated by the Mittelstand and its apparent achievements. In 2014, for example, Britain's Trade Minister opened a conference to which business leaders had been invited to come and "Meet the Mittelstand", impressing upon his audience "the importance of a strong UK Mittelstand in rebalancing the UK economy".[16] Conservative politician Michael Heseltine's *No Stone Unturned in Pursuit of Growth* highlighted elements of the German economic

---

11   *The Economist, Mittelstand or Mittelfall?*, 17 October 1998, referenced in Entrepreneurship and Innovation course notes, Judge School of Business (2011) [accessed 4 November 2012].

12   Hermann Simon, 'Lessons from Germany's Midsize Giants', *Harvard Business Review* (March-April 1992), 115–123.

13   Simon, 'Lessons', 116.

14   See for example Herman Simon, 'You Don't Have To Be German To Be A "Hidden Champion"', *Business Strategy Review*, 7.2 (1996); Blackstone and Fuhrmans, 'The Engines of Growth'; 'Germany's Mittelstand – Beating China', *The Economist* (30 July 2011), 59; Olaf Storbeck Waldachtal, 'Mittelstand Celebrated as Hidden Champions', *The Financial Times* (London, 17 October 2018), p. 13.

15   Federal Ministry for Economics Affairs and Energy, *The German Mittelstand: Engine of the German Economy* (Berlin, 2014), p. 8. <https://www.bmwi.de/Redaktion/EN/Publikationen/wirtschaftsmotor-mittelstand-zahlen-und-fakten-zu-den-deutschen-kmu.html> [Data drawn from the Deutsche Weltmarktführer database 2.3.1, survey of 29 June 2012].

16   'Meet the Mittelstand: How German Mid-Sized Companies Went Global | All-Party Parliamentary Manufacturing Group' <https://www.policyconnect.org.uk/apmg/events/meet-mittelstand-how-german-mid-sized-companies-went-global> [accessed 16 February 2019].

model which British managers and policymakers should follow.[17] Labour Party leader Jeremy Corbyn wanted "to see a new, co-operatively owned 'British Mittelstand' created: high-investment, high-productivity smaller firms that provide high-quality employment in those sectors where we have the greatest potential: digital technology, healthcare, high-value added manufacturing."[18] Others have shared their enthusiasm. The Confederation of British Industry's leader wanted the UK "to have its own version of the German 'Mittelstand' – a backbone of medium-sized firms which export, innovate and generate growth."[19] At a regional level, "a version of what the Germans refer to as the Mittelstand" has been promoted as the solution to the economic woes of the West Midlands.[20] For Britain's mid-size company owners, *The Daily Telegraph* presented the Mittelstand as the source of "secrets of growth",[21] while Labour peer Stewart Wood urged the post-Brexit British Government to look to the Mittelstand and Germany as "the gold standard for a high-productivity economy".[22]

What *Is* The Mittelstand?

Given its global reputation and the enthusiasm of British decision-makers to copy it, it made sense in this study to review the origins of the Mittelstand's particular characteristics, and to use them as a lens through which to view both Mittelstand firms themselves and the British companies with which we are comparing them. But what *is* the Mittelstand, and how should it be defined?

---

17   Michael Heseltine, *No Stone Unturned In Pursuit of Growth* (London, October 2012).

18   Jeremy Corbyn, 'Reckless Tories Wandered into Brexit - Now They Are Scurrying Away from the Mess', *Labour List* (2016) <https://labourlist.org/2016/09/jeremy-corbyn-reckless-tories-wandered-into-brexit-now-they-are-scurrying-away-from-the-mess/> [accessed 31 July 2019].

19   Helen Power, 'Britain's Forgotten Army of Firms Must March like the Germans, Says Cridland', *The Times* (London, 24 October 2011), p. 47, The Times Digital Archive.

20   Steven McCabe, 'Exploring the Realities of Manufacturing in Birmingham', *Birmingham Post* (Birmingham, 3 February 2014), Online edition <https://www.birminghampost.co.uk/business/business-opinion/steven-mccabe-exploring-realities-manufacturing-6663271> [accessed 16 February 2019].

21   Marion Dakers, 'Secrets of Growth: The Power of Germany's Mittelstand', *The Telegraph* (11 May 2017) <https://www.telegraph.co.uk/connect/small-business/driving-growth/secrets-growth-power-of-germany-mittelstand/> [accessed 15 February 2019]; also cited in: 'Diagnose Mittelstand - Winter 2018' (Finanzgruppe Deutscher Sparkassen- und Giroverband, 18AD), p. 16 <https://www.dsgv.de/sparkassen-finanzgruppe/publikationen/diagnose-mittelstand.html> [accessed 14 February 2019].

22   Stewart Wood, 'Why Brexit Britain Should Embrace a European-Style Economic Model', *New Statesman* (2021) <https://www.newstatesman.com/world/europe/2021/10/why-brexit-britain-should-embrace-a-european-style-economic-model> [accessed 31 December 2021].

Originally referring to a middling class of the self-employed, entrepreneurs, and owners of small businesses, the term Mittelstand is now understood to refer to a specific section of German (as well as Austrian and Swiss) business, made up mostly of small and medium-sized enterprises (SMEs) which have remained in private ownership. The European Union has a specific definition of SMEs: they are companies with fewer than 250 employees, less than €50 million in turnover, and with an annual balance sheet value of less than €43 million.[23] The longstanding definition of the Institute for Mittelstand Research (IfM) in Bonn was slightly different, allowing German SMEs up to five hundred employees and €50 million Euros in turnover.[24]

In the study that follows, we will not be restricted to these numerical desig-nations (even though the companies we examine would have been included within them at some, or every, point in their history) because it is clear that the Mittelstand is about much more than a statistical categorisation. The IFM cites the architect of Germany's postwar economic miracle, Ludwig Erhard, who in 1954 insisted that the Mittelstand was not something which could easily be defined in material terms. It was, rather, something to be understood by reference to its members' ethos, attitudes, and mindset.[25] A contemporary commen-tator described the Mittelstand of forty years later as "a phenomenon without definition", that nevertheless had distinctive attributes – such as creativity, independence, a willingness to take risks and to put company owners' own capital at risk – which were widely understood by all political, economic, and institutional actors in Germany.[26] To these attributes historian Jeff Fear adds the emotional commitment to the business of the owning family, an attachment to their region, a patriarchal culture that enables a sense of independence and 'family', and a commitment to achieving excellence in particular niche products.[27] Hartmut Berghoff points as well to Mittelstand leaders' commitment

23 Industry Directorate-General for Internal Market, *User Guide to the SME Definition* (LU: Publications Office of the European Union, 2020), p. 10 <https://data.europa.eu/doi/10.2873/255862> [accessed 5 August 2022].

24 'IfM Bonn: KMU Definition Des IfM Bonn' (Institut für Mittelstandsforschung, 2014) < https://www.ifm-bonn.org/definitionen-/kmu-definition-des-ifm-bonn/> [accessed 5 August 2022].

25 'IfM Bonn: Mittelstandsdefinition Des IfM Bonn' (Institut für Mittelstandsforschung, 2019) <https://www.ifm-bonn.org/definitionen/mittelstandsdefinition-des-ifm-bonn/> [accessed 14 February 2019].

26 Susanne Ensser, 'Die Bedeutung Der Treuhandanstalt Für Die Wiederbelebung Des Industriellen Mittelstandes in Den Neuen Bundesländern: Eine Ordnungspolitische Betrachtung', *Schriften Zur Wirtschafts- Und Sozialgeschichte* (Berlin, 1998), BAND 53, pp. 34–36.

27 Jeffrey Fear, 'Straight Outta Oberberg: Transforming Mid-Sized Family Firms Into Global Champions 1970–2010', *Jahrbuch Für Wirtschaftsgeschichte*, 2012.1 (2012), 125–68 (p. 129).

to focused, long-term strategies, to generational continuity, and to independence.[28] All these definitions are echoed and validated in a recent publication by the national *Sparkasse* organisation, bankers to the Mittelstand for decades. It defines the Mittelstand as those "enterprises that are characterised, on the one hand, by close ties to their region and their employees and, on the other hand, by high-quality, competitive goods produced for the world market. These enterprises provide local training and employment opportunities and, at the same time, global sources of income."[29]

It is important to note that those attitudes have persisted even as companies have increased their sales and the size of their workforce: there are many Mittelstand companies which have outgrown definitions based on business size but remain members of the Mittelstand because their founding mentality and attitude persist, as we will see with RECARO below. In acknowledging this reality, the IfM has recently changed its definition: a Mittelstand company is now considered to be one in which up to two living people or members of their family own, directly or indirectly, at least 50% of the shares, and participate in its management. Consequently, "the meanings of Mittelstand, family business, owner-managed business, and family-managed business are, according to the IfM's definition, to be seen as synonyms."[30] This is an important correction. After all, a company which has been owned and operated by the same family according to the same philosophy since its inception cannot become "another kind" of company simply by growing: if an owner-manager believes that the "task I took over from my father is to successfully prepare the company for the future, to secure existing jobs and create new ones" and he "counts in decades rather than quarters", then his remains a Mittelstand company, even when it has grown to have 5,000 staff and revenues of €800 million.[31]

German and British Approaches to Business

It is helpful at this point to consider briefly some of the scholarship on approaches to business in Britain and Germany as an aid to understanding similarities and differences in philosophy and practice. The distinction between German and British business organisation and performance was most famously made by the American business historian Alfred D. Chandler in his seminal *Scale and Scope: The Dynamics of Industrial Capitalism*. Analysing the evolution of

---

28   Berghoff, 'The End of Family Business?', 272–75.
29   Finanzgruppe Deutscher Sparkassen- und Giroverband, p. 16. Also published as 'SME Diagnosis', in which all page and paragraph locations and URL are identical.
30   'IfM Bonn: Mittelstandsdefinition Des IfM Bonn'.
31   Olaf Storbeck Waldachtal; the article refers to Fischer: 'Fischer Group' (2019) <https://www.fischer.group/de-de> [accessed 16 February 2019].

managerial capitalism and the modern industrial enterprise in both countries and the United States after 1870, Chandler argues that economies of scale allowed the large organisations he studied to produce ever-increasing amounts of product at ever-reducing cost, affording them the opportunity to exploit economies of scope to market and distribute different products through the same facilities.[32] He examines the generic approach of each country as well as specific performance in several key industries, concluding that success was derived from a "three-pronged investment" by entrepreneurs in manufacturing, marketing, and management.[33]

Chandler criticises British business performance, which was limited by the persistence of what he calls "personal capitalism".[34] Unlike German and American enterprises, most British companies failed to make adequate "three-pronged" investments and failed to install adequate management organisations, preferring to retain family control.[35] They were motivated by a desire to preserve "a steady flow of cash to owners" and "a large and stable income for the family" rather than committing, as their American counterparts did, to "long-term profit and growth".[36] In Germany, entrepreneurs behaved differently. They quickly recruited professional managers and also made early investments in manufacturing and marketing, in what Chandler calls "cooperative managerial capitalism". From the outset, German manufacturers differentiated themselves from the Americans by concentrating on manufacturing products for producers rather than for consumers. They aligned themselves with Germany's universities and technical schools, far more advanced than those in Britain, and involved financial institutions from the beginning in their determination to invest in the appropriate asset base.

Chandler's work has dominated subsequent debate, attracting both praise[37] and criticism.[38] For the purposes of this book, it offers some useful guidance

32   Alfred D. Chandler, *Scale and Scope: The Dynamics of Industrial Capitalism* (Cambridge, 1994). See chapter 2, 'Scale, Scope, and Organizational Capabilities', especially p. 31.

33   Chandler, *Scale and Scope*, p. 8.

34   Chandler, *Scale and Scope*, pp. 235–37.

35   See for example, Chandler, *Scale and Scope*, pp. 262, 273, 275.

36   Chandler, *Scale and Scope*, p. 390.

37   For example, David Teece argues that *Scale and Scope* "ought to influence, if not shape, the research agenda for work in business history, industrial organization, the theory of the firm, and economic change for decades to come": David J. Teece, 'The Dynamics of Industrial Capitalism: Perspectives on Alfred Chandler's Scale and Scope', in *Management Innovation: Essays in the Spirit of Alfred D. Chandler, Jr*, ed. by William Lazonick and David J. Teece (Oxford, 2012), p. 30.

38   In Gary Herrigel and Jonathan Zeitlin, 'Alternatives to Varieties of Capitalism', *The Business History Review*, 84.4 (2010), 667–74 (p. 667) [accessed 28 May 2019], the authors call for a move away from Chandler's thinking: "to contribute fruitfully to the understanding

for examining the companies under review: the "three-pronged investment" is necessary in any industrial business, after all. But in comparing British SMEs and the Mittelstand, accepting that Chandler's conclusions have universal validity is problematic. *Scale and Scope* is US-centric; it focuses exclusively on huge corporations, the largest 200 manufacturing firms in core industries in each country, whereas we are only concerned with much smaller enterprises; it is dismissive of personal capitalism within family-managed firms.[39] Nevertheless, the weight of Chandler's authority and the widespread acceptance of his conclusions demand consideration of his arguments. In the analysis which follows I argue that our smaller firms did make the appropriate "three-pronged investments", and show that while Chandler's concerns about personal capitalism are valid in some instances, they are an inappropriate summary of the family-dominated organisations we will review.

The German 'System'
The work of the American political economist Gary Herrigel is an important aid to understanding how smaller companies than those considered by Chandler operated during the period of our study. In his examination of "the sources of Germany's industrial power" he places "dynamic regional systems" of SMEs in their rightful position at its centre, alongside the great industrial concerns that captivated Chandler. Herrigel identifies the Mittelstand[40] as the "decentralized form of industrial order", initially thriving in parallel with larger companies rather than being subordinate to them.[41] He depicts a dense network of relationships between small enterprises that grew out of a tradition of independent smallholder property and craft skills, financed by locally funded savings banks, and centred on certain regions including Baden-Württemberg.[42] In other regions, where the network of supportive SME suppliers was less strong, larger corporations formed what Herrigel calls the "autarkic form of industrial order", incorporating most of the stages of manufacture under their own control.

---

of the variety-producing dynamics of capitalist development, business historians need to shed – if they have not done so already – the old Chandlerian paradigm of a teleological hierarchy among global business systems, where the best and most competitive paths lead in the direction that the United States has already traversed."

39   Chandler, *Scale and Scope*, p. 10.

40   My term: Herrigel seldom uses the word Mittelstand in this or other works himself, other than to refer to "the industrial Mittelstand" as an aggregate concept, referring instead to small firms.

41   Gary Herrigel, *Industrial Constructions: The Sources of German Industrial Power* (Cambridge, 1996), pp. 19–20.

42   Also examined, with reference to Herrigel, by Francesca Carnevali, *Europe's Advantage: Banks and Small Firms in Britain, France, Germany, and Italy Since 1918* (Oxford, 2005; online edn, Oxford Academic, 1 September 2006), pp. 41–42 < https://doi.org/10.1093/019 9257396.001.0001> [accessed 15 February 2014].

Consequently, they developed close relationships to major national "universal" banks in order to fund primary industry's huge capital investments.[43]

Baden-Württemberg and its SMEs have been extraordinarily successful thanks to their high levels of flexibility and specialisation, utilising new technologies to produce high quality, specialised products. They coexist with larger, mass-production companies in the region in symbiotic relationships thanks to "a clear set of institutional arrangements, both in the government and in society, that bring order to their mutual relations."[44] Those arrangements allow small firms to benefit from the socialisation of risk. Educational institutions – from technical universities to *Fachhochschulen* (local technical colleges) to *Berufsschulen* (vocational training schools) – are closely tied into surrounding industry through informal and formal arrangements.[45] Business associations provide information on markets and support programmes, and coordinate technical standards, a "practice of using collusion to further the competitive character of the industry" unknown to Anglo-American firms who "invariably find their stable intermingling difficult to grasp".[46]

Mittelstand firms are funded by local banks, whose boards include local entrepreneurs and are therefore able to encourage good practice and make informed investment decisions.[47] The regional government offers support through the Steinbeis Foundation, linking businesses to education, and provides additional funding. The Chambers of Industry and Commerce (IHK (*Industrie-und Handelskammer*)) play a critical coordinating and enforcing role. This complex of supporting institutions underpins the practice of "collaborative subcontracting", where firms pool resources and know-how to make more rapid technological advances in dynamic, fast-changing markets.[48] There is a spirit of openness between firms and institutions, buttressed by mutual trust.[49] In short, Herrigel's thesis is that one cannot look only at the firms themselves to understand their operations, "one has to view the system as a whole. It

---

43   Herrigel, *Industrial Constructions*, pp. 20–21.
44   Gary Herrigel, 'Large Firms, Small Firms, and the Governance of Flexible Specialization: The Case of Baden-Württemberg and Socialized Risk', in *Country Competitiveness: Technology and the Organizing of Work*, ed. by Bruce Kogut (Oxford and New York, 1993), pp. 15–35 (p. 15).
45   Herrigel, 'Large Firms, Small Firms', pp. 17–18.
46   Herrigel, 'Large Firms, Small Firms', p. 19.
47   Herrigel, 'Large Firms, Small Firms', p. 19.
48   In one study specifically focused on these networks, though, it is argued that business owners were much less willing to cooperate with competitors; joint development was more likely in this view to have occurred with customers and suppliers: Reinhold Grotz and Boris Braun, 'Territorial or Trans-Territorial Networking: Spatial Aspects of Technology-Oriented Co-Operation within the German Mechanical Engineering Industry', *Regional Studies*, 31.6 (1997), 545–57.
49   Herrigel, 'Large Firms, Small Firms', pp. 19–21.

is much greater that the sum of its parts." All of the elements he describes here will become evident in the histories of our case-study companies and the ecosystems surrounding them.

The other, critical element of the Baden-Württemberg Mittelstand's operating system, Herrigel argues, is its relationship with the region's large firms. He offers a case study of the ascent of Daimler Benz and its gradual subsumption of processes previously completed by specialist Mittelstand suppliers;[50] we will see evidence of their hardening attitude in the study of Reutter below. But Herrigel also explains how the Mittelstand, even if it only occupied the so-called *verlängerte Werkbank* (the extended workbench, a metaphor in wide use to describe subcontractor relationships), remained indispensable to Daimler Benz: as its growth accelerated, Mittelstand subcontractors provided particular expertise, or more production capacity, or optimised production flows.[51] His scepticism about the future of the Mittelstand (his study was written in 1996), faced by accelerating technological change, was echoed by other authors including Hartmut Berghoff and is reasonable in some respects.[52] But in other ways his arguments are unnecessarily negative. We will see in Chapter 9 that Reutter, for example, did become increasingly driven by Porsche's unceasing growth, as Herrigel suggests such firms did. But it did not lose its autonomy, or its creativity. It did not become servile; on the contrary, it created new technologies of its own. Customer relationships were robust but not always, as Herrigel implies, choking. Wandel and firms like it were never merely subordinates of "autarkic" giants. If Mittelstand firms really had "wallowed in a marginal backwater of inefficiency", how would any of them have survived?[53] How would so many have flourished in the export markets identified by Simon? Herrigel's work is tremendously comprehensive and in many ways persuasive, but Mittelstand firms in Baden-Württemberg and elsewhere are seen only as elements in a system rather than as individual entities with horizons beyond their region. As we will see below, the 'system' in Baden-Württemberg was critical to the progress of our companies, but each of them, and their owners, had distinctive and independent personalities.

An alternative perspective to Herrigel's scepticism is provided by Christel Lane. She reviews contemporary studies by German organisational scholars to understand the Mittelstand's efforts during the 1980s to become more competitive through "flexible specialisation".[54] Staff skills were turned to new challenges, unions generally supported job enrichment activities, and managers

50   Herrigel, *Industrial Constructions*, pp. 149–63.
51   Herrigel, *Industrial Constructions*, pp. 153–55.
52   Herrigel, *Industrial Constructions*, pp. 176–80; 193–203; 204.
53   Herrigel, *Industrial Constructions*, p. 182.
54   An approach identified by Charles F. Sabel and Michael J. Piore, *The Second Industrial Divide - Possibilities for Prosperity* (New York, 1984).

were competent to anticipate and deliver the necessary changes.[55] Lane's study is particularly relevant to our own review, because it contrasts the German approach to an increasingly competitive and testing manufacturing market with that of British firms: "Such energetic technological innovation requires not only the commitment of considerable financial resources but also a high level of technical expertise among management and support staff at all levels. Neither precondition typically exist[ed] in British industrial organisations" of the 1980s, a situation whose roots we will discern below.[56]

Political and Social Standing

Francesca Carnevali identifies another key difference between British small business and the Mittelstand: their respective political influence. In the political turmoil of interwar Germany, the Mittelstand "were able to achieve an identity as a group, to make their voices heard, by associating at a national, regional, and sectoral level."[57] In Britain, in contrast, the SME sector was undervalued by successive governments[58] – in fact, "Labour's attitude towards small firms was a fundamentally hostile one"[59] – from which the banks took their cue for the indifference we will see in Chapter 3 below. It was the Mittelstand's ability to organise and engender mutual respect which underpinned the regional networks and relationships identified by Herrigel and Varieties of Capitalism (VoC) scholars. For Carnevali, its importance was exceptional: "The Mittelstand could be all things to all people, both in economic and social terms: a more humane version of capitalism, a symbol of the values and aspiration of good German citizens".[60] In Britain, in contrast, the small-business sector saw its influence – and the number of firms – decline as successive British governments pushed for American-style consolidation and mass-production practices, despite their unsuitability for the smaller markets served by British firms that demanded greater product flexibility.[61]

Varieties of Capitalism

In exploring the environment in which the Mittelstand and British SMEs operated, the VoC debate, initiated by Peter Hall and David Soskice and their

---

55   Christel Lane, 'Industrial Change in Europe: The Pursuit of Flexible Specialisation in Britain and West Germany', *Work, Employment and Society*, 2.2 (1988), 141–68 (pp. 143–58).
56   Lane, 'Industrial Change in Europe', p. 160.
57   Carnevali, p. 46.
58   Carnevali, chap. 6, 'The Demise of Small Firms in Britain'.
59   Carnevali, p. 91.
60   Carnevali, p. 137.
61   Carnevali, pp. 86–91.

collaborators in 2001, is important.[62] It is relevant to the present work because Britain, which Hall and Soskice define as a Liberal Market Economy (LME), and Germany, a so-called Coordinated Market Economy (CME), are seen to embody two very different arrangements of economic and social institutions which sustain dissimilar approaches to business. Though it has subsequently attracted criticism from some scholars for failing to allow for the change in economies over time or for the heterogeneity in firm strategies or modes of governance,[63] the VoC paradigm has also attracted sustained support as a framework for distinguishing between divergent approaches.[64] Hall and Soskice identify five principal "spheres" which are decisive for the conduct of business: industrial relations; vocational training and education; corporate governance and its relationship to funding and investment; inter-firm relationships, especially those with suppliers and clients; and an enterprise's employees and their knowledge and commitment.[65] Relationships within the five spheres are critical to firms' exploitation of their core competencies and dynamic capabilities. But the nature of relationships is fundamentally dissimilar in the two approaches. In LMEs like Britain and the United States, firms coordinate activities through hierarchies and market arrangements, often transactional in nature, whereas in CMEs like Germany, non-market, longer-term relationships are fostered.[66] All of those spheres were important in the histories of the businesses reviewed in Part Two.

These differences in approach, and in the nature of institutions which frame them, generate systematic differences in firms' strategy[67] and entrepreneurial

---

62   Peter A. Hall and David Soskice, 'An Introduction to Varieties of Capitalism', in *Varieties of Capitalism* (Oxford, 2001).

63   See, for example: Wolfgang Streeck, 'Varieties of Varieties: "VoC" and the Growth Models', *Politics & Society*, 44.2 (2016), 243–47; Michael J. Piore, 'Varieties of Capitalism Theory: Its Considerable Limits', *Politics & Society*, 44.2 (2016), 237–41; Herrigel and Zeitlin; Matthew M.C. Allen, *The Varieties of Capitalism Paradigm. Explaining Germany's Competitive Advantage?* (Basingstoke, 2006).

64   See, for example: *Beyond Varieties of Capitalism: Conflict, Contradictions, and Complementarities in the European Economy*, ed. by Bob Hancké, Martin Rhodes, and Mark Thatcher (Oxford Scholarship Online, 2008) <https://www.oxfordscholarship.com/view/10.1093/acprof:oso/9780199206483.001.0001/acprof-9780199206483> [accessed 1 June 2019]; William Lazonick, 'Varieties of Capitalism and Innovative Enterprise', *Comparative Social Research*, 24 (2007), 21–69; Michael A. Witt and Gregory Jackson, 'Varieties of Capitalism and Institutional Comparative Advantage: A Test and Reinterpretation', *Journal of International Business Studies*, 47.7 (2016), 778; Carola Frege and John Godard, 'Varieties of Capitalism and Job Quality: The Attainment of Civic Principles at Work in the United States and Germany', *American Sociological Review*, 79.5 (2014), 942.

65   Hall and Soskice, pp. 6–8: Their 'spheres' and my themes overlap; common areas are explored in Part 1 of this book and in relation to the case-study companies.

66   Hall and Soskice, pp. 8–9.

67   Hall and Soskice, p. 16.

behaviour: within CMEs, incremental innovation is the norm, whereas LME entrepreneurial activity favours radical innovation.[68] In Germany, firms are willing to invest in the development of high skills that enable long-term, incremental innovation because institutional arrangements – such as the vocational education system, trade associations, and chambers of commerce – encourage a widespread commitment to skills development.[69] The investment in skills is further validated by a CME-specific approach to funding, whereby "patient capital" is invested by long-term funders able to monitor firms' performance and reputation through mutual participation in those institutions.[70] In LMEs, by contrast, institutions are arranged to facilitate rapid engagement and dismissal of staff, and financial market structures facilitate short-term investment in riskier ventures. The differences in political economic structure and business practices derived from them are encapsulated in the concept of "comparative institutional advantage";[71] competitive success is achieved in areas of business which are best enabled by the prevailing institutional arrangements.

In this environment of fundamentally different approaches, William Lazonick sees Germany as the "high-quality, high-cost producer" and Britain as the "low-quality, high-cost producer" among leading Western industrial nations. If Germany has fared better, it is because for it and other countries like it, "the interaction between the innovative enterprise and the developmental state" has been of critical importance: companies innovate and perform, but they do so in an environment in which government plays an active role in creating and sustaining enabling institutions.[72] The chosen approach of German managers and business leaders has aided them in their approach. Whereas the British business elite of the early twentieth century rejected technical education for themselves[73] (Geoffrey Jones finds similar prejudices in Britain's trading companies, whose selection policies followed "the general British preference for 'character' and social skills as the main qualification for management."),[74] top executives in Germany were scientists or engineers who had risen through the company. Since then, German companies have flourished by the inculcation

---

68   Hall and Soskice, pp. 37–38; See also the analysis of differences between present-day entrepreneurial approaches in André Pahnke and Friederike Welter, 'The German Mittelstand: Antithesis to Silicon Valley Entrepreneurship?', *Small Business Economics* (2018), 1–14 <https://doi.org/10.1007/s11187-018-0095-4> in Chapter 11 below ; and also the analysis of Andrea Herrmann, 'A Plea for Varieties of Entrepreneurship', *Small Business Economics*, 52.2 (2019), 331–43, reviewed in this chapter.

69   Hall and Soskice, pp. 24–25.

70   Hall and Soskice, p. 22.

71   Hall and Soskice, p. 36.

72   Lazonick, pp. 18–19.

73   Lazonick, pp. 18–19.

74   Geoffrey Jones, *Merchants to Multinationals, British Trading companies in the Nineteenth and Twentieth Centuries*, (Oxford, 2000), p. 208.

of technical skills and the advancement of technical experts into management positions. Institutional differences also affect "varieties of entrepreneurship", Andrea Herrmann argues, for "the regulated institutional environment is at the basis of the success of Germany's *Mittelstand* and its core export industries. A highly qualified workforce with firm-specific skills is essential for incremental innovations and, thus, for the development of sophisticated high-quality products, which are so typical of Germany's engineering and metal-working industries."[75] We will see in the histories of the case-study companies and their environments whether a particular variety of capitalism proved to be more beneficial.

Approach and Methodology

I set out to discover the origins of the Mittelstand's strengths by comparing German companies' approach during the post-war decades with that of small and medium-sized businesses in Britain, reviewing their respective business philosophies and the commercial practices which encapsulated them. Though scholarship on relative macroeconomic change is well developed,[76] less attention has been paid to the companies whose performance actually drove both national economies, and very few studies indeed have examined the smaller firms which have been so fundamentally important to both nations' economic development.

---

75   Herrmann, p. 340.
76   See, for example: Alan Booth, 'The Manufacturing Failure Hypothesis and the Performance of British Industry during the Long Boom', *Economic History Review*, LVI.1 (2003), 1–33; Stephen Broadberry, 'The Performance of Manufacturing', in *The Cambridge Economic History of Modern Britain, Vol. III, Structural Change and Growth, 1939–2000*, ed. by Roderick Floud and Paul Johnson (Cambridge, 2004); Michael Kitson, 'Failure Followed by Success or Success Followed by Failure? A Re-Examination of British Economic Growth since 1949', in *The Cambridge Economic History of Modern Britain, Vol. III*, ed. by Roderick Floud and Paul Johnson (Cambridge, 2004); Nick Crafts, 'Competition Cured the "British Disease"', VoxEU.Org <http://www.voxeu.org/article/competition-cured-british-disease> [accessed 5 February 2015]; Michael Kitson and Jonathan Michie, 'The Deindustrial Revolution: The Rise and Fall of UK Manufacturing, 1870–2010', in *The Cambridge Economic History of Modern Britain: Volume 2*, ed. by Roderick Floud and Paul Johnson (2012) <https://michaelkitson.files.wordpress.com/2013/02/kitson-and-michie-the-deindustrial-revolution-oct-20121.pdf> [accessed 13 May 2016]; Stephen N. Broadberry and Karin Wagner, 'Human Capital and Productivity in Manufacturing during the Twentieth Century: Britain, Germany and the United States', in *Quantitative Aspects of Post-War European Economic Growth*, ed. by Bart van Ark and Nicholas Crafts (Cambridge, 1997); Stephen Broadberry and Nick Crafts, 'UK Productivity Performance from 1950 to 1979: A Restatement of the Broadberry-Crafts View', *Economic History Review*, LVI.4 (2003).

Using archival evidence from both countries, the following study examines what it is that the managers of individual Mittelstand companies actually did to make their enterprise a success or failure. We will review the external environments in which Mittelstand managers managed – what might be termed their companies' ecosystems – and the bearing they had on the Mittelstand's success. We will consider how the management of similar British companies compared with the Mittelstand approach, and how that performance was in turn affected by the context in which the British firms themselves operated. In taking a perspective over several decades, it is possible to evaluate whether the 'Mittelstand model' was a formula for long-term sustainable business success within companies. We will also review whether it represented a way of living and working which was achievable only in Germany and its German-speaking neighbours, or whether history shows that British companies were able to achieve similar results by conducting themselves in a similar manner. Finally, we will consider whether the Mittelstand's approach to doing business in the past offers any useful guidance to present-day entrepreneurs.

These questions are addressed in two parts. Part One provides an appraisal of the ecosystems within which regional businesses operated. Drawing on research undertaken in external archives, such as those of banks and regional universities, Chapters 2 to 4 provide context for each company's operations and help to assess the validity of source materials uncovered at the company level.[77] In Part Two we will explore the histories of six companies from the second half of the 1940s until around 1980. For consistency, I compared similar regions, the West Midlands around Birmingham and the Stuttgart region of Baden-Württemberg. For each business, a comprehensive review of available primary archival materials was undertaken in regional business archives.[78] Few records of SMEs are available, so the choice of company was necessarily limited, but I matched each UK firm with a business in Germany which served the same or related markets.[79] The industries included are paper (papermaking equipment manufactures Chr. Wandel & Co. KG of Reutlingen, and printers and stationery

---

77   Stephanie Decker, 'The Silence of the Archives: Business History, Post-Colonialism and Archival Ethnography', *Management & Organizational History*, 8.2 (2013), 155–73 (p. 165); Matthias Kipping, R. Daniel Wadhwani, and Marcelo Bucheli, 'Analyzing and Interpreting Historical Sources: A Basic Methodology', in *Organizations in Time: History, Theory, Methods*, ed. by R. Daniel Wadhwani and Marcelo Bucheli (Oxford, 2014), pp. 305–29 (pp. 316–19).

78   The principal company-related archives for the companies listed are at the Wirtschaftsarchiv Baden-Württemberg in Stuttgart (WABW), Sandwell Community History and Archives Service in Smethwick (Sandwell), and the Modern Records Centre, University of Warwick (MRC).

79   West Germany, or the Federal Republic of Germany (FRG) during the period under investigation.

manufacturers Kenrick & Jefferson Ltd. of West Bromwich);[80] steelwork (steel fabricators Julius Schneider GmbH & Co. KG of Ludwigsburg, and Braithwaite & Co. Engineers Ltd. of London, Newport and West Bromwich); and automotive (coachbuilders and seat manufacturers Karosseriewerk Reutter and its successor RECARO of Stuttgart, and coachbuilders and luxury car makers Jensen Motors Ltd. of West Bromwich). Supplementary analysis of several other companies from each region is used to illuminate particular points.

Though scholars trying to recreate company histories are urged to investigate multiple "memory phenomena" inside and outside each firm, this is often not possible for smaller companies active several decades ago.[81] In general, of course, small firms simply produce fewer documents to study than corporations do. Their records are fragmented, incomplete, and inconsistent within themselves, let alone in comparison with those of other companies. Employees are – with few exceptions – dead or impossible to locate. Firms which are still active present the challenge of gaining information about their past performance, relating it to present outcomes, and respecting the current desire for confidentiality. For the case-study companies, sources varied in quantity, quality, and scope, which complicated both the original analysis and the subsequent writing: the arrangement of each chapter consequently differs according to the availability of material related to specific areas of interest. Given the challenges experienced in recreating the six companies' histories, the following health warning is relevant: "Like all reconstruction, it suffers from uneven, complex and confusing evidence, multiple explanations, the eventual choice to prioritize one account over another, the bias inherent in the intellectual framework of the researcher, and the fundamental silence of some historical sources."[82]

Readers might reasonably argue that conducting a comparative historical analysis by reference to Mittelstand characteristics is problematic: on the face of it, judging British and German firms according to characteristics derived from German firms is likely to result in judgements which favour the German firms. Yet there are two reasons to conduct the analysis in this way. First, it is impossible to evaluate the appropriateness of calls for a 'British Mittelstand' unless one conducts an analysis of the German one and measures the British equivalent against it. Second, an evaluation of Mittelstand firms' culture and practice is by definition necessary for a review of the German firms examined here. Using Mittelstand characteristics as a framework of analysis is not an assertion of their innate superiority, as examples of better British practice in the cases below demonstrate.

---

80 Regrettably the archives of stationery manufacturer Louis Leitz at WABW, which would have allowed a more direct comparison with the history of K&J, were not accessible.

81 Philip Scranton and Patrick Fridenson, *Reimagining Business History* (Baltimore, 2013), p. 215.

82 Decker, pp. 160–61.

One related consideration must be taken into account. As we have already seen, some Anglo-American writing about the Mittelstand has been rather enthusiastic in its tone. In the study that follows, I have remembered Christian Homburg's admonition that "the English language literature on Mittelstand companies consists of a remarkable mixture of war stories and pep talks with a very limited amount of reliable information. Many authors' attitude towards Mittelstand companies in Germany may be characterized as a rather uninformed naive admiration."[83] I have also borne in mind the danger of *Mittelstandsromantik*, romanticising the experience of individual entrepreneurs and their businesses.[84] The risk of becoming persuaded of the Mittelstand's infallibility, while giving insufficient credence to the potential of British companies to compete effectively against it, must be resisted. While these warnings are necessary and have been heeded, there remains a special value in conducting research like that which follows. That is the opportunity to recall the working lives of entrepreneurs and business leaders in both countries who gave employment to many and created businesses which they hoped would make a difference to their communities or markets, and of the workers who made their achievements possible. Their individual and collective histories are, regrettably, all too often overlooked and uncelebrated.

---

83   Christian Homburg, *Structure and Dynamics of the German Mittelstand*, (Heidelberg, 1999), p. v.
84   'The romanticization of small and medium-sized owner-run businesses': Armin Grünbacher, *West German Industrialists and the Making of the Economic Miracle: A History of Mentality and Recovery* (London, 2017), p. 175.

PART ONE: OPERATING CONTEXTS

Prologue

As they began to rebuild their businesses after the Second World War, company owners and managers in the West Midlands and Baden-Württemberg faced multiple challenges. Some were close to home and personal: how to manage the relationship between family and family firm, how to plan for succession, how personal values would impact the conduct of company affairs, whether one's standing within the local community would boost business – or vice versa. Other challenges depended on what we might call the external ecosystem and were consequently harder to control: how to find the most capable staff, how to fund a growing – or struggling – business, whether it was located in the most appropriate place for business success. In Part One we consider these challenges in relation to the companies examined in the following case studies, to help us understand one fundamental question: which mattered more for business success, the ability of individual entrepreneurs, or the advantages of the ecosystem in which they conducted their business? We begin with a brief overview of each region's situation at the beginning of our period.

Post-war Circumstances

Both countries faced extraordinarily challenging conditions after the end of the war in 1945.[1] Britain had suffered 358,950 war dead, 63,635 of them civilians.[2] Some 75,000 shops, 42,000 commercial properties, 25,000 factories and 450,000 homes had been destroyed or made unusable by German bombing. Material and labour shortages constrained rebuilding efforts, and Government policies focused less on local needs than on external challenges such as ongoing

---

1   I explore these themes in more detail in David W. Paulson, 'British and German SMEs and the Memory of War: A Comparative Approach', *Management & Organizational History*, 13.4 (2018), 404–29 (pp. 2–4).

2   Peter Howlett, 'The War-Time Economy, 1939–1945', in *The Cambridge Economic History of Modern Britain*, ed. by Roderick Floud and Paul Johnson (Online edition, 2004), pp. 1–26 (p. 24) <https://doi.org/10.1017/CHOL9780521820387.002>.

military commitments and the generation of income from exports,[3] all made more difficult by the "almost indecent swiftness" with which the American Government ceased its Lend-Lease financial support programme at the war's end.[4] Ministers believed they could plan the country's way out of its economic difficulties, failing to respond to the public's desire for more material goods and fewer restrictions;[5] wide-ranging restrictions on consumption were still in place in 1951.[6] Business leaders were frustrated throughout the late 1940s and 1950s by Government demand-management policies, the manifestation of the difficulty of achieving both sustainable domestic growth and external stability during the Cold War.[7]

Germany's situation after the war was, however, apparently much worse. The country was occupied by the four Allied victors. Over five million young men had been killed on military service. By one estimate, 400,00 civilians had been killed and 800,000 injured by Allied bombing.[8] Nine million refugees were trying to return to their hometowns within Germany while fourteen million ethnic Germans, expelled from Eastern Europe, were arriving there. Eleven million German combatants were now in captivity. Some 3.8 million apartments had been destroyed.[9] In Stuttgart, home to two of the companies studied in Part Two, fifty-three Allied air raids had left 4500 inhabitants dead and 9000 injured. Thirteen out of fourteen river bridges and 57% of buildings had been destroyed, leaving 4.9 million cubic metres of rubble.[10] Industrial production had reached only 44% of 1936 levels by 1947, there were demands for reparations and the dismantling of plants, and denazification programmes had temporarily removed many managers and business leaders from the economy.[11]

3   Catherine Flinn, '"The City of Our Dreams"? The Political and Economic Realities of Rebuilding Britain's Blitzed Cities, 1945–54', *Twentieth Century British History*, 23.2 (2012), 221–45 (pp. 225–29); Nick Tiratsoo, 'The Reconstruction of Blitzed British Cities, 1945–55: Myths and Reality', *Contemporary British History*, 14.1 (2000), 27–44 (pp. 34–35).

4   Howlett, p. 16.

5   M.J. Daunton, *Wealth and Welfare, An Economic and Social History of Britain, 1851–1951* (Oxford, 2007), pp. 593–602.

6   Daunton, *Wealth and Welfare*, p. 600, table 17.1.

7   Peter M. Scott and James T. Walker, 'The Impact of "Stop-Go" Demand Management Policy on Britain's Consumer Durables Industries, 1952–65', *The Economic History Review*, 70.4 (2017), 1321–45 (p. 1323).

8   Ian Kershaw, *The End: Germany, 1944–45* (London, 2012), p. 379.

9   Adam Tooze, *The Wages of Destruction: The Making and Breaking of the Nazi Economy* (London, 2007), p. 672.

10   Manfred J. Enssle, 'The Harsh Discipline of Food Scarcity in Postwar Stuttgart, 1945–1948', *German Studies Review*, 10.3 (1987), 481–502 (p. 486).

11   Richard Overy, 'The Economy of the Federal Republic Since 1949', in *The Federal Republic of Germany Since 1949: Politics, Society and Economy before and after Unification*, ed. by Klaus Larres and Panayi Panikos (London and New York, 1996), pp. 3–34 (pp. 4–5).

Yet there was cause for German hope. Allied bombing had had a less destructive effect than intended on Germany's production capabilities.[12] As we will see in our case-study companies, some firms suffered losses of plant and equipment to military action or subsequent dismantling for reparations. But at a national level, most machine tools had not been irreparably damaged and the value of net industrial fixed assets after depreciation and war damage was 20.7% higher than in 1936: its value in 1948, after punitive actions, was still 11.1% higher than in 1936.[13] A 1944 analysis by the US Office of War Information had reported "an unexpectedly favorable impression of the German scene" with management training, time studies, and work "rais[ing] industrial morale by friendly treatment of the workers and by offering opportunities for advancement".[14] Many workers were highly skilled, thanks to Nazi apprenticeship programmes and the demands of war-work.[15] Manufacturing businesses retained competencies.[16] For example, supplier capabilities that had sustained aircraft production had survived the war, and many SMEs used to working closely with larger manufacturers within a robust supply network would soon be able to continue their transition from pre-war automotive work to military work and back into the automotive industry.[17] The Western occupying powers' policies also favoured industrial renewal. The American Government wanted to counter East-West tensions by the promotion of private capitalism,[18] and the financially constrained British Government wanted a rapid return to full production so that its occupation would become self-funding. Given these

---

12   Werner Abelshauser, 'Kriegswirtschaft Und Wirtschaftswunder. Deutschlands Wirtschaftliche Mobilisierung Für Den Zweiten Weltkrieg Und Die Folgen Für Die Nachkriegszeit', *Vierteljahrshefte Für Zeitgeschichte*, 47.4 (1999), 503–38.

13   Werner Abelshauser, *Deutsche Wirtschaftsgeschichte von 1945 bis zur Gegenwart*, 2nd edn (Munich, 2011), pp. 66–69; 70, table 2.

14   H.L. Ansbacher, 'German Industrial Psychology in the Fifth Year of War', *Psychological Bulletin*, 41.9 (1944), 605–14 (pp. 605, 614) <https://doi.org/10.1037/h0058291>.

15   Abelshauser, *Deutsche Wirtschaftsgeschichte*, pp. 49–50.

16   For insights into the way in which German businesses favoured skills that would ensure quality, rather than deploying technologies that would enable mass production, see Raymond G. Stokes, 'Technology and the West German Wirtschaftswunder', *Technology and Culture*, 32.1 (1991), 1–22. His observation that companies were able to build export success using older technology, and only incrementally and deliberately add new technologies, suggests both innate business strengths and confidence in the ecosystems that supported their tradition of excellence.

17   Jonas Scherner, Jochen Streb, and Stephanie Tilly, 'Supplier Networks in the German Aircraft Industry during World War II and Their Long-Term Effects on West Germany's Automobile Industry during the "Wirtschaftswunder"', *Business History*, 56.6 (2014), 996–1020.

18   Volker R. Berghahn, *The Americanisation of West German Industry 1945–1973* (Cambridge, 1986), pp. 88–110; Barry Eichengreen, *The European Economy since 1945: Coordinated Capitalism and Beyond* (Princeton and Oxford, 2007), pp. 54–58.

pressures, and the lobbying of restored trade and employers' associations and chambers of commerce,[19] most business leaders, especially in the Mittelstand, were soon able to regain control of their companies.

Aid for the German economy's recovery came from the $13 billion Marshall Plan in 1948, which underpinned finance minister Ludwig Erhard's removal of price controls.[20] The German currency reform in June 1948 encouraged businesses to release previously hoarded goods into the market and encouraged consumers to buy them: economically, "the results were nothing short of miraculous".[21] In September 1949 voters elected conservative Konrad Adenauer as the first Chancellor of the new German Federal Republic, with Erhard as his Finance Minister. Adenauer chose to focus on social integration rather than recrimination.[22] To deliver the national wellbeing that would allow the new West Germany to look forwards rather than backwards, they chose not to plan the economy, as their British counterparts were trying to do, but to present the 1949 electorate with an alternative approach:[23] they would enable renewal through the free operation of markets coupled with welfare policies, an approach that would come to be called the social market economy.[24] Erhard's declared goal was "Wohlstand für Alle", prosperity for everyone.[25] The consequence was a virtuous circle: West Germans wanted to consume after years of restraint,[26] and growth was fuelled by West German workers' "proud consciousness of achievements, based on their own efforts, often expressed in the acquisition of modern, technological goods" produced by German manufacturers.[27] Transformation was not immediate: by 1953 Germany's per capita GDP was only 63% of Britain's.[28] But Britain's production in 1951 was 32% higher

19   Berghahn, *The Americanisation of West German Industry 1945–1973*, pp. 64–69; Rainer Schulze, 'Representation of Interests and Recruitment of Elites. The Role of the Industrie-Und Handelskammern in German Politics After the End of the Second World War', *German History*, 7.1 (1989), 71–91.

20   Eichengreen, pp. 59–69.

21   Eichengreen, p. 70.

22   Jeffrey K. Olick, *The Politics of Regret. On Collective Memory and Historical Responsibility* (London and New York, 2007), p. 46; C.M. Clark, 'West Germany Confronts the Nazi Past: Some Recent Debates on the Early Postwar Era, 1945–1960', *The European Legacy*, 4.1 (1999), 113–30 (p. 126).

23   Mark E. Spicka, *Selling the Economic Miracle: Economic Reconstruction and Politics in West Germany, 1949–1957: 18*, Illustrated edition (New York, 2007), p. 49.

24   Spicka, *Selling the Economic Miracle*, chap. 2; James C. Van Hook, *Rebuilding Germany: The Creation of the Social Market Economy, 1945–1957* (Cambridge, 2004).

25   Ludwig Erhard, *Wohlstand für Alle*, ed. by Ludwig Erhard, 2009 reissue (Köln, 1957).

26   Enssle, p. 501.

27   Lutz Niethammer, '"Normalization" in the West: Traces of Memory Leading Back into the 1950s', in *The Miracle Years. A Cultural History of West Germany, 1945–1968*, ed. by Hanna Schissler (Princeton and Oxford, 2001) pp. 237–65 (pp. 259–60).

28   Daunton, *Wealth and Welfare*, p. 167, Table 5.1.

than in 1947, while West Germany's had risen by 312% in the same period.[29] This would set the pace for what became known as the *Wirtschaftswunder*, West Germany's economic miracle.[30] This was the environment in which the Mittelstand businesses reviewed in Part Two operated.

Conditions in Succeeding Decades

If the conditions described above shaped the responses of managers and workers in the immediate aftermath of the war, how had their working environments changed by the end of the period covered by our study? In the West Midlands, Birmingham and the Black Country were completely dominated by industry. In Birmingham, 51,000 houses had been declared unfit after the end of the war. By the late 1960s, 38,000 of them had been demolished. The city's 1960 Development Plan revealed a shortage of open spaces and an inadequate road system.[31] Though changes were underway, workers' self-confidence and belief in the future might have been affected by what *The Economist* described in 1966 as "the full awfulness of the area, where a rampant demand for labour [was] matched by unequalled squalor in the landscape, and a desperate shortage of houses."[32] Indian and Pakistani immigrants travelled "by jet from the sixteenth to the nineteenth centuries" to a "town whose physical structure [was] entirely outdated".[33] By the end of the following decade, local inhabitants faced further social and economic deterioration. For those resident in public housing, for example, one analysis estimated in 1979 that some £210 million per year would need to be spent for the next ten years by the West Midlands' authorities to rectify poor conditions in pre-1919 and publicly-owned dwellings. However,

---

29   Eichengreen, p. 57, table 3.1.
30   For valuable summaries, see for example: Lothar Kettenacker, *Germany Since 1945* (Oxford and New York, 1997), pp. 80–96; Tony Judt, *Postwar: A History of Europe Since 1945* (London, 2011), pp. 354–59; Deeper analyses are available in works such as: Barry Eichengreen and Albrecht Ritschl, 'Understanding West German Economic Growth in the 1950s' (London School of Economics, 2008) < http://eprints.lse.ac.uk/22304/ > [accessed 5 August 2022]; Rolf H. Dumke, 'Reassessing the Wirtschaftswunder: Reconstruction and Postwar Growth in West Germany in an International Context', *Oxford Bulletin of Economics & Statistics*, 52.4 (1990), 451–92; Steven Tolliday, 'Enterprise and State in the West German Wirtschaftswunder: Volkswagen and the Automobile Industry, 1939–1962', *The Business History Review*, 69.3 (1995), 273–350; an excellent overview of the evolution of the West German economy throughout the postwar decades is provided in Overy.
31   Leigh Michael Harrison, 'Factory Music: How the Industrial Geography and Working-Class Environment of Post-War Birmingham Fostered the Birth of Heavy Metal', *Journal of Social History*, 44.1 (2010), 145–158, 309–310 (pp. 146–47).
32   'Doubts in West Brom', *The Economist* (12 March 1966), p. 979.
33   'Facing Up To Colour', *The Economist* (2 April 1966), p. 23.

the total government allocation for all public housing, including building new houses, was £77 million per annum, to be reduced annually, and it was anticipated that increasing numbers of people would be "trapped" in poor housing.[34]

In the workplace there were also difficulties. The three-week strike at the Servis washing machine factory in October 1979, which cost the company £3.5 million after workers turned down a 28% wage increase was, on the face of it, a good example of the "British disease".[35] But their actions could have been those of frightened people observing local events: over six months and within seven miles of K&J's factory at West Bromwich, local newspapers reported – these are just some examples of many stories of economic decline – the loss of 630 foundry jobs in Wednesbury and 600 auto castings jobs in Smethwick,[36] fifty-seven skilled men made redundant at a week's notice at a machine makers in West Bromwich,[37] and 3100 redundancies at British Steel plants,[38] not to mention the hundreds of jobs lost at Braithwaite Engineers and earlier at Jensen Motors, whose histories we will see in Part Two. Adverse reactions to the loss of so much skilled employment should have been understandable, as should workers' scepticism at the promise of new jobs being created on the former Jensen site and the also-closed Chance Brothers glass factory[39] or the prospective development of new works on the Braithwaite site.[40]

West Midlands residents had survived the war feeling self-confident about the region's future. West Bromwich suffered little damage in contrast to Stuttgart, where Allied bombing caused great destruction and loss of life.[41] But by 1979, relative fortunes had changed. Housebuilding had been "state priority number one" in Baden-Württemberg since the war, and by 1968 45% of the state's dwellings had been built between 1949 and 1967. Total residential

34   Alexander Johnston, 'Metropolitan Housing Policy and Strategic Planning in the West Midlands', *The Town Planning Review*, 53.2 (1982), 179–99.

35   'Servis Men Turn Down £100 A Week Pay Packet', *Sandwell Evening News* (Sandwell, 2 October 1979), Sandwell Archive, 63/219; 'Servis Strikers Vote to Go Back', *Sandwell Evening News* (Sandwell, 24 October 1979), Sandwell Archive, 63/224.

36   'Foundry Jobs Axe for 400 Workers', *Sandwell Evening News* (Sandwell, 19 July 1979), Sandwell Archive, 63/190.

37   'Storm as 57 Told: Quit on Friday', *Sandwell Evening News* (Sandwell, 30 October 1979), Sandwell Archive, 63/224.

38   '600 To Lose Jobs As Axe Falls On Steel Works', *Evening Standard* (23 January 1980), Sandwell Archive, 63/203.

39   'Hundreds of New Jobs on Factory Estate', *Sandwell Evening News* (Sandwell, 4 January 1980), Sandwell Archive, 63/250.

40   'New-Look Car Firm Lines Up Big Jobs Boost', *Sandwell Evening News* (Sandwell, 4 January 1980), Sandwell Archive, 63/251.

41   Paulson, 'Memory', pp. 7, 10–11, 13–15; Brendan Jackson and Moreen Wilkes, eds, *West Bromwich at War 1939–1945* (West Bromwich, 2016) pp. 46–69; Enssle, p. 486.

stock grew from 1.6 million to 3.6 million units between 1952 and 1980.[42] The state's unemployment rate was 2.1%, its economy had grown by 3.1% annually over the past ten years, and "Stuttgart [was] a nice, bright, modern industrial city", "industrially well placed, at the heart of the EEC".[43] Not everything was perfect. The workers of IG Metall had gone on strike in 1978, but were expecting to return to work in the booming Baden-Württemberg automotive industry after a pay settlement of just over 5%.[44] In contrast, their West Midlands colleagues feared the consequences of British Leyland's prospective collapse.[45] *The Economist* returned to the subject of housing in 1984, reminding West Midlands readers that "'*Schaffe, Schaffe, Häusle baue*' is the motto of the industrious Swabians who do indeed work and work, thus getting their little houses built." They worked in an economy in which the state premier "had cajoled industry into financing research institutes for micro-electronics, data processing and molecular biology in his state", and was implementing "what may be Europe's most ambitious clean-up targets" for power-plant pollution, in "the home not only of Mercedes-Benz but also of many small firms that enjoy global renown in their particular specialities".[46]

The actions and outlooks of all of the actors in the case studies which follow should be considered against this backdrop.

---

42   Willi A. Boelcke, *Wirtschaftsgeschichte Baden-Württembergs von Den Römern Bis Heute* (Stuttgart, 1987), pp. 531–32; Statistisches Landesamt Baden-Württemberg, *Statistische Bericht: Bautätigkeit Und Wohnungen* (Stuttgart, 18 May 1983) <https://www.statistisch-ebibliothek.de/mir/servlets/MCRFileNodeServlet/BWHeft_derivate_00014336/3734_82001.pdf> [accessed 8 January 2022].

43   'Southern Comfort', *The Economist* (8 November 1980), section A Survey of the West German Economy, p. 13, The Economist Historical Archive.

44   'Showing Its Metall', *The Economist* (18 March 1978), p. 80, The Economist Historical Archive.

45   Thames Television, *British Leyland Cars | British Car Manufacturing | TV Eye | 1980* <https://www.youtube.com/watch?v=SsizoYrceOg> [accessed 18 February 2019].

46   'South-Western Star', *The Economist* (17 March 1984), p. 56+, The Economist Historical Archive.

2

Culture, Community, and Continuity

In this chapter we look at some of the cultural and environmental influences on businesses and their leaders, and consider leaders and their firms within their local networks. We also review the challenge of succession, critical to the generational continuity that has been identified as a core element of Mittelstand and family-business values.

Regions, Clusters and Networks

In a study which examines activity in two distinct regions, it makes sense to start with understanding what impact location and surrounding business ecosystems had on the conduct of business.[1] Since the economic collapse of the 1980s, scholars have tried to explain the West Midlands' economic decline and the ongoing difficulties of reviving its fortunes. From the Industrial Revolution until the decline in manufacturing which accelerated under the Thatcher government after 1979, the region was dynamic and entrepreneurial: in 1955, for example, the MP for Wednesbury urged the government not to impose credit controls which would hurt the ten thousand small manufacturing businesses in the surrounding Black Country.[2] The various districts of Baden-Württemberg

---

1 See, for example, over a forty-year timescale, works like David B. Audretsch and Erik E. Lehmann, 'Small Is Beautiful', in *The Seven Secrets of Germany: Economic Resilience in an Era of Global Turbulence* (Oxford Scholarship Online, 2015) < https://doi.org/10.1093/acpro f:oso/9780190258696.001.0001> [accessed 5 August 2022] for considerations of modern-day regional investment; both David Keeble, *Industrial Location and Planning in the United Kingdom* (London, 1976) and Andrew K.G. Hidreth, 'In Search of Profits: An Investigation Into the Manufacturing Locational Shift From the West Midlands Conurbation 1880–1986' (unpublished Ph.D. thesis, University of Cambridge, 1991) for considerations of planning and location; N. Flynn and A. Taylor, 'Inside the Rust Belt: An Analysis of the Decline of the West Midlands Economy. 2: Corporate Strategies and Economic Change', *Environment and Planning A*, 18.8 (1986), 999–1028 on considerations of regional decline; *De-Industrialisation and New Industrialisation in Britain and Germany*, ed. by Trevor Wild and Philip Jones (London, 1991) for comparative analysis of regional transformations.
2 Carnevali, pp. 94–95.

were similarly vibrant, sustaining high levels of small-business activity after the Second World War as they had done for a century or more before it. But why should two distinct regions each provide such fertile ground for growing businesses? Clues can be found in the work of economist Alfred Marshall, who at the turn of the twentieth century had identified the advantages of regionally specific business activity. Firms stay where their "good work is rightly appreciated", new ideas are shared and improved, and subsidiary trades support further business development.[3] Skilled labour is readily available: in regions where industries are the same or similar, businesses will cluster together where they think there are skilled staff wanting to join them, and skilled workers will use improving transportation to wherever there are the most employment opportunities. Marshall cautioned, however, against over-specialisation within a single district, which invites companies there to fall victim to any disruption to supply or demand.[4] This was a risk then as it remains today: should local businesses become increasingly expert in a single product, developing a technology-specific ecosystem in which entrepreneurs successfully trade off local competition against mutually reinforcing sector advancement? Or should entrepreneurs retain independence and flexibility and avoid the risk of one day joining their neighbours on a sinking ship?

Writing a century after him, Harvard economist Michael Porter reinforced Marshall's arguments: world-leading industrial competitiveness is enabled by companies clustering together where their strengths become mutually reinforcing. Often there are distinct clusters of companies from a specific industry in one particular location.[5] Companies derive benefits from these locations, including the availability of specialised employees, who are incentivised to stay in the area where their skills will be most valued. They are also able to work with expert and responsive local suppliers; have access to specialised information through local networks; benefit from local educational and training infrastructure and other institutions; and share in investment by regional and national governments.[6]

These benefits could be seen in the clustering of the Baden-Württemberg Mittelstand in the second half of the twentieth century. In a 1996 review of contemporary innovation practices, British firms were seen to be informally organised and focused on responding rapidly to changing market demands.

---

3   Alfred Marshall, *Principles of Economics*, 8th edn (London, 1920), p. 156.
4   Marshall, pp. 157–58.
5   Michael E. Porter, *The Competitive Advantage of Nations* (Basingstoke, 1998), pp. 148–59.
6   Michael Porter, 'Clusters and the New Economics of Competition', *Harvard Business Review* (November–December 1998), 77–90 (pp. 77–90); the importance of clusters and business districts in Britain is explored in *Industrial Clusters and Regional Business Networks in England, 1750–1970*, ed. by John F. Wilson and Andrew Popp, 1st edition (Burlington, 2003).

In contrast, Mittelstand firms were innovating strategically, their stronger technological orientation delivered by skilled in-house staff, and supported by external mutual networking mechanisms.[7] As we shall see below, Reutter exemplified these advantages from the early 1950s onwards. Located next to its key customer Porsche in the automobile manufacturing industry centred around Stuttgart, Reutter had grown by differentiating itself through its high level of intra-firm expertise and knowledge. When circumstances caused it to change strategic direction, that expertise allowed Reutter to quickly reinvent itself as a market-defining specialist seating company in the 1960s. Contemporary commentators saw the knowledge held within Mittelstand firms as a key asset, further strengthened by their commitment to working with their customers in product development.[8] But caution was also urged. Though another contemporary observer saw the advantages to Baden-Württemberg of its industrial districts with their cooperative industrial networks and supportive institutional environment,[9] he also warned that there can be advantages and disadvantages to regional location, with a risk of "lock-in effects, path dependencies, and technological trajectories".[10] As we shall see in the case studies below, by the 1990s this fate had befallen Wandel and its competitors in Reutlingen's paper-making-equipment industries, as Wandel remained committed to its expertise in ageing technology and its now-unsuitable town-centre location. Steelwork fabricator Schneider had already gone, slow to adapt in a period of increasing competition and changing building technologies. In the West Midlands, metalworking automotive suppliers which had all pursued the same technologies and ways of working declined in step with the car manufacturers they were dependent on. Nevertheless, despite the very real risks involved in local specialisation, countless long-lived Mittelstand businesses benefited from their regional networks and derived strength from them even in times of economic difficulty.

An additional source of strength for individual Mittelstand companies was their membership of their respective trade association, and of their local Chamber of Industry and Commerce (IHK). The latter had an immediate impact in 1945 and afterwards in representing local business interests.[11] Gary Herrigel shows how the textile machinery industry was restored through IHK and trade association coordination between 1945 and 1952,[12] and explains

7   Stephen Roper, *Product Innovation and Small Business Growth: A Comparison of the Strategies of German, UK and Irish Companies* (Belfast, 1996), pp. 14–15.

8   Grotz and Braun.

9   Martin Heidenreich, 'Beyond Flexible Specialization: The Rearrangement of Regional Production Orders in Emilia-Romagna and Baden-Wuerttemberg', *European Planning Studies*, 4 (1996), 401–19 (p. 410).

10   Heidenreich, p. 412.

11   Schulze.

12   Herrigel, *Industrial Constructions*, pp. 166–68.

how IHKs "provided firms with information about changing government regulations, markets, technology, and organization at the same time that they provided regional authorities with information on the changing needs of local industry" as well as overseeing vocational training standards.[13] The various IHKs actively promoted Mittelstand growth[14] and facilitated financial support for it.[15] While each case-study company's archive contains little or no detail on its own regular interactions with its trade association or IHK (which are therefore not considered separately here) representatives of both attended their key events and celebrations, emphasising the bond between institutions and firms. Though strong claims have been made for the importance of Chambers of Commerce in Britain, there is no evidence of their involvement with our case-study businesses, possibly because they were not required, as their Baden-Württemberg counterparts were, to join their local Chamber.[16]

Values and Motivations

Though the mediating role of formal trade institutions was less apparent in Britain, networking activity was nevertheless important. Historians have shown that in early nineteenth-century British cities, there was value in networks of "businessmen associating, often publicly, to pool resources, to share information, to spread risk, to investigate investment opportunities, to expand their local infrastructure, and to reduce distribution and service costs in their core trades."[17] These relations developed through the nineteenth century, in many cases becoming a feature of business owners' participation in civic affairs and entry into local politics.[18] By the twentieth century, participation in formal business organisations like the Chambers of Commerce may have been less important for business-related networking – or for the securing

13   Herrigel, *Industrial Constructions*, p. 169.

14   See, for example, documentation on support programmes in 'Correspondence on "Mittelstandsprogramm", June 1976 - August 1977' (Industrie- und Handelskammer Stuttgart, 1977), WABW A16/ Bü 87.

15   'Closed Files Relating to Ongoing Subsidy and Support Programmes for Mittelstand Businesses' (IHK Ostwürttemberg, 1988), WABW A15/ Bü 263, 264, 266, 271, 289, 318.

16   R.J. Bennett, *Local Business Voice: The History of Chambers of Commerce in Britain, Ireland, and Revolutionary America, 1760–2011* (Oxford and New York, 2011).

17   R. Pearson and D. Richardson, 'Business Networking in the Industrial Revolution-Riposte to Some Comments', *Economic History Review*, LVI (2), 2003, p. 366. See also: R. Pearson and D. Richardson, 'Business Networking in the Industrial Revolution', *Economic History Review*, LIV (4), 2001; John F. Wilson and A. Popp, 'Business Networking in the Industrial Revolution – Some Comments', *Economic History Review*, LVI (2), 2003.

18   E.P. Hennock, *Fit and proper persons : ideal and reality in nineteenth-century urban government*, Studies in Urban History, 2 (London, 1973).

of one's class position or status – in the West Midlands than philanthropic or religious engagement. This is observable in the histories of two of our case-study companies, Kenrick & Jefferson and Braithwaite & Co. Engineers. The Kenrick family, Unitarians like the Jeffersons, were engaged in all areas of Birmingham and West Bromwich civic life:[19] Frederick Jefferson was Treasurer of the local hospital, as his son would also be, a Justice of the Peace, and a Liberal political activist.[20] James Hulse Humphryes, born and apprenticed in Wednesbury, later chairman and majority shareholder of Braithwaites, shared his business neighbours' sense of obligation: in his will in 1927, he left £4000 to be shared between four hospitals, including the West Bromwich District Hospital.[21] It seems likely that the Jeffersons and the Kenricks shared with Humphryes a sense of moral obligation to the community, whether for religious or secular reasons. This may have brought them into contact with each other in this early manifestation of corporate, as well as family, social responsibility. Unfortunately there is no remaining evidence within our individual companies' archives to enable the recreation of their owners' networks, or to understand whether the changes in civic engagement noted by historians might in any way have attenuated local business owners' influence on public affairs where they lived and worked.[22]

Their social position and civic contribution may have been important considerations for individual owners building West Midlands businesses in the first half of the twentieth century. But in the period after the Second World War, the health of those businesses depended increasingly on the attitudes of those employed in them. Our companies' archives also contain little or no detail on trade union-management interaction, so industrial relations are not considered separately here. But we will see in the individual case studies below how working culture evolved over the post-war decades. The prevalent spirit among many West Midlands workers, either exhausted by the war or made arrogant by victory and now maintaining a sense of entitlement, was complacency.[23] Elements of previously paternalistic management practices within each business persisted for a while, but gradually declined as pre-war standards of worker deference faded and employees pursued their leisure interests away from company sports fields and social clubs.

19   R.A. Church, *Kenricks in Hardware – A Family Business 1791–1966* (Newton Abbot, 1969), p. 228.

20   Kenrick & Jefferson, 'Their Work Shall Endure' (Kenrick & Jefferson, 1934), p. 5, Sandwell, BS/KJ/5/4/1.

21   'RECENT WILLS - James Hulse Humphryes', *The Manchester Guardian* (Manchester, 8 November 1927), p. 8.

22   Hennock, *Fit and Proper Persons*, pp. 323–24.

23   Paulson, 'Memory' reviews evidence of these attitudes among West Midlands' businesses.

Attitudes in what would soon become West Germany were, perhaps under-standably given the scale of loss and destruction there, different. In his 1946 analysis of 'The German Question' and his consideration of the postwar reordering of Germany, Wilhelm Röpke saw work, founded in the values learned through religious faith, as the means by which many Germans could distance themselves from their recent past.[24] German workers were not merely diligent in their work, they immersed themselves in it in a spirit of social conscience and personal consolation. And while "merchant's honour", a term first used in medieval Hanseatic trade, standing among one's peers, and the maintenance of bourgeois values were all important elements of the conduct and self-image of the Ruhr's post-war industrial elite, it was the more down-to-earth values of thrift and hard work that were central to the self-perception and conduct of the Swabian Mittelstand of Baden-Württemberg.[25]

This mindset was evident in the small city of Reutlingen, home to Christian Wandel. A 1959 regional industrial history, written to introduce young workers to Reutlingen's principal companies and industries, drew attention to "the spirit which produced this industry, and which sustains it ... What it has become, it has become through sacrifice and tenacity, hard work and capability, the guiding lights of our future fate."[26] Wandel had explained to the world in 1958 that global demand for their products had been fulfilled by their factory, rebuilt after the war "with true Swabian graft" [Fleiss].[27] This word is repeated in a guide, published a quarter of a century later, to Reutlingen as an industrial location that "lies in the middle of the industrial region, known for Swabian initiative and Swabian industriousness [Fleiss], at the foot of the Swabian Alps in the heart of Württemberg."[28] In his speech at Julius Schneider's 50th anniversary celebrations, the company's owner Rolf Walz refers seven times to "Fleiss", the industriousness of Schneider workers past, present and future.[29]

24   Wilhelm Röpke, *The German Question*, trans. by E.W. Dickes (London, 1946), p. 125 < https://mises.org/library/german-question > [accessed 5 August 2022].
25   Armin Grünbacher, '"Honourable Men": West German Industrialists and the Role of Honour and Honour Courts in the Adenauer Era', *Contemporary European History*, 22.2 (2013), 233–52 (p. 236); See also Grünbacher, *West German Industrialists and the Making of the Economic Miracle*, chap. 5.
26   'Vorwort' to Adolf Reitz, *Werke Und Köpfe: Aufstieg Und Bedeutung Der Südwestdeutschen Industrie: Leistung Und Auftrag* (Reutlingen, 1959), Stadtbibliothek Reutlingen.
27   Fachgemeinschaft Druck- und Papiermaschinen, 'Der Maschineningenieur: Im Papierherstellungsmaschinenbau Und Papierverarbeitungsmaschinenbau' (VDMA Fachgemeinschaft Druck- und Papiermaschinen, 1958), p. 37, WABW B79/Büg.
28   Stadt Reutlingen, *Industriestandort Reutlingen* (Reutlingen, 1984), p. 3, Stadtbibliothek Reutlingen.
29   Rolf Walz, 'Speech by Rolf Walz for 50th Anniversary Celebrations', 1960, WABW B4/Bü3.

What were the origins of this regional self-identity? A 2016 *Stuttgarter Zeitung* article on the 'Mentality of the Württemberger' explores the origins of "Swabian Respectability" and present-day values. A meritocratic mentality, implanted by competition to enter prestigious church schools, combined with the Swabian attributes of industriousness [*Fleiss*, again], thrift and orderliness, has been reinforced by centuries of secular and religious authority.[30] The lines of these long-established influences can be traced through the histories of our case-study companies. For example, the impact of religious faith on working life in Baden-Württemberg was traditionally strong and especially marked among Pietists like the Reutter family, whose company principles were defined by the family's religious values.[31] And while the workplace culture of Reutter's competitor and eventual acquirer, Keiper, was not overtly religious, the beliefs and practices of its founding family underpinned their company's value system. Their most obvious values were industry and integrity. Founder Fritz Keiper was, like his brothers, apprenticed to his blacksmith father. Their workday was from 6am to 8pm, and on four days each week they also went to apprentice school (*Fortbildungsschule*) from 8pm to 9pm. They went to apprentice school again on Sundays from 8.30am to 9.30am, after they had cleaned the forge between 7am to 8am, and before they went to church.[32] Their father "fulfilled various honorary offices and until his death the religious office (*das kirchliche Amt*) of a Presbyterian."[33] There is no recorded evidence of religious practice by Fritz Keiper himself or his own family. But subsequent developments in the Keiper business, even under the youthful, hard-driving Putsch brothers in the 1960s and 1970s, appear to have been characterised not only by extremely hard work but also by respectful and humane treatment of the company's workforce and the continuation of a locally based, family-business culture, suggesting that their grandfather's values had been retained.[34] No matter what their motivation, it was consistent with widely understood Mittelstand values which are socially constructed and codified into German law, predating by decades 21st-century management thinking on the virtues of stakeholder capitalism. This long-maintained way of thinking and working was summarised in 2018 by a regional bank: "The traditional model of the German mid-sized business is based on a

---

30   Werner Birkenmaier, 'Mentalität der Württemberger: Die schwäbische Ehrbarkeit', stuttgarter-zeitung.de (Stuttgart, 17 March 2016), Online edition <https://www.stuttgarter-zeitung.de/inhalt.mentalitaet-der-wuerttemberger-die-schwaebische-ehrbarkeit.46062bea-1ae5-46e2-8015-302849383ff8.html> [accessed 11 December 2018].
31   See Chapter 5 below.
32   Fritz Keiper, 'Mein Weg' (Unpublished typed manuscript, 1939), pp. 33–34, Graciously provided by Herr Frank Jung, then Head of Tradition, RECARO Holding GmbH).
33   Keiper, p. 45.
34   The sons of Keiper's daughter, who became joint managing directors of the family business: see Chapter 9.

long-term approach, in which ownership and the resulting responsibility are paramount. This is entirely in line with Article 14 of Germany's Constitution, which reads: 'Ownership of property comes with responsibility. Its use shall also serve the common good.'"[35]

Succession and Governance

That long-term approach requires continuity in ownership and leadership. Achieving it is particularly important in Germany, where one long-term historical study shows that only 10% of German firms are held in diffuse ownership, in contrast to the United Kingdom where 60% are. Analysing data on 310 German firms from 1960, its author shows how family ownership "was not only highly concentrated but was also understood to be a long-term commitment" by families which continued to prefer private forms of legal ownership. There are benefits to closed forms of governance, enabling owner-families to operate in a stable context, focused on their strategy and with a commitment to long-term investment and to training managers who are often drawn from within the family.[36] What the study does not explain is how such families were able to find new ideas and maximise management inventiveness, nor how they ensured that managers were adequately trained to meet the company's future needs. These questions will be addressed below.

In Britain, the notion of entrepreneurial talent and energy not reaching the third generation is commonplace, reflected in the longstanding adage that entrepreneurs' families go from "clogs to clogs in three generations".[37] Inadequate planning for succession could destroy Victorian companies and the wealth of their shareholding families.[38] In the 1950s, Harvard Business School professor C. Roland Christensen warned that anointing a next-generation family member as the new business leader was risky: "Such a practice restricts the opportunities that can be offered to nonfamily management talent, and places the company at a disadvantage in respect to competitors who can draw upon wider markets for their leaders."[39] This suggests an inevitable tension in Mittelstand firms

---

35   Cited in: Finanzgruppe Deutscher Sparkassen- und Giroverband, p. 16.
36   Christina Lubinski, 'Path Dependency and Governance in German Family Firms', *Business History Review*, 85 (2011), 699–724 (pp. 705, 712, 716).
37   As examined by, for example, Tom Nicholas, 'Clogs to Clogs in Three Generations? Explaining Entrepreneurial Performance in Britain since 1850', *Journal of Economic History*, 59 (1999), 688–713.
38   Martin Daunton, 'Inheritance and Succession in the City of London in the Nineteenth Century', *Business History* 30.3 (1988), pp. 269–286.
39   C. Roland Christensen, *Management Succession in Small and Growing Enterprises* (Boston, 1953), p. 168.

pursuing generational continuity, though this eventuality may not even arise in situations when company owners refuse to retire or cannot find a replacement.[40] The preoccupation of Mittelstand, indeed all, family firms with succession planning is therefore not surprising. Between 2004 and 2009, one study shows, 354,000 German family firms faced a succession issue; 8% of them closed down for want of a successor, threatening in the opinion of its authors not only jobs and productivity but also the principle of respectable capitalism.[41]

As we will see later, succession questions played a part in the fate of all our German case-study companies. The more successful Mittelstand firms, however, have been shown to take pragmatic responses to succession crises. World-leading businesses Stihl and Siegwerk Druckfarben chose to recruit external CEOs when their strategies demanded a supplement to their family gene pool. At machine-tool manufacturer Trumpf, CEO Berthold Leibinger had originally been chosen as the business heir of founder Christian Trumpf not only for his ability (and his willingness to buy equity), but also because he was Frau Trumpf's godson.[42] A generation later Leibinger was able to maintain the family commitment by passing the company's leadership to his daughter.[43] Such pragmatic strategies demonstrate the need for flexibility if family firms are to prosper and survive. Research on intra-family succession in present-day Mittelstand firms highlights, in addition, the requirement to sustain external social capital during any transfer to the next generation:[44] as historian Hartmut Berghoff suggests, a refusal of a business owner to concede his dominant position – and by extension share his networks – can have fatal consequences.[45] The case-study firms faced similar options, and failure rates. Braithwaites, though a public company, contrived to pass their chairmanship from father to son twice, until the Humphryes family subsequently bowed out. K&J suffered for their insistence on having only family managing directors, and RECARO, Wandel, and Schneider all expired or were taken over because of their failure to find an heir or appoint a competent outsider.

40   Berghoff, 'The End of Family Business?', pp. 286–93.

41   Susanne Hilger et al, 'Von Generation zu Generation: der Nachfolgerprozess in Familienunternehmen', in *Familienunternehmen im Rheinland im 19. und 20. Jahrhundert: Netzwerke, Nachfolge, soziales Kapital*, Schriften zur rheinisch-westfälischen Wirtschaftsgeschichte, Bd 47 (Köln, 2009), pp. 177–87 (p. 177).

42   Berthold Leibinger, *Wer wollte eine andere Zeit als diese: Ein Lebensbericht*, 2. (Hamburg, 2011), secs 798, 1469.

43   Fear, 'Straight Outta Oberbueg', pp. 144–49.

44   Sabrina Schell, Miriam Hiepler, and Petra Moog, 'It's All about Who You Know: The Role of Social Networks in Intra-Family Succession in Small and Medium-Sized Firms', *Journal of Family Business Strategy*, 9.4 (2018), 311–25 (p. 321).

45   Berghoff, 'The End of Family Business?', pp. 292–93.

Succession was undoubtedly critical, but even the best-managed firms fortunate enough to have great management talent within the family's gene pool are dependent on critical supporting resources. The most important of those resources for long-term business success were the availability of adequate funding and the quality of their employees. We explore both in the following chapters.

3

Banking

Introduction

Every small-business owner is likely to feel dependent on their bank to some extent. Irrespective of whether the business needs to count on consistent support during hard times or feels it has backing for its growth plans when new opportunities present themselves, bank–business relationships matter. Throughout the post-war period, British SMEs' relationships with their banks were likely to reflect the general indifference of those banks to the SME sector and to local conditions. In contrast, bank–business relationships have been identified as one of the critical elements in comparative German economic success, along with vocational education and industrial relations.[1] Though it is the participation of great 'universal' banks in the affairs of major corporations that is most often seen to have been the special feature of German industrialisation,[2] there was in fact a distinctive three-pillar system of national, local, and cooperative banks that emerged after the Second World War to serve the particular needs of different types of business.[3] German banks provided long-term funding, especially to smaller firms, within a stable financial system that permitted banks to provide consistent support. That system relied on prudent regulation and a "federalist form of corporatism", which allowed smaller, regional institutions to modernise and develop in support of the SME sector, funded by savers.[4]

A comparative analysis of the evolution of SME and banking relationships in Britain, France, Italy, and Germany shows that as British SMEs increasingly

---

1   Wendy Carlin, 'West German Growth and Institutions, 1945–90', *Economic Growth in Europe since 1945*, ed. by Nicholas Crafts and Gianni Toniolo (1996), pp. 484, 487–89.
2   Understanding of this structure has been reassessed by historians, See Jeffrey Fear and Christopher Kobrak, 'Banks on Board: German and American Corporate Governance, 1870–1914', *The Business History Review*, 84.4 (2010), 703–36 (p. 705).
3   Herrigel, *Industrial Constructions*, pp. 20–22: see pp. 158–159 for his analysis of the way Deutsche Bank's relationship with Daimler Benz worked; see Alex Brunner et al, *Germany's Three-Pillar Banking System: Cross-Country Perspectives in Europe*, Occasional Papers (Washington, DC, 2004) for an appraisal of the system by the International Monetary Fund.
4   Sigurt Vitols, 'Are German Banks Different?', *Small Business Economics*, 10 (1998), 79–91 (pp. 79–80).

struggled, Mittelstand companies continued to thrive into and beyond the 1970s. The support of their *Hausbank* (house bank, a term in universal usage) was fundamental to each company's success,[5] and the much larger number of small firms in Germany reflected – and sustained – the more segmented banking system.[6] Small firms were additionally supported by public policies to strengthen their position in post-war West German society, including tax concessions, low-interest funds, and support for trade associations, chambers of commerce, and professional quality standards. When the economic crises of the 1970s struck, financial support was strengthened still further.[7]

West Germany

The West German approach was based on the principle of state support for companies' long-term, stable relationships with their banks, so that firms could pursue long-term objectives such as the research and development (R&D) and training necessary to deliver diversified quality production.[8] In comparison to Britain, the German banking system was less concentrated and had many more banks. The close relationships between larger firms and the national "universal" banks, offering a range of advisory services and embedded in firms' strategic decision-making, continued in the post-war period. By the 1970s, those national banks were also pursuing Mittelstand business, adding to the options available to Mittelstand leaders;[9] as we will see, Chr. Wandel banked with both national and local banks. But the market share of locally focused *Sparkassen* (savings banks owned by local governments) and cooperative banks continued to increase, reflecting their local focus and their deep knowledge of their customers' businesses. Small firms' financing and growth are often constrained by banks' reluctance to lend when there are "information

---

5   Carnevali, pp. 133ff, 140. She shows that there were many more small craft manufacturers in West Germany. In 1963, for example, there were 366,000 such firms (employing fewer than 10 staff) in West Germany versus 31,000 in Britain (p. 139). There were also differences in the number of larger SMEs. In 1967, 43.5% of West Germany's manufacturers (equating to more than 3.9 million firms) had fewer than 200 staff (p. 139); in 1968, in contrast, Britain had almost 2.3 million SMEs, or 29% of all businesses, employing fewer than 200 staff (p. 86).
6   Carnevali, p. 146.
7   Carnevali, pp. 141–42, 147–48.
8   Carnevali, p. 142.
9   Carnevali, pp. 143–44, tables 8.2 and 8.3; For examples of the increasing interest of national banks in the Mittelstand, see also Ralf Ahrens, *Die Dresdner Bank 1945–1957: Konsequenzen Und Kontinuitäten Nach Dem Ende Des NS-Regimes* (Munich, 2007), p. 266; Commerzbank AG, 'Geschäftsbericht Für Das Jahr 1964' (Commerzbank AG, 1964), p. 26 <https://www.commerzbank.com/media/de/konzern_1/geschichte/download_8/geschaefts-bericht_1964.pdf> [accessed 2 February 2019].

asymmetries" between them and prospective borrowers. In Britain, this problem had grown since the banks had begun to consolidate in the 1920s.[10] In West Germany, in contrast, local relationships and mutual confidence sustained long-term interdependence.

British bankers were themselves conscious of the different provision for SMEs in each country. Timothy Bevan, later chairman of Barclays Bank, analysed the West German system in a 1978 Cambridge development seminar for British bankers. The description he provided for participants helps us to understand the differences between the two approaches. In West Germany, each of the eleven Länder (states) had credit guarantee companies dealing with SMEs. They were backed by the state, institutions, and various chambers of trade, and were able to provide funds at up to 2% below market rates. This system was also supported by the decentralised network of savings and local cooperative banks, lending long-term funds to SMEs with state guarantees. Other institutions supporting SMEs were the reconstruction bank Kreditanstalt für Wiederaufbau (KfW) and the Industriekreditbank AG – Deutsche Industriebank, the latter providing eight- to fifteen-year term loans to industry. Bevan's summary was: "The German approach to small business has been very methodical; not only has the sector been encouraged by cheap finance, it has also benefited from the various policies and programmes that have been introduced by the government over the years."[11] In Britain, there were no provisions for subsidized bank lending to small firms and no systems which would have allowed local bank branches to control it. Instead, Britain's five major clearing banks operated a centralised model to which SMEs were of relatively little importance. When the British Government finally became interested in SMEs in the late 1970s, its free-market stance persuaded it only "to remove, or compensate for, market imperfections".[12] In West Germany, however, support for SMEs had been an integral part of economic policy for both national and regional (a tier missing altogether in Britain) governments since 1945. In both countries, then, banking arrangements have reflected political will. Germany has persisted with its approach even in the face of other European countries' resistance to

---

10   Carnevali, p. 8; Others concerned with information asymmetries in these relation-ships include: Lucy Newton, 'Trust and Virtue in English Banking: The Assessment of Borrowers by Bank Managements at the Turn of the Nineteenth Century', *Financial History Review*, 7.2 (2000), 177–99; Timothy W. Guinnane, 'Delegated Monitors, Large and Small: Germany's Banking System, 1800–1914', *Journal of Economic Literature*, 40.1 (2002), 73–124; Timothy W. Guinnane, 'Cooperatives as Information Machines: German Rural Credit Cooperatives, 1883–1914', *The Journal of Economic History*, 61.2 (2001), 366–89; Martin Binks and Christine Ennew, 'The Relationship between UK Banks and Their Small Business Customers', *Small Business Economics*, 9.2 (1997), 167–78.
11   Timothy H. Bevan, 'British Banks and Small Businesses', in *The Banks and Small Businesses. Cambridge Seminar 1978* (London, 1978), pp. 29–52 (p. 47).
12   Carnevali, p. 150.

its arrangement of state guarantees for both *Landesbanken* and *Sparkassen*.[13] But the German way of banking has worked, and we will see below the consequences for small businesses of these differing approaches.

One view of the differing national approaches to banking is that they mirrored differences in business culture. In Britain, family-owned firms were of less significance to the overall economy than was the case in West Germany. There, it took thirty-two years for the number of corporations to rise from 2500 in 1961 to 3000 in 1993; it needed the opening of the stock market for this number to increase to 14,000 by 2008. The long-term nature of business thinking in Germany, even among companies which intended to trade their shares, is evident in the approach to incorporation. British companies which listed in 1995 had on average been in existence for eight years. American companies went public after fourteen years. In Germany, however, the small number of companies seeking an initial public offering did so on average fifty-five years after they had been founded.[14] Such long-term thinking also characterised Mittelstand businesses, which consequently valued close, long-term relationships with their Hausbank.[15] Bank support enabled Mittelstand firms to make extended commitments to R&D and high-quality products, backed by both loan and equity capital and by the provision of comprehensive business information.[16] The evolution of those relationships had begun in the mid-nineteenth century with the development of credit cooperatives, which still exist today, notably in the form of Raiffeisen banks. They offered both short- and long-term loans, in some cases of twenty years or more, and did not always demand collateral, relying instead on their knowledge of the borrower and co-signer.[17] Local banks "succeeded in large part because of their ability to capitalize on the information and enforcement capabilities implicit in their small size and local organization."[18] In the interwar period, provincial private bankers also funded industrial SMEs. For them too, local networks and local knowledge were fundamental to the lender-borrower relationship.[19]

13   Guinnane, 'Delegated Monitors', p. 92 and p. 92 n. 25.

14   Lubinski, 'Path Dependency', p. 716.

15   Christina Lubinski, *Familienunternehmen in Westdeutschland. Corporate Governance Und Gesellschafterkultur Seit Den 1960er Jahren* (Munich, 2010), p. 47.

16   Richard Deeg, 'What Makes German Banks Different', *Small Business Economics*, 10 (1998), 93–101 (pp. 94, 98).

17   Guinnane, 'Delegated Monitors', pp. 379–80.

18   Guinnane, 'Delegated Monitors', p. 386.

19   Harald Wixforth and Dieter Ziegler, 'The Niche in the Universal Banking System: The Role and Significance of Private Bankers within German Industry, 1900–1933', *Financial History Review*, 1.2 (1994), 99–119 (pp. 116–17); a finding echoed by Carsten Burhop, Timothy W. Guinnane, and Richard Tilly, 'The Financial System in Germany, 1800–1914', in *Handbook of Finance and Development*, ed. by Thorsten Beck and Ross Levin (Cheltenham, 2018), pp. 154–55.

For Mittelstand companies, relationships with their local *Sparkassen* (savings banks) were, and remain, particularly significant. Originally intended to help the poor to save, *Sparkassen* had restrictions on their asset holdings, but also guarantees from their chartering entities, meaning that they were both conservative and secure. Initially they played only an indirect role in industrial development through the funding of urban infrastructure projects,[20] but the *Sparkassen* became more active following legislation that allowed them to offer chequing accounts and underwrite securities by 1921.[21] Their position was further strengthened through arrangements made with state-owned *Landesbanken* and state governments to back their liquidity,[22] and by the establishment of *Gironzentrale*, regional coordinating bodies which enabled transfers between *Sparkassen* based in separate regions. As inflation hurt regional economies in the interwar years, the federal states permitted local banks to lend to local Mittelstand firms, thereby easing local hardships and consolidating the Mittelstand's politically influential position.[23]

Sparkasse funding continued after the Second World War, but despite the good will of the Adenauer government, whose tax policy was very pro-Mittelstand [*mittelstandsfreundlich*], companies were initially able to carry out only limited and inadequate investments for want of funds.[24] These limitations were due partly to a cultural resistance to borrowing, shared by all members of the community including entrepreneurs, and partly to the scarcity of external funding in the late 1940s and early 1950s. Medium- and long-term credit was barely available, so business owners relied initially on short-term loans and overdrafts even for longer-term capital investments: in the Rhineland, for example, 80% of all short-term Sparkasse loans went to Mittelstand companies between the 1948 Currency Reform and 1957.[25] This situation changed, however. In Baden-Württemberg the severely limited postwar funding opportunities and the concomitant financial burdens on SMEs eased as local institutions' ability to lend was boosted by the thrifty Swabians' high savings rates.[26] Business borrowers also benefited from the replacement of collateral-based

---

20   Burhop, Guinnane, and Tilly, pp. 160–61; This point is made in Hans Pohl, *Die Rheinischen Sparkassen. Entwicklung Und Bedeutung Für Wirtschaft Und Gesellschaft von Den Anfängen Bis 1990* (Stuttgart, 2001), p. 103; Guinnane, 'Delegated Monitors', pp. 86–88 reflects more widely on the early history of the Sparkassen and develops this theme.
21   Guinnane, 'Delegated Monitors', pp. 88–89.
22   The origin of other EU countries' concerns about unfair state support.
23   Carnevali, pp. 34–38.
24   Hans Pohl, Bernd Rudolph, and Guenter Schulz, *Wirtschafts- und Sozialgeschichte Der Deutschen Sparkassen Im 20. Jahrhundert* (Stuttgart, 2005), pp. 274–76.
25   Pohl, Rudolph, and Schulz, p. 275.
26   Willi A. Boelcke, *Wirtschaftsgeschichte Baden-Württembergs von Den Römern Bis Heute* (Stuttgart, 1987), pp. 560–62.

credit (*Beleihungskredit*) by company credit (*Wirtschaftskredit*) from the early 1960s onwards.

With the rapid growth of the West German economy fuelling companies' demand for support, total Sparkasse lending to Mittelstand companies had reached DM86 billion in 1986,[27] and as the savings banks' share of bank business grew from 30.8% to 38.5% between 1950 and 1977, the share held by private banks fell from 36.4% to 24.9%.[28] With their local knowledge and similar mentality to their customers, the *Sparkassen* had been able to extend their network – most West German businesses were close to one of nearly 18,000 Sparkasse branches[29] – and to resist the competitive incursions of national banks.[30] But what made the *Sparkassen* so successful over an extended period? For one commentator, their lack of interest in profit maximisation or trading their customers' debt has made their business model more economically beneficial and sustainable than that of the national banks.[31] Writing in 2013, a Sparkasse director explained their traditional way of working and its continuing validity: a Sparkasse is "married" to its locality, and must therefore do all it can for it. This means that a Sparkasse in a predominantly agrarian area may have nothing to do with export trade, whereas one in an area specialising in the production of machine tools "will develop all the competences necessary to accompany its clients to the end of the world". If the Sparkasse cannot offer all the support required, its regional Landesbank will provide the missing resources. Mittelstand entrepreneurs are matched with Sparkasse leaders who are themselves local entrepreneurs, mix in the same social circles as their clients, and know them well enough to trust them to manage through economically difficult periods: this assurance of ongoing, comprehensive support encapsulates "what a Hausbank is" to its customers.[32]

Mittelstand business owners could also turn to regional banks for support. A history of the Baden-Württembergische Bank (BWB) over 125 years shows how this regional bank (formed in 1977 from the merger of the Württembergische Bank with the Handelsbank Heilbronn and the Badischer Bank) and its antecedents supported Mittelstand growth through long-term relationships,

---

27   Pohl, Rudolph, and Schulz, p. 365.
28   Daniel Detzer et al, *The German Financial System*, Studies in Financial Systems (Leeds, 2013), p. 40, table 1.1; quoting Jeremy Edwards and Klaus Fischer, *Banks, Finance and Investment in Germany* (Cambridge, 1994), p. 100.
29   Pohl, Rudolph, and Schulz, p. 419, table 7.
30   Pohl, Rudolph, and Schulz, p. 366.
31   Harald Wixforth, 'Das Universalbanksystem – Ein Erfolgsmodell Auf Den Finanzmärkten?', *Jahrbuch Für Wirtschaftsgeschichte / Economic History Yearbook*, 58.2 (2017), 583–612 (pp. 610–11).
32   Frank Eloy, 'Le rôle des banques régionales dans le financement de l'économie allemande', *Réalités Industrielles*, 2013, 56–60 (p. 58). Eloy was at the time of writing the director of a Sparkasse in the Saar responsible for the French market.

again founded on trust and local knowledge. BWB's strongpoint was its focus on Mittelstand needs. Though it did not ignore opportunities to work with larger firms, it was able to maintain profitable short- and medium-term lending with smaller businesses for which it could offer a "home advantage". To do this, BWB counted on the "intensive care of customer relationships in the region and on the individualisation of advisory functions" such that "the customer must be convinced that the banker makes the worries, problems, and interests of the customer his own"[33] and will stand by the company even in difficult times when the bank's risk increases.[34] In some cases, the banks' commitment to their customers extended to the provision of equity funding and the maintenance of a stake in a company's shareholding.[35]

BWB's commitment to Mittelstand relationships was reflected in its governance structure, which illustrates how the bank's directors understood its customers, and how Mittelstand networks were interlocked by shared knowledge and experience. For example, Klaus Scheufelen was a member of the Württembergischer Bank's supervisory board from 1956 onwards, then on BWB's supervisory board from the 1977 merger until 1982.[36] Politically active and influential within the CDU (Christian Democratic Union), Scheufelen was the owner of a paper company, using products made by Chr. Wandel or its competitors.[37] He was also a director of a machinery company. Wandel, or any other company working in a paper- or machinery-related industry, could therefore be confident that Scheufelen and others like him in the bank's senior management understood intimately their needs. Though no bank correspondence remains in Wandel's archive, it is also possible BWB provided it with the advisory support it needed for its very vibrant export programme.

The backing offered to owners and managers of small firms was not confined to the regional banks, credit unions and *Sparkassen*. Support for the Mittelstand had been a specific part of the Kreditanstalt Für Wiederaufbau's (KfW) remit since it was established in 1948. Support came with fixed interest rates – which the KfW ensured were no less favourable than those which large companies could negotiate on the financial markets – for extended periods. For export activities, the bank offered extended, fixed terms to allow investment in

---

33   Willi A. Boelcke, *125 Jahre Baden-Württembergische Bank* (Stuttgart, 1996), p. 178, wording which recalls Eloy's portrayal of Sparkasse-customer relations in 2013.

34   Willi A. Boelcke, *125 Jahre*, p. 179.

35   Willi A. Boelcke, *125 Jahre*, pp. 180–81.

36   'Klaus Scheufelen', Wikipedia (2018) <https://de.wikipedia.org/w/index.php?title=Klaus_Scheufelen&oldid=177045753> [accessed 5 February 2019]; Willi A. Boelcke, *125 Jahre*, p. 207; 'Über Uns - Papierfabrik Scheufelen' <http://www.scheufelen.com/unternehmen/ueber-uns/> [accessed 5 August 2017].

37   'Scheufelen, Klaus Heinrich', *Konrad Adenauer Stiftung*, 2013 <https://www.kas.de/o/webfriend-to-liferay-url-rest-endpoint/urlredirect/resolve-liferay-rpk/1139347/de/252038> [accessed 2 August 2020].

the machinery and equipment required to deliver the borrower's international business plan. In a later period, a key element of the KfW's post-reunification activity was support for the emerging, or redeveloping, Mittelstand in the new states, targeting DM18 billion in 1993 (approximately £7.6 billion at 1993 rates) in support.[38]

It seems reasonable to conclude that for any Mittelstand business owner, one's relationship with one's bank has been a source of long-term strength. Trust was and has remained a critical element of that relationship, as "in credit relationships where trust is high, banks are less likely to pursue a fully-fledged instrumental risk approach but instead tend to incorporate parts of a social risk evaluation, with relationship managers gathering soft information by integrating entrepreneurs' social networks."[39] In consequence, bank-company social networks are considered to be the most important social capital element in any inter-generational transfer of Mittelstand company leadership.[40] This environment has enabled Mittelstand leaders to have the confidence and resources to expand and to pursue long-term plans: "the firms themselves still concentrate[d] on their rightly focused product development and innovation but a network of supporting institutions [including their bank] provide[d] the necessary knowledge and financing to go global."[41] As we will see next, the support of their banks was consistent in the business lives of our case-study companies, but it was not unconditional and open-ended; performance and business viability were required.

Case Studies
Though no bank–company correspondence or other documentation remains in their archives, the general nature of relationships between our case-study companies and their own banks can be discerned. For example, Chr. Wandel seems, from the limited available evidence, to have received sympathetic support from its banks over decades. In 1955, just after its new factory had been built, it had loans from two banks (one local, one the Industrie Kredit-Bank AG) totalling DM331,000. During the year it repaid DM28,000 and paid loan interest of DM20,000, or 5.8%.[42] Over the next 14 years, the company held accounts at four different banks – Württembergische Bank, LZB, Deutsche

38   Gert Vogt, 'Die Kreditanstalt Für Wiederaufbau: Ein Unterenehmensporträt', *Zeitschrift Für Öffentliche Und Gemeinwirtschaftliche Unternehmen*, 17.3 (1994), 373–78.
39   Bernhard Hirsch, Christian Nitzl, and Matthias Schoen, 'Interorganizational Trust and Agency Costs in Credit Relationships between Savings Banks and SMEs', *Journal of Banking & Finance*, 97 (2018), 37–50 (pp. 48, 46).
40   Schell, Hiepler, and Moog, pp. 320–21.
41   Fear, 'Straight Outta Oberberg, p. 152.
42   Chr. Wandel, 'Accounts Ledger, Showing Activa + Passiva, with Profit and Loss Calculations and Profit Shares, 1940–55' (Chr. Wandel, 1955), WABW B79/Bü233.

Bank, and Dresdner Bank – showing that support was readily available for Mittelstand firms like Wandel which faced the challenge of managing cash flow in a business with long machinery delivery lead times, significant export business, and high wage bills for skilled staff.[43] For example, though Wandel's order book at 28 February 1969 stood at DM952,000, and they had received DM380,000 in cash in the previous four weeks, account balances in their four banks were already down to DM13,000, DM1,200, DM11,000, and DM0, respectively.[44] The previous month cash receipts were DM500,000, but again the bank accounts held between DM10,000–DM11,000.[45] Bank support was longstanding, but it was not unlimited. When Wandel eventually closed its doors in 1995, it claimed it was because "the bank stopped everything".[46] Wandel's elderly owner could not understand "the men from the bank" any longer: though Wandel's assets were far more valuable than its debts, Deutsche Bank had terminated its credit and made it impossible to pay the wages.[47] As Wandel's competitors were failing in a shrinking industry, and the company was in financial difficulties itself, the bank's response was surely reasonable after twenty-five years or more of support: it and other banks backed their customers over the long term, but ultimately prioritised prudence and risk-management over sentimental attachment. And while we do not know the details of its final days, the transfer of Wandel's assets and staff to its competitor suggests that the banks supported a managed, principled exit.

Julius Schneider's relationship with its banks followed a similar trajectory. The steel- and glass-fabricator had worked with only one local savings bank, Stuttgart's Städtische Girokasse, before the Second World War. During the war it worked with Deutsche Bank as well, adding the local Feuerbacher Volksbank after the war and subsequently dropping Deutsche Bank after the 1948 Currency Reform.[48] Schneider's cash accounts held RM193,000 at the

---

43   In fact, by 1997 Mittelstand firms typically had 2–4 banks, including the *Hausbank*, securing multiple financing offers, dependent on company turnover. This suggests either that Wandel's relationships were normal, or that mid-1990s Mittelstand firms felt as financially constrained as Wandel had done earlier. See: Ulrich Hommel and Hilmar Schneider, 'Financing the German Mittelstand', *EIB Papers*, 8.2 (2003), 53–90 (p. 64), table 7.

44   'Aktennotiz, Auftragsbestand und – Eingang Weberei/Maschinenfabrik, 12.3.69' in Chr. Wandel, 'Analysis Sheets: Annual Turnover by Product and Country' (Chr. Wandel, 1986), WABW B79/Büi91.

45   'Aktennotiz, Auftragsbestand und – Eingang Weberei/Maschinenfabrik, 14.2.69' in Chr. Wandel, 'Analysis Sheets: Annual Turnover by Product and Country'.

46   'Bank stoppte alles', *Schwäbisches Tageblatt* (Reutlingen, 3 March 1995), p. 10, WABW A7/Bü Fi L/1997 Wandel, Chr.

47   'Trauerspiel Um Traditionsbetrieb', *Reutlinger Nachrichten* (Reutlingen, 15 March 1995), WABW A7/Bü Fi L/1997 Wandel, Chr., A7/Bü Fi L/1997 Wandel, Chr.

48   Kurt Hege, 'Geschichte der Firma J. Schneider GmbH & Co. KG, Ludwigsburg' (Privately printed, 1977), p. 32, WABW B4/Büi.

war's end – an indication of the extent to which the bomb-damaged company had still been able to conduct business right up to the point that Allied forces arrived in Stuttgart – and the company appears to have maintained positive relations with its two banks over the next three decades. Finances were managed prudently: in 1972, turnover reached DM13.7 million, and the same two banks held Schneider's DM845,000 deposits, but the company had chosen to protect its cash reserves by using, and steadily repaying, two long-term loans from Allianz to pay for its factory-building programme and its new crane.[49]

Following the 1973 recession, however, the steel fabrication market went into rapid decline. In 1975, turnover had fallen to DM8.7 million and Schneider had made a loss. It asked its two longstanding banks for a long-term loan of DM1.5 million, having to top up its current account by almost DM1 million just to meet its day-to-day obligations. In consequence, Schneider's 1975 interest payments were DM194,000, and the company attempted to turn its short-term funding facilities with the two banks into a long-term arrangement. The banks were supportive in principle, but cautious, insisting on an asset valuation. And ultimately, they were also realistic: by the end of 1975, when the industry's decline was so deep that Schneider's survival seemed impossible, both banks advised that the company be liquidated while its assets still had value.[50] Having made its decision, however, the Stuttgarter Volksbank ("our real house bank") committed itself to supporting Schneider's efforts to complete a sale of its assets, finish its outstanding contracts to generate revenues, and implement a DM800,000 social plan to ensure that its workforce and pensioners were generously treated. Even when moribund, Schneider could count on the support of its house bank to the end, provided profligacy was avoided, risks mitigated, and business conducted honourably.[51]

Water-purification equipment manufacturer Philipp Müller Nachf. Eugen Bucher GmbH & Co, based in Stuttgart, was apparently (again, bank–customer correspondence is not available) also able to rely on the support of its bankers throughout the postwar period. Like Schneider and Wandel, Müller held accounts with a variety of banks. This was sometimes to facilitate local payments for complex installation projects undertaken at a distance from Stuttgart. In 1950, for example, the company had cash holdings with its local Sparkasse, the state bank (Landeszentralbank) and with the Südwestbank in Stuttgart, as well as with the Sparkasse and Bayerische Vereinsbank at Schwandorf in Bavaria, some 270km away.[52] By 1957, Philipp Müller still held cash in a variety of local, regional, and national banks, but was funding its growth and

---

49 Hege, 'Geschichte', p. 72.
50 Hege, 'Geschichte', pp. 81–82.
51 Hege, 'Geschichte', pp. 83–88.
52 'Vorläufige Vermögensrechnung Auf 31.12.1950' (Firma Philipp Müller Nachf. Eugen Bucher GmbH & Co, 1952), WABW B38/ Bü11.

rebuilding programme through a subsidised KfW loan of DM150,000 and a European Reconstruction Programme (ERP) loan of DM100,000 provided by Württembergische Finanz-AG in Stuttgart.[53] In 1965, DM64,000 of ERP loan remained outstanding, together with DM122,835 of lending from the Württembergischer Kreditverein, a regional credit union. But the company, which achieved a turnover in 1965 of DM8.6 million and net profit of DM96,000, also had outstanding loans of DM390,000 in a special loan account for a development programme, a DM230,000 loan from the state of Baden-Württemberg, and almost DM202,000 from Deutsche Bank in Stuttgart.[54] Philipp Müller had consistently shown itself to be adept at offering high-quality, high-price, high-margin niche products to a global customer base and periodically reorientating its expertise to meet changing market conditions with new, patentable innovations.[55] Its ability to do so must have been in some part due to the availability of supportive funding; equally, the level of financial commitment from its lenders appears to indicate a high degree of trust in the company's management and confidence in its future. Both turned out to be warranted; after merging as a minority partner with a much larger French company in 1967, Philipp Müller continued to innovate in the creation of complex technologies, and is still extant as part of an international group.[56]

At Karosseriewerk Reutter, the founding culture was based on Pietist principles, which meant honouring all agreements punctiliously and paying debts immediately they fell due. This mindset had helped Reutter to achieve considerable financial strength in the interwar years, but it found itself in a challenging position in the initial postwar period until its relationship with the Porsche company began to be both busy and financially rewarding. Although most of the very large and recurrent investment needs for keeping up with Porsche's growth could be funded out of the business, Reutter also needed bank support. In 1950, as production for the Porsche 356 was starting, Allbank granted Reutter a discount credit (*Wechselkredit*) of DM200,000 and an overdraft of DM50,000. At the same time, the Württembergische Landessparkasse (regional savings bank) granted them a DM100,000 mortgage

53 'Bilanz Zum 31. Dezember 1957' (Firma Philipp Müller Nachf. Eugen Bucher GmbH & Co, 1961), WABW B38/ Bü38.

54 'Jahresabschluss Auf 31. Dezember 1965' (Firma Philipp Müller Nachf. Eugen Bucher GmbH & Co, 1967), WABW B38/ Bü66.

55 The company's history is detailed in 'Festschrift Zum 90jähriges Firmenjubiläum' (Firma Philipp Müller Nachf. Eugen Bucher GmbH & Co, 1986), WABW B38/ Bü22; evidence of its innovativeness is confirmed by the 23 patents granted up to 1962: see 'Philipp Müller Nachf. Eugen Bucher GmbH & Co: Patents Granted', Espacenet, 2020 <https://worldwide.espacenet.com/patent/search?q=Philipp%20M%C3%BCller%20Nachf.%20Eugen%20Bucher%20> [accessed 27 July 2020].

56 Hager & Elsässer, 'About H+E Group', *Hager & Elsässer* (2020) <https://www.he-water.group/en/about-h-e.html> [accessed 28 July 2020].

against their property.[57] Relationships were with these local institutions rather than national banks – the Unterstützungskasse (which offered support for pensions), the Württembergische Landessparkasse, and the largest creditor, the Württembergische Kreditverein (Credit Union). It had lent Reutter DM800,000 for five years in 1955;[58] the relationship had clearly grown to support factory expansion requirements, as the debt was by 1962 DM1.8 million and shown as a mortgage. Interest charges on total debt totalled DM202,000 (around 6.2%), though interest receipts on its financial assets were DM303,000:[59] like Philipp Müller, Reutter appeared to be using financing strategically, rather than to fund daily operations. As a rapidly growing business with significant needs, even if its preference was normally to fund its own capital expenditure, Reutter could turn to local banks familiar with both its own operations and those of its principal customer Porsche.

Like so many other Mittelstand enterprises, our case-study companies thrived during the years of the economic miracle, rebuilding themselves after the devastation of the war and sustaining themselves during three decades and more of growth and intermittent economic downturns. They were able to do so by investing in the people and resources necessary to develop and sell high-quality niche products. This approach was bolstered by the long-term support of banks that provided a range of funding solutions and could be relied on as a trusted partner for as long as their business was viable.

Britain

The situation in the West Midlands was rather different. While the long-term funding and business-support services provided by a variety of financial institutions were helping Baden-Württemberg's mid-century Mittelstand to flourish, British business owners and entrepreneurs were living through "the demise of small firms in Britain".[60] Their decline was attributable to several factors, including the preference of successive post-war governments for US-style consolidation through mergers (including those in the steel industry which adversely affected supplies to Braithwaites and others, as we shall see in Chapter 8). In addition to general Government disdain for the small-business sector, SMEs also faced severe funding difficulties thanks to both government and bank

57 Uta Jung and Helmut Jung, *Stuttgarter Karosseriewerk Reutter: Von Der Reform-Karosserie Zum Porsche 356* (Bielefeld, 2006), p. 172.
58 Jung and Jung, p. 211.
59 Stuttgarter Karosseriewerk Reutter & Co. G.m.b.H., 'Bericht Über Das 56. Geschäftsjahr 1962' (Stuttgarter Karosseriewerk Reutter & Co. G.m.b.H., nd), RECARO Holding GmbH archives, Anlage 1.
60 Carnevali, chap. 6.

policies.[61] Banks were concentrated in a centralised system that suited relations with big business but was physically and mentally distant from the smaller firms the banks were also supposed to serve. The inconsistency of government approaches to credit controls caused ruinous uncertainty among SMEs, to which lending fell by 40% between 1951 and 1958. A 1956 survey showed that SME growth and innovation depended on the availability of funding, but thanks to government monetary policy funding was both scarce and unpredictable, making it impossible for firms to invest in change and innovation[62] and causing a damaging effect on business output.[63] Francesca Carnevali argues that failures to support SMEs "were the direct consequence of the structure of the banking system ... The near absence of local or regional banks meant that there were no institutions whose economic interests rested with small firms and who could soften the blow of credit restrictions."[64] The absence of any political desire to help small business meant that there was no pressure applied to banks to make this change, and the banks themselves would have resisted any effort to make them more competitive.[65] In other words, the British approach was diametrically opposed to the various commitments made to the Mittelstand.

How did this situation come about? Historians have identified a gradual change for the worse between the mid-nineteenth century and the interwar period. Ironically, British banking's evolution was largely characterised by a move *away* from the local model which was proving to be so instrumental to Mittelstand success. During the nineteenth century, entrepreneurs who "possess[ed] intimate knowledge of industrial circumstance and personalities" often participated in local banks, which duly "were willing to advance a certain amount of long-term as well as short-term capital to industry."[66] But those local shareholders were also exposed to any downturn in the concentrated local industry they served, and as private individuals they found it difficult to continue serving expanding businesses with increasing capital requirements. Accordingly, consolidation followed until by the mid-twentieth century, five major clearing banks dominated British business. The effect was to reduce bank risk by diversifying portfolios, but also to reduce local knowledge and shorten lending periods.[67] The consequence was that at "a time when substantial new long-term investment in British industry was necessary to match international

61   Carnevali, pp. 88–90.
62   Carnevali, pp. 92–95.
63   Carnevali, pp. 95–97.
64   Carnevali, p. 127.
65   Carnevali, p. 129.
66   Michael Best and Jane Humphries, 'The City and Industrial Decline', in *The Decline of the British Economy*, ed. by Bernard Elbaum and William Lazonick (Oxford, 1986), pp. 222–39 (p. 227).
67   Best and Humphries, p. 228.

competition, the clearing banks sought to sever any long-term commitment to industry."[68]

This lack of commitment had already been evident during the interwar decades. Bank decisions on lending were taken centrally, without the benefit of local knowledge, emphasising short-term lending and high collateral.[69] The banks were already suspected of operating interest rate cartels, and had made it clear that their goal was not to make steady income through the long-term support of SMEs, but to maximise profits through support for companies which they considered big enough to seek an early Initial Public Offering (IPO).[70] Credit for Industry, a private enterprise in which the Bank of England was a 50% shareholder, was prevented from making a significant impact by the clearing banks' tactics and determination to preserve the "super-normal profits" they earned from smaller firms.[71]

By the postwar period, according to one analysis, British banks were operating an "arms-length approach to corporate finance".[72] Their insistence on protection against all lending risks made for enviable stability across the banking system by international standards, but the banks were not required to take any active interest in their clients' business. According to this analysis, the "Victorian" mentality of Britain's clearing bankers produced a "cognitive inertia that limited [banks'] strategic possibilities and commercial potential"[73] and might have been partly responsible for Britain's slow post-war growth.[74] The consequences of this post-war approach for bank–SME relationships were reviewed in a 1988 study conducted by academics on behalf of business groups.[75] They concluded that SMEs faced high interest rates and charges, unreasonable demands for security, and a lack of understanding by banks of their business. Banks' risk aversion and ignorance of their affairs forced companies to use overdrafts to finance long-term growth, which banks were not keen to fund or would do only if offered punitive personal guarantees.[76]

---

68   Best and Humphries, p. 230.

69   Peter Scott and Lucy Newton, 'Jealous Monopolists? British Banks and Responses to the Macmillan Gap during the 1930s', *Enterprise and Society*, 8.4 (2007), 881–919 (p. 892).

70   Scott and Newton, pp. 900–08.

71   Scott and Newton, pp. 913–14.

72   Mae Baker and Michael Collins, 'English Commercial Banks and Organizational Inertia: The Financing of SMEs, 1944–1960', *Enterprise and Society*, 11.1 (2010), 65–97 (p. 66).

73   Baker and Collins, p. 94.

74   Baker and Collins, pp. 93–95.

75   Martin Binks, Christine Ennew, and Geoffrey Reed, *The Survey By The Forum of Private Business on Banks and Small Firms. Report to the Forum of Private Business* (Nottingham, 12 July 1988); see also Graham Bannock and E. Victor Morgan, *Banks and Small Business: An International Perspective* (London, 10 August 1988).

76   Binks, Ennew, and Reed, pp. 74–80.

However, another contemporary analysis pointed to the increased risks to the banks associated with funding the large number of poorly managed new SMEs which had sprung up under the Thatcher government.[77] The conclusion drawn from these differing perspectives was that there was a need for improved relationships and information-sharing between banks and those SME customers requiring their support.[78]

In general, then, company–bank relationships in the UK appeared to be very different from the closer Mittelstand–bank partnerships in West Germany. And differences had widened as earlier restrictions on funding were compounded by the constant pursuit of mergers and consolidations among British banks. While Barclays and National Westminster accounted for 60% of total liabilities among the five remaining clearing banks by 1977, European countries had continued with a system in which the size of a bank matched the size of its commercial customers, and enabled it to reduce transaction costs through knowledge of customers' businesses. Francesca Carnevali identifies the issue of transaction costs, born out of information asymmetries, as being key to the difference between British and German banking provision. The Government-appointed Bolton Committee on Small Firms in 1969 concluded that they were a "fact of life" and were unavoidable. Carnevali rejects this argument completely. Transaction costs certainly affected small firms, but they were paying the price of the banks' structures and way of working: as "one of the consequences of banking concentration was to create larger, more centralized organizations … which increased the distance between the banker and the borrower", British bankers had little knowledge of industrial SMEs' business or management, unlike their German counterparts, and were willing to pass their ignorance on in the form of relatively higher costs.[79]

Carnevali shows how this ignorance, or indifference, manifested itself at Midland Bank, whose performance in the West Midlands is reviewed below.[80] By linking the purchase prices of machine tools to the very low number of similarly valued loans offered by the bank, she suggests that putatively innovative SME manufacturers were being underfunded. Though it was publicising its commitment to making longer-term loans, Midland Bank did not in practice increase its lending, compounding its ongoing failure to support its manufacturing customers.[81] Midland Bank's approach differed from that of Barclays, whose Birmingham Local Board consisted of three local businessmen as well as a banker. The autonomy and local knowledge of that Board contributed to the

77   Kevin Keasey and Robert Watson, 'The Bank Financing of Small Firms in UK: Issues and Evidence', *Small Business Economics*, 6 (1994), 349–62.
78   Binks and Ennew.
79   Carnevali, pp. 112–13.
80   Carnevali, pp. 113–17.
81   Carnevali, pp. 124–26.

relative success of Barclays' Birmingham operation, hinting at the possibility that British banks could have adopted the approaches which their German counterparts were using so successfully.[82] In practice, they had little incentive to do so. Lloyds Bank, for example, was flourishing financially in the late 1950s, even though advances to some business borrowers fell by 40% while advances as a whole fell by 18%.[83] Reducing advances to smaller customers was, the chairman of Lloyds Sir Oliver Franks candidly admitted, much easier than denying credit to larger, corporate businesses.[84]

Local Practice

Evidence from the banks' own archives reinforces the conclusion that West Midlands business leaders faced very different conditions from their Mittelstand counterparts and competitors. Local bank managers and their SME clients faced frustratingly inconsistent policies, often driven by the banks' corporate reactions to Government policy swings, but also reflecting the systemic bias against SMEs. In 1951, for example, Lloyds' West Midlands branch managers were instructed to restrict lending to all but farmers and exporters as part of "a policy of urgent national importance".[85] Within a little over a year, though, it had "now been agreed ... to restore some measure of flexibility" by offering advances to some categories of customer. Managers were reminded that "reducing interest and commission rates" would damage the banks, whose "heavy and increasing overhead commitments" apparently required them to engage in mutually-supportive uncompetitive practices.[86] The flexibility in regard to advances disappeared following a statement from the Chancellor in the Commons in July 1955 on the need for a "positive and significant" reduction in lending. Any West Midlands company owner who saw growth opportunities or a requirement to compete against Mittelstand businesses with their newer equipment would now be disappointed, because "[p]roposals to be firmly turned aside would include any for the financing of capital expenditure, for

82   Carnevali, pp. 116–22.
83   J.R. Winton, *Lloyds Bank 1918–1969* (Oxford and New York, 1982), p. 157.
84   Carnevali, p. 94; Sir Oliver Franks, establishment figure, former British Ambassador to Washington and Provost of Worcester College, Oxford. He found Lloyds conservative and somnolent. He himself, however, had no training in economics, like many professional bankers; nor did he have any experience of running a bank. But he concluded that "If you can run an Oxford college you can run anything": Alex Danchev, *Oliver Franks, Founding Father* (Oxford, 1993), p. 143.
85   Letter from chief general manager to branch managers, 5.12.1951, in 'File of Manager's "Confidential Letters", Lloyds Bank, Sparkbrook Branch, 1948–72' (Lloyds Bank), Lloyds Banking Group Archives, B/1307/a/2.
86   Letter from chief general manager, 26.1.1953, in 'File of Manager's "Confidential Letters", Lloyds Bank, Sparkbrook Branch, 1948–72'.

building up stocks beyond basic levels or for increasing the production or sale of consumer goods."[87]

Inconsistencies continued during the following decade. Midland Bank responded to the easing of credit restrictions with a promising commitment to new growth in 1959: "We are prepared to give generous support to customers of character, integrity, and business ability." As the bank was looking for long-term relationships, "goodwill should be built up with the present generation of young people." Lending for plant, machines, and property could all be offered if the business prospered, and increased if it grew. Managers were urged to be enthusiastic and to avoid forming "the habit of approaching every proposition as if liquidation of the customer's business were imminent."[88] In 1959, then, any entrepreneur or existing business could have felt reasonably confident of the support of their Midland branch manager in pursuing their growth plans. Their confidence must not have lasted for long. Within fifteen months, the Midland's support had been withdrawn, and by mid-1961 the bank was writing to its managers again following an instruction from the Chancellor.[89] Funding for exports was permitted if "urgently needed" but managers were "to discourage proposals for the financing of capital expenditure". Encapsulating the difference between British bankers' thinking and that of their West German counterparts, Midland's chief general manager thought it important to remind staff of the bank's role in financing business: "our proper function in the field of lending is the provision of short-term credit on a revolving basis."[90] Business owners who banked with Lloyds had to endure the same unpredictability. Their Birmingham branch managers were told in 1961, in response to the latest Government restriction and Lloyds' own diminishing liquidity ratio, that £5 million must be recovered from borrowers within the region by the year end and that long-term lending was specifically prohibited.[91] This message was reinforced in 1964, in a time of Government-imposed "abnormal stringency" – other than for needed exports.[92] By 1967, though, West Midlands branch

---

87 'Circular S. 180/1955, Memorandum to Branch Managers Re: Credit Restriction' (Midland Bank, 1955), HSBC Group Archives, London 0193–0004–0002.

88 'Circular S. 163/1959, Memorandum to Branch Managers Re: Lending Policy' (Midland Bank, 1959), HSBC Group Archives, London 0200–0074b.

89 'Circular S.C. 236/1960, Memorandum to Branch Managers Re: Credit Conditions' (Midland Bank, 1960), HSBC Group Archives, London 0200–0074b.

90 'Circular S. 180/1961, Memorandum to Branch Managers Re: Credit Restrictions' (Midland Bank, 1961), HSBC Group Archives, London 0200–0074b.

91 Minute note, regional manager's meeting, 16 August 1961, 'File of Manager's "Confidential Letters", Lloyds Bank, Sparkbrook Branch, 1948–72'.

92 Letters to all managers of branches from Lloyds Bank Head Office, 1 December 1964 and 5 January 1966, in 'File of Manager's "Confidential Letters", Lloyds Bank, Sparkbrook Branch, 1948–72'.

managers were being enjoined not to lose accounts, and in particular to pay attention to the needs of "younger men making business progress".[93]

How were bank–business relationships actually managed in the face of these frequent changes in policy? We have some sense of them from the Private Memoranda in which local managers continued to record observations on their customers,[94] as they had done since they began using "character books" in the nineteenth century to record information on their customers and mitigate the banks' risk of lending to them.[95] Very few post-war Memoranda are left in the archives, but an investigation of those which remain offers a means of understanding the scope of branch interests in their customers' businesses. We find that managers' analyses seem to be more concerned with social standing and character than with business plans. For example, when a group of businessmen purchased a firm in Alcester, Warwickshire in 1945 with the intention of turning it into a limited company, Lloyds' branch manager recorded that one partner, a local farmer, was "not too strong financially" and "should be encouraged not to take a very active role in the business as it may be detrimental to his farming." The manager had more confidence in another partner, "proprietor of [another company] our customers – a splendid worker and keen businessman who will give the co good advice and a steadying influence, very reliable and considered worth £7500." One director had moved from another Lloyds branch, which reported: "We consider him highly respectable and trustworthy … We have no further knowledge of his means but his wife who we understand has means, guaranteed his account to the extent of £100 in 1940." The effort to understand this man's "means" continued: when he requested a mortgage two years later, the Alcester branch manager felt it necessary to record that he was "v well connected", and gave extensive details of his family's background and social position.[96] Perhaps mindful of future collateral requirements, he concluded: "I believe that they possess some nice old family silver, but have no idea of its value."[97] One perspective on this record is that in order to protect the bank's interests, the branch manager had made himself intimately aware of his customer's personal and family situation, as well as his performance within his business, and based his support for him and his company on that

---

93 'Memorandum by District Manager, Birmingham: "Business Development Notes"' (Lloyds Bank, 1967), Lloyds Banking Group Archives, B/1307/a/2.
94 David Paulson, Interview with John Saynor, retired senior manager, Newcastle-under-Lyme group, Lloyds Bank, 2016.
95 Newton; see also Victoria Barnes and Lucy Newton, 'Constructing Corporate Identity before the Corporation: Fashioning the Face of the First English Joint Stock Banking Companies through Portraiture', *Enterprise & Society*, 18.3 (2017), 678–720, for commentary on the presentation of the branch manager as a figure in local society.
96 Removed here to prevent identification of the family.
97 Entry for 3/5/47, 'Private Memoranda Book, Alcester Branch, 1919–49' (Lloyds Bank), Lloyds Banking Group Archives, B/19/a/1.

understanding. The counterargument is that the bank remained preoccupied with character and social standing; details of the family silver are noted, but there is no mention in the record of the company's business plan or of this individual's execution of it, let alone of any ways in which the bank intended to support it.

This distance from the reality of business performance did not always apply, and there are instances of conduct which show how British banks could act in the more supportive fashion practised by their West German counterparts. To assist another branch's customer with due diligence, for example, Lloyds' Brierley Hill's manager was asked by a counterpart in Shropshire to comment on a local firm of engineers: whether it was well managed, had plentiful labour, whether its premises and plant were in good condition, and what valuation could be put on the business as a going concern.[98] In his reply, Brierley Hill's manager highlights the high reputation of the late owner and gives details of remaining shareholders.[99] Over the course of the next month, Brierley Hill's manager apparently played an active role in sounding out potential purchasers of the company, reporting on progress to the district manager in Birmingham.[100] In this situation, branch staff show knowledge of their customers' businesses and are willing to take actions which will advance a customer's position: this is much more like the "all-finance" relationship between Mittelstand firms and their "house banks", but it appears to have been the exception rather than the norm.

Though central policies dominated the banks' regional approach, it is possible that managerial limitations also affected banks' local conduct. Provincial managers' independence and capability in the immediate post-war years were limited by their personal background. In the post-war decade, mechanisms existed within Barclays to advance competent "singled-out" men of talent up to local and national director level. They had to compete against "special entry" recruits from the forces or universities, who were required to demonstrate social skills and qualities of character and leadership. On neither career path were branch management or banking examinations initially stipulated.[101] At Barclays, "local directors and branch managers continued to make shrewd lending decisions, but had no desire to be involved in details of company management. They backed horses, not courses" and "still had few technical,

---

98 'Private Memoranda Book, Brierley Hill Branch, 1914–49' (Lloyds Bank), Lloyds Banking Group Archives, B/186/a/4, memo dated 2.3.1949.
99 'Private Memoranda Book, Brierley Hill Branch, 1914–49', memo dated 4.3.1949.
100 'Private Memoranda Book, Brierley Hill Branch, 1914–49', memos of May 1949.
101 Margaret Ackrill and Leslie Hannah, *Barclays. The Business of Banking 1690–1996* (Cambridge, 2001), pp. 127–29.

scientific or production skills."[102] It is difficult to imagine such men adding much value to a local entrepreneur or growing engineering business.

Lloyds Bank actually found recruitment for manager positions difficult in the years following the war.[103] One recruit was John Saynor, who joined Lloyds in 1960, having left school aged fifteen. His experience during the 1960s and 1970s in the East and West Midlands offers an insight into the bank's culture and the reality of branch relationships with local businesses.[104] His initial posting in a small mining town encompassed a six-week introductory course, which included coaching on dress and deportment. Somewhat paradoxically, given their employers' general indifference to SMEs, bank managers' education included not only training in the bank's systems but also a proper understanding of SME financing. The Institute of Banking's 1964 examination in banking practice required candidates to assess several SME-related problems, such as an overdraft (but not, significantly, a long-term funding) request from a manufacturing company wanting to buy plant and extend its factory.[105] The Lloyds' six-week Senior Course also included instruction on how to appraise and assess businesses.

Engagement in community activities was important. Lloyds expected their managers to become members of associations such as Rotary Clubs and the Chamber of Trade;[106] in this respect, those managers were doing what their predecessors had practised during the nineteenth century and their German counterparts had been doing for decades. In fact, by the late 1970s, other aspects of bank managers' local conduct had also begun to resemble German practices. As branch manager at Burslem in 1979, Saynor recalls that working with SMEs, such as pottery manufacturers, was the most important part of his job. He personally visited all of his SME clients to judge their dependability. As with his predecessors, though, the chief criteria for assessing customers remained "Character (the primary determinant)", along with "Capability", and "Capital" (whether they owned their own home and business property). Managers were also trained to look at clients' balance sheets and take a view over three years, looking at control of stock and debtors, movements in sales and working capital, and key ratios relevant to their industry. Saynor also recalls working with start-ups, and he and other managers were tasked with building their branches, with their personal rewards being promotion or increased status.

102   Ackrill and Hannah, pp. 142–46, 147.
103   Letter to Managers of Branches and Heads of Departments, 'Staff Recruitment and Training', 21.9.1949, in 'File of Manager's "Confidential Letters", Lloyds Bank, Sparkbrook Branch, 1948–72'.
104   Paulson, 'Interview with John Saynor'.
105   'The Institute of Bankers: Banking Diploma Examination, Part II. "The Practice of Banking", September 17, 1964' (Institute of Bankers, 1964), Private collection, J. Saynor.
106   As was the case for Barclays' branch managers: Ackrill and Hannah, p. 159.

Saynor's experience was reflected in the Institute of Banking's management development seminar at Christ's College, Cambridge in 1978 on dealing with SMEs. Students were aged thirty to forty and their participation was by selection.[107] They were taught by John Bolton, recent chairman of the Parliamentary report on small businesses, and Timothy Bevan, subsequently chairman of Barclays Bank, his family's business.[108] As we have already seen, Bevan reflected on the differences between West German and British approaches to small-business banking. He also reviewed various challenges facing SMEs, relationships between them and local branch managers, the recent transition by banks to medium-term lending, services such as leasing and HP, and support for exporting. Seminar students then worked on case studies, including a small manufacturing company with limited resources, and on a discussion syllabus, which included considerations of the burden of increased legislation.[109] The seminar's approach was commendable, but the focus on small businesses was unique to the 1978 edition of a series of annual seminars. One may ask in any case whether professional bankers approaching the age of forty should have been introduced to the problems of SMEs only at this stage of their career, when so many of their West German counterparts had from the beginning of their own career seen Mittelstand firms as the critical element – perhaps even the raison-d'être – of their banks' existence.

While their training, advertising, and the professional orientation of their branch managers at last showed British banks taking a serious interest in SME development, their apparent commitment actually lasted for only a very brief period in post-war British banking history.[110] Saynor recalls that "the best years were when the branch manager was involved hands-on with the customers", but by the 1990s, the job had become "more of a sales role". He was retired at age 57 because senior managers were no longer required in branches. His disappointment in the underlying cultural and strategic shifts is echoed in Pal Vik's review of the changes to branch banking. Managers had been principally focused on lending to businesses, seeing themselves "as autonomous

107   Edwin Green, *Debtors to Their Profession: A History of the Institute of Bankers 1879–1979* (London, 2012), p. 175.
108   J.E. Bolton, 'The Financial Needs of the Small Firm', in *The Banks and Small Businesses*, Cambridge Seminar 1978 (London, 1978), pp. 1–28; J.E. Bolton, *Report of the Committee of Enquiry into Small Firms* (London, 1971).
109   The Institute of Bankers, *The Banks and Small Businesses*, Cambridge Seminar 1978 (London, 1978).
110   As contemporary advertisements confirm: see for example 'Westminster Bank Advertisement: "How to Make a Little Business into a Big One"', *The Economist* (30 September 1967), p. 1158, The Economist Historical Archive; 'Lloyds Bank Advertisement: "When You've Got the Idea, Here's How to Get the Money"', *The Economist* (4 August 1979), p. 14, The Economist Historical Archive.

and authoritative craftsmen".[111] But a three-fold transformation marked the
end of the branch manager careers enjoyed by Saynor and Vik's interviewees,
and also marked a deterioration in those SME relationships which had been
briefly fostered: the banks moved lending to central branches or processing
centres, which depersonalised SME relationships; they introduced business
credit scoring, which undermined managers' knowledge of the client SME; and
they became increasingly focused on sales and targets, reflecting their preoccupation with their own growth rather than their clients'.[112] Indeed, British
banks' commitment to their own profitability was contrasted at the time by the
International Monetary Fund, which found that "profit maximization [was]
not the primary motivation" for participants in the three-pillar banking system
in Germany.[113]

Case Studies
In practice, how did these bank attitudes manifest themselves in the funding
of our case-study companies? Unfortunately no company's archive contains
much material on bank relationships, but it is evident that all the companies
got access to some finance. For example, Jensen Motors Ltd. met Barclays
Bank in 1947. The loan amount requested was £20–£30,000. With assets
of £192,000, an additional £60,000 of capital available within six months,
and estimated profits of £115,000 over the next three years, the bank still
required a debenture.[114] Details of the final arrangement are not known, but
future accounts show secured loans of £20,800 in 1949 increasing to £85,000
in 1959.[115] In 1951/52, total bank and debenture charges amounted to 8.7%
of the average outstanding loan, 50% higher than the rates charged to Chr.
Wandel at a similar period.[116] Though these costs were substantial, it does not
appear that Jensen's bankers failed to support the company through this final
period under family ownership, possibly because that support was approved
by Barclays' more autonomous Local Board in Birmingham.[117] As with the

111   Pal Vik, '"The Computer Says No": The Demise of the Traditional Bank Manager
and the Depersonalisation of British Banking, 1960–2010', *Business History* (2016), p. 14.
112   Vik, pp. 11–13; Midland commissioned a report on increasing profit. Though it showed
most margin coming from SMEs, it recommended no SME strategy: 'Report by McKinsey
& Co. Inc. : "Strengthening Midland's Ability to Grow Profitably"' (Midland Bank, 1971),
HSBC Group Archives, London 0126–0003.
113   Brunner et al, p. 1.
114   'Handwritten Duplicate Book' (Jensen Motors Ltd., 1942), pp. 36–37, MRC, MSS
215/6/1.
115   'Jensen Motors Limited: Summary of Accounts, 1949–58' (Blakemore, Elgar & Co.,
1958), MRC, MSS.215/2/10.
116   'Handwritten Profit and Loss Account Summary, 1951/52 to 1955/56' (Jensen Motors
Ltd., 1954), MRC, MSS.215/3/, author's calculations.
117   As described in Carnevali, pp. 116–17.

other British businesses examined below, however, there is no evidence of any additional support or strategic advice.

Braithwaite & Co. Engineers Ltd. depended on Lloyds Bank for support in the form of an overdraft, for which they were ultimately offered a £600,000 facility. Originally they were supported by the West Bromwich branch, but the larger facility later came from Lloyds' head office; there are no records of long-term lending, only a continuing overdraft facility. Braithwaites became a public company in 1927 – a model which would automatically have endeared it to British banks – even though it remained under the control of the Humphryes family.[118] It had the option of generating funds through stock issues, meaning that the overdraft sufficed for all day-to-day management, but this was a clumsy, expensive, and potentially risky arrangement.[119] On the face of it, the bank was supportive as the uncertainties of managing public engineering contracts ebbed and flowed. But Braithwaites was well run and profitable, and often had sizeable cash holdings, which should have mitigated bank concerns. And having the overdraft facility did not mean long-term investments were automatically possible: for example, while Braithwaites' board were conscious of the dangers involved in managing an overdraft which was forecast to reach £652,000 in October 1969 at 9% interest, in the same period the company was unable to make a needed investment of £25,000 in a new sandblasting plant.[120] The overdraft facility could in any case, by definition, be withdrawn at any time and it was not inexpensive: the 1975 balance sheet, for example, show an overdraft of £250,260 and overdraft interest payments of £37,829 at a time when the company's net current assets exceeded £2 million – a relatively low risk to the bank.[121] Though Braithwaites' relationship with Lloyds may have been helped by the "character" of its public-school educated chairmen, it should not have had to depend on it. Theirs was a fundamentally solid business which could have benefited from stronger bank support, such as when they were unable to

118   Midland, for one, was much more interested in SMEs with plans to float than in others requiring ongoing support: A.R. Holmes and Edwin Green, *Midland: 150 Years of Banking Business* (London, 1986), p. 241.

119   'Resolution of Braithwaite & Co. Engineers, 21/9/1972 Re: Increase in Capital and Sale of Shares' (Companies House, 1949), Companies House, archive disk 00175912–03; 'Special Resolution of Braithwaite & Co. Engineers, 24/12/1949 Re: Borrowing and Issue of Securities' (Companies House, 1949), Companies House, archive disk 00175912–03.

120   Minutes for 22 October 1969 in Braithwaite & Co. Engineers Limited, 'Board of Directors' Meetings, 10 July 1968 to 11 December 1974' (Braithwaite & Co. Engineers Limited, 1974), Sandwell, BS-B1/1/10.

121   Braithwaite & Co. Engineers Ltd., 'Report and Accounts for the Year Ended 31 March 1975' (Braithwaite & Co. Engineers Ltd., 10 July 1975), Companies House, archive disk 00175912–21.

complete a bid on a major power station contract in 1973 because the bank would not provide a performance bond.[122]

Kenrick & Jefferson also banked with Lloyds, of which the Kenrick family had been directors. It was a cash-rich company throughout its early life: in 1950, after a rewarding war, K&J had £205,000 in their Lloyds deposit account.[123] This position deteriorated over time. By the end of the 1970s, K&J's shareholders were prospering but its managing director was warning divisional managers of deteriorating profitability and dependence on overdrafts, which had risen from zero to £587,000 during the decade. At no point in the company's accounts is there any record of bank lending or long-term indebtedness. This suggests that during the period 1973 to 1980, for example, the increase in sales from £2.6 million to £11.1 million, and the increase in fixed assets from £1.76 million to £3.2 million, were funded only by retained profit and by the bank overdraft which grew from nothing to £587,000 over the same period. This was a costly approach: in 1981, K&J's pre-tax profit was £72,000; its overdraft interest was £95,000.[124] And throughout this period, the company was required to provide guarantees for overdraft facilities run by its subsidiaries. Like Braithwaites, K&J was a fundamentally sound, well-run business. But it was in a rapidly evolving, highly competitive marketplace. And while some of its failures to repeat previous international product successes or match growing competitors were attributable to leadership shortcomings, as we shall see below, it seems reasonable to suggest that a more supportive arrangement with its bankers might have enabled it to build better on its past achievements.

Unfortunately, archival evidence is insufficient for a detailed understanding of bank–company relationships in either country. The evidence from the banks' archives and our case-study companies seems to contradict the suggestion that British banks were not willing to lend money. But that money was in the form of overdrafts, the most precarious level of support, with little evidence of the long-term backing from multiple sources enjoyed by Mittelstand counterparts. It is clear that for individual managers like John Saynor, supporting local SMEs was important. But interest in client businesses seems to have related to specific lending opportunities rather than to ongoing relationships in which wider advice and sustenance were provided. Support was inconsistent at best, and secondary to the banks' commitment to advancing their own wellbeing. In

---

122   Minutes for 20 September 1973 Braithwaite & Co. Engineers Limited, 'Board of Directors' Meetings, 10 July 1968 to 11 December 1974'.

123   Kenrick & Jefferson, 'K&J Cash Ledger' (1935), Sandwell, BS/KJ1/2/11, entry for 30/6/1950. Ledger records of their Lloyds deposit account continue to 1963, but there is no correspondence.

124   Kenrick & Jefferson, 'Accounts to 27 June 1981' (Kenrick & Jefferson, 1981), Companies House, archive disk 0006471_04.

any case, the window in which SMEs seem to have been offered valuable, local assistance closed very soon after it had been opened.

In contrast, the *Sparkassen* and other local banks appear to have offered consistent support throughout the lives of their Mittelstand customers. The value of that broad support was also acknowledged by Midland Bank in its 1994 report into 'The Mittelstand, the German Model, and the UK'. Its authors found fundamental differences which went beyond banking: "the provision of finance must be put in the wider context of a more restrained and thoughtful business culture, moving away from the 'lifestyle' company approach, a more developed training ethos for all sections of the economy both initially and on a continuing basis, together with (most importantly) greater overall economic stability."[125] Ironically, financial innovation *was* present in this period in the shape of Britain's building societies, which stimulated both house-ownership and house-building.[126] It is paradoxical that eighty years ago, Britain, like Germany, possessed a network of locally-owned financial institutions, which drew on local savers' deposits to make loans which boosted the local economy. Like Germany today, Britain still has that network. Then as now, however, the German variant was dominated by *Sparkassen* committed to boosting local industry, whereas Britain's regional building societies have continued to restrict their activities to consumer-lending for house purchase.

---

125   Midland Bank PLC Corporate Finance Department, *The Mittelstand. The German Model & the UK* (London, September 1994). Quotation from p. 2.
126   Best and Humphries, pp. 234–36.

4

Recruitment and Training

Funding was of no value to a company unless it had adequate staff, and for some observers, the quality of personnel was the key differentiator between post-war British and German business performance. In a 1988 report the Confederation of British Industry (CBI) concluded that British companies were less productive than the similar German companies which they investigated. They found, however, that R&D expenditure was not significantly less than in West Germany; plant and machines were no older; product design was not noticeably inferior. Instead, the CBI concluded that "the only area where our West German companies retain a clear-cut advantage is in the educational level attained by their employees." Whereas 52% of German workers had a post-secondary education, only 18% of their British counterparts had; to make matters worse, the British workers had "had an inferior secondary education in the first place, particularly in subjects of a technical nature." Furthermore, "not to be outdone by their workers, UK managers are also less qualified than their German counterparts."[1]

Alfred Chandler argues that German universities and technical education were a key enabling factor in Germany's economic development from the beginning of the twentieth century, "providing the best technical and scientific training in the world", which "pioneered in institutionalizing the acquisition and transfer of knowledge." Whereas in Britain in 1913 there were only 1129 students of engineering in all English and Welsh universities, there were 16,568 engineering students just in Germany's *Technische Hochschulen*, without considering its universities.[2] Engineering training was not the only differentiator. In international trade, for all Britain's success over centuries, "it was generally believed that German commercial education was superior to that available in Britain": embarrassingly, "Anglo-German merchants were in the vanguard of the movement to improve technical education in England."[3]

---

1   Confederation of British Industry, *Tales of Two Companies : A Comparison of Industrial Performance in the UK and West Germany* (London, 1988), pp. 28–29.
2   Chandler, *Scale and Scope*, p. 425.
3   Stanley Chapman, *Merchant Enterprise in Britain From the Industrial Revolution to World War 1* (Cambridge, 1992), pp. 288–89.

The educational historian Michael Sanderson sees evidence of educational failings across all areas of business. In his *Education and Economic Decline in Britain, 1870 to the 1990s* he argues that there was no sustained success in any educational initiative after 1914 which effectively allowed Britain to compete comprehensively against Germany and other leading economies.[4] Sociologist Christel Lane analyses the system of vocational education and training which existed in both countries during the 1980s, concluding that "in Germany industrial training [was] regarded as a matter of public interest and as a valuable societal resource". British training, however, lacked rigour and structure at the post-secondary level for the third of British teenagers offered any vocational training before entering employment, and offered minimal opportunity for older workers to upgrade their skills.[5]

Given the challenges facing post-war business, first of scarce material resources and skills shortages, and then of growing international competition and quickening technological change, human resources counted: skilled, motivated workers were needed in the right numbers, and leadership needed to be applied where it could be most influential. Numerous factors were involved.[6] The importance of management education has been studied in detail elsewhere, and will not be considered here. Nor will industrial relations: clearly they have been seen by contemporary and later commentators – not to mention successive governments – as a critical factor in Britain's economic performance, but there is little or no specific material in our case-study companies' archives relating to union–management relations. Instead, we will take a different perspective. My contention is that supervisory management and a supply of well-qualified engineering talent were critical differentiators between the two countries' approach to manufacturing, and have been analysed in insufficient detail in relation to SMEs. But those individuals could only deliver productivity and quality when they were working with skilled workers who were trained and motivated. In this chapter, therefore, we consider apprenticeships, first-line management, and engineer recruitment. We review the approach in each country and, to the extent that evidence is available, within the case-study businesses.

4   Michael Sanderson, *Education and Economic Decline in Britain, 1870 to the 1990s* (Cambridge, 1999), pp. 81, 83–90.
5   Christel Lane, 'Vocational Training and New Production Concepts in Germany: Some Lessons for Britain', *Industrial Relations Journal*, 21.4 (1990), 247–59 (pp. 62–85); for a detailed study of comparative developments, see Kathleen Thelen, *How Institutions Evolve: The Political Economy of Skills in Germany, Britain, the United States, and Japan* (Cambridge, 2004).
6   Thelen reviews the German approach to apprenticeships in the postwar period. It was notable for the coalition of stakeholders, including unions, which affirmed their importance and facilitated the 'dual system' that combined workplace and classroom training: Thelen, pp. 240–53.

Apprenticeships

If skilled workers were the basis of relative economic success, it makes sense to start with examining those employees who would form the foundation of any business in the post-war years, its youngest staff members. In this section, we consider the importance of apprenticeships as a source of supply and development for this essential pool of talent. In both Britain and Germany, apprenticeships had been a feature of economic activity since the Middle Ages. In Bernard Elbaum's view, the institution of apprenticeship brought national economic advantages that explained its continued place in the British economy over centuries.[7] Apprenticeship improved economic efficiency by certifying training and competency in valued skills, helping employers recoup their investment in that training, and giving apprentices assurances of stability of employment, and content and duration of training, during their apprenticeship.[8]

Yet despite its supposed importance in Britain, Stephen Broadberry concluded in 1997 that "Germany ha[d] retained a commitment to apprenticeships which ha[d] evaporated in postwar Britain",[9] as Figure 1 illustrates.[10]

The question of apprenticeship attracted a substantial amount of academic interest in the 1990s and early 2000s, as scholars and policy makers in both Britain and the newly-united Germany debated the most suitable youth-development mechanisms to meet the changing economic challenges of the times. Some scholars questioned its continuing validity within a German economic model that they now considered to be superannuated. Sceptics questioned whether the implicit rigidity in craft training was suited to a new era of rapid technological change, and highlighted the value of more flexible approaches to apprentice training that inculcated team-based approaches to problem solving.[11] For other commentators, however, the organisation and delivery of apprenticeships remained fundamental to what some termed the "high-skill equilibrium".[12]

Scepticism about the German model, ironically, was countered in Britain by a call for greater investment in apprenticeships. One influential report pointed

---

7   Bernard Elbaum, 'Why Apprenticeship Persisted in Britain But Not in the United States', *The Journal of Economic History*, 49.2 (1989), 337–49.

8   Elbaum, pp. 342–45.

9   S.N. Broadberry, *The Productivity Race: British Manufacturing in International Perspective, 1850–1990* (Cambridge, 1997), p. 112.

10   Broadberry, pp. 110–14. Compiled by the author from tables 8.4, 8.5, 8.7.

11   Gary Herrigel and Charles F. Sabel, 'Craft Production in Crisis: Industrial Restructuring in Germany during the 1990s', in *The German Skills Machine: Sustaining Competitive Advantage in a Global Economy*, ed. by Pepper D. Culpepper and David Finegold (New York and Oxford, 1999), pp. 77–114.

12   Pepper D. Culpepper, 'The Future of the High-Skill Equilibrium in Germany', *Oxford Review of Economic Policy*, 15.1 (1999), 43–59.

Britain	Engineering Apprentices (000s)	Engineering Employment (000s)	Apprentices as % share of Engineering employment	Manufacturing Apprentices (000s)	Manufacturing Employment (000s)	Apprentices as % share of Manufacturing employment
1950	64.8	1,480.2	4.40	240.4	8,067.9	2.98
1964	152.5	3,461.1	4.41	243.7	8,158.0	2.99
1966	170.4	3,550.8	4.80	218.6	8,033.0	2.72
1970	151.2	3,539.2	4.27	149.5	6,519.4	2.29
1980	101.3	3,026.5	3.35	53.6	4,953.1	1.08
1989	34.1	2,130.3	1.60			

West Germany	Metals & Engineering Apprentices (000s)	Metals & Engineering Employment (000s)	Apprentices as % share of Engineering employment	Whole Manufacturing Apprentices (000s)	Whole Manufacturing Employment (000s)	Apprentices as % share of Manufacturing employment
1950	203.6	2,553.0	8.00	304.7	6,576.0	4.60
1960	339.7	4,739.0	7.20	553.9	10,016.0	5.50
1970	289.2	5,393.0	5.40	447.3	10,181.0	4.40
1980	363.2	5,095.0	7.10	611.7	9,017.0	6.80
1988	374.0	5,004.0	7.50	621.1	8,499.0	7.40

Figure 1 Apprenticeships, Britain and West Germany, 1950–88.

to "serious skill shortages and enduring gaps at the skilled crafts, technician and associate professional level" which could be remedied by a doubling of apprentice starts as a first step in recovering from the "failure to modernise and reform in the 1970s and 1980s" that had caused a serious decline in apprentices trained.[13] Whereas only 10 percent of British eighteen-year-olds were joining the Modern Apprenticeship programmes launched by the British Government in 1993, two-thirds of their German counterparts were entering apprenticeships.[14] Regrettably, there was also limited interest from employers, which the report's authors attributed partly to the high cost of apprentice wages in Britain compared to those in Germany. The authors called for both a reduction in apprentice wages to a lower proportion of the skilled-worker's wage, and for greater public investment in the educational infrastructure that in Germany was sophisticated and provided for free to German apprentices and their employers.

History and Context

Though apprenticeships were founded in a tradition of craft training dating back to medieval guilds, the German dual system, encompassing both vocational education outside the workplace and on-the-job training within it, was formalised in the late nineteenth and early twentieth centuries. Recognising the difference between 'industry' (*Industrie*) and 'craft' (*Handwerk*), the responsibilities of participating institutions – companies, labour, and government – were enshrined in laws such as the 1953 Craft Regulation Act (*Handwerksordnung*) and 1969 Vocational Training Act (*Berufsbildungsgesetz*). One commentator argues that the dual system is distinguished by two key principles. The first is that the use of dual learning sites "fosters a training culture that regards vocational training not only as a specific form of employment, but also as a form of education." The second "is the vocational principle (*Berufsprinzip*) which stands for a holistic notion of competence referring to more than just a specific workplace."[15] This can be contrasted with the British tradition of an apprenticeship based in and suited to one employer, teaching the skills required for its organisational needs.

---

13   Hilary Steedman, Howard Gospel, and Paul Ryan, *Apprenticeship: A Strategy for Growth* (London: Centre for Economic Performance, London School of Economics and Political Science, October 1998), p. 7.
14   Steedman, Gospel, and Ryan, p. 28.
15   Thomas Deissinger and Silke Hellwig, 'Apprenticeships in Germany: Modernising the Dual System', *Education & Training*, 47.4 (2005), 312–24 (p. 314); the cultural and historical foundations of the dual system are lucidly described in Thomas Deissinger and Philipp Gonon, 'The Development and Cultural Foundations of Dual Apprenticeships – a Comparison of Germany and Switzerland', *Journal of Vocational Education & Training* (2021).

While German institutions were committing themselves to compulsory vocational training organised to national standards for multiple trades and supported by government, employers, and trade unions through a combination of workplace and vocational-school training, coordination was lacking in interwar Britain. Its employers were offering mostly low levels of unregulated, informal workshop training with only a minority of firms requiring apprentices to attend evening classes, giving rise to such a level of dissatisfaction among the apprentices themselves that a national apprentices strike took place in 1937. Among the apprentices' demands was paid day release to participate in external classes that would add some theoretical grounding to their often mundane workshop work. By the eve of the Second World War, German youth and business were benefiting from an established system of vocational training to national skill standards, achieved collaboratively among all stakeholders. In Britain, instead, employers and unions devoted their energy to issues of demarcation and workplace control.[16]

One example of British employers' attitude is instructive. In 1937, steel fabricators Dorman, Long, a competitor of and occasional collaborator with Braithwaites, received a copy of a letter from the British Association for Commercial & Industrial Education, enquiring whether they would be in favour of children staying on at school until the age of fifteen. They were also asked whether they would support compulsory day-release training for young workers as a condition of employment. Though the Committee's members included a range of industrialists and educators, the Iron and Steel Trades Employers' Association indignantly urged Dorman, Long not only to resist the idea, but to refuse to reply to the letter.[17] What makes this resistance to employee learning, in an industry dependent on internationally competitive skills, so incongruous is that two weeks later, the managing director of Dorman, Long was replying to an acquaintance at Barclays Bank who had asked him for help finding a job for a qualified draughtsman: "I will do what I can to see that he is found a position. We are in fact in need of first rate Draughtsmen at present and they are extremely hard to come by."[18]

Other companies, however, supported local education, out of both a sense of social responsibility and an awareness of their future need for capable recruits. In 1934, K&J's directors were contributing three-quarters of the cost of courses at Kenrick Technical College, where 212 boys and girls were in evening classes.

---

16   Thelen, pp. 140–46.

17   Dorman, Long, 'Correspondence between British Association for Commercial & Industrial Education and Iron & Steel Trades Employers' Association' (1937), Teesside Archives, Middlesbrough, BS.DL/3/2/1/2/11.

18   Dorman, Long, 'Correspondence between Colonel E.H.W. Bolitho of Barclays Bank Penzance and J.G. Goodenough, managing director of Dorman Long Ltd.' (1937), Teesside Archives, Middlesbrough, BS.DL/3/2/1/2/11.

They had done this, they told the company's staff, because so many were leaving local elementary and secondary schools with no employment prospects. K&J had already taken on eighty boys and apprenticed many, though trade unions had restricted the numbers of apprentices allowed.[19]

Post-war Developments

The distinction between British and German approaches would unfortunately be resumed after the Second World War. Following the national commitment after the First World War to skills training through the state Labour Administration, German businesses had become habituated to the notion that business success was founded on the capabilities of a company's workforce. Thus even in the immediate aftermath of the Second World War, German companies were offering more apprentice vacancies than there were available trainees, evidence that "German firms planned for a long-term future in which, they expected, a high-skilled workforce would be one of their greatest assets."[20] West Germany refined and revised its dual-training commitment and required those 15- to 18-year-olds not in full-time education to participate in compulsory vocational training at least one day per week. By the 1970s, less than one tenth of German youth entered the workforce as unskilled labour. In Britain in 1973, in contrast, 26% of 16- to 19-year-olds were in full-time education, 10% were on voluntary, part-time vocational courses, but fully 60% were undergoing no education or training of any sort. The median British youngster would join the labour market without skills, while less than a tenth of their German counterparts would, providing "one of the sharpest contrasts between Britain and Germany".[21] And those who *did* undertake training in Britain were not required to pass any national examination, or any examination at all, to be classified as a skilled worker, whereas their German counterpart would have to pass written and practical examinations assessed to national standards for every trade.[22] Moreover, the inclusion of general principles and theories in the German apprentices' vocational education would then afford their employers easier adoption of new, more advanced

19   Kenrick & Jefferson, 'K&J Boys', *K&J News* (15 December 1934), Sandwell, BS/KJ4/1/5.

20   David Meskill, *Optimizing the German Workforce: Labor Administration from Bismarck to the Economic Miracle*, Open access ebook (New York and Oxford, 2010), p. 287. Meskill's study reviews the development of a coordinated national labour policy over several decades, to which the direction of youths to apprenticeships was fundamental.

21   S.J. Prais, *Productivity and Industrial Structure: A Statistical Study of Manufacturing Industry in Britain, Germany and the United States* (Cambridge, 1981), pp. 29–31.

22   Thelen shows how these were developed in the interwar years by DATSCH, the Deutscher Ausschuß für Technisches Schulwesen (German Committee for Technical Education): Thelen, chap. 2 and pp. 233–34.

technologies and methods than would be possible for British workers trained only to perform currently applicable tasks.[23]

West Germany

How did this come about in practice for the companies we are interested in? Advancement of the Mittelstand and its competitiveness had been a key element of state policy in south-west Germany since the beginning of the industrial age. After the foundation of Baden-Württemberg in 1952, this policy continued, and investment in skills training and the improvement of technical qualifications were central to it.[24] With national agreement that vocational education was central to Germany's prosperity, several regional chambers of industry and trade (IHK) had formed the Office for Industrial Vocational Training in 1947. In 1951 it became the national Office for Business Vocational Training (*Arbeitsstelle für betriebliche Ausbildung*), which acted as a unified organisation to establish vocational training standards and educational materials.[25] A history of the IHKs of Baden-Württemberg in the post-war period sets out the terms by which they committed themselves in 1949 to "Training and Education". They are worth quoting in full:[26]

1. Intensification of professional training and education in the commercial and industrial area.
2. The development of instructors through courses and work-circles.
3. Training of industrial supervisors and master-craftsmen (*Industriemeister*).
4. Development and expansion of technician training.
5. Analysis of all activities that relate to training and education in the economy.

They were determined from the outset to ensure the highest standard of delivery and assessment, recruiting in 1949 a specialist in pedagogy and initiating a programme of "train the trainer" activities which connected local trade instructors with each other through seminars, study-circles, and meetings with university teachers. The IHKs' primary aim was to ensure uniformly high teaching standards and programme content. By the creation of a central office that collected and disseminated teaching and assessment materials from

---

23   Prais, pp. 180–83.
24   Boelcke, *Wirtschaftsgeschichte*, p. 542.
25   Meskill, p. 303.
26   Harald Winkel, *Geschichte Der Württembergischen Industrie- Und Handelskammern Heilbronn, Reutlingen, Stuttgart/Mittlerer Neckar Und Ulm 1933–1980: Zum 125jährigen Bestehen* (Stuttgart, 1980), p. 604, Stadtbibliothek Reutlingen. As will be explained later in this chapter, the title *Meister or Industriemeister* incorporates the joint meaning of master craftsman and, in British terminology, foreman: a person would occupy the foreman's role by virtue of having achieved the nationally recognised qualification certifying mastery of his craft.

1948 onwards and was gradually expanded, they ensured that final examinations were also of a uniformly high standard, which meant that qualifications would have identical value across Baden-Württemberg. By 1979, this office was sending out examination materials to 69 IHKs across the country, widening the acceptability and universality of the trade qualifications awarded.[27] From 1973 onwards, the region's IHKs had also begun to experiment with training models that combined university-based learning with work experience, the so-called Stuttgart Model or dual apprenticeship, combining theory with practice in an alternative to university-only education.[28] Only several decades later would this dual apprenticeship-degree model begin to be offered in Britain.

At the company level, it is important to note that all sizes of German company were committed to apprenticeships, seeing them as a public good but pragmatically managing them according to their own needs and circumstance. Mittelstand companies saw the opportunity for a collective commitment that would be of reciprocal benefit. In a retrospective analysis of the evolution of apprenticeships, one study identifies the difference between "collectivist" and "segmentalist" notions of training: large firms tailored their training to suit their own internal labour markets, whereas skill-intensive Mittelstand firms "that were not able to sustain internal labour markets sought (and actually established, on a voluntary basis) a more genuinely solidaristic system of skill formation premised on labour mobility and skill standardization across firms."[29] Firms responded to changing external circumstances, gradually moving away from a "monolithic" approach to standards, to provide an element of tailored training within a more modular approach.[30] But they did so with an eye to sustaining mutually beneficial industry standards, a collaborative approach that can be contrasted with the free-riding and poaching by many British firms that frustrated the minority of their counterparts who were fully committed to training.

The continuing commitment of Mittelstand firms to skills development occurred in the context not only of the IHKs' organisation of training and assessment, but of the presence of technical universities and colleges (*Technische Hochschulen* (TH) and *Fachhochschulen* (FH)), local institutions which supported local businesses through the delivery of technical training and the dissemination of technological knowledge.[31] For Gary Herrigel, developing

27 Winkel, pp. 604–05.
28 Winkel, pp. 614–15.
29 Kathleen Thelen and Marius R. Busemeyer, *From Collectivism towards Segmentalism Institutional Change in German Vocational Training* (Cologne, 2008), p. 8.
30 Thelen and Busemeyer, pp. 16–17.
31 Gary B. Herrigel, 'Industrial Order and the Politics of Industrial Change: Mechanical Engineering', in *Industry and Politics in West Germany Toward the Third Republic*, ed. by Peter J. Katzenstein (Ithaca: Cornell University Press, 1989), pp. 185–220 (p. 201).

workers' skills contributed to the maintenance of trust in the workplace because "the education each worker receive[d] instill[ed] a sense of pride in the product of his or her labor and, more important, a sense of the integrity and indispensability of skilled trades."[32] Added to the sense of shared community obligation that suffused Mittelstand businesses – and was a critical element of local bank–business relationships, as we have seen – this mindset enabled a high-quality, high-value culture.

This thinking was universal in large and small firms at the regional and national level across West Germany. For example, Bayer was by 1969 a very substantial business – turnover was almost £1.1 billion and it was West Germany's second-largest exporter. It is notable that in their annual report for 1969 the company stated that, with more than 3000 apprentices currently in training for 50 different trades and professions, "productivity per head [had] more than doubled in the last 10 years, due to rationalisation and extensive training programmes."[33] Training and the influx and development of young talent were, in other words, known to be fundamental to business success. Likewise apprentice numbers were increased within the West German automotive industry in response to global competition. A "virtuous circle" was recreated in the 1970s through a restructuring approach which included a large-scale training and retraining effort. In the second half of the 1970s, apprentice recruitment was increased in West German automobile manufacturing as it was being cut in other countries, which contributed to "firms' stock of human capital, increasing their capacity to absorb technological change and giving them a competitive edge over foreign producers."[34]

Among the case-study companies in Part Two below, Wandel considered apprentices to be important and employed them throughout their history. In the immediate post-war years, day-to-day business was directed by its young *Prokuristen*,[35] both of whom had joined the firm as apprentices and had quickly risen through it. RECARO's eventual acquirer, Keiper, was also strongly committed to apprenticeships. Their family history exemplified the German tradition. As we have already seen, Fritz Keiper became the third of his blacksmith father's sons to be apprenticed to him and faced intense demands.

---

32   Gary B. Herrigel, p. 203.

33   'Bayer (Germany) 1969', *The Times* (London, 23 June 1970), p. 26, The Times Digital Archive.

34   Wolfgang Streeck, 'Successful Adjustment to Turbulent Markets: The Automobile Industry', in *Industry and Politics in West Germany Toward the Third Republic*, ed. by Peter J. Katzenstein (Ithaca, 1989), pp. 113–56 (pp. 129–30).

35   A Prokurist's 'powers are for all practical purposes equivalent' to a managing director's, and 'the position of Prokurist carries considerable prestige in Germany': Baker & McKenzie, 'Doing Business in Germany' (Baker & McKenzie, 2015), sec. 3.2.2 <https://www.baker-mckenzie.com/-/media/files/insight/publications/2015/05/doing-business-in-germany/doing_business_in_germany_29april2015.pdf?la=en> [accessed 19 August 2019].

Even as village blacksmiths, the curriculum in their classes at Fortbildungsschule (Continuation School) included bookkeeping, physics, commercial calculations, and technical drawing.[36] This work ethic and education formed the basis, further developed through specialised *Meister* training, of Fritz Keiper's career as an entrepreneur manufacturer. It was therefore natural for his heirs to see apprentices as an integral part of the family firm's future. They established a dedicated learning centre in an old mill near their home office in the small rural Palatinate town of Rockenhausen. By offering local young people training as good as that offered by the large automotive employers, Keiper gave themselves a strong base of skilled local people in an area where there were few competitors and little enthusiasm among locals for relocating to industrial cities. Keiper's rationale for investing in apprentice training was simple. They produced around 2500 parts, each of which required its own tool; some needed as many as twelve tools, so with 5000 tools in total they were in constant need of toolmakers for changes and for new developments. In their new learning unit, they initially recruited thirty apprentices, twenty-eight boys, including toolmakers, and two girls in technical drawing, telling the surrounding community: "We pamper our apprentices, not by indulging them, but by a strict and thorough training programme with first-class training masters (*Lehrmeistern*)." By 1966 they had sixty apprentices, fifty of them toolmakers. To emphasise the esteem in which the new craftsmen and -women were held and to affirm the Mittelstand business's values, Keiper held celebratory ceremonies which included the works choir, poetry readings by apprentices, and motivational speeches by former apprentices now in leadership positions.[37] This was a fully committed strategy of recruiting for the long term and training for excellence – exemplifying and enabling, in other words, the high-skill equilibrium.

How did these apprenticeships work in practice? The apprentice contract (*Lehrvertrag*) for a technical draughtsman at water-treatment manufacturer Philipp Müller demonstrates the approach.[38] The contract is drawn on a template provided by the local chamber of commerce, the *Industrie- und Handelskammer Heilbronn*. The apprentice was 19 years old, and the contract was to last for two years, as he had previously spent some time as an apprentice engineer. The training period was in practice extended to three years, by the requirement for practical learning in the workplace, so that he would achieve competence in all the skills and knowledge specified by the state in its

36   Keiper.
37   Ulrich Putsch and Martin Putsch, *In Bewegung. Der Automobilzulieferer Keiper: Geschichte Und Geschichten Aus Den Jahren 1920 Bis 2011* (Kaiserslautern, 2011), pp. 152–53.
38   '"Lehrvertrag" (Apprentice Contract) for Technical Draughtsman' (Firma Philipp Müller Nachf. Eugen Bucher GmbH & Co, 1957), WABW B38/ Bü193.

occupational profile (the *Berufsbild*) for the role and set out in an addendum
to the contract.

The contract sets out the apprentice's obligations to the business and
vice-versa, stipulating the commitment of both parties to his regular attendance
at college and requiring the company to offer him every support to pass the
state apprentice examination and to attain the standards specified in the
occupational profile. Pay was modest and shown on the contract as a range,
according to external norms: in year one, DM150–DM210, and in year two
DM230–DM250.[39] In contrast, in 1962 the company paid an engineer approximately five times the apprentice's maximum rate (DM1272) and a *Richtmeister*
(steelwork-erection foreman) three times as much (DM752).[40] For Müller, the
engagement was an affordable investment in the company's future skill-base.
For the apprentice himself, the low wage or learning allowance was fair compensation for the learning he was undergoing and the promise of a long-term
engagement with the company supporting it. Evidence that an apprenticeship
could form the basis of a successful business career can be seen in biographies
of Müller's top management team in 1986, among whom two of the company's
three *Prokuristen* had begun their careers as apprentices in other companies
before joining Müller and being promoted to its leadership team 22 and 23
years, respectively, after starting their apprenticeship as boys.[41]

Britain
The British approach was less structured and less consistent. Though apprenticeships had been established for centuries as an accepted way of learning a
trade, they were not universally seen as beneficial. Many industrial workshops
in nineteenth-century Birmingham, for example, were based on piece-rate
working. This incentivised the use of unskilled boys on simplified tasks. There
was no apprenticeship system and little opportunity for a worker to develop such
a range of skills that he could become a skilled journeyman.[42] Of course, many
of those apprenticeships which *were* in place were valuable. Roderick Floud has
shown that machine tool entrepreneurs who built successful companies before
the First World War had "almost without exception" served an apprenticeship
as a mechanical engineer. Some came from poor backgrounds and financed
their own apprenticeship. Others, like Alfred Herbert who subsequently built
Britain's largest machine-tool manufacturer, came from more prosperous homes

---

39   '"Lehrvertrag" (Apprentice Contract) for Technical Draughtsman', sec. 6.
40   'Payroll 1961–65' (Firma Philipp Müller Nachf. Eugen Bucher GmbH & Co), WABW
B38/ Bü182.
41   'Management Biographies: Philipp Müller Nachf. Eugen Bucher GmbH & Co.' (Firma
Philipp Müller Nachf. Eugen Bucher GmbH & Co, 1986), WABW B38/Bü12.
42   Alan Fox, 'Industrial Relations in Nineteenth-Century Birmingham', *Oxford Economic
Papers*, New Series, 7.1 (1955), 57–70 (pp. 58–60).

and became "premium apprentices", financed by their families or working in a firm owned by a relative. In all cases, though, their business success grew out of the technical ability that had, for all but one of the leading machine-tool entrepreneurs, been developed during an initial period of apprenticeship.[43]

Floud resists the claim that the British system of technical education, based on apprentices learning in the workplace, and in some cases going to evening classes, was inferior to its Continental dual-system counterparts. As his analysis of members of the Institute of Mechanical Engineers shows, the reliance on workplace apprenticeships was a rational method within a dynamic market of producing engineers who were internationally competitive in the decades before the First World War.[44] Among our own companies, the Jensen brothers had begun their own working lives as apprentices in the motor trade, and James Humphryes started as an engineering apprentice in Wednesbury before going on to achieve international success leading Braithwaites. However, it can reasonably be argued that these men and the individuals identified by Floud were a tiny minority of the general workforce, were distinguished from it by their outstanding entrepreneurial talent, and were at the apex of the employment pyramid. As the twentieth century unfolded, what would differentiate national economic performance would not be the technical capabilities of a few leaders, but those of the workforces they led and the consistent quality of the training they undertook.

For Michael Sanderson, it was shortcomings in technical education that were at the root of Britain's relative economic decline. There were opportunities in the interwar years for continuation schools to develop the skills of those who had left school at fourteen to join the workforce, or for junior technical schools to offer high levels of training for all those heading towards careers in manufacturing. In practice, the continuation schools (an important element of skills development in Germany, as we have seen for Fritz Keiper in the 1890s) never took off after funding cuts in the 1920s, and junior technical schools faced opposition or apathy from multiple sides.[45] The attempt to establish secondary technical schools in the 1950s also came to naught, and they were gradually phased out by merger with the new comprehensive schools: for Sanderson, their "deliberate neglect and demise ... was one of the most harmful developments of the post-war years. It lay at the heart of many of the difficulties in the formation of an effective labour force in other areas."[46]

43   Roderick Floud, *The British Machine Tool Industry, 1850–1914*, 1st edition (Cambridge, 1976), pp. 46–49.

44   Roderick Floud, 'Technical Education and Economic Performance: Britain, 1850–1914', *Albion: A Quarterly Journal Concerned with British Studies*, 14.2 (1982), 153–71.

45   Sanderson, pp. 60–61.

46   Sanderson, p. 81.

Having failed to ensure that an adequate basic education was provided for the future workforce, an additional national failing was the decline of apprentice-ships from the 1960s onwards. In 1973 *The Times* reported on "The search for industry's missing craftsmen", noting that engineering apprentice intakes had fallen to 18,000 in 1972 from 30,000 a few years previously, and claiming that companies and industries appeared to be relying on Government efforts to train the required numbers of staff, rather than investing in their own futures: this mentality was now holding back industries in a time of economic expansion.[47] Britain differentiated itself from West Germany by firms' short-term thinking and reluctance to invest in training, according to Sanderson, perhaps because they themselves were largely in low-skilled industries which were seen not to warrant investment in high-skills training.[48] The consequence, another analysis has concluded, was that Britain found itself trapped in a "low-skills equilibrium, in which the majority of enterprises staffed by poorly trained managers and workers produce low-quality goods and services".[49]

How had this come about? Concerns had first been raised in the West Midlands in 1955, when the Birmingham Productivity Association sent a delegation made up of educators, employers, and trade union officials to West Germany to study its apprenticeship system. Their detailed report, which they entitled 'Gaining Skill', is worth examining in detail as an objective evaluation of the West German system and, by implication, a realisation of the oppor-tunity for beneficial change in Britain. While they acknowledged the existence of many excellent training schemes within individual firms in Britain, the report's writers nevertheless "recognised the need for a wider adoption of systematic and improved training of craftsmen if British industry were to have this valuable personnel available in sufficient numbers and of the right quality to maintain Britain's position in the face of increasing competition for world markets."[50]

The visiting team described the historical development of the German system of vocational education and apprenticeships, acknowledging the cooperative efforts of multiple institutions and the structure of technical education.[51] They found that German apprentices were closely supervised by a qualified *Lehrmann* or apprentice tutor, and were tested every six months before being

---

47   Eric Wigham, 'The Search for Industry's Missing Craftsmen', *The Times* (London, 3 July 1973), p. 23, The Times Digital Archive.
48   Sanderson, pp. 84–90.
49   David Finegold and David Soskice, 'The Failure Of Training in Britain: Analysis and Prescription', *Oxford Review of Economic Policy*, 4.3 (1988), 21–53 (p. 22); quoted by Sanderson, p. 89.
50   Birmingham Productivity Association, 'Gaining Skill: A Report of an Investigation into the Training of Industrial Apprentices in Western Germany' (1955), p. 1, MRC, MSS.289/VB/5/3/3.
51   Birmingham Productivity Association, pp. 2–6.

formally examined in a three-part national examination – practical, written, and oral – at the end of their apprenticeship (sample examination questions were appended to the report). The delegates were complimentary about their findings on their numerous factory visits. As industrial relations problems and quality deficiencies began to predominate within the West Midlands automotive industry, the visitors found that at Opel, for example, "it was almost incredible to us that boys at work could be so clean, tidy and orderly in their methods, appearance and surroundings and also produce work of excellent quality and finish", including weekly written reports of an "astonishingly high" standard.[52] In their summary of the study tour, which included visits to numerous factories and institutions and interviews with many stakeholders including apprentices themselves, they found that employers' representatives and trade union officials unanimously asserted "the great contribution systematic training of operators and craftsmen can make to productivity, to quality of production and to a higher standard of living."[53] The delegation concluded that the West German approach was a "nationally accepted, efficiently organised and, in so far as achieving its purpose is concerned, eminently successful system."[54]

Though they were evidently greatly impressed by what they found, the visiting delegation were reticent on recommendations for change back home. They argued that in view of "conditions which differed materially from those in England, such as climate of opinion, native temperament and traditional methods", they "considered it desirable neither to make comparisons between apprenticeship systems in the two countries nor to make recommendations for the adoption of a scheme of education and training of craft apprentices in this country based, in whole or in part, on the German pattern."[55] Given their apparently wholehearted enthusiasm for their findings, the presumed motivation for sending them to West Germany in the first place, and the deficiencies that would plague West Midlands industry for decades to come, this outcome surely represented a lost opportunity.

The need for change – which the Birmingham delegation failed to act on – was summarised by *The Engineer* in 1960, noting that companies had traditionally expected apprentices to learn entirely on the job, but there was increasingly "an appreciation that a less haphazard method produces better results more quickly."[56] Inconsistencies in training provisions are evident in personal recollections from this period. David Hall's oral history of post-war British working lives contains many references to individuals' apprenticeships. What is striking is the variability in quality among them. In the absence of

52   Birmingham Productivity Association, p. 47.
53   Birmingham Productivity Association, p. 26.
54   Birmingham Productivity Association, p. 25.
55   Birmingham Productivity Association, p. 1.
56   'Models for Apprentices', *The Engineer*, 210.5453 (1960) 170.

defined national standards for particular apprenticeship outcomes, individual apprentices could face different experiences, as two did at a single ship-repair yard, for example. One trained as an electrician and found "there was no formal training"; he was simply to follow an older worker's practices. He found that the mandated evening classes did not have "any relevance between what [he] was learning in the evening and what [he] was doing in the day." The other trainee served his apprenticeship as a draughtsman in the same yard. The five-year engagement was highly structured and required an additional two years as an "improver" as well as mandatory work in manual trades around the yard to provide "invaluable experience". In his case, external classes were highly valuable, as he "could see that the tuition was related to [his] work. [He] could see why he was doing it and that made [him] take a greater interest."[57]

Among the case-study companies in Part Two, we will see that Jensen sent their own apprentices to West Bromwich College as well as providing on-the-job training in the factory. Braithwaites were enthusiastic recruiters and developers of apprentices. Faced with post-war skills shortages, its management committee recognised the urgent need to send apprenticeship brochures into local schools.[58] The company was keen to advance those capable of further development, as their award of two engineering scholarships to Birmingham University to former apprentice draughtsmen showed. But its directors noted with frustration at the end of the 1960s that the majority of those they trained were subsequently leaving the drawing office to join other businesses. On the face of it, this substantiates the traditional reluctance of British firms to train apprentices because of the risk of them being poached by free-riding compet-itors who were unwilling to pay for apprentice-training themselves. This might not always have been true in Braithwaites' case: of the 122 factory employees made redundant during 1978 and 1979, twenty-five had originally joined the company as apprentices.[59] But the poaching concern was real and was also a function of supply and demand: if Britain was consistently training fewer skilled people than were needed, the risk of trained staff being enticed away was unavoidable.

K&J also continued to recruit and value apprentices, and their value is mentioned occasionally in the company's records. In common with other British companies, and unlike their German counterparts, they had tradi-tionally required their apprentices to endure an extended apprenticeship which

57   David Hall, *Working Lives: The Forgotten Voices of Britain's Post-War Working Class* (London, 2012), pp. 188, 190.
58   Minutes of 14 June 1950 meeting. Braithwaite & Co. Engineers Limited, 'Minutes of Joint General Managers' Meetings, 21 January 1949 to 13 May 1952' (Braithwaite & Co. Engineers Limited, 1952), Sandwell, BS-B1/1/3.
59   Braithwaite & Co. Engineers Ltd., 'Employee Record Cards' (1980), Sandwell, BS-B/3/2/1; analysis by author.

did not, as it did in West Germany, result in a certificated qualification or guarantee high-quality training.[60] Like other companies, K&J still faced union restrictions on the number of apprentices they could employ relative to skilled labour: the 1959 national printing strike included what the unions termed "protective practices" and the employers "restrictive practices", intended largely to preserve craft trades, partly through restriction on the intake of apprentices.[61] Other restrictions specified pay levels, for example for bonus amounts by apprentice age.[62]

Nevertheless, apprentices' place in the company seems to have remained important. In 1967 Albert Smart joined its board as finance director, forty years after joining as an apprentice.[63] The previous December, twenty-six apprentices representing all K&J crafts including commercial trades attended the annual apprentice prize-giving and were warned by chairman Peter Kenrick: "The tempo of industrial change demands that you keep an open mind on developments for you surely will not be printing at the end of your working life as we print today."[64] This awareness seems to have influenced K&J's approach over the next decade: company policy by 1977 was "more and more to reduce the period of apprenticeship", but K&J's training manager saw "training is a continuous operation. With changing technology we have to be on our toes to make sure that our people have proper re-training."[65] The commitment was such that in 1978 managing director Tom Jefferson could tell his directors that with thirty-two new apprentices, they had continued to take their "full quota", partly in response to the ongoing loss of skilled workers across the business even in times of high unemployment.[66] Though it does not sound like K&J fully endorsed the learning culture of their German counterparts, their approach was more far-sighted than many of their competitors, who had been criticised

60   Thelen, pp. 114–15.
61   As described by Alf Robens in the Commons debate: Hansard, HC Deb 06 July 1959 vol 608 cc 893–963. See also John Gennard and Peter Bain, *A History of the Society of Graphical and Allied Trades* (London, 1995), pp. 452–57.
62   Sandwell, BS/KJ3/3/3. Letter to K&J dated 16 June 1961 from The Federation of Master Process Engravers.
63   'New Talents Allied to Fresh Business Skills', *Birmingham Post* (Birmingham, 12 April 1967), p. 1, Sandwell, 35A/131.
64   Kenrick & Jefferson, 'Prizes to Apprentices', *K&J News* (December 1966), Sandwell, BS/KJ4/1/27.
65   'New Jobs for New and Old Stagers', *K&J News* (Summer 1977), p. 1, Sandwell Archive, BS/KJ4/1/31.
66   Kenrick & Jefferson, 'T. Jefferson, Year-End Report, 1977/78' (Kenrick & Jefferson, 1978), Sandwell, BS/KJ8/2/1.

for failing to fill 1700 of the printing industry's 3000 available apprenticeship places in 1977.[67]

By the early 1990s, the German apprenticeship system could be seen to have created, over decades, a "virtuous circle" in comparison with its British counterpart. Standards were high, assessment reliable, and the content relevant to the trainees' companies. These factors justified students' investment in three or more years of training on low wages. In Britain's low-level equilibrium, trainees were unwilling to accept low wages because the qualification that would result from their period of apprenticeship was "of little economic value": the required skill levels were low, the qualification was "narrowly industry-specific", and the absence of externally controlled assessment made it "an unreliable indicator of an individual's actual skills". And because trainees were unwilling to accept low wages, British employers had little incentive to improve the training offer.[68] In West Germany, in contrast, a high-skill, high-education equilibrium was made possible by students working hard at school to win a competitive apprenticeship and then committing to that apprenticeship. They made that commitment because it offered a high chance of a job in the training company. But their apprenticeship also offered them a strong element of general education, with nationally recognised standards; an insurance policy for future career security, and ticket to further career advancement. Companies therefore could employ individuals whose basic qualifications were higher, motivations stronger, and adaptability more certain than those of their British competitors.[69] And when the time came for those individuals to seek further advancement, their employers could support their progress into the equally well structured *Meister* system of first-line management, creating the next generation of apprentice-instructors to perpetuate the high-skills equilibrium.[70]

67   Edward Townsend, 'Printing Groups Censured over Recruitment Figures', *The Times* (19 December 1977), p. 15, The Times Digital Archive.

68   Nicholas Oulton and Hilary Steedman, 'The British System of Youth Training: A Comparison with Germany', in *Training and the Private Sector*, ed. by Lisa M. Lynch, National Bureau of Economic Research Comparative Labor Markets (Chicago, 1994), pp. 61–76 (p. 74).

69   David Soskice, 'Reconciling Markets and Institutions: The German Apprenticeship System', in *Training and the Private Sector*, pp. 25–60.

70   First-line manager: 'A person at the bottom of the management hierarchy responsible for day-to-day operations in an organization. Traditionally this role was labelled supervisor or foreman': *Oxford Reference* <https://www.oxfordreference.com/view/10.1093/oi/authority.20110803095820966#> [accessed 5 August 2022].

First-Line Management

In 1983–84, Britain's National Institute of Economic and Social Research conducted a pilot inquiry across thirty-two matched metalworking SMEs in Britain and West Germany of productivity, investments in and the effective use of machinery, and skills. They discovered that, on average, labour productivity in the German plants was 63% higher, and highlighted as the major gap between approaches "the technological capabilities of those of foreman or chargehand status, where the German level of competence was far ahead.[71] The foreman in Britain is typically appointed for his managerial or human skills; the German foreman is primarily a technically qualified person who in addition has acquired further experience and the requisite managerial qualifications." This mattered, they concluded, because "to organise production *efficiently*, and to produce goods that are preferred for their *quality*, a technically qualified foreman was highly desirable" and consequently in Britain "there was a need for a strong policy initiative … in relation to the appropriate training, qualifications, and incentives for foremen."[72]

This gap was all the more worrying because it existed alongside a "drastic" fall in the number of craft and technician trainees beginning training supervised by the Engineering Industries Training Board from 28,000 in 1967 to 9000 in 1983;[73] we have reviewed these differences in the preceding section. But the greatest contrast the researchers found in their study, having examined the use and maintenance of machinery in the pursuit of productivity, was between the technical qualifications of foremen: in Germany, most "had taken advanced courses beyond that of craftsman level", affording "great advantages to production efficiency of combining in one person technical and managerial skills", whereas in England only a minority of foremen had attained even a craftsman's qualification.[74]

Their evidence for these conclusions was their discovery that in fourteen of the sixteen British firms they visited, foremen "had acquired their position purely as a result of experience on the shop floor; in only two cases had they served an apprenticeship." In the sixteen German firms studied, production foremen had all passed craftsmen examinations, thirteen had achieved certification as *Meister*, a Master Craftsman, and three were studying for the *Meister*

---

71   A. Daly, D.M.W.N. Hitchens, and K. Wagner, 'Productivity, Machinery and Skills in a Sample of British and German Manufacturing Plants: Results of a Pilot Inquiry', *National Institute Economic Review*, 111 (1985), 48–61 (p. 51). In addition to 16 metalworking plants in each country, they also visited 13 machinery suppliers, to understand from their perspective how installed equipment was being used and maintained.
72   Daly, Hitchens, and Wagner, p. 60.
73   Daly, Hitchens, and Wagner, p. 60.
74   Daly, Hitchens, and Wagner, p. 61.

qualification.[75] In British comparator plants, the limited capabilities of foremen required the employment of several individuals with discrete responsibilities, with tasks being divided among several that in Germany would have been completed by a single person. And their work was more onerous, and more necessary, because the workers operating the machines did not themselves have the skills to operate them efficiently and ensure the high up-time achieved by their apprentice-trained German counterparts.[76]

West Germany

How did the German system of developing and employing first-line managers work? Following the National Institute of Economic and Social Research study, Sigbert Prais and Karin Wagner reviewed the differences between foremen and *Meister* training in 1988, asking to what extent the higher productivity and smoother operation of German plants were attributable to the skills of first-line management.[77] Writing in the same period, Christel Lane asserted that *Meister* (master craftsmen) made a decisive difference to productivity, adaptability, and quality.[78] In the following section, we will look at the training offered to *Meister* in Baden-Württemberg from the 1950s onwards as part of an overall review of the relative importance of foremen and *Meister*, nominally at the same level within their organisations, to our case-study companies and to industry more widely.

The *Meister* system dates back to medieval guilds. Some scholars trace the origins of Mittelstand companies in the nineteenth century to the continuation of master–journeymen–apprentice relationships within small, family-owned businesses: those origins are evident in Fritz Keiper's personal progression from blacksmith's son to *Meister* to factory owner.[79] Keiper epitomised the classic Mittelstand entrepreneur: humble beginnings with a strong work ethic; manual work and training leading to a *Meister* qualification, engendering a high level of technical skills; a decision to commercialise those skills; and the establishment of his own company, in which he took personal financial risks to enable heavy investment in innovative, patentable products.[80] Likewise, Wilhelm Reutter

75   Daly, Hitchens, and Wagner, p. 56.
76   Daly, Hitchens, and Wagner, pp. 56–58.
77   S.J. Prais and Karin Wagner, 'Productivity and Management: The Training of Foremen in Britain and Germany', *National Institute Economic Review*, 123.1 (1988), 34–46 (p. 1).
78   See Christel Lane, *Management and Labour in Europe: The Industrial Enterprise in Germany, Britain and France* (Aldershot, 1989), pp. 45–46 for a very clear explanation of the relative advantages of the Meister system.
79   Marcel Hoogenboom et al, 'Guilds in the Transition to Modernity: The Cases of Germany, United Kingdom, and the Netherlands', *Theory and Society*, 47.3 (2018), 255–91 (p. 272).
80   Keiper, pp. 125–39.

was a *Meister* in another coachworks before setting up his own business and following a similar path to high quality, patentable innovation.

Before considering the importance of *Meister* to each of our case-study businesses, we should examine institutional engagement with the standing and education of *Meister* within Baden-Württemberg. As we have seen, *Meister* had been central to the conception of craft organisation for centuries. After the war, with a need to fill the gap in industry created by the loss of so many young men, it was deemed critical to Germany's recovery to educate successors to the *Meister* already in industry, who were now fifty to sixty years old. Qualified craftsmen were invited to apply for a new *Meister* training programme: "the ability of 'Made in Germany' to stand for German quality once more depends on the capability, knowledge and experience of the *Meister*", a newspaper article claimed.[81] The programme was to be run by the IHK Karlsruhe (Karlsruhe Chamber of Industry and Commerce), which in 1950 circulated a suggested outline, shown in Figure 2, from the Handelskammer Nürnberg for a preparatory course for the *Werkmeister* examination.[82]

In this original conception, the preparatory and full courses would comprise 600 and 240 hours respectively, covering basic science, mathematics, electronics, geometry and trigonometry, technical drawing, and commercial subjects including law and economics. They would culminate in the *Industriemeister* examination, which would represent the apex of the candidate's achievement. This thinking was further developed and elaborated in considerably more detail by IHK Frankfurt, which shared it with IHK Stuttgart in 1956.[83] The approach they set out would form the basis of future training, setting an aspirational target for skilled workers.[84] It is worth reviewing in detail, to illustrate the professional rigour expected of all aspiring *Meister*, and to highlight the contrast with English foremen, who even thirty years later would typically not be qualified craftsmen, whether time-served or examined, and not have any type of examined supervisory qualification.[85]

81 'Berufsausbildung Für Industrie-Facharbeiter', *Ettinger Zeitung* (19 October 1950), Ettingen edition, WABW A16/ Bü 850, Bd. I.

82 Industrie- und Handelskammer Karlsruhe, 'Vorbereitungskurs Für Werkmasterprüfung' (Industrie- und Handelskammer Karlsruhe, 1950), WABW A16/ Bü 850; Illustration taken from Appendix to letter: Industrie- und Handelskammer Karlsruhe, 'Skizze: Industriemeister Ausbildung' (Industrie- und Handelskammer Karlsruhe, 1950), WABW A16/ Bü 852, Bd. III.

83 Both institutions thereby playing the critical coordinating role identified by Herrigel, *Industrial Constructions*, pp. 169–70.

84 'Industriemeister - Ein Aufstieg Für Facharbeiter', Passauer Neue Presse Niederbayerische Zeitung (Passau, 30 July 1965), 173 edition <http://digipress-beta.digitale-sammlungen.de/de/fs1/calendar/0-0-0.all/bsb00051146_00459.html?spellcheck=true&qt=dismax&hl=true&mode=comfort&fulltext=industriemeister&zoom=1.0> [accessed 19 September 2017].

85 Prais and Wagner, p. 41.

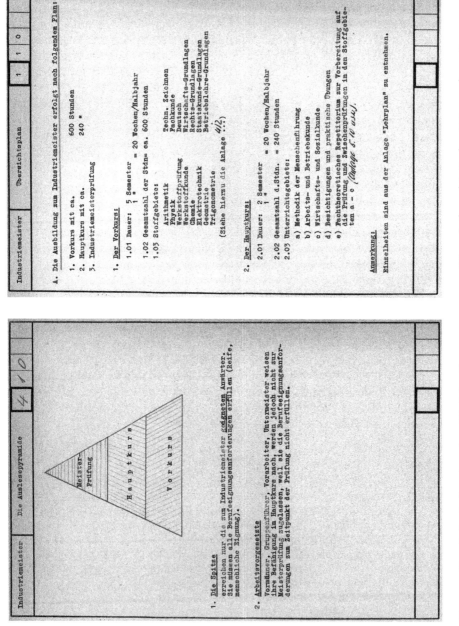

Figure 2 Sketch for *Industriemeister* Training Programme, 1950. Wirtschaftsarchiv Baden-Württemberg, Stuttgart-Hohenheim (WABW), Bestand A16/ Bü 852, Bd. III.

Participants had to be certified craftsmen aged 24 or over, with a good educational grounding in mathematics and writing, and five years' experience after an approved apprenticeship. The defining philosophy of the German approach is immediately evident: the overall purpose of the training was "to entrust the *Meister* with the latest and most successful methods of handling and leading people, to develop him into a valued member of the organisation's leadership level."[86] The example training plan for *Meister* in metalwork industries covered a comprehensive range of topics, and was intended to last for ten months, with participants attending for two hours a day after work, four days a week. The work was broken down as follows:

- **58 hours of Management,** including:

    - Organisational development
    - Accounting
    - Planning and Calculations (*Arbeitsvorbereitung*)
    - Rationalisation, including REFA techniques
    - Pay and rewards
    - Health and Safety
    - Training and education

- **40 Hours of Personnel Management,** including:

    - The enterprise as living space (*der Betrieb als Lebensraum*)
    - Care of the company atmosphere, introduction of newcomers
    - Aptitude testing
    - Differences in human relationships as individuals, in groups, and en masse
    - Treatment of colleagues
    - Job instruction
    - The *Meister* as teacher and educator

- **242 Hours of Technical Training,** including:

    - Technical calculations, 40 hours
    - Basics of electronics, 20 hours
    - Technical drawing, 42 hours
    - Materials science, 20 hours
    - Mechanics, 20 hours (taught by a university lecturer)
    - Machine tools, measurement and testing, and machines in the workplace, 80 hours (taught by an engineer from Opel)

- **Discussion evenings,** 10 hours

86   Industrie- und Handelskammer Frankfurt am Main, 'Letter to Dr. Steuer, IHK Stuttgart Re: "Industriemeisterausbildung"' (25 September 1956), WABW A16/ Bü 1299.

All *Meister* training was to end with examinations, and "in view of the high demands which must be placed on an *Industriemeister* in metalworking" (the emphasis was in the original instruction) the following marking scale was applied:[87]

Below 70	not passed
70–80	successfully passed
81–88	satisfactory performance
89–95	good performance
95–100	very good performance

Thus the bar was set very high: *Meister* were required to have an extremely high standard of knowledge across all areas on the course, with an examination that tested that knowledge rigorously. This outcome can be compared with the situation in Britain three decades later, where Prais had been unable to get estimates of the proportion of skilled workers who had ever passed an examination, commenting drily that the lack of data was "in itself a sad reflection on an entrenched distrust of 'book-learning'", and concluding that it was "likely that the majority [had] never passed any written examination, and that only a small proportion [had] undergone a series of tests comparable to those of the German *Facharbeiter*."[88]

Nor did the education of *Meister* necessarily stop there: a recent study has shown that *Meister* participated in management training at the *Bad Harzburger Akadamie für Führungskräfte der Wirtschaft*, a favoured destination for tens of thousands of German junior and middle managers which taught the principles of devolved authority and bottom-up management.[89]

Were there any disadvantages to the deployment of the *Meister*? Could their influence effectively act as a brake on innovation in firms where a *Meister* might feel that his status would be undermined by the adoption of new technology and processes, or a move to group working?[90] It is conceivable that reluctance among Wandel's *Meister*, for instance, might have impeded the move from

---

87 'Bewertungschlüssel Für Die Ergebnisse Aus Den Industriemeisterprüfungen Metall' (Industrie- und Handelskammer Region Stuttgart, 1956), WABW A16/ Bü 1299, underlining in the original.

88 Prais, p. 181: A 'Facharbeiter' was a skilled worker below the level of Meister.

89 Grünbacher, *West German Industrialists and the Making of the Economic Miracle*, pp. 104–09; Keiper adopted the Harzburger model in 1967 to foster 'competence, individual initiative, and self-management by the employee': Putsch and Putsch, p. 168.

90 Holger Bargmann, 'Innovationshemmnis Industriemeister?', *Zeitschrift für Soziologie*, 13.1 (1984), 45–59; for an analysis of the consequences of omitting foremen/supervisors/ Meister from the consideration of workplace changes affecting their future status, see Muriel Ray, 'Les équipes semi-autonomes et la maîtrise: Le cas d'un atelier de bobinage', *Revue française de sociologie*, 20.3 (1979), 590–604 (pp. 601–05); Ogilvie argues that guilds

steel to plastic weaving. At Schneider, the company's all-steel structures were gradually superseded by steel-reinforced concrete, and it is similarly conceivable that Schneider's steel-trained *Meister* might have been unenthusiastic about mastering the new technology.[91] However, we have no evidence of resistance to change happening among our companies' *Meister*, and a comparative study of automotive component and machinery factories in the 1990s found that while there was *some* resistance to the introduction of team working, *Meister* in the German plants continued to be better qualified than their British counterparts, adapted their leadership approach to suit new team-working regimes, and continued to add value in the workplace.[92]

Notwithstanding the theoretical possibility of occasional intransigence, the contribution of their *Meister* to our German companies seems to have been fundamental to business success. *Meister* occupy an important place in the collective memories of Reutter and Keiper. As we have seen, both were founded by former *Meister*, whose values permeated their businesses and offered an honourable route to career advancement as the companies developed: Theo Wolff began his career at Keiper as an apprentice toolmaker, becoming in the 1960s a *Maschinenbaumeister*, a master machine-builder, and retiring as Keiper's director of production.[93] In both firms, specifically dedicated *Meister* were responsible for leading the apprentice training schools. Reutter's company histories highlight their central importance to the effective operation of key areas of production and development; Figure 3 shows the white-coated *Meister* Kurt Wagenknecht and his team working on Porsche 356 bodyshell production.[94]

At Schneider, the *Meister* are all named at various points in the company's history, including the eight master-riggers on site and the two *Betriebsmeister*, identified in 1951 as members of the company's leadership team.[95] At Wandel, the company's core product was shown to be so complicated that it had to be produced by a *Meister*,[96] and Wandel's seven *Meister* managed 86 production staff.[97] At Philipp Müller, efforts were made to persuade *Richtmeister* HG to join the company in 1954, their letter highlighting their esteem for him. His personal file contains his "German Engineer's Calendar" of 340 pages of

often opposed innovations that threatened their present situation: Sheilagh Ogilvie, 'The Economics of Guilds', *Journal of Economic Perspectives*, 28.4 (2014), 169–92 (pp. 183–84).

91   Hege, 'Geschichte', pp. 73–74.

92   Geoff Mason, 'Production Supervisors in Britain, Germany and the United States: Back from the Dead Again?', *Work, Employment & Society*, 14.4 (2000), 625–45 (p. 640).

93   Putsch and Putsch, p. 181.

94   Frank Jung, *Porsche 356 Made by Reutter* (Bielefeld, 2011) p. 230.

95   Hege, 'Geschichte', pp. 44, 38.

96   'Reutlinger Metalltücher Gehen in Alle Welt', *Reutlinger General-Anzeiger* (14 March 1953), p. 216, WABW B79/Bü10.

97   Chr. Wandel, 'Monatlicher Stand Der Betriebsangehörigen Vom 1 Okt 1962 Bis 31 Okt 1966' (Chr. Wandel, 1962), WABW B79/Bü40.

Figure 3 *Meister* Kurt Wagenknecht with his Karosserie Reutter Work Team.
Source: Frank Jung, Private Collection.

analytical geometry, mechanics, chemistry, into which he has pasted 20 pages
of handwritten tables and formulae: HG was "only" a site foreman, but it is
evident that his technical education and expectations of himself were both
considerable.[98]

The capabilities of *Meister* benefited their employers, and the wider Baden-
Württemberg economy, in several ways. They trained their company's apprentices, the next generation of technical workers, and provided a role model
for them. They ensured the highest standards of product quality that allowed
Mittelstand businesses to produce niche products to world-class quality
standards. They ran factories efficiently. They provided an additional level of
management strength which allowed for flatter hierarchies, within a leadership
structure that combined technically qualified business leaders with technically qualified engineering managers and them as superbly qualified foremen.
And when the company needed to change direction, the *Meister* offered the

98   *Deutscher Ingenieur Kalendar* in: 'Personal Folder of HG' (Firma Philipp Müller Nachf.
Eugen Bucher GmbH & Co), WABW B38/ Bü190. Name withheld for confidentiality reasons.

capabilities required to implement new products, materials or processes. As we will now see, few or any of these advantages were available to British counterparts whose largely amateur managers (who themselves had quite possibly had less formal business education than the shop floor *Meister* of their German competitors) struggled with craft demarcation and the limited flexibility of poorly educated first-line supervisors and workers, problems which were compounded by their struggle to find appropriately qualified engineering talent.

Britain

In the post-war Anglo-American work world, the notion of the first-line supervisor and his role being problematic was commonplace,[99] beginning with Fritz Roethlisberger's widely cited 1945 analysis of the American foreman as a man with increased responsibility and decreased status.[100] In studies conducted in the early 1980s, one identified the "foreman's predicament", his loss of authority, the diminishing distinctiveness of his expertise, and – in Britain – the precariousness of his class status. It compared him unfavourably to his German counterpart.[101] In their study of two Birmingham manufacturing plants, John Child and Bruce Partridge argued that the "problem" lay in the decline in status and responsibility over one hundred years, exacerbated by the increasing educational accomplishments of post-war management, which effectively formed a social and professional barrier to the advancement of supervisors who had often not even served an apprenticeship.[102] In an extended, comparative study of supervision in Sweden and Britain, Keith Thurley and Hans Wirdenius asked, "Why is supervision a problem?", common to "all organizations."[103] For them, the British conception of a foreman was someone whose responsibility was to put into operation innovations produced by managers. However, the latter frequently found their foremen either incompetent or not committed to implementing management's new ideas, hence the "problem".[104] In practice, Thurley and Wirdenius concluded, studies showed

99   "His" is used in this section to reflect the overwhelming predominance on men in foremen/*Meister* roles during the period under review.
100   F.J. Roethlisberger, 'The Foreman: Master and Victim of Double Talk', *Harvard Business Review* (September 1965) <https://hbr.org/1965/09/the-foreman-master-and-victim-of-double-talk> [accessed 9 February 2019] a reprint of the original 1945 article.
101   Peter Lawrence, *Managers and Management in West Germany* (London, 1980), pp. 154–55.
102   John Child and Bruce Partridge, *Lost Managers: Supervisors in Industry and Society* (Cambridge, 1982), p. 10.
103   Keith Thurley and Hans Wirdenius, *Supervision: A Reappraisal* (London, 1973), p. 217; Keith Thurley and Hans Wirdenius, *Approaches to Supervisory Development* (London, 1973), p. 83.
104   Thurley and Wirdenius, *Supervision: A Reappraisal*, p. 216.

"the most critical aspects" of foremen's roles "were the responses made to contingencies or unanticipated events".[105]

Supervisors themselves argued that the "problem" was in their being given insufficient authority and not being considered by management to be part of management. A 1967 study placed the foreman within the context of industrial relations in the motor industry, arguing that "slackness" by managers and foremen, and the limited responsiveness of the former to the latter, was leading to the trade union shop steward – or workplace organiser – becoming more influential. To avert the industrial relations problems which might ensue, "the foreman must be given his proper place and status as a member of line management", responsible for negotiating on management's behalf with the unions' shop stewards.[106] A later analysis of the engineering industry suggests that it was already too late to make these changes, as foremen's authority had been gradually usurped during the 1950s by the increasing power of the shop steward. Opportunities to advance a company by appointing technical specialists to foreman positions were precluded by unions' insistence that "only tradesmen could supervise other tradesmen." Notwithstanding his credibility as a tradesman, the foreman's authority depended on "the reciprocal exchange of 'gifts' between the foreman and his shop workers"[107] (which does not sound like a position of strength) and was remorselessly undermined by shop stewards' efforts to change the politics of production.[108] Behind these deteriorating circumstances there lay in any case the strong opposition of the Engineering Employers' Federation (EEF) and its member firms to any inclusion of workforce representatives in production planning.[109] Even in enlightened

---

105   Thurley and Wirdenius, *Supervision: A Reappraisal*, p. 217; an argument they repeat in their analysis of development opportunities: Thurley and Wirdenius, *Approaches to Supervisory Development*, p. 14. Curiously, to modern observers familiar with Japanese and derivative management philosophies, not to mention contemporaneous German approaches, they do not seem to conclude that companies would be better reducing the occurrence of unforeseen problems.

106   A.W. Dickinson, *Industrial Relations in Supervisory Management* (London, 1967), pp. 8, 2. Dickinson had first-hand knowledge of his subject and its inherent frustrations; he was the training services manager of the British Motor Corporation.

107   Alan McKinlay and Joseph Melling, 'The Shop Floor Politics of Productivity: Power and Authority Relations in British Engineering, c.1945–1957', in *British Trade Unions and Industrial Politics 1945–1978: Vol. 1, the Post-War Compromise, 1945–1964*, ed. by Alan Campbell, Nina Fishman, and John McIlroy (Aldershot, 1999), p. 232.

108   McKinlay and Melling, pp. 237–39; see also Joseph Melling, '"Non-Commissioned Officers": British Employers and Their Supervisory Workers, 1880–1920', *Social History*, 5.2 (1980), 183–221 for an exploration of the changing nature of the foreman's role in earlier decades.

109   McKinlay and Melling, pp. 228–29.

West Midlands firms like Cadburys, it is not clear that foremen were consulted much before the 1980s.[110]

Clearly the foreman occupied a difficult place within British industry. His tenure was the result of his craft experience but his position in the workplace was compromised by the attitudes of those above and below him. An example of this is evident in the compliment paid in 1949 by the Coventry machine tool manufacturer Sir Alfred Herbert to his foremen, "a body of men for whom I have great respect and with whom I have very real sympathy in the difficult and exacting duties they have to perform in their position as buffers between management and workers." Though Sir Alfred "wonder[ed] if they fully realise the great extent of their influence" being a "buffer" does not seem to be the best use of capable men.[111] Herbert's managing director Colonel C.W. Clark reiterated his chairman's conception, patronisingly telling the company's foremen: "[You] occupy a position between Management and Labour and are apt on occasion to be damned by both. But, we understand your difficulties, arising largely from the changed conditions in Industry to-day, and we admire the cheerful way you tackle and dispose of them."[112] The foremen saw qualities in themselves – "diplomacy, tact, psychology, discipline, salesmanship and above all a good knowledge of human nature" – which suggested they could offer more than this.[113] Five years later, however, Herbert's foremen seem to have grown tired of being a "buffer" and being "damned", with their qualities under-appreciated: the earlier speaker's foreman colleague bemoaned the "couldn't care less" attitude which now prevailed among them.[114]

Given post-war industry's demands, with increasing competition and limited availability of skilled resources, what efforts were being made to build on the qualities Herbert's foremen saw in themselves? As Thurley and Wirdenius observed, "traditionally supervisors [had] been left very much to run their own shops and [had] picked the job up by observation of other foremen and by learning from their own mistakes."[115] With this unsystematic approach, it would have been rational for progressive companies, especially any reflecting on the approach taken in Germany (from where Herbert saw increasing competition),

---

110   Chris Smith, John Child, and Michael Rowlinson, *Reshaping Work: The Cadbury Experience* (Cambridge, 1990), pp. 146, 174.
111   Sir Alfred Herbert, 'Speech to BTH (Rugby) Foremen's Association' (1949), MRC, MSS.242/BT/15.
112   C.W. Clark, 'Speech to Alfred Herbert Ltd. Annual Foremen's Dinner, 1949' (1949), Coventry History Centre, PA1270/23/8.
113   The views of one of the foremen, speaking at the previous year's gathering: 'Speech to Foremen's Annual Dinner 1948', *The Alfred Herbert News* (October 1948), 66–69, Coventry History Centre, JN621.9.
114   'Speech to Foremen's Annual Dinner 1953', *The Alfred Herbert News* (December 1953), 183–84, Coventry History Centre.
115   Thurley and Wirdenius, *Approaches to Supervisory Development*, p. 14.

to have considered investing in the development of their foremen as business became more difficult.[116] In practice, how were foremen treated and trained in our case-study companies and other West Midlands businesses? The first issue to note is how little information is available, in any company archives, of relevant material on foremen or supervisors as a group, let alone on efforts to develop them (there are no development materials in the Herbert archive, for example). The lack of data on foremen in company archives cannot, of course, be claimed to prove a lack of company commitment to them. But it is reasonable to conclude that the material which *is* available is representative of a generally prevalent culture. It does not paint a convincing picture of company views of their staff, or of their response to the approach taken by increasingly successful German competitors.

One example: in 1962 the Humber motor company in Coventry introduced training for "The Foreman in the Modern Technological World", asserting that the "new technologies demand that the foreman be an organiser skilled in the art of man management" and confirming that "modern progressive industrialists recognise his status as that of a 'Junior Executive'". This enthusiasm sounds convincing. In fact, the training was concerned mainly with the industrial relations difficulties the company was facing. Three hours' training was provided for 137 candidates. An external organisation, the Industrial Welfare Society, was engaged to run residential weekends for small groups. Their purpose was, as one participant reported to management, "to bring Shop Stewards and Foremen together in an attempt to promote better relations and understanding at shop floor level ... Some useful advice was also given on ways of dealing with coloured employees, young lads just out of school, and older men approaching retirement". No further technical or commercial training appears to have been offered.[117]

Within our case-study companies, we will see later that Jensen's foremen appear to have been appointed according to experience and length of tenure, and to have been preoccupied with protecting their territory. At K&J, post-war supervisors and foremen had to retrain veterans or induct recruits. They were all enrolled in instructor courses in 1947 as "a sure and dependable method of passing on to others the skills we have learnt in our particular trades or professions." Management hoped to put all supervisors onto these courses, which ran for two hours per day for one week. The course was "not concerned in any way with those actual skills, but it does show us how to instruct others in acquiring them", raising the question of how supervisors had been passing

---

116 'German Competition in Machine Tools', *The Alfred Herbert News* (December 1952), 159, Coventry History Centre; Sir Alfred Herbert, 'German and Continental Competition', *The Alfred Herbert News* (August 1952), 86, Coventry History Centre.

117 'Internal Correspondence: Humber and Rootes Training for Foremen' (Rootes Group, 1962), Coventry History Centre, Rootes Archive, 1690/1/16/52.

on their learning to their staff and apprentices until that point, and indeed how the skills taught were validated.[118]

Although K&J's training of recruits apparently improved over time, such that commercial apprentices joining in the 1960s were offered a good, all-round training, the development of existing senior staff appears to have lagged behind.[119] In 1968, K&J's Board announced a scheme of Management and Supervisory Development for all managers and supervisors. The training offered seems not have been particularly constructive or focused. Chairman Peter Kenrick was at pains to point out that no criticism of their current performance was implied: "For the most part the training will take place on the job and basically will consist of making sure that each one of us knows what our jobs involve, what our strengths and weaknesses are and then endeavour to help where help is required." The extent to which management considerations were divorced from the need for development can be gauged from their statement that even for such an apparently superficial commitment, "it [had] taken the Board some time to crystallise its ideas on what is a very big subject indeed."[120] It is not clear how the company expected its first-line managers, without any preparation other than experience with the status quo, to initiate new products and processes or ensure consistent product quality. Company veteran Ivan Walker, who had joined in 1932 for a seven-year apprenticeship assigned to a journeyman, was appointed supervisor of the new greetings card department in the 1960s, with 200 outworkers. He recalled that he was just "thrown in at the deep end."[121]

While this lack of effort by employers seems troubling, it should be related to the attitudes and background of foremen themselves. A study of the steel industry in 1966 revealed that one British company had 243 foremen, of whom six had basic skills qualifications, two had lower-level college certificates, five higher-level certificates, and one a professional certificate; in the other company, 124 foremen had three, three, one, and none respectively. The steel companies did in fact offer foreman's courses; unusually for British industry, some foremen attended more than one.[122] The lack of provision and qualification seems alarming. In the Birmingham manufacturing plants reviewed

118 '"TWI" Training Within Industry', *K&J News* (31 January 1947), p. 1, Sandwell Archive, BS/KJ4/1/18.

119 David Paulson, Interview with Jeremy Plimmer, former business development manager, K&J, 2014.

120 'Management & Supervisory Development Programme', *K&J News* (28 June 1968), p. 1, Sandwell Archive, BS/KJ4/1/18.

121 David Paulson, Interview with Ivan Walker, former production supervisor K&J, 2013.

122 P.W. Musgrave, *Technical Change: The Labour Force and Education* (London, 1967), pp. 211–12. The qualifications referred to here were, in order, City & Guilds; ONC; HNC; and ARTC (Glasgow).

by Child and Partridge, however, foremen's "attitude to training, given that a majority had not received any training for the job, suggest[ed] that they consider[ed] personal qualities and experience to be of greater importance in carrying out their work."[123]

The tragedy of the British situation was that during and immediately after the Second World War, some efforts were made to raise the profile and productive potential of foremen. One interesting thinker on the subject was A.P. Young, works manager of engineers British Thomson-Houston in Rugby, who saw foremen as the "backbone of industry".[124] In 1949, in a speech to the Institute of Industrial Supervisors, he argued:

> Every Works Manager, if he is doing his job in the right way, has to depend increasingly on the work done by the foreman, a line of leadership that bears directly on the workers ... If we could only inculcate the feeling that they were called to a great task ... to radiate the human principles of management and thus cause the team spirit to blossom, what a transformation scene would we witness in British industry.[125]

Young was not alone in the West Midlands. The aspiration for greater recognition and training for foremen and supervisors had been voiced by a study group within the Birmingham Technical College, made up of managers from regional companies. They published *A Code of Management Practice Relating to the Status of the Foreman* in 1948. In it, they identified the foreman as a critical element in the conduct of operations, a "part of management [whose] quality as an individual must be judged by management standards."[126] They called for a period of initial training, involving some exposure to management and financial principles within the employer's business, and participation in local college courses concentrating on personnel-management practices and organisational behaviour. This would be combined with work as an assistant to an experienced foreman. The study group's recommendations were incorporated by David Bramley, recently appointed to lead the Business Department of the Technical College, forerunner of Aston Business School, into the foremen's training programme he had set up in 1947. Its 1950/1 syllabus extended over

123 Child and Partridge, p. 98.
124 A.P. Young, 'Unpublished Manuscript: My Thoughts on Management' (nd), MRC, MSS.242/MP/4/18.
125 A.P. Young, '"The Foreman and Works Management": Speech to the Institute of Works Managers, Smethwick' (1949), MRC, MSS.242/IW/8.
126 *A Code Of Management Practice Relating To The Status Of The Foreman, Being Suggestions Arising From The Work Of A Management Study Group* (Birmingham: Institute of Industrial Supervisors and Industrial Administration Group, Birmingham Central Technical College, 1948), p. 8, Aston University, David Bramley Archive, Folder Box 3, S19.F1.

the "technical aspects" and the "human aspects" of supervisory management, with the following courses:[127]

	Technical Aspects	Human Aspects
First Year	Factory Organization	Industrial Relations
	Work Study	Psychology for Supervision
Second Year	Factory Costing & Estimating	Personnel Administration
	Industrial Law	Industrial Psychology

The programme lasted a total of 240 hours over two years of part-time study. Teaching faculty all had industrial experience in the subjects they taught, a requirement of Bramley's Department. The teaching was not superficial – individual course elements included, for example, consideration of "Revenge and moral indignation in maintaining social order" and the interpretation in production planning of design and sales requirements – and students were required to engage in discussion groups on Management Principles and Practice led by senior local business leaders.

The course's creators proclaimed that it was "one of the most comprehensive available for supervisory management in the country" and was "designed and conducted so as to be appropriate for the foreman who is likely to become superintendent or departmental manager."[128] There were some similarities to the *Meister* training programmes in aspects of their attention to personnel management. Yet Bramley's programme was very different in aspiration, scope, and expectation – the pass mark for each element was 40% – than was the much more comprehensive programme delivered over 840 or more hours to German *Meister* candidates – whose own pass mark was 70%. It demonstrates little of the *Meister* training's ambition of setting the highest standards of technical excellence (the study group had downplayed the importance of craft skills versus personal qualities) and general business awareness, both of which might combine to form the basis of progression into senior management. And the different starting point of his students, lacking the skills of their German counterparts and without the opportunity to benefit from the technical "pre-course" within the *Meister* training programme, meant that students passing Bramley's course were likely to offer much less all-round competence to their employer, had their employer been interested.

---

127 College of Technology Birmingham, *Course of Management Studies in Workshop Supervision* (Birmingham: College of Technology Birmingham, 1950), Aston University, David Bramley Archive, Folder Box 1, C3.1.F2.
128 College of Technology Birmingham, *Progress Report 1947–1952* (Birmingham: College of Technology Birmingham, 11 July 1953), p. 14, Aston University, David Bramley Archive, Folder Box 1, C3.1.F2.

Moreover, attendance on Bramley's programme appears to have been disappointing. Although 270 students enrolled in the first cohort of the course in 1947, only seventy-five of them appeared in the second year of study. By 1951/2, first-year enrolment was fifty-eight, with thirty-nine joining the second year. Far from being a cause for celebration, the huge interest in its first year was a concern, as it "overwhelmed the Department and unsatisfactory teaching conditions resulted." Rather than expanding provision, enrolments were thereafter managed by a policy of not publicising the course and maintaining contact only with senior executives of companies which sent other students to the Department.[129]

In 1954, a House of Commons Committee of Inquiry, chaired by a civil servant and with members drawn from employers' associations, industrial institutions, and the Trades Union Congress (TUC), reported on the national importance of training foremen and supervisors.[130] The committee found that training was offered on a variety of bases in numerous technical colleges across the UK to 2800–3300 supervisors annually (the lack of accurate data being perhaps indicative of policy shortcomings). It noted that The Institute of Industrial Administration offered a Certificate in Foremanship and Supervision, a course requiring attendance at college two evenings per week over two years.[131] However, the syllabus appears not to have been rigorous in comparison with what was offered in West Germany – "the purpose of the first-year course is largely to give experience in written and spoken expressions" – with some introduction to the principles of production, planning, estimating and costing in the second year. In any case, in 1952/3, only 438 Certificates were issued nationally.[132]

Whether there would have been greater ongoing interest in Bramley's programme if enrolment had been more widely encouraged cannot be known, though *A Code of Management Practice Relating to the Status of the Foreman* went through three impressions totalling 7000 copies in 1948/9.[133] But it is notable that the Parliamentary Committee found that "[T]wo facts stand out very clearly ... first that only a very small proportion of supervisors are yet receiving any training outside their firm, and secondly, that all the places at present available for outside courses for training foremen are not fully occupied."[134] In its conclusions, the committee called for greater management

129   College of Technology Birmingham, *Progress Report 1947–1952*, p. 26.
130   Ministry of Labour and National Service, *Report of Committee of Inquiry on The Training of Supervisors* (London: HMSO, 1954), Aston University, David Bramley Archive, Folder Box 3, O15.F3.
131   For which there are no substantive archival records available.
132   Ministry of Labour and National Service, pp. 14–15.
133   *A Code Of Management Practice Relating To The Status Of The Foreman, Being Suggestions Arising From The Work Of A Management Study Group.*
134   Ministry of Labour and National Service, p. 28.

commitment to foremen's training, internally and in cooperation with local technical colleges, and to the assertion of foremen's place within company management structures.

Yet while it was able to cite a few examples of good courses and excellent in-company training programmes, the committee was "unable to reach a definite decision on the quality or type of outside course needed generally."[135] Its recommendation for the colleges themselves was vague, calling for more short courses without examination and further emphasis on in-company training sponsored by the Ministry of Labour and National Service under its Training Within Industry Scheme.[136] While the *Meister* training programmes were being rolled out across West Germany, establishing an aspirational culture for skilled workers keen to achieve the high national standard, their British counterparts experienced a combination of individual or employer apathy and national policy incoherence. Notwithstanding the efforts of regional educators like Bramley, the vast majority of Britain's first-line managers would continue to rely on their seniority and the customs of their workplace, rather than on targeted education and training within a national system of excellence.

The potential benefit of a programme like Bramley's, had it been developed further regionally and nationally, is evidenced by German workers' and employers' investment in professional development. Over the two decades after the proposed schema for *Meister* training was first presented, its national acceptance had become firmly established: in 1977, 4788 candidates took the national *Meisterprüfung* (Master Craftsman's examination) for industry in West Germany. An additional 30,147 candidates took the examination in their craft trade, which included work in the trades carried out by some of our subject companies.[137] Though there have been some variations over time in the number of candidates presenting themselves for the *Meister* qualification, still in 2018 there were 13,319 candidates from various branches of industry,[138] and a further 20,100 from craft trades,[139] evidence of Germany's continuing national commitment to excellence in technical first-line management.

---

135   Ministry of Labour and National Service, p. 28.
136   Ministry of Labour and National Service, pp. 33–35.
137   Statistisches Bundesamt Wiesbaden, *Berufliche Bildung 1977*, Bildung Und Kultur (Wiesbaden, 1978), pp. 108–12 <https://www.statistischebibliothek.de/mir/receive/DEHeft_mods_00131152> [accessed 5 August 2022].
138   Deutscher Industrie- und Handelskammertag, *IHK- und DIHK-Fortbildungsstatistik 2018* (Berlin, June 2019) <https://www.dihk.de/de/themen-und-positionen/fachkraefte/aus-und-weiterbildung/weiterbildung/weiterbildungsstatistiken--2742> [accessed 26 May 2020].
139   Zentralverband des deutschen Handwerks, 'Meisterprüfungsstatistik - Detailauswertung 2019' (Berlin, 25 May 2020) <https://www.zdh-statistik.de/application/index.php?mID=3&cID=814> [accessed 26 May 2020].

Engineering Graduates

Critical to the Mittelstand's development of niche products of the highest quality was the interplay, in their development and manufacture, between a *Meister* and his company's engineers. To evaluate the assumption that differences in the availability and technical competence of young engineers were factors in the comparative development of companies in the two regions, we must understand the constraints and opportunities available to would-be employers of graduate engineers in the West Midlands and Baden-Württemberg.[140]

The shortcomings in British engineering training have been highlighted by Chandler and others. Over time, Braithwaites and their neighbours could draw on an expanding regional pool of graduates to help them grow: one study argues that by 1964, the Conservative Government had made great progress in higher education, promoting the advancement of the university sector.[141] However, it also highlights the concern of the university establishment that teaching technology would be "subverting the ideal of a genuinely liberal education" and that increasing "the 'Germanic' vices of 'specialisation' risked moral decay by privileging technical training and a narrow form of educational utilitarianism."[142] It was in this environment that Birmingham University's Science faculty grew from the late 1960s onwards. In 1950, there had been 198 Science faculty members in total, including 65 Engineering teachers; by 1960 there were 301 and 120 respectively; in 1970, 559 and 209; and in 1979, 725 and 241.[143] Aston University now also began to develop, along with Warwick and Loughborough, so that by 1971 a West Midlands company could in principle recruit students from one of eleven universities or polytechnics within a fifty-mile radius.[144] Unfortunately for ambitious businesses, that provision was not available in previous decades. As the analysis in figure 4 shows, a local firm could choose from one of forty-eight Birmingham University graduates

---

140   Future research would be beneficial in local technical colleges in both localities, to establish the relative numbers and qualification levels of non-graduate engineers.

141   M.T.F. Finn, 'The Political Economy of Higher Education in England, c. 1944–1974' (unpublished Ph.D. thesis, 2009), p. 170.

142   Finn, pp. 21, 34.

143   Analysis by the author, from: University of Birmingham, *The University of Birmingham Calendar for the Session 1950–51* (Birmingham: Cornish Brothers, 1950); University of Birmingham, *The University of Birmingham Calendar for the Session 1960–61* (Birmingham: Cornish Brothers, 1960); University of Birmingham, *The University of Birmingham Calendar for the Session 1970–71* (Birmingham: Cornish Brothers, 1970); University of Birmingham, *The University of Birmingham Calendar for the Session 1979–80* (Birmingham: Cornish Brothers, 1979), courtesy of the Cadbury Research Library, University of Birmingham.

144   Regrettably, Aston University's archives were not available to me, preventing a comparison with Birmingham University and an aggregate comparison with their Baden-Württemberg counterparts.

Summer 1957 Enrolments, Baden-Württemberg

Subject	Technische Hochschulen			Universities				University of Birmingham Graduates, 1956
	Karlsruhe	Stuttgart	Mannheim	Heidelberg	Tübingen	Freiburg	Totals	
Physics	190	291		167	745	169		31
Chemistry	355	411		399	255	235		49
Architecture	368	432						
Civil Engineering	616	451						31
Surveying	52	60						
Machine/Mechanical Engineering	1,017	1,135						22
Electrical Engineering	534	511						26
Business Studies			1,061					34
All Subjects	4,238	4,049	1,089	6,393	6,533	7,000	27,270	
"Industry-Relevant" Subjects	3,132	3,291	1,061	566	1,000	404	9,454	
Total Enrolled Students – Baden-Württemberg							27,270	
Total "Industry-Relevant" Students – Baden-Württemberg							9,454	
Subjects Studied at Birmingham only								
Chemical Engineering								35
Petroleum Production Engineering								2
Metallurgy								17
Total "Industry-Relevant" Graduates – Birmingham								**247**
Total Science Undergraduates – Birmingham, 1960								**1772**

Figure 4 Enrolments at Baden-Württemberg Institutions and the University of Birmingham.

in Electrical or Mechanical Engineering in 1956, whereas their counterparts in Baden-Württemberg could recruit one of the 3197 students who enrolled in the *Technische Hochschulen* at Stuttgart or Karlsruhe in the same subjects.[145]

It was not only a question of quantity, but of quality, as the Civil Engineering curriculum at *Technische Hochschule* (TH) Stuttgart showed at the time of Julius Schneider Eisenkonstruktion und Glasdachbau's foundation in 1910. Teaching comprised a heavy hourly load each week in practical elements of engineering – including hydraulics, earthworks, railway and road construction, bridge engineering – as well as elements of management and economics, as the extract in Figure 5 from the 1910 course calendar for the second and third years shows.[146]

TH Stuttgart's Mechanical Engineering programme in 1910 was equally demanding. Before they could enrol in the programme, students were required to have a minimum of one year's practical experience in a workshop and a thorough ability in calculation, scientific knowledge, technical drawing and visualisation. Their own curriculum comprised a comprehensive range of courses and lectures in subjects ranging from aerodynamics to technical drawing, machine tools to electronics, steam engines to pumps. In each of their three years of learning, students were also urged to pursue additional studies in practical geometry, chemistry, and English, French, and Italian; those wishing to deepen their expertise were also free to attend lectures in any other programme in the university or to engage in practical study in its various research institutes.[147]

The interruption of the Second World War and the exigencies of reconstruction did not ease the demands on students. The 1948 Study Plan for Mechanical Engineering, which would have been identical to the programme followed by Berthold Leibinger before joining Trumpf, and Rolf Walz before joining Schneider, was comprehensive, practically orientated (with a heavy emphasis on practical exercises), but intellectually extremely demanding. As well as mandatory participation in rubble clearance and the rebuilding of the

145   Table compiled by the author from: University of Birmingham, *The University of Birmingham Calendar for the Session 1956–57* (Birmingham: Cornish Brothers, 1956); Statistisches Landesamt Baden-Württemberg, 'Statistische Bericht B I 3 und 4: die Studierenden an den wissenschaftlichen Hochschulen und Kunsthochschulen im Wintersemester 1956/57 und Sommersemester 1957' (Statistisches Landesamt Baden-Württemberg, 1957) <https://www.destatis.de/GPStatistik/servlets/MCRFileNodeServlet/BWHeft_derivate_00003819/BIII_j_WS56_57_SS57.pdf> [accessed 24 April 2016].
146   Technische Hochschule Stuttgart, *Programm der Königlich Württembergischen Technischen Hochschule in Stuttgart für das Studienjahr 1910–1911*': (Stuttgart, 1910), pp. 67–68 < https://digibus.ub.uni-stuttgart.de/viewer/image/1530689129952_1910_1/36/> [accessed 5 August 2022].
147   Technische Hochschule Stuttgart, *Programm Der Königlich Württembergischen Technischen Hochschule in Stuttgart Für Das Studienjahr 1910–1911*, pp. 75–80.

	Weekly Hours			
	in Winter		in Summer	
Second Year	Lecture	Tutor-ials	Lecture	Tutor-ials
Practical Geometry I	3	2	-	4
- - II	-	-	5	4*)
Mechanical engineering	4	-	-	-
Exercises in the materials research laboratory	-	4**)	-	-
Graphical analysis in bridge construction	2	2	-	-
Analytical theory of engineering structures	4	4	4	4
Building design II	4	4	-	5
- - III	-	-	2	-
Highway engineering	-	-	2	-
Hydraulic engineering	3	-	-	-
Water supply	-	-	3	-
City sewage systems	-	-	3	-
Metallurgy for civil engineers	1	-	-	-
	21	15	19	17
Second Year				
Exercises in geodetic surveying	-	2	-	-
Fundamentals of electrical engineering	2	-	-	-
Civil engineering III	-	4	-	-
Bridge engineering I	3	6	4	7
Foundations for civil works	1	-	1	-
Earthwork	2	-	-	-
Alignment	-	-	2	-
Railway engineering I	4	-	4	6
Railway construction I	2	-	-	4
Dams	1	-	-	-
Hydroelectic installations	1	-	-	-
Rural engineering	2	-	-	-
Hydraulic engineering II	2	-	-	-
Exercises in hydraulic engineering	-	4	-	4
Law	-	-	2	-
	20	16	13	21
Seventh Semester				
Bridge engineering II and tunnel engineering	3	6		
Railway engineering II	2	-		
Exercises in railway- and highway engineering	-	8		
Railway construction II	-	4		
Exercises in hydraulic engineering	-	4		
Administration	2	-		
Economics	3	-		
	10	22		

*) On the surveying fieldtrip, see p.29
**) These exercises can also be completed in a later semester if it suits an
individual student's study plan better.
For additional subjects, see the explanatory note on p. 70.

Figure 5 Extract from study plan – Civil Engineering, Technische Hochschule
Stuttgart, 1910–11. Universität Stuttgart. Translated by author.

bomb-damaged university, students had to manage lectures and seminars in
a wide range of courses, including higher mathematics, mechanics, thermo-
dynamics, machine-building, and turbine technology, over the years of their
degree programme, as the abbreviated extract in Figure 6, showing hours of
instruction in the summer semester, shows.[148]

Leibinger remembers the demands placed on students: "I had to exert myself
to manage it ... mastering a Mechanical Engineering course is hard graft." The
large lecture theatre, with 500 seats, was "always overflowing" and the "tempo
in the lectures, for example in Higher Mathematics, was breathtaking."[149]

At Birmingham, the practical aspects of Engineering were not ignored.
Students were "required to spend a satisfactory proportion of the summer
vacation in practical work with engineering firms."[150] But it seems reasonable
to assume that Birmingham's Final Examination in Mechanical Engineering,
which required students to write two essays, one on 'Power presses and
their tools, including rubber pad pressing', might have taxed Leibinger and
Ulrich Putsch of Keiper less than their own final examinations in mechanical
engineering at TH Stuttgart and TH Karlsruhe respectively.[151] Even without
these concerns, the potential value of Birmingham University as an engineering
talent pool for regional SMEs seems to have been limited by the chosen career
paths of its graduates. As the analysis in Figure 7 shows, only twenty-seven
of forty-three science and engineering graduates from 1950, who might have
become the region's business leaders of the 1960s and 1970s, are identifiable
and/or remained in the UK. Of them, only one was working in an SME eight
years after graduation, and only eight remained in the Midlands.[152]

Of course, it cannot be known whether the class of 1950 chose their careers
because they disdained work in SMEs or in private-sector, technology-orien-
tated enterprises, or because those enterprises were not interested in recruiting
them. Prais suggests, however, that even by 1981, British universities still did

148   Technische Hochschule Stuttgart, *Programm der Technischen Hochschule Stuttgart für
das Sommersemester 1948* (Technische Hochschule Stuttgart, 1948), pp. 7, 38–39, <https://
digibus.ub.uni-stuttgart.de/viewer/image/1530689129952_1948_1/1/> [accessed 5 August
2022]. The programme for the Winter semester was published separately; what we see here
is therefore one half of each year's study requirements.

149   Leibinger, sec. 707.

150   University of Birmingham, *University of Birmingham Syllabuses 1960–1961*
(Birmingham: University of Birmingham, 1960), p. 155, Cadbury Memorial Library.

151   Birmingham University, *University of Birmingham Examination Papers 1960 -
Medicine and Science* (Birmingham: University of Birmingham, 1960).

152   Table compiled by the author from: University of Birmingham, *The University of
Birmingham Calendar for the Session 1950–51*; Guild of Graduates of the University of
Birmingham, *The University of Birmingham Register of Graduates Up to December 1957,
With a Supplementary List of Those Who Graduated in July 1958*, 6th edn. (Birmingham:
Guild of Graduates of the University of Birmingham, 1958).

III. Faculty of Mechanical Engineering
1. Department of Mechanical Engineering

	Hours		
2nd Semester	Lecture	Seminar	Practicals

	Lecture	Seminar	Practicals	
Higher Mathematics II, Descriptive Geometry B II, Experimental physics II see under I, 1. Chemistry see under I. 2				
Engineering mechanics II (for mechanical and electrical engineers as well as mathematicians and physicists)	3	2	-	Grammel
Engineering technology II	2	-	3	Gottwein
Structures	2	-	1	Wellinger
Introduction to mechanical engineering II	1	-	4	Ehrhardt
Introduction to electrical engineering	2	-	-	Wolman
4th Semester				
Higher mathematics II, graphical and numerical Methods see under I. 1. Engineering mechanics II (for mechanical engineers, mathematicians und physicists)	3	2	-	Grammel
Thermodynamics	3	1	-	Grammel
Machine components II	3	-	6	Rembold
Machine laboratory	-	-	3	N. N.
6. Semester				
Reciprocating engines II	2	1	6	Rembold
Fluid mechanics II	2	1	-	Weise
Hydraulic motors II	2	1	6	Braun
Steam- and gas turbines	3	1	6	Jansen
Materials handling technology II	2	1	6	Müller
Machine tools II	2	1	6	Ehrhardt
Special laboratory in the Institute for Machine Tools	-	-	4	Ehrhardt
Factory management I	2	2	6	Gottwein
Rail vehicles I	2	-	-	Hiller
Motor vehicles	2	1	6	Riekert, Eisele
Materials engineering	2	-	1	Siebel
Applied materials science	2	-	1	Siebel
Elasticity theory (higher dynamics)	3	1	-	Kauderer
Gears	3	-	-	Widmaier
Precision engineering for instrument building II	1	-	6	Kell
Machines	2	-	-	Kniel

Figure 6 Extract from Schedule of Lectures and Exercises – Mechanical Engineering, Technische Hochschule Stuttgart, 1948. Universität Stuttgart. Translated by author.

Degree	Class	Job Title / Role	Industry	Private or State	Midlands Resident	SME
Chemical Engineering	1	Ph.D.	Hydrocarbons	Private	No	No
Chemical Engineering	1	Chemical Engr	Hydrocarbons	Private	No	No
Chemical Engineering	2.1	Refinery Designs Engr	Hydrocarbons	Private	No	No
Chemical Engineering	2.1	Process Engineer	Hydrocarbons	Private	No	No
Electrical Engineering	2.1	Project Engineer	Automotive	Private	No	No
Electrical Engineering	2.1	Management Consultant	Consulting	Private	No	No
Electrical Engineering	1	Principal Engineer	Automotive	Private	No	No
Industrial Metallurgy	1	Asst Melting Shop Mgr	Metals	Private	No	No
Industrial Metallurgy	1	Technical Manager	Metals	Private	No	No
Mechanical Engineering	1	Head	Armaments	Private	No	No
Mechanical Engineering	1	Leader	Aviation	Private	No	No
Mechanical Engineering	2	Technical Officer	Chemicals	Private	No	No
Physics	1	Ph.D. Technical Staff	Telecoms	Private	No	No
Physics	1	Trials Analyst	Armaments	Private	No	No
Chemistry	1	Senior Scientific Offr	Government	State	No	No
Chemistry	1	Ph.D.	Armaments	State	No	No
Chemistry	1	Ph.D. Scientific Officer	Infrastructure	State	No	No
Electrical Engineering	1	District Engineer	Infrastructure	State	No	No
Mechanical Engineering	1	Senior Scientific Offr	Agriculture	State	No	No
Chemistry	1	Research Biochemist	Pharma	Private	Yes	No
Chemistry	1	Ph.D. Research Chemist	Ceramic	Private	Yes	No
Chemistry	1	Research Chemist	Plastics	Private	Yes	No

Degree	Class	Job Title / Role	Industry	Private or State	Midlands Resident	SME
Civil Engineering	1	N/L	Eng Consultants	Private	Yes	No
Electrical Engineering	2.1	Electronic Engineer	Aviation	Private	Yes	No
Mechanical Engineering	2	Company Director	Road Transport	Private	Yes	Yes
Chemistry	1	Ph.D. Senior Scientific Offr	Government	State	Yes	No
Civil Engineering	1	Senior Engineering Asst	Infrastructure	State	Yes	No

Figure 7 Career Destinations, 1950 Science and Engineering Graduates, the University of Birmingham.

not deliver the same value to industry as their German counterparts "in terms of numbers of qualified engineers produced and research undertaken".[153]

If privacy laws and available data permitted, determining the destinations and eventual career achievements of TH Stuttgart and TH Karlsruhe graduates would allow a full and comparative understanding of each institution's contribution to its region's business. In contrasting those two institutions with those in the West Midlands, however, it is important to remember that they form just two parts of an intensive research infrastructure which is in place today for Baden-Württemberg. It was also available, if not always on the same scale, to the state's Mittelstand businesses during the period under review: around them were numerous research institutes, including eleven Max Planck Institutes, conducting world-leading scientific research;[154] thirteen institutes of the Fraunhofer-Gesellschaft, focused on the development of key technologies and their commercial exploitation;[155] ten industrial joint research institutes, and eight contract research institutions, plus seven other universities and nineteen technical colleges (*Fachhochschulen*), with relationships between business and academia all facilitated by the Steinbeis Foundation.[156]

153   Prais, p. 184.
154   Max-Planck Gesellschaft, 'Short Portrait of the Max Planck Society', *Max-Planck Gesellschaft* (2021) <https://www.mpg.de/short-portrait> [accessed 29 December 2021].
155   Fraunhofer-Gesellschaft, 'Profile / Structure', *Fraunhofer-Gesellschaft* (2021) <https://www.fraunhofer.de/en/about-fraunhofer/profile-structure.html> [accessed 29 December 2021].
156   Günter von Alberti, *Steinbeis 1971–1991*, 2nd edn (Stuttgart, 2010), p. 46; 'Steinbeis-at-a-Glance' (Steinbeis Foundation, 2019) <https://www.steinbeis.de/fileadmin/content/

West Midlands businesses were at a significant disadvantage compared to their Baden-Württemberg counterparts in the number and quality of engineers available to them, and the competence and motivation of first-line managers able to turn the engineers' creations into products of the highest quality. The combination of both these sources of talent made a decisive difference between the ability of Mittelstand businesses to create excellent, niche products, and their British counterparts' efforts to do the same. The surrounding infrastructure further added to their relative advantage.

Epilogue

The preceding analysis inevitably begs the question of whether the advantages claimed here were merely transitory. In the interests of fairness it makes sense to consider briefly whether academic studies conducted in the economically turbulent, post-unification 1990s stand as a potential corrective to my conclusions about the earlier period.[157] Gary Herrigel and Charles Sabel argued that the mentality and methods of training described above were once ideally suited to the demand for flexibly produced, customised goods but were inappropriate in the rapidly changing working environments of the 1990s. Difficulties in adjustment were bringing "extremely dramatic and pervasive social transformation" to Germany, and industries and companies were threatened with extinction.[158] They showed that piecemeal attempts to introduce team-based working in Baden-Württemberg firms were failing, though they saw some cause for optimism within businesses where change had been embraced. And although the restructuring process was "difficult and treacherous", the continuation of the external institutions which helped deliver the Mittelstand's previous high standards offered a "ray of hope".[159] Karin Wagner argued that adaptation of the dual system (apprenticeships combined with university study) of industrial/ commercial education would be required, but that *Meister* would remain important to developing businesses[160] as they aided restructuring efforts.[161] David Finegold cautioned that *Meister* training must be continually updated

Publikationen/unternehmenspublikationen/Publication_Steinbeis_at_a_Glance.pdf > [accessed 17 February 2019]; see also Roper for an assessment of the way firms in each country approached innovation and utilised networks and institutional resources.

157   *The German Skills Machine: Sustaining Competitive Advantage in a Global Economy*, ed. by Pepper D. Culpepper and David Finegold (New York and Oxford, 1999).

158   Herrigel and Sabel, pp. 78–81, 94.

159   Herrigel and Sabel, pp. 112–14.

160   Karin Wagner, 'The German Apprenticeship System Under Strain', in *The German Skills Machine*, pp. 37–76 (pp. 68–70, 76).

161   David Finegold and Karin Wagner, 'The German Skill-Creation System and Team-Based Production: Competitive Asset or Liability?', in *The German Skills Machine*, pp. 115–55 (p. 153).

to reflect their evolving responsibilities, which he suggested should include the maintenance of high-quality apprentice training within firms.[162]

Advancing another twenty years, changes in German industry have indeed taken place, but the value placed on its apprentices and *Meister* has remained. RECARO Aircraft Seating, now a €600 million per annum business,[163] still recruits engineers through its dual-study programme.[164] It still employs as a Module Engineer an individual who completed his apprenticeship with the firm in 1988, was retained and sponsored through a degree programme throughout the crisis described by Herrigel and Sabel, and advanced through various team leader and *Meister* roles in the intervening two decades.[165] Only RECARO remains of our German case-study companies. But a twelfth-generation Swabian Mittelstand engineering company still recruits *Stahlbaumeister* in the same way that Schneider did fifty years ago, and with them continues to win global contracts in niche markets.[166] Across German industries and craft trades, over 33,000 *Meister* completed their examinations in 2018.[167] Recent studies have considered the critical role to be played by companies' *Meister* in the digitalisation of the Mittelstand and the rollout of Industry 4.0.[168] After six decades it would appear that traditional conceptions of skills and first-line management in the workplace are, mutatis mutandis, still valid.

162   David Finegold, 'The Future of the German Skill-Creation System: Conclusions and Policy Options', in *The German Skills Machine*, pp. 403–30 (pp. 416, 424).

163   'Recaro "Pulverized" Previous Revenue Records in 2018', *Aircraft Interiors International* (2019) <https://www.aircraftinteriorsinternational.com/news/industry-news/recaro-pulverized-previous-revenue-records-in-2018.html> [accessed 29 April 2019].

164   'DH-Student (m/w/d) Maschinenbau - Produktionstechnik - Beginn 2020 - RECARO Aircraft Seating' <https://www.recaro-as.de/de/job-karriere/jobs/details/dh-student-m-w-d-maschinenbau-produktionstechnik-beginn-2020–22853.html> [accessed 4 August 2019].

165   'Klaus Wieland | LinkedIn' <https://www.linkedin.com/in/klaus-wieland-30329282/> [accessed 4 August 2019].

166   'Meister Produktion Stahlbau (m/w/d) | PFEIFER Group | LinkedIn' <https://www.linkedin.com/jobs/view/meister-produktion-stahlbau-m-w-d-at-pfeifer-group-1299032574/?originalSubdomain=de> [accessed 4 August 2019]; 'PFEIFER Group of Companies' <https://www.pfeifer.info/en/pfeifer-group/company/pfeifer-group-of-companies/> [accessed 4 August 2019].

167   Zentralverband des deutschen Handwerks, 'Meisterprüfungsstatistik - Detailauswertung 2018', *ZDH Statistik-Datenbank* <https://www.zdh-statistik.de/application/stat_det.php?LID=1&ID=MDQ1OTI=&cID=00787> [accessed 26 May 2020].

168   Benjamin Schneider et al, 'Der Meister in Industrie 4.0-Fabriken', in *Die Digitalisierungshürde lässt sich Meister(n): Erfolgsfaktoren, Werkzeuge und Beispiele für den Mittelstand*, ed. by Thomas Knothe et al (Berlin, Heidelberg, 2020), pp. 13–40 <https://doi.org/10.1007/978-3-662-60367-3_3>; Hajck Karapetjan, 'Die Erfassung der Kompetenzen von Industriemeistern als Teil des betrieblichen Kompetenzmanagements - Ein systematischer Ansatz zur Erfassung der Kompetenzen von Industriemeistern im Kontext der Digitalisierung einer Spritzgussproduktion' (Institut für Berufspädagogik und Allgemeine Pädagogik, 2020) <https://doi.org/10.5445/IR/1000121947>.

PART TWO: COMPANY CASE STUDIES

Prologue

Part Two contains the histories of six businesses, three each from Baden-Württemberg and the West Midlands, loosely connected in three industries and chosen to enable a comparison to be made between them. The themes addressed above in Part One are demonstrably critical to small-business success, and they show that, in most respects, the business ecosystem in Baden-Württemberg offered advantages to its resident businesses which their counterparts in the West Midlands did not enjoy. In the case studies that follow we will see more about the ecosystems within which each business operated, and will be able to consider the way they were managed and the culture that prevailed within them. The exploration of each company's history, and the consequent arrangement of each case study, have been dictated by the availability of archival sources. Though I have attempted so far as possible to pay attention to the same themes, the relative emphasis of one series of events over another is reflective of the information that was available to me.

In Chapters 5 and 6 we explore two family-owned companies which were indirectly connected through the paper industry. They shared some similarities: both remained attached to their original location, both shared a patriarchal culture and remained independent across changing generations. Both also ultimately declined when they proved unable to master changing business environments.

The first, Chr. Wandel KG of Reutlingen (Wandel), was a specialist manufacturer of equipment used in paper-making. Founded in 1869 it was owned and managed by its founding family throughout its existence until insolvency in 1995. In many ways the quintessential, small Mittelstand company, it rebuilt itself after near-destruction in the Second World War, regaining a large export market. Wandel's history is interesting because of the extent to which management failings are obvious in its documentary record, providing a valuable corrective to stereotypical assumptions of Mittelstand managerial infallibility. Yet its continuing competitiveness in world markets over several decades speaks to the innate strengths of the business's culture and surrounding ecosystem.

Kenrick & Jefferson Ltd. (K&J) of West Bromwich was a user of paper, as a specialist printer and stationery manufacturer.[1] Founded nine years after Wandel, it was owned by its founding families throughout its existence. It became a powerhouse in the first half of the twentieth century, employing over 1000 people (around seven times more than Wandel), though at any given point it could itself have reasonably been described as a British Mittelstand company, driven by hands-on owners pursuing excellence in specialist, niche products. After the Second World War, though, it struggled to regain its pre-war glory despite having itself suffered no damage and prospering financially during the war. Though dissimilar in many ways, it shared with Wandel the committed family ownership that was resistant to outside managerial influence and declined, albeit from a greater height and within a different industry, for similar reasons.

In Chapters 7 and 8 we see two very different approaches to management, in businesses which also bear some strong similarities. Both manufactured and erected steel structures but on different geographical scales. Both ran fabrication and contracting operations but with a completely different philosophy of leadership engagement. Both were dominated by one family but with completely different models of governance. Both were successful and became frustrated, leading to closure, but found some continuity within very different conceptions of capitalism.

Julius Schneider GmbH & Co. KG (Schneider), based first in Stuttgart then in nearby Ludwigsburg, was a designer, producer, and installer of steel-framed buildings and glass roofing. It celebrated its 50th anniversary in 1960 but by 1976 had closed its doors. Schneider's leadership passed from father to son. They were resilient and committed, and took pride in a paternalistic company culture which relished hard work in adverse conditions. Though their single-minded commitment to family ownership ultimately deprived the company of the flexibility it required to survive following the early death of its owner,

---

1   I have dealt with K&J's history up to 1940 here: David Paulson, 'The Professionalisation of Selling and the Transformation of a Family Business: Kenrick & Jefferson, 1878–1940', *Business History*, 62.2 (2020), 261–91. For postwar history, archival research was supplemented by personal interviews with Hugh Jefferson, former senior director and shareholder, who spent his entire career in the company; Ivan Walker, a 47-year veteran of the company who joined it in the 1930s and retired as a factory supervisor; and Jeremy Plimmer, who joined as an apprentice in the 1960s and left as its business development director in 1994. All were able to offer perspectives into business life at different levels, which usefully supplement the available documentary evidence.

Schneider's history offers a compelling insight into the values that governed the performance and culture of smaller Mittelstand firms.

Braithwaite & Co. Engineers Ltd. (Braithwaites), established in 1884 in West Bromwich, was very different from its German counterpart, though their output was very similar. It was run as a public company from head offices in London, then Surrey,[2] but had been founded by, and was subsequently always controlled and managed by, one family.[3] It had factories in South Wales and West Bromwich. We focus on the latter, which made bridges and other steel structures, often for major infrastructure projects. Until its closure in 1979 its products were sold in Britain and overseas, where Braithwaites enjoyed considerable success. The group was radically transformed in the 1980s through financial engineering, and its successor remains active – albeit it in unrecognisable form – today.

In Chapters 9 and 10 we meet two automotive companies, Stuttgarter Karosseriewerk Reutter (Reutter), later renamed RECARO, and Jensen Motors Ltd. (Jensen), which began in very similar ways. Having started well they each created iconic automotive brands in different fields. But, after subsequently facing difficulties, they ended up in very different circumstances which can be said to have reflected distinctive aspects of their respective national business cultures.

RECARO Aircraft Seating is a world leader in its market and part of the family-owned RECARO Group whose origins date back to 1906 and the Stuttgarter Karosseriewerk Reutter. Business values have been consistent since then, even after one family acquired the business of another.[4] During that period the respective families' companies have sometimes been very large, with international manufacturing operations. But the commitment to Mittelstand values has remained and, as we will see, those values are evident at all points

---

2   Archival material for Braithwaites is limited. The dominance of meeting minutes offering 'official' views has added to the task of reconstruction, and required attention to Decker's concerns regarding evidence of this sort: Decker, pp. 161, 165.

3   The author's letters to the chairman and a director of the company in 1979 and to the later purchaser of its Newport subsidiary were not acknowledged. The relevant professional archive does not contain information from the late 1970s, preventing a separate view of Braithwaites and/or its industry: 'Engineering Employers' Federation - Archives Hub' <https://archiveshub.jisc.ac.uk/data/gb152-eef> [accessed 10 January 2019].

4   The history of the Reutter family's businesses is told in: Jung and Jung: Uta Jung is the granddaugher of interwar shareholder and business leader Albert Reutter and the daughter of joint managing director Theodor Koch; Jung, *Porsche 356 Made by Reutter*: Frank Jung is the great-grandson of Albert Reutter, and the former Head of Tradition for Recaro Holding GmbH; the history of Keiper, which acquired and still owns Recaro, is told in: Putsch and Putsch; Ulrich Putsch was the business owner at the time of the Recaro acquisition, and his son Martin Putsch is the current business owner of Recaro Holding GmbH.

of the history which follows, demonstrating that dynamism and growth are not inconsistent with long-term thinking and humane management.

In its brief heyday, Jensen Motors participated in what one study has identified as one of Britain's economic success stories, the customised production of sports cars in the 1950s and 1960s.[5] In its pursuit of excellence in a niche market, Jensen and firms like them sounded, in fact, like Mittelstand businesses. In Jensen's case, there was an apparent resemblance to Reutter: founded and initially run by two brothers, who started with coachbuilding, their company became famous for a series of iconic sports-touring cars. Jensen's eventual decline following the brothers' departure did not mirror Reutter's experience, however: a series of takeovers revealed that, despite their similar origins, the experience of each company was guided by different values and philosophies, and ended in different outcomes.

5   Stephen Broadberry, p. 83.

5

Chr. Wandel KG, Reutlingen

In March 1953, the local newspaper in Reutlingen, 30km south of Stuttgart, celebrated the success of one of the town's specialist industries, the weaving of fine metal cloth or mesh utilised in the production of paper, which had once again reached production levels not seen since before "the lost war" (*dem verlorenen Krieg*).[1] The four competitors in the town produced what had become a Reutlingen speciality, manufacturing between them 60% of total German production: those in Reutlingen could quite easily cover the whole German requirement and still have capacity to manufacture exports. Reutlingen was renowned for its textile trade, and its metal-cloth manufacturers drew on the town's traditional expertise in weaving. Threads 0.07mm thick were produced, and a *Meister* would take up to two weeks to prepare them. They were then woven on huge looms up to 8.5m wide which could produce cloths of up to 240m² for use in paper-making machines: the paper pulp mixture was run along the fine mesh, and the liquids all drained through it while the paper dried out on top of it. As the machines used in mesh manufacture were so sophisticated the industry employed relatively little labour, but those it did employ had to be all the more skilled. According to the newspaper, "this precision work demand[ed] long experience, a very sure hand, very good eyes, and complete attention in every second."[2] The Reutlingen metal cloth trade, in other words, embodied the precision manufacturing within a clustered niche industry by which Mittelstand businesses had been differentiating themselves from their competitors outside Germany for decades.

Company and Industry Developments, 1860 to 1945

The smallest of the four competitors was the family-owned Christian Wandel, founded in 1869. It is worth reviewing in some detail the history of the business up to 1945 because it shows the way in which expertise was accumulated, family members' own destinies were tied into the business, and future path

---

1 'Reutlinger Metalltücher Gehen in Alle Welt'.
2 'Reutlinger Metalltücher Gehen in Alle Welt'.

dependencies were created.³ Christian Wandel himself had been the seventh child of a sieve-maker, whose family had been in the Reutlingen region since 1494, a century after Ulman Stromer had founded the first German paper mill near Nuremberg; a "sieve" (subsequently to become wire cloth) was always necessary for the production of paper. His journey to becoming an independent entrepreneur was, like that of engineer Karl Walz at Julius Schneider in the following century, a long one in which extensive experience was accumulated and refined. In 1836 Christian was apprenticed to a sieve-maker at Reutlingen, but soon departed on an international tour to learn more about the paper-making industry. He spent the following decades acquiring technical expertise and manufacturing experience, developing customer relationships around Europe, and winning plaudits for his products.⁴ After periods in partnership with others, in 1869 Christian Wandel became sole owner of his factory at the age of forty-eight, having recently been awarded a silver medal at the Paris world exhibition. Wandel's was not the story of a young entrepreneur launching a new business idea: he took his time and built funds and expertise and reputation and chose not to go it alone until he had spent over thirty years at his trade.

Once in control, he patented an important new machine that transformed the industry, and with his three sons developed business with Russia and America as well as throughout Europe. The business continued to be successful and grew steadily. But when Robert Wandel, by then running the company alone, died in 1913, the third generation had to assume control "at the most unfortunate point possible". Nevertheless, Erich and Hugo, Robert's nephews, took over "and set new standards in the production of the factory". New looms were built which were nearly twice as fast, and fine seams, which had previously depended on a woman's hand, were now welded. When, in the 1930s, the paper industry began using beech pulp, Wandel began building new machines with additional condensing equipment which were still an important product line in the late 1960s.⁵

Reutlingen and Chr. Wandel KG, 1945 to 1954

There is no archival record of the company's activities during World War Two, but the imprisonment and subsequent death in captivity of Hugo Wandel in France in November 1945 suggests either a link with the Nazis' war effort or the

---

3   Chr. Wandel, '100-Jähriges Firmenjubiläum' (Chr. Wandel, 1969), WABW B79/Bü11.

4   See Jürgen Kocka, *Unternehmer in Der Deutschen Industrialisierung* (Göttingen, 1975), pp. 59–62 for a discussion of the way in which foreign travel informed the professional development of many nineteenth century German entrepreneurs.

5   Chr. Wandel, '100-Jähriges Firmenjubiläum'.

use of slave labour.[6] Though we do not know whether Wandel employed any of them, at least 1000 of the 4000 foreign civilians in the town were identified by the French Red Cross as forced labourers.[7] Reutlingen's industry was in a difficult state at the war's end. Allied bombing had damaged infrastructure, including 164 industrial buildings, fifty-seven of which – including three-quarters of Wandel's own buildings – were totally destroyed.[8] Under French occupation Reutlingers were subsisting on a ration of 669 calories per day.[9] Road transport was difficult on damaged or unmaintained roads, though the French restored the rail connection to Strasbourg and some other services. Only one twentieth of pre-war electricity provision was available at the war's end, and some 7500–8000 workers were without homes.[10] Looting was rife: one French observer noted, "Since 15 June there has been no order in the district."[11]

It was this situation that Erich Wandel faced in 1945 as he "stood with a few of his workers next to the pile of smoking rubble that had once been his factory." As his nephew Kurt recalled at the company's centenary celebrations in 1969, "it really needed an unshakeable belief in the future to not give into despair in this situation." The bad situation worsened: "To cap it all, they then had to drag the few recoverable looms and machines out of the rubble and deliver them to the victorious powers. It was Zero Hour (*Es war die Stunde Null*)."[12] Wandel and his staff had their smallest loom running again in March 1946, but shortly afterwards a French requisition team took away the two newest metal-cloth looms, the newest lathe, and several tons of metal wire. This was a "really costly takeover" which was made worse when the firm found itself, in 1947, on the "dreaded" dismantling list.[13] One member of the economic section of the French occupation force wished to "reduce Reutlingen to the level of a colony or a third-world country" by allowing its world-class manufacturers – including those in the metal-cloth industry – to manufacture only basic goods required for the survival of the German people, and to permit what the Minister-President of the American zone termed in 1947 "the intellectual robbery of German industry by the representatives of foreign

---

6   Or acknowledgement of the war and its impact in later recollections. See Paulson, 'Memory'.

7   Gerhard Junger, *Schicksale 1945: Das Ende Des 2. Weltkrieges Im Kreis Reutlingen* (Reutlingen, 1991), pp. 453–59, 460–61.

8   Junger, p. 310.

9   Junger, pp. 299, 301–09. Junger's data is drawn from a mixture of contemporary submissions to local authorities and reports written by French officials.

10   Junger, pp. 399–402.

11   Junger, p. 455.

12   Kurt Wandel, 'Speech at 100th Anniversary Celebrations' (Chr. Wandel, 1969), WABW B79/Bü11.

13   'Jubiläen 85 Jahre Chr. Wandel Reutlingen', *Wochenblatt Für Papierfabrikation* (1957), 2nd edition, WABW B79/Bü10.

firms."[14] Although all removal of machines was required to cease by edict of the Allied Control Council on 15 June 1946, the French "kept that date secret" and continued to remove machines and materials from Reutlingen until 1949.[15] Wandel and its competitors were in a fortunate position insofar as the strong demand for paper in the post-war economy had to be fulfilled and both this and the undamaged condition of the French metal-cloth trade did not make their "dismantling" a priority.[16] But realising that removing machines did not also transmit the know-how required to operate them, the French authorities insisted the industry act as "compensation businesses"; the reparations demanded were so significant that the city of Reutlingen established a Compensation Office and arranged for the Chamber of Commerce to act as mediator and broker.[17]

Following his brother's death in captivity, Erich Wandel did everything possible to prevent the *Totaldemontage* (total stripping of the business) but then died, aged 61, in November 1949. The company was run by its *Prokurists*, Alfred Maier and Arthur Maurer, both of whom had joined as apprentices,[18] until at the beginning of 1951 Erich's daughter Dr Erna Wandel and Hugo's son Kurt Wandel took over.[19] In Kurt's words, "like our fathers my cousin and I, without having the ability to draw on the experience of the previous generation, were put in the difficult position of needing to drive the continuation of the firm forwards by all means."[20] Given the presence of experienced managers in situ, it is not clear why Erna and Kurt chose to assume daily control of the business. Erna Wandel was a chemist with a doctorate, and could presumably have continued in her chosen profession. But their fathers also took over at an unpropitious time, and perhaps Erna and Kurt felt that they consequently had no excuse not to do the same. The business was paternalistic, providing a sickness fund and family holiday trips,[21] which added perhaps a further sense of obligation. They might also have felt that they held some sort of covenant, a responsibility to their families both alive and dead: in the company's 85th anniversary history, published in 1954, their roots are traced to Hans Wandel, the first sieve-maker in 1626. In a very conscious and public

14   Junger, pp. 452–53; Hans-Georg Wehling, 'Reutlingen - Kontinuität Und Bruch Nach 1945', in *Die Zeit Nach Dem Krieg: Städte Im Wiederaufbau*, ed. by Karl Moersch and Reinhold Weber (Stuttgart, 2008), pp. 311–38 (pp. 325–26).
15   Wehling, p. 325.
16   Junger, p. 450.
17   Wehling, pp. 325–26.
18   Robert Oberhauser, *85 Jahre Chr. Wandel Metalltuch- Und Maschinenfabrik Reutlingen* (Darmstadt, 1954), p. 26, Stadtbibliothek Reutlingen. The Prokurist, a role carrying considerable prestige in Germany, is a company officer with signatory powers, able to deputise for the company's managing director. For a helpful definition, see Baker & McKenzie, p. 29.
19   'Jubiläen 85 Jahre Chr. Wandel Reutlingen'.
20   Kurt Wandel.
21   Oberhauser, pp. 29–31.

statement of their link to the past, Erna and Kurt asserted: "The history of the Wandel company is the history of the performance of a family. The deeds of the fathers thereby provide an example for all those currently employed in the factory they founded."[22] More prosaically, Christina Lubinski has argued that many family firms continued in this way because "the ideal of preserving the family fortune for current and future generations not only influenced the choice of legal form [in Germany] but [was] also a fundamental principle in German inheritance law." After generations of family ownership, in other words, the next generation often felt they had no choice but to accept that their fate was decided, dictated by an ineluctable path dependency and validated by securing the family's finances.[23]

Though the Wandel cousins might have been accused of looking too much to the past rather than the future, they found themselves in fortunate circumstances: "the reconstruction of the entire German economy brought us advantages too. Productivity grew across the board", to such an extent that they were able to invest in a new factory building.[24] In December 1953, the local newspaper reported on the opening ceremony for the new Wandel factory. "For various reasons rebuilding had been slow, but it [had] recently picked up pace" and would now open for business early in 1954. The new building was substantial: 2500m² of new workspace plus 1200m² of new warehousing. Specific mention is made of the new toilet block, with separate facilities for male and female staff; it is not clear whether this was a new experience for German workers in this period, but the change, and the enthusiasm with which it was greeted, recalls the move away from self-admittedly "primitive" conditions at J. Schneider's Stuttgart factory. Prominently positioned on its original site at a road junction in the restored town, the external aspect of the new Wandel works would "give a peacetime feel to the location" as well.[25] It would also constrain the company's future development and illustrate another example of path dependency: in apparently wanting to honour their legacy by rebuilding on the historic site at the crossroads, the Wandels invested in a facility whose prominent position would allow drivers and pedestrians in the city centre to respect the Wandel name, but whose shape and boundaries would soon inhibit essential productivity improvements.[26]

---

22   Oberhauser, p. 5.
23   Lubinski, 'Path Dependency', p. 710.
24   Kurt Wandel.
25   'Am Montag Richtfest Bei Chr. Wandel', *Reutlinger General-Anzeiger* (19 December 1953), p. 216, WABW B79/Bü10.
26   Schwäbische Treuhand AG Wirtschaftsprufungsgesellschaft, 'Bericht Über Die Untersuchung Der Betriebsorganisation Der Firma Chr. Wandel, Metalltuch- Und Maschinenfabrik, Reutlingen' (Schwäbische Treuhand – Aktiengesellschaft, 1959), p. 3, WABW B79/Bü25.

Their decision and its ramifications stood in contrast to their competitors, Bruderhaus, whose extensive works were built on the edge of the town and were updated and improved after the war with added training space for apprentices,[27] and to the machine-tool manufacturer Burckhardt & Weber, which by this time was celebrating not the provision of staff lavatories but the implementation of an innovative, highly automated modular-production process in the factory which it had built just outside the town, allowing for steady expansion, in the 1930s.[28] Despite this and other manifestations of their inexperience (or self-confidence), however, Erna and Kurt began to build on promising growth at Wandel. This was reflected in industry data held by the Chamber of Commerce on the four players in the Reutlingen metal-cloth industry, all of which could point to increasing sales, improving manpower productivity, and strong exports – and to the Chamber's active monitoring of its members' businesses.[29]

The *Stuttgarter Nachrichten* newspaper reported that the four Reutlingen firms had 60% of the total West German metal-cloth industry, but capacity was too high in West Germany, hence the need to export 50% of their production. Output was now back to 1938 levels, though prices were 2.3 times higher than then. The companies' key concerns were the very high tax burden and the uncertainty of export trade, the risks of which they now sought to reduce.[30] The Chamber of Commerce's data shows that they were much more active in exporting than their peers in other iron- and metalwork industries. For example, in January 1948 their turnover was only 8% of the whole Reutlingen metalwork industry's, yet they were shipping 26% of its total exports.[31]

Of the four companies, Wandel was the smallest, and its performance lagged behind that of the others. The next largest company had between 11% and 17% more staff, but 21% to 80% higher turnover, dependent on which month's data is measured. Their largest competitor, Wangner, had no more than three times as many staff, but up to five times the monthly turnover.[32] Nevertheless, achievements were real enough to encourage the boast made in a 1958 trade

---

27   *100 Jahre Maschinenfabrik Zum Bruderhaus: Maschinen Für Die Papier-, Pappen-Und Zellstoffherstellung, Eisen- Und Metallgiesserei* (Reutlingen: Maschinenfabrik zum Bruderhaus, 1951), p. 21, Stadtbibliothek Reutlingen; Dr. Martina Schroeder, 'Nicht Ein Stein Ist Übrig', *Reutlinger General-Anzeiger* (Reutlingen, 16 September 2009) <http://www.gea.de/region+reutlingen/reutlingen/nicht+ein+stein+ist+uebrig.163534.htm> [accessed 23 February 2017].

28   *Vielspindlig Denken: Eine Festschrift Zum 75-Jaehrigen Bestehen Der Firma Burckhardt & Weber*, ed. by Karl Langebacher (Reutlingen: Burckhardt & Weber KG, 1963), Stadtbibliothek Reutlingen.

29   'Die Metalltuchindustrie Reutlingen' (IHK Reutlingen, 1950), WABW A16/Bü563.

30   'Metalltuch-Industrie Wieder Voll Beschäftigt', *Stuttgarter Nachrichten*, 15 March 1953, WABW A16/Bü563.

31   'Die Metalltuchindustrie Reutlingen'.

32   'Die Metalltuchindustrie Reutlingen'.

publication: at Wandel "we started our rebuilding without delay and with true Swabian hard work" and now had a factory that was "capable of meeting the great demand for Wandel products which came right after the war from all corners of the world." There was little sense, within a decade, of the Wandels or their industry peers losing the war; its outcome seems only to have inspired them to get better.[33] Their financial results seem to bear this out. Wandel was profitable each year after 1948's turbulence, though profit levels varied. Sales trended steadily upwards, though with some variability that may have reflected some inconsistencies in management or product availability.[34]

It is important to note that while they were personally committed, both in terms of their careers and of their personal liability (Chr. Wandel was, like Julius Schneider, a *Kommanditgesellschaft* in which Kurt and Erna bore personal liability), each of the four shareholding members of the Wandel family benefitted financially from the growth of the business. Profit shares for 1954 and 1955, for example, were DM37,082 and DM65,448 each, while Erna and Kurt also took DM12,000 each in annual salary.[35] Other company owners might have chosen to take less out, and it is possible that they were more motivated to maintain the social standing which had been achieved through the company's past achievements than they were to maximise its future potential by investing in new technologies.

Sales and Business Development, 1950 to 1970

Market Context
Wandel entered the 1950s as niche participants within a booming, wider paper-processing industry that grew by an average of 8.2% per year between 1951 and 1962.[36] When at the end of the decade the Industry Association for Printing and Papermaking Machinery launched a specialist training programme in Munich for engineers and apprentices, they reviewed West Germany's position in global markets in which increasing wealth and literacy were bringing an ever-growing demand for paper. Only a handful of countries boasted expertise in paper-making equipment, and among them West German firms were producing around 40% of paper-making machinery and almost 50% of paper-processing

---

33 Fachgemeinschaft Druck- und Papiermaschinen, p. 37.
34 Chr. Wandel, 'Accounts Ledger, Showing Activa + Passiva, with Profit and Loss Calculations and Profit Shares, 1940–55'; Chr. Wandel, 'Analysis Sheets: Annual Turnover by Product and Country'.
35 Chr. Wandel, 'Accounts Ledger, Showing Activa + Passiva, with Profit and Loss Calculations and Profit Shares, 1940–55', pp. 175, 185, 204, 219.
36 Heinz Schmidt-Bachem, *Aus Papier, Eine Kultur- und Wirtschaftsgeschichte der Papier verarbeitenden Industrie in Deutschland* (Berlin, Boston, 2011), p. 355.

machinery (*Papierverarbeitungsmaschinen*). These two branches were among the most export-intensive of German machine-building branches: 55–60% of manufacturing machines and 75–80% of processing machines were by then being exported to 121 different countries, the two complementary segments growing sales by 40% to DM380 million between 1954 and 1956 alone.[37] The 36 firms producing paper-manufacturing machines employed 10,000 staff in West Germany in enterprises ranging from 50 to 5000 employees. As every paper-making factory had its own characteristics and needs, and produced so many different kinds of paper for such varied applications, the industry offered an ideal world for the machine manufacturers: the huge variety of papers "meant in practice that every single paper machine has to be custom-built – a manufacturer's dream."[38] This was, in other words, another perfect Mittelstand industry: high skill levels, high demand at home and abroad, and all products specialised and different.

Within the paper-processing equipment branch, where the products of companies like Wandel complemented those of the manufacturing-machine producers, there were one hundred firms employing 12,000 staff in West Germany. Here, the industry was very varied. Some of the machines were mass-produced (*Serienbau*) with the most modern production methods and highest quality, securing a world-leading position. Individually produced machines also held what the Association called a first-rate position. Such complicated machines could, however, "only be economically produced if a capable sales force [made] it possible for them to be produced in increasing volumes", which meant Wandel and other German firms had to be active on world markets and needed to recruit and direct capable, motivated, and ambitious sales people.[39]

Sales Culture

Erich Wandel and his brother had monitored competitive information as it was received from the marketplace over several decades.[40] But to be able to resurrect his business immediately after the end of the war, Erich needed to restore his selling capability. He made strenuous efforts to secure the release from custody of his pre-war *Prokurist* Karl Schlegel. Wandel argued to the authorities that Schlegel and Hugo Wandel shared all the commercial responsibilities, and noted the special difficulties of re-establishing relationships with customers at home and abroad, the latter having been Schlegel's responsibility.

37   Fachgemeinschaft Druck- und Papiermaschinen, pp. 5, 7.
38   Fachgemeinschaft Druck- und Papiermaschinen, p. 6.
39   Fachgemeinschaft Druck- und Papiermaschinen, p. 7.
40   Chr. Wandel, 'Sales-Related Record Book' (Chr. Wandel, 1955), p. 13, WABW B79/ Bü202.

His request was resisted, implying that Schlegel had been an active Nazi.[41] By April 1951, though, Schlegel had been released, and was attending a sales meeting with Wandel's other representatives.[42] The meeting was taking place shortly after the appointment of Kurt and Erna Wandel, both present at the meeting, and it is clear from the minutes that the six salesmen were committed, but insistent on the need for improvements. They expressed concern that the increase in manufacturing capacity had seemed also to cause an increase in lead times for delivery, making it impossible to win new contracts before existing contracts had been fulfilled; they urged the directors to begin manufacture of a cardboard-making machine; they demanded action on the loss of sales commissions when sieves were sold to a machine manufacturer rather than to the end-user; they called for the recruitment of a technical specialist with knowledge of the paper industry who could accompany them on sales visits; and they insisted that aggressive action should not be taken against late-paying customers. This would seem to have been a capable and experienced team, the "battle-hardened sales force" that Norbert Helmes of RECARO thought was so essential to business success, but their observations on Wandel's shortcomings should have been a concern to the directors.[43]

The sales team's coverage of the German and neighbouring markets was matched by an extensive network of foreign representatives: the list of representative agents and distributors outside West Germany, dating from the mid-1950s, covers twenty-two countries including several in South America; the Italian distributor had represented Wandel since 1906, and all but one representative had worked for Wandel since before the war.[44] Their relationships were required to be formalised through the grant of a Representation Authorisation, issued by the regional government.[45] Many of Wandel's international representatives participated in a sales conference in March 1956 for which, unfortunately, the hotel and restaurant bills (Erna Wandel was a scrupulous collector of cost minutiae) but no meeting minutes survive.[46] Subsequent records suggest,

41   It is not clear whether Schlegel and other salesmen like him benefited from postwar commercial relationships among erstwhile Nazis. See Pamela E. Swett, *Selling Under the Swastika: Advertising and Commercial Culture in Nazi Germany* (Stanford, 2014), pp. 139, 162ff for an analysis of their work during the regime. Swett was not able to provide information on postwar selling (email to author, 23/2/2017).

42   Chr. Wandel, 'Memo: Besprechung mit den Vertretern bei Uns' (Chr. Wandel, 1951), WABW B79/Bü195.

43   Norbert Helmes, *RECARO – unternehmenspolitische Entscheidungen 1969 und ihre Konsequenten* (Leonberg, 1 August 1977), p. 19 (p. 7), Jung Family Archive.

44   Chr. Wandel, 'Vertreterverzeichnis' (Chr. Wandel, nd), WABW B79/Bü195.

45   Chr. Wandel, 'Allgemeine Vertretergenehmigung: Ing. Anton Wultech' (Land Württemberg-Hohenzollern, Wirtschaftsministerium, 1951), WABW B79/Bü195.

46   Chr. Wandel, 'File on 8–9 March 1956 Sales Conference' (Chr. Wandel, 1956), WABW B79/Bü195.

however, that they were active and successful, selling, for example, 469 units of one type of machine into thirty-three countries between 1955 and 1984.[47] This is borne out by the files on individual representatives, maintained by Erna. For example, her very detailed file on relations with her Cape Town representative demonstrate, like her other records, comprehensive market knowledge, formally noted, and meticulous.[48]

There are many of these memos spread across various folders in the archive. Relationships were clearly friendly and caring, occasionally paternalistic: gifts were sent each Christmas and New Year, and wives and daughters were invited to stay with the representatives in the hotel for each sales conference. Though friendly, relations were apparently also businesslike and professional. Dr. Wandel's notes from the September 1962 sales meeting (*Vertretertag*) are very detailed, covering many points. Representatives were asking for improved marketing material, especially individual specification sheets for specific products. They discussed Christmas gifts for customers in some detail. She seems to be constructive, happy for them to be generous to the customer, but also conscious of the costs, which are all meticulously recorded. In fact, as we shall see, although she was a scrupulous manager of detail, there is a growing sense as the company's history unfolds that Erna Wandel could not see the wood for the trees.

There followed a detailed discussion on commissions, which again appears to have produced a constructive and amicable solution. It is notable in this instance that the representatives were apparently well rewarded for a successful deal, with agreement on a 6% sales commission being paid on machines costing DM75,000.[49] The salesmen's report on their visit to the fourth International Textile Machine Show in Hannover in September 1963, following which they give extremely detailed reports of conversations with nine different firms on the show, confirms their professionalism.[50] There is a suggestion at one point in the archive that Wandel defined 'professionalism' quite broadly and was not above offering incentives to employees of a potential customer to facilitate attractive deals: a memo from March 1966 reports that a long-time Wandel representative had paid a cash commission of 2% of the contract value to a named individual at one of Wandel's largest customers, who had helped the company sell a machine to his colleagues at another company location. The memo records no

---

47 'Analysis Sheets: Gelieferte Zylinder 1955–85, Werkstatistik 1975–84, Export 1976–1982' (Chr. Wandel, 1985), WABW B79/Bü190.
48 Chr. Wandel, 'Folder of Correspondence with Representatives L-Z' (Chr. Wandel, nd), WABW B79/Bü198.
49 Chr. Wandel, 'Notes from "Vertretertag", 11 September 1962' (Chr. Wandel, 1962), WABW B79/Bü198.
50 Chr. Wandel, 'Report of Visit to 4th Internationale Textilmaschinen-Austellung in Hannover, September 1963' (Chr. Wandel, 1963), WABW B79/Bü197.

negative comment on this transaction, matter-of-factly mentioning only that the manager in question had promised to reserve in Wandel's name any future requirement for metal cloths.[51] In the handwritten accounts ledger for each year between 1950 and 1955, there is an entry for "extraordinary expenses" (*ausserordentliche Aufwendung*) averaging over DM40,000 per year.[52] In such a very comprehensive series of itemised expense lines, it is possible that these *were* just "extraordinary" expenses. But the lack of detail, in an environment in which Dr. Erna Wandel kept the receipts for hosted restaurant meals for thirty years, suggests the possibility that this was money used for facilitation payments or other, possibly dubious, means of influencing customers.

Dr. Wandel kept a detailed analysis of sales. On the face of it, Chr. Wandel performed well for most of the period, achieving an average of 10% annual sales growth over the period in current prices, in many years growing faster than the West German economy as a whole, and at all points maintaining an impressive export output as part of the booming paper-equipment industry, as Figure 8 shows.[53]

These summary records were reinforced by detailed analyses, of which the following samples give a sense of their apparent attention to performance. At all points, a distinction is made between woven products and machinery sales, and from 1962 onwards, sales are further broken down to show which proportion of sales originated from the new subsidiary site in the nearby town of Öschingen. The analysis for machinery sales by foreign country for 1963, for example, shows total foreign sales of DM1.1 million, 52% in Europe. Each country's record shows substantial achievements, with a protective spread of business across several markets, appearing to show that

51   Chr. Wandel, 'Memo: Telephone Conversation between Dr. Wandel and Herr Grashof' (Chr. Wandel, 1966), WABW B79/Bü197.
52   Chr. Wandel, 'Accounts Ledger, Showing Activa + Passiva, with Profit and Loss Calculations and Profit Shares, 1940–55'.
53   Table created by the author from: Chr. Wandel, 'Analysis Sheets: Annual Turnover by Product and Country', WABW, B79/Bü190, B79/Bü191; Statistisches Bundesamt, 'Publikation - Preise - Preise Und Preisindizes Für Gewerbliche Produkte (Erzeugerpreise) - Statistisches Bundesamt (Destatis)' (2017) <https://www.statistischebibliothek.de/mir/receive/DEHeft_mods_00070482> [accessed 6 August 2022]; Statistisches Bundesamt, 'Publikation - Preise - Verbraucherpreisindex Für Deutschland - Lange Reihen Ab 1948 - Statistisches Bundesamt (Destatis)' <https://www.destatis.de/DE/Publikationen/Thematisch/Preise/Verbraucherpreise/VerbraucherpreisindexLangeReihen.html> [accessed 27 January 2017]; 'Publikation - Bruttoinlandsprodukt, Bruttonationaleinkommen, Volkseinkommen - Statistisches Bundesamt (Destatis)' (2022) <https://www.destatis.de/DE/Themen/Wirtschaft/Volkswirtschaftliche-Gesamtrechnungen-Inlandsprodukt/Tabellen/inlandsprodukt-volkseinkommen1925-pdf.html> [accessed 6 August 2022].

Chr. Wandel KG	1949	1950	1951	1952	1953	1954	1955	1956	1957	1958	1959
Weaving sales	499,360	640,616	917,833	839,644	830,734	1,119,613	1,508,782	1,431,785	1,598,880	1,592,896	1,814,196
Home											
Export											
Machinery sales	672,678	1,041,885	1,348,650	1,871,093	1,080,672	1,351,740	1,622,745	1,832,346	2,400,013	2,223,169	1,927,516
Home											
Export											
Total sales	1,172,038	1,682,601	2,266,483	2,710,736	1,911,406	2,471,353	3,131,528	3,264,132	3,998,894	3,816,066	3,741,712
Inland	922,840	1,206,776	1,656,952	1,759,346	1,525,528	1,502,003	2,072,392	2,178,516	2,987,248	2,859,688	2,679,151
Export	249,148	475,825	609,530	951,390	385,877	969,350	1,059,136	1,085,615	1,011,645	956,378	1,062,561
% Export	21%	28%	27%	35%	20%	39%	34%	33%	25%	25%	28%
Sales Growth vs Prior Year		44%	35%	20%	-29%	29%	27%	4%	23%	-5%	-2%
Germany: GDP Growth			9.7%	9.3%	8.9%	7.8%	12.1%	7.7%	6.1%	4.5%	7.9%
Germany: Industrial Prices (2010=100)							32.1	32.6	33.2	33.0	32.8
Germany: Consumer Prices											

Chr. Wandel KG	1960	1961	1962	1963	1964	1965	1966	1967	1968	1969	1970
Weaving sales	2,075,542	2,312,736	2,063,662	1,926,236	1,660,391	1,843,176	1,953,758	1,631,207	1,629,000	1,697,061	1,380,133
Home		1,659,932	1,539,368	1,433,206	1,295,292	1,292,308	1,377,929	1,098,478	1,152,890	1,211,123	1,191,519
Export		652,804	524,293	493,030	365,099	550,867	575,828	532,729	476,110	485,937	188,613
Machinery sales	2,150,405	3,234,941	2,855,654	2,253,917	2,420,908	2,199,558	2,463,436	2,600,945	2,027,455	2,582,232	3,228,096
Home		2,174,477	1,871,628	1,119,014	1,329,700	1,336,608	1,314,036	1,334,643	1,258,435	1,670,024	2,281,243
Export		1,060,014	984,026	1,134,902	1,091,207	862,950	1,129,400	1,266,301	769,020	912,207	946,852
Total sales	4,225,948	5,547,677	4,919,316	4,180,153	4,081,299	4,042,734	4,417,194	4,232,152	3,656,455	4,279,293	4,608,229
Inland	3,032,142	3,834,409	3,410,996	2,552,220	2,624,992	2,628,916	2,691,965	2,433,121	2,411,325	2,881,147	3,472,762
Export	1,193,805	1,712,818	1,508,319	1,627,932	1,456,306	1,413,817	1,705,228	1,799,030	1,245,130	1,398,144	1,135,465
% Export	28%	31%	31%	39%	36%	35%	39%	43%	34%	33%	25%
Sales Growth vs Prior Year	13%	31%	-11%	-15%	-2%	-1%	9%	-4%	-14%	17%	8%
Germany: GDP Growth	8.6%	4.6%	4.7%	2.8%	6.7%	5.4%	2.8%	-0.3%	5.5%	7.5%	5.0%
Germany: Industrial Prices (2010=100)	33.2	33.7	33.9	34.1	34.6	35.4	35.9	35.5	35.4	36.0	39.4
Germany: Consumer Prices				3.0%	2.3%	3.2%	3.3%	1.9%	1.6%	1.8%	3.6%

Figure 8 Chr. Wandel KG, Sales Performance 1949–70.

Wandel's representatives were active and its products were saleable.[54] Sales outside Europe are to a considerable range of countries in the Middle East, Asia, North and South America, and South Africa. The biggest market outside Europe is America with sales of DM345,904, implying a serious presence in that market. The analysis for woven-product sales in 1966 shows total foreign sales of DM980,000, 61% in Europe but with significant sales to thirteen countries across Asia and the Middle East and to South Africa.[55]

These levels of performance appear, without being able to analyse the comparative performance of its three Reutlingen-based competitors, to indicate a business which was well managed and competitive on home, European, and world markets. But negative sales growth in several years, notably in 1966 to 1968 (when there were admittedly general economic difficulties, faced by Julius Schneider and RECARO too), suggest the possibility that all was not entirely well at Chr. Wandel. This impression is reinforced by a note in the sales file analysing the sales position at the end of February 1969.[56] Again, initial impressions are positive: the order book on 28 February stood at DM925,000, of which DM356,000 was from abroad. The order intake in March to date is DM140,000, and turnover DM70,000. The unidentified writer then itemises key products and order values, and concludes that the total order book currently stands at around DM1 million, which means with current capacity lead times will be at least six months. The writer then goes on to review where this leaves Chr. Wandel with some customers and products vis-à-vis the competition. One customer is demanding machine performance that Wandel cannot meet, and the order might therefore be lost. Other machines are available immediately from competitors, but not from Wandel, which had only managed to produce 1.5 machines per month over the past year and had shown itself to be incapable of mass production.

The writer's analysis and prognosis are interesting: on the face of it, Chr. Wandel are doing well, but this is a very competitive market and they appear incapable of changing their business model or production processes, or making model variations, to meet demand. It is not clear who wrote the report or for whom, but this seems to be a culture of plain speaking. Unfortunately, as the following review of the company's operations and management will reveal, acknowledgement of the facts in 1969 came long after weaknesses outside the sales area had been identified; the lead-time problem had first been identified at the 1951 sales meeting referred to above. There is a discernible difference in

---

54 'Maschinenfabrik: Aufteilung des Auslandversandes nach Ländern', in Chr. Wandel, 'Analysis Sheets: Annual Turnover by Product and Country' dated 25.6.1964.

55 'Weberei: Aufteilung des Auslandversandes nach Ländern', in Chr. Wandel, 'Analysis Sheets: Annual Turnover by Product and Country' dated 6.1.1967.

56 'Aktennotiz, Auftragsbestand und – Eingang Maschinenbau', in Chr. Wandel, 'Analysis Sheets: Annual Turnover by Product and Country', p. 2.

the underlying sentiments in this file note, and the words (which were understandably positive, given the occasion) of Kurt Wandel at the company's centenary celebrations later in 1969. Chr. Wandel could attribute its success over a century, three wars, inflation and numerous crises to "the unrelenting initiative, unbelievable courage to take on risks, to industry and to frugality, as well as the clear recognition of the constant need to properly appreciate economic opportunities and necessities."[57] The following review of the company's operational performance since 1950, and of his and his cousin's management abilities, will enable us to evaluate the accuracy of Wandel's words.

Operations and Company Management, 1950 to 1970

The motivation for the establishment of the paper-machinery engineering training programme in Munich had been the requirement for specialists who could respond to the paper-manufacturing industry's global needs. All this demanded, in the words of the Industry Association for Printing- and Papermaking Machinery, a great deal of engineers. They needed to have a "gift for construction", but also "empathy for the technical needs of machines" whose development was "in permanent movement".[58] It was in this environment that Wandel proclaimed their own competence, with their new factory "ready to meet the great demand for Wandel products which grew right after the end of the war."[59] In fact, contemporaneous events were showing that while the company may have been satisfying international customers, it was facing a crisis within. In October 1959, a management consultancy which had been brought in by the Wandels (to their credit) issued a damning report on their business. The consultants began with the observation that the factory's position on the crossroads in town militated against the necessary reorganisation of production flows, with inefficient organisation of tasks limiting the output of metal cloth and producing significant tensions within the workforce:

> Given the acute shortage of skilled labour and the tendency towards decreasing work hours it is urgently necessary to find a form of organisation which secures the orderly cooperation of all employees, promotes initiative and drive, and creates the bases of good human relationships.[60]

Having started on the shop floor, the consultants progressed to the leadership of the business. Its leaders were supported by two *Prokurists*, but there was

57   Kurt Wandel.
58   Fachgemeinschaft Druck- und Papiermaschinen, p. 7.
59   Fachgemeinschaft Druck- und Papiermaschinen, p. 37.
60   Schwäbische Treuhand, 'Wandel', p. 3.

no clear division of tasks. In consequence, the interests of the machine-building division and all its development, construction, sales, purchasing, and production had been taken on by the factory manager (*Betriebsleiter*), while the interests of the weaving mills and its purchasing, sales, production, despatch, and bookkeeping were represented by the commercial manager (*kaufmännischer Leiter*); it is implied, but not stated, that these positions were held by the respective *Prokurists*. This division did not follow industry best practice and frequently caused friction. As the two *Prokurists* were longstanding employees but were younger than the company's directors, there frequently arose differences of opinion which disrupted the whole flow of the business. At a personal level, it appeared that both Kurt and Dr. Erna Wandel were simply not competent as directors of the company:

> We recommend the leadership of the business to take its control more firmly in hand and to secure the future of the business through constant improvements to the existing fabrication programme and further new-product manufacturing. Every hold-up is dangerous today.[61]

Their detailed and wide-ranging report went on to identify significant failings in every area of the company. They recommended that a qualified engineer be appointed to take care of the technical office, hitherto the responsibility of the overburdened factory manager. Procurement must be controlled by one leader, and access to the warehouse must be strictly controlled (loose control of stores being then, as now, a standard indicator of lax management), as must the issue of tools. In the machine-production area, workflow was too slow, machines were old and hindered the workflow and needed replacement, staff were unsupervised and not required to clock in or out. The company's *Meister* were not working effectively and in the weaving mill entire shifts often worked without supervision. Identifying a current practice that serves as a metaphor for the company's mindset, the consultants urged that "beer sales should be moved out of the warehouse and only permitted on special occasions." The recommendations continued, covering everything from the urgent need for a new machine park to the adoption of card systems in the office and a reorganisation of office staff. There was, however, one predominant problem; the absence of leadership and control:

> All these organisational measures will not bring the desired progress unless at the same time the personnel situation is sorted out ... tight, controlling man-management is the precondition for better performance and will be respected by the staff ... workers who disrupt the business with their negative comments should be sacked ... We are now at the point where the future of

---

61   Schwäbische Treuhand, 'Wandel', p. 4.

the company is at stake. Success can only be achieved through the combined efforts of both leaders and workers.[62]

There is a sense that, in this era of almost insatiable demand for both consumer goods and, from Wandel and others, the machinery that produced them, Wandel's boat was rising with the tide. But this was also a time of full employment, and satisfactory sales revenues, notably those earned overseas, masked a state of crisis within the business. It was occasioned by staff who, if they were competent, lacked commitment, and by directors who may have been committed but were not apparently competent. In an environment in which the technical expertise of the Mittelstand was revered, Wandel's managerial expertise was worryingly deficient: staff did not know how to organise themselves, had distant leaders, saw friction between the *Prokurists* who were responsible for the day-to-day management of the business, and were either the victims or the beneficiaries of poor controls in the workplace. But surely this account should also cause us to question clichés about the *Wirtschaftswunder*-era German worker. He or she was not socially programmed to work only to world-class standards, to be self-disciplined enough to need to no supervision, to be respectful and never question authority. Instead, he or she required leadership and proper management at all levels within a structured way of working, It is the perhaps surprising absence of those things from Wandel that reaffirms the excellence of their daily practice – by *Meister* as well as by managers and directors – at Reutter and other high-performing Mittelstand businesses. The *Treuhand*'s report usefully serves as a detailed template for the best practices elsewhere which were making that high performance possible.

It was to this environment that the consultants returned, six months after their initial review. They had been asked to implement the changes they recommended in the previous November's report – a request which would seem to reinforce the sense that Kurt and Erna Wandel were incapable of being the hands-on, directive leaders which the company needed. (A contrasting example of the necessary leadership – and the background which enabled it – was being experienced at this time by the staff of neighbouring machine-tool builder Burkhardt & Weber, whose own managing director Louis Weber had spent over forty years in charge following a four-year spell in the United States learning every technical detail "from the ground up" of the machine-tool industry, and personifying a mindset of constantly evolving operational and technical improvements which persists today.)[63] The consultants' report was comprehensive and divided into a series of separate instructions, arranged by

---

62 Schwäbische Treuhand, 'Wandel', pp. 5–7.
63 Langebacher, pp. 13–14; BURKHARDT+WEBER, 'Geschichte', *BURKHARDT+WEBER* (2015) <http://burkhardt-weber.de/unternehmen/geschichte> [accessed 23 February 2017].

functional area. The first action was telling: "The leadership and direction of the business will be taken in hand by the two personally liable shareholders, Herr Kurt Wandel and Dr. Erna Wandel."[64] Their respective tasks were to be divided, with Kurt responsible for all aspects of sales, distribution, development, and construction while his cousin was to look after workshops including buildings, all HR and pay matters, work preparation, purchasing, and accounts. Rather embarrassingly for the cousins, the report went on to suggest that "the works council should help the directors to learn about processes and measures in the personnel area. Close human relations will underpin the solution of given tasks in the interest of the business." This statement raises questions over the quality of personal relationships within the firm, and between the cousins, given that their responsibilities had to be spelt out in this way. It also calls into doubt their innate capabilities as leaders and businesspeople: *surely* these things were obvious? The fact that they were not allows us to discard another Mittelstand cliché, namely that Swabian family firms in this era benefited from a succession of excellent leaders whose natural flair for tight management was genetic. Again, the absence of high-quality leadership at Wandel throws into useful relief its presence at Burckhardt & Weber, Keiper, and elsewhere.

Other functional managers' responsibilities are set out in the report in great detail, the numerous overlaps with the Wandels' stated responsibilities suggesting that the two cousins would fulfil roles which oversaw the activities of their more technically competent managers rather than directly managing operational staff themselves. The two *Prokurists'* responsibilities are particularly emphasised, with Arthur Maurer, the Commercial Leader, being provided with two pages of single-spaced instructions on the necessity of working tightly together with the Technical Leader in a constructive, results-oriented fashion. Maurer's responsibilities were to include "creating sufficient sales and selling the products profitably", "remaining in tight contact with the sales representatives through ongoing communication and demanding thorough reporting", and "overseeing, directing, and facilitating the activities of the sales team" – in addition to many other specified tasks, demonstrating his own initiative and reading of the situation, and maintaining close relations with the joint managing directors.[65] Fundamental improvements were to be implemented right across the business, with instructions provided on areas such as cost-management, production-planning, technical compliance and contract management, all of which were to be run from new or reorganised offices. In August 1960, a summary progress report was provided by the consultants, who noted that new machines and handling equipment had been purchased and security had been improved in the stores, but there was still insufficient

---

64   'Procedure 1' in 'Organisationsplan' (Schwäbische Treuhand – Aktiengesellschaft, 1960), WABW B79/Bü25.
65   Schwäbische Treuhand, 'Organisationsplan'.

progress on workflow, although the engagement of staff was seen to be good and full results would in any case be seen only after a year. However, they felt constrained to mention yet again their concerns about the Wandels' personal engagement: "We recommend the company's directors put man-management first, sharing the responsibility [for it] with those below them, but maintaining the leadership of the business tightly in their own hands": only in this way would previous costly mistakes, arising from the over-burdening of managers, be avoided.[66] Now it seemed not only that the Wandels lacked innate leadership qualities or management acumen, but also that they were unable or unwilling to act when things were spelled out to them.

Whether Arthur Maurer was one of the managers who felt "over-burdened" is not known. We only know that he had spent all his career to this point within Chr. Wandel, and that the consultants' recommendations conferred on him complete responsibility for all market-knowledge and customer-management activities. We also know that in 1962, one Arthur Maurer (whose provenance cannot be confirmed) founded a competing manufacturer of metal cloth in Reutlingen, a company which claims to have had a history of relentless operational innovation until the present day, and which in 1995 bought out of bankruptcy all that remained of Chr. Wandel.[67] The archive contains no mention of Maurer's departure from Chr. Wandel nor of any changes in his disposition towards the company, but it can be imagined that his must have been a frustrating job. Originally identified as a problem in 1951, machine lead-times were still highly unsatisfactory in 1962. A file memo shows that Wandel's most rapidly produced machine would not be delivered in less than 17 weeks from order; spare parts would take 10 weeks; one machine would take 49 weeks. Confirming an average lead time for their whole range of machines which exceeded 31 weeks, there are no negative comments in the memo: this seems to have been what they had always been used to.[68] But with 1962 machinery sales exceeding DM2.8 million, achieving a 10-week lead time would have generated over DM1 million of additional cash flow through the business annually.[69] We see no evidence of action to address this in the archives, even though by 1969 the company's liquidity still appeared to be very constrained, with the largest of their four bank accounts holding only DM11,000 out of gross cash receipts of DM500,000.[70]

66   Schwäbische Treuhand AG Wirtschaftsprufungsgesellschaft, 'Aktenvermerk' (Schwäbische Treuhand – Aktiengesellschaft, 1960), WABW B79/Bü25.
67   Siebfabrik Arthur Maurer GmbH & Co. KG, 'Eine Geschichte Mit Zukunft' <http://www.siebfabrik.de/de/unternehmen/geschichte/> [accessed 23 February 2017].
68   Chr. Wandel, 'Arbeitsanweisung Nr. 6' (Chr. Wandel, 1962), WABW B79/Bü26.
69   Chr. Wandel, 'Analysis Sheets: Annual Turnover by Product and Country'.
70   'Aktennotiz, Auftragsbestand und – Eingang Weberei/Maschinenfabrik', dated 14 February 1969, in Chr. Wandel, 'Analysis Sheets: Annual Turnover by Product and Country'.

In the only remaining Works Council (*Betriebsrat*) minutes, from 1962, instead of constructive discussions on productivity or falling sales in the metal-cloth division, we find numerous personnel-related disagreements and a difficult relationship between Erna Wandel and the chairman of the Works Council and his colleagues. At various points in the minutes (written in the first person by Erna) we see evidence of disagreements over pay and working hours, unhappiness with the new piecework bonus programme (which had been approved 18 months earlier by a Works Council containing several different members, suggesting some turnover in membership), an "energetic resistance" by Erna to the suggestion by another Council member that foreign workers were being given privileged treatment by being allowed to work for an extra hour each day, and Erna "allowing herself to appear amused by the concerns shown by the Council members".[71] In addition to the possibly acrimonious relationships between the managing director and her key staff members, there is evidence of substantive problems in the workplace: "no sooner do we succeed in employing a new turner or fitter than he's gone again", a problem which the Council members blame on the poor pay for new starters, a view which Erna again contests.[72] The minutes reveal a company leader who does not appear to have the confidence of her staff, or vice versa. The situation at Chr. Wandel in this period resembles that at Julius Schneider in this respect: the idealised Mittelstand family firm was being shown not to work without clear and qualified leadership, and thorough organisation of motivated, directed staff at all levels; neither Rolf Walz's passion for his father's company nor Erna Wandel's strong intellect and commitment to her inheritance were automatic guarantors of employee respect or essential technical change. But the available evidence suggests that Walz more clearly recognised his own limitations and, without in any way resiling from his obligations to the company, sought assistance with its management. He was, moreover, *obsessively* committed to Schneider's success. In contrast, it may be reasonable to wonder whether either Wandel's heart was in the business in quite the same way, or whether they were there to honour their family and its legacy.

Despite its owners' shortcomings, however, the flourishing economy ensured that the business continued to grow. Although orders for the loom shop were down 6.9% in 1962, the increase in machinery orders outweighed the loss by over DMo.5 million, with export orders 118% higher.[73] Staff numbers increased as well, and recruitment difficulties were eased by the decision to

---

71   Chr. Wandel, 'Board Minute: "Einführung Neuer Vorgabezeiten in Der Weberei"' (Chr. Wandel, 1962), WABW B79/Bü53.

72   Dr. Erna Wandel, 'Protokoll Der Betriebratssitzung Am 28.9.1962' (Chr. Wandel, 1962), WABW B79/Bü53.

73   Auftragsbestandvergleich, 31. Dez 1961 und 28. Dez. 1962 in Chr. Wandel, 'Analysis Sheets: Annual Turnover by Product and Country'.

set up the subsidiary plant at Öschingen, 15km away. Records were meticulously maintained, as ever, and showed a high point of 133 staff in 1964,
which was reduced to 125 in 1966. Nine of the staff were *Meister*, and the
company maintained a high level of trained staff: 19% of its workforce were
unskilled helpers in 1966, but 22% were highly skilled and a further 30% semi-
skilled, characteristic of the Mittelstand's high-skill industrial culture.[74] Over
the course of the decade, shortages of staff appear to have been addressed by
recruiting increasing numbers of foreign workers: a review of the reports on
employee numbers submitted to the authorities shows an increase from 10% to
21% of the unskilled and semi-skilled workforce who were "guest workers".[75]

By the end of the decade, Chr. Wandel confidently celebrated its centenary
with the good wishes of all its major competitors,[76] with the presence of many
guests entertained for expensive dinners and given specially designed gifts, and
with the confidence of Kurt Wandel in his company's ability "always to make
good judgements on economic opportunities and necessities."[77] In the new
decade, that confidence slowly began to appear misplaced.

The Long Decline of Chr. Wandel, 1970 to 1995

It appeared that Chr. Wandel had prospered during the 1960s. Total sales had
grown from DM4.2 million to DM6.5 million. Export sales had grown by 86%
to DM2.2 million. But West Germany's economy had grown too, and in real
terms Chr. Wandel's performance had not kept pace.[78] In the first year of the
new decade, internal sales reports showed foreign machine sales of DM946,000.
While the company's achievement in spreading its sales exposure across eleven
European countries and five continents was laudable, sales had actually declined
by DM320,000 in current prices over two years.[79] As the decade unfolded, the

---

74   Figures for 31.10.1966 in Chr. Wandel, 'Monatlicher Stand Der Betriebsangehörigen
Vom 1 Okt 1962 Bis 31 Okt 1966'.

75   Workers with non-German names identified by the author and assumed to be immigrant
workers, taken from 'Aufteilung Für Industriebericht' (Chr. Wandel, 1960), WABW B79/
Bü39, WABW B79/Bü39.

76   Chr. Wandel, 'Letter of Heartfelt Congratulation' (Treuhandstelle der Metalltuch-
Industrie, 1969), WABW B79/Bü11.

77   Kurt Wandel.

78   Chr. Wandel, 'Analysis Sheets: Annual Turnover by Product and Country'; 'Historic
Inflation Germany – Historic CPI Inflation Germany' <http://www.inflation.eu/inflation-
rates/germany/historic-inflation/cpi-inflation-germany.aspx> [accessed 23 February 2017];
Volker R. Berghahn, *Modern Germany: Society, Economics and Politics in the Twentieth
Century*, Second edition (Cambridge, 1987), p. 280, Table 12.

79   'Maschinenfabrik - Aufteilung des Auslandversandes nach Ländern', for 1967 and 1970
in Chr. Wandel, 'Analysis Sheets: Annual Turnover by Product and Country' dated 16 January
1969 and 19 April 1971.

situation appeared to worsen. The archive holds no sales records for the period 1971 to 1974, and the positive sales data held on file for 1975 onwards appear to be contradicted by a report in the local newspaper in December 1976 entitled 'Wandel is still behind 1974'. In it, the company reported that 1976 sales were better than the "very bad" 1975, in which Julius Schneider and other businesses experienced difficulties and the whole West German economy contracted by 2.7%, but were very variable by month.[80] The company's shipper had refused to hold any finished stocks, which had constrained capacity, and Wandel's capital investment was lower than the annual depreciation charge. Profitability had fallen in comparison with earlier years, driven by the increasingly high personnel charges; foreign competitors, who were very active, did not face these costs and could therefore sell more cheaply. Those contracts which were available in the marketplace now had short delivery lead times, which had reduced the size of Wandel's order book, and the company's foreign trade was made more challenging by slow cash receipts from overseas, frequently accompanied by substantial foreign exchange losses.[81] Although there is no archival record of the challenges presented by changes in the Deutsche Mark's international value, it seems likely that the decline in the US Dollar's value against it must have caused Chr. Wandel either to lose international market share, or to reduce its prices in order to maintain it, during a period when its internal, DM-denominated costs continued to rise following the oil-shock crisis and the Schmidt Government's reforms.[82]

In fact, sales fell steadily in real terms over the decade. Though the West German economy was no longer the powerhouse of the *Wirtschaftswunder* years, it grew by an average of 2.28% between 1976 and 1983. Chr. Wandel's sales did not match it. Unfortunately the archival records contain no sales data after 1984, though later meeting notes suggest that the downward trend continued and the positive performance of 1983 itself did not mark the beginning of a turnaround. In Figure 9, the inconsistency in the company's sales performance is evident.[83]

80   Berghahn, *Modern German*, p. 280, Table 12.
81   'Wandel Liegt Noch Hinter1974 Zurück: Auftragseingang Hat Sich 1976 Gegenüber Vorjahr Verbessert', *Reutlinger General-Anzeiger* (Reutlingen, 22 December 1976), WABW A7/Bü Fi L/1997 Wandel, Chr.
82   DM to US$ conversion, 1960–75, at 'Historical Exchange Rates from 1953 with Graph and Charts' <http://fxtop.com/en/historical-exchange-rates.php?A=100&C1=DEM&C2= USD&YA=1&DD1=01&MM1=01&YYYY1=1960&B=1&P=&I=1&DD2=01&MM2= 01&YYYY2=1975&btnOK=Go%21> [accessed 24 February 2017]; Abelshauser, *Deutsche Wirtschaftsgeschichte*, pp. 267–69.
83   Table compiled by the author from: Chr. Wandel, 'Analysis Sheets: Annual Turnover by Product and Country'; Berghahn, *Modern Germany*, p. 280, Table 12; 'Historic Inflation Germany – Historic CPI Inflation Germany'.

	1975	1976	1977	1978	1979	1980	1981	1982	1983
Weaving sales DM	3,636,803	4,003,983	3,668,733	3,291,254	3,059,753	3,005,280	3,071,201	2,649,010	2,367,078
Home		1,539,368	1,719,096	1,906,282	1,768,878	1,970,055			
Export		524,293	553,112	983,933	1,023,137	1,279,016			
Machinery sales DM	5,484,641	4,262,269	4,890,827	3,915,771	3,801,223	3,742,685	3,478,707	3,946,025	5,928,437
Home		1,871,628	1,329,700	1,314,036	1,258,435	2,281,243			
Export		984,026	1,091,207	1,129,400	769,020	946,852			
Total sales DM	9,121,444	8,266,252	8,559,560	7,207,395	6,868,976	6,747,965	6,549,908	6,595,035	8,295,515
Inland		3,410,996	3,048,796	3,220,318	3,027,313	4,251,298			
Export DM	ND	1,508,319	1,644,319	2,113,333	1,792,157	2,225,868	ND	ND	ND
% Export	ND	66%	50%	63%	66%	75%	ND	ND	ND
Sales Growth, 2 Years	ND	-9.4%	3.5%	-15.8%	-4.7%	-1.8%	-2.9%	0.7%	25.8%
Inflation, FRG		3.69%	3.41%	2.54%	5.40%	5.54%	6.69%	4.55%	2.71%
Economic Growth, FRG Annually		5.80%	2.70%	3.30%	4.50%	1.80%	-0.20%	-1.00%	1.30%
Net Real Sales Growth		-15.18%	0.85%	-19.10%	-9.20%	-3.56%	-2.74%	1.69%	24.48%
Economic Growth, FRG 1975–83									19.50%
Net Real Sales AAGR, 1976–83									-19.50%

Figure 9 Chr. Wandel KG, Sales Performance 1975–83. ND = No data in archive.

The company's log of products sold shows this decline at the product level. One item continued to sell well after 1975, but it had been introduced only in 1968. The other two mainstays of the cylinder product line had been on sale since 1955 (and may well have been modified in the interim, though there is no record of any changes in the archive) and their sales dropped alarmingly from the mid-1970s onwards.[84]

In the absence of explicit internal documentation or external correspondence, it is difficult to reach a clear conclusion for the reasons that the business was unable to reverse its incipient decline. Hints may be found in a detailed survey document, sent to Chr. Wandel by the Baden-Württemberg Ministry for Work, Health and Social Order in 1973.[85] Wandel's response showed a decline in staff numbers over the previous seven years to 117. Wandel said that they were engaged in custom manufacture rather than series production. Worryingly, they then confirmed that during the past five years they had not brought in any significant technical innovations which had "had an impact on the number, the qualifications and/or the productivity of our workers." The suspicion that they were not being sufficiently innovative appears to be confirmed in their negative answers to questions on R&D. It may be that the lack of answers meant only that Chr. Wandel objected to the questionnaire (thereby living up to *Mittelständlers*' reputation for secretiveness). But it is clear that the Ministry were genuinely engaged and it seems reasonable to assume, given the dearth of new products and the continuing challenges of internal organisation and productivity, that Chr. Wandel simply were not doing any, or sufficient, R&D. It is also apparent, from the final section of the questionnaire, that the business had continued to find it difficult to recruit staff locally, as over 13% of current employees were "guest workers". Wandel's answers suggest that the company sought to treat its workers fairly: its foreign employees did not "do tasks that German workers would do only unwillingly" and they would be dismissed only on performance grounds. It is clear that they were essential to the business's future, even with its smaller workforce, because the company responded "No" to the question, "If all your foreign workers left, could you cover the reduction in workload by rationalisation or technical advancements?", although their response may also be taken to mean that the business had no concept of opportunities for further automation or productivity enhancements.

Archival evidence is limited for the 1970s and a detailed review of the succeeding decades is limited by archival sources. It is, in any case, outside the scope of this study. But the records for annual sales conferences reveal concerns among the sales force about responsiveness to technical demands. Someone

---

84   'Analysis Sheets: Gelieferte Zylinder 1955–85, Werkstatistik 1975–84, Export 1976–1982'.
85   The following section is drawn from Chr. Wandel, 'Response to State Ministerium Für Arbeit, Gesundheit Und Sozialordnung's "Untersuchung Der Qualititiven Auswirkungen Des Technischen Wandels Auf Die Arbeitskräfte"' (Chr. Wandel, 1973), WABW B79/Büg.

asks where the focus of the company's sales efforts should be, and how they should go about increasing sales revenues, suggesting there was either a lack of clarity in the management of sales or an unequal level of performance or commitment amongst the sales force.[86] One of the company's long-serving staff members was promoted to deputy managing director on the 25th anniversary of his "tireless and selfless engagement". The atmosphere was apparently cordial, as in previous sales conferences, but there is little sense of urgency on the part of Kurt Wandel. Although the following year's conference introduced a new sales manager to the team, the agenda is leisurely.[87] Despite there being explicit concerns about several of the company's products, there is no indication in the extant archival material of any sense of alarm within the company's leadership.

By 1986, staff numbers had declined to seventy-five, plus eleven apprentices.[88] A memorandum from consultants asks for details of the company's staff, relationships with customers and suppliers, and manufacturing performance data. There are hints that the company was being prepared for sale.[89] This was the only logical way forward. In 1981 Wandel's competitor Bruderhaus had gone into liquidation and had been restructured on a smaller scale by its acquirer. In a "metal-cloth industry in which the tendency for consolidation was clear and in progress", another competitor, Peter Villforth, had been acquired by the British giant Scapa PLC.[90] Villforth itself, with 200 employees and DM25 million in 1987 sales, was three times larger than Wandel, but was itself dwarfed by Scapa, with 100 business units and DM700 million in annual sales. By now, "David was growing tired in his fight against Goliath". As development times had shortened dramatically and new products were being brought into the market now at a rate decades faster than previous sieve-types had lasted, it was not surprising the "founder generation" of Mittelstand companies' owners, dependent for decades on their own capital but now faced with huge investment costs and price reductions if they were to survive, "were getting tired".[91]

We have only newspaper records of Chr. Wandel's last days. Dr. Erna Wandel celebrated her 70th birthday, still in control of the company, in 1989.[92] How it

86   Chr. Wandel, 'Notes from "Vertretertag", 11–12 January 1984' (Chr. Wandel, 1984), WABW B79/Bü196.
87   Chr. Wandel, 'Notes from "Vertreterkonferenz", 2 May 1985' (Chr. Wandel, 1985), WABW B79/Bü196.
88   Chr. Wandel, 'Strukturdaten Über Die Firma' (Chr. Wandel, 1986), WABW B79/Bü12.
89   Chr. Wandel, 'Data Analysis Completed by Wandel Management in Response to a Questionnaire from Dr. Ebner, Dr. Stolz & Partner, Wirtschaftsprüfer Und Steuerberater, Stuttgart.' (Chr. Wandel, 1986), WABW B79/Bü12.
90   Franz Pfluger, 'David Wird Im Kampf Gegen Goliath Müde', *Reutlinger General-Anzeiger* (Reutlingen, 31 December 1987), p. 10, WABW B79/Bü8, B79/Bü8.
91   Pfluger.
92   'Birthday notice, Erna Wandel', in *Nachrichten aus Chemie, Technik und Laboratorium* (Verlag Chemie, 1989), p. 536.

struggled on for the following years is not clear, but in March 1995 it declared its insolvency. In the words of one newspaper, it had "been on the pilot light for a long time". The deputy managing director appointed in 1985 was still in place, and had hoped that the situation could be rescued, but they had been unable to pay February's wages. Surprisingly, the local manager of Deutsche Bank commented publicly on Wandel's financial problems.[93] The German paper industry had lost DM3 billion in sales since 1991 with a 27% reduction in prices, and the Reutlingen metal-cloth makers were either already insolvent, forced into technical cooperation with each other, or facing a difficult battle with foreign competitors from Eastern and Northern Europe who enjoyed currency and cost advantages.[94] In the face of all these challenges, Dr. Erna Wandel seemed to be in denial. Now aged 75 and in control of her grandfather's business for forty-four years, she said she "could not understand the world any more".[95] After a period in which contract wins were sluggish, the bank had withdrawn its financial support. Erna insisted that, with 50% of its sales still being exported, Chr. Wandel had been holding its own in the market until the "great breakdown" of the previous summer, but nevertheless the company's "numbers were not so dreadful". She now hoped that the workforce, only fifty strong, would not "be sold down the river" and could be taken on by a new buyer.[96] They were: the buyer was the firm founded by her former employee three decades earlier, by now run by a new management team following Arthur Maurer's withdrawal from day-to-day management in 1988.

Without the benefit of primary source material for its final decade, it is difficult to draw unequivocal conclusions about Chr. Wandel's fate. But it seems clear that its elderly owner, supported by an executive manager who had himself been in the business for over thiry-five years, had not had the energy or the desire to make the necessary radical changes which had originally been highlighted in the 1960s. Employee relations, at least with the foreign sales representatives, continued to be cordial. But longstanding problems with deliveries were not solved, new products were not introduced, new managers were not developed and given responsibility. An apparent attempt to find a trade buyer in the mid-1980s had foundered, and Dr. Erna Wandel had pushed on (the fate of her cousin is not known). Credit must be given to her and her staff for maintaining customer relationships at home and overseas over decades, in the face of impending industry consolidation and aggressive foreign competition.

93   'Schon Länger Auf Sparflamme. Sprecher Der Deutschen Bank: Kreditgewährung War Nicht Mehr Zu Vertreten', *Schwäbisches Tageblatt* (Reutlingen, 4 March 1995), WABW A7/Bü Fi L/1997 Wandel, Chr., A7/Bü Fi L/1997 Wandel, Chr.
94   'Chr. Wandel Beantragte Konkurs', *Reutlinger General-Anzeiger* (Reutlingen, 4 March 1995), p. 10, WABW A7/Bü Fi L/1997 Wandel, Chr.
95   'Bank stoppte alles'.
96   'Bank stoppte alles'.

Yet in honouring her family's past, she had paid insufficient attention to their company's future needs, and placed herself at the centre of a business which she had never seemed fully competent to lead. With no family successors apparently available, she persisted, no doubt for honourable reasons, to lead the business to its inevitable fate.

6

Kenrick & Jefferson Ltd., West Bromwich

Kenrick & Jefferson was a British printer and stationery manufacturer, founded in West Bromwich in 1878 and remaining there until its closure in 2000. In the first half of its life, K&J was remarkably successful, delivering consistent sales growth with impressive rates of profitability.[1] It did so while continually investing in the business's technical capabilities and sustaining a performance culture among staff members who could be confident that consistent personal performance meant a job for life. After World War Two, K&J found circumstances more challenging. Despite managing to retain elements of its paternalistic ethos while simultaneously investing in new equipment and processes, the company struggled to sustain pre-war standards.[2] In this chapter, we review K&J's performance between 1949 and 1979, assessing the importance of key elements of the business, most notably sales, innovation, and management. To reflect the main periods of change, and for ease of organisation, these elements are examined across three time periods: up to the mid-1950s; from 1955 to the late 1960s; and from 1970 to 1979. As we follow this timeline we will discover those strengths which sustained K&J beyond its 100th anniversary, and the weaknesses which ultimately overcame them and ensured its eventual demise twenty-one years later.

Management and Organisation to 1955

Between its foundation in 1878 and the end of the Second World War, K&J had retained a paternalistic culture in which both those who owned and led the business and those who worked in it frequently referred to their membership of the "K&J Family". "Mr. Fred" Jefferson (members of the owning families were addressed in this style), second-generation chairman and joint managing

---

1 The company's early history, organisation, and performance are reviewed in David Paulson, 'The Professionalisation of Selling and the Transformation of a Family Business'. This article also reviews postwar sales performance until the 1960s, which therefore receives less attention in this chapter.

2 The company's postwar attitudes are reviewed in Paulson, 'Memory', pp. 10–11.

director with his brother Edward, combined a focus on the company's performance with a commitment to its members' wellbeing. On his death in 1940, K&J was in good financial and operational condition. It prospered through the Second World War, producing ration books and similar government-procured products in huge quantities. The immediate post-war years had been prosperous too, but there were signs that this good fortune could not last and that K&J was no longer the company it had been. On the eve of the company's 75th anniversary, the business boom of the immediate post-war years had passed; neighbouring countries, notably Germany, had begun to rebuild their economies; the future of trade with Britain's colonies was uncertain. "What of the future", asked one K&J staff member rhetorically in an article in *K&J News*, "Now that competition is with us once again and every order has to be fought for?"[3]

The patronising tone of chairman 'Mr. Edward's Christmas Message to the K&J Family' in December 1952 may have been appropriate in earlier decades – he himself had been with the company 47 years – but took no account of the gradual decline of earlier models of deference and institutional loyalty in the years after the 1945 election, or of the cultural changes occurring elsewhere in a fast-modernising business world. Hugh Jefferson, a future director himself, considered in retrospect that K&J's directors were doing too little to prepare for the future. Little thought was given to succession or to building organisational strength.[4] Longevity of service was a source of great pride. The 75th anniversary booklet names each of the 525 staff members whose service exceeded ten years. The six directors, one by then non-executive, boasted 230 years' service between them. Among the sales force sixty-eight men had been employed for more than ten years; the average tenure across this senior group was 32.2 years.[5] There was value in this foundation of enormous loyalty and experience, grounded in Fred Jefferson's obsession with quality and customer service. But there was also a risk of stasis: too many staff members stuck in their ways, not troubled by new ideas brought in by new thinkers.

The company's potential failings seemed to be personified by its directors, even the youngest ones. Though K&J were "always good nepotists",[6]

---

3   Kenrick & Jefferson, 'A Few Memories', *K&J News* (28 November 1952), Sandwell, BS/ KJ4/1/21.

4   David Paulson, Interview with K. Hugh Jefferson, 2013. Hugh was the senior director of the company at the time of its closure in 2000 and the great-grandson of F.T. Jefferson.

5   Walter H. Cartwright, *The House of K&J – a Booklet Issued to Celebrate the 75th Anniversary of Our Foundation in 1878 for Private Circulation Among Our Friends* (West Bromwich: Kenrick & Jefferson, 1953), Appendix.

6   An expression which recalls Alfred Chandler's criticism that "in the United States, nepotism had a pejorative connotation. In Britain it was an accepted way of life." Chandler, *Scale and Scope*, p. 286; quoted by Brian R. Cheffins, *Corporate Ownership and Control: British Business Transformed* (Oxford, 2008), p. 223.

welcoming any family member who wanted to join, they also insisted that they work their way up and quickly removed those who did not perform.[7] In this, K&J's owners appeared to have followed the "fundamental principle" identified by Martin Daunton of "employing only those family members who were competent".[8] Peter Kenrick and Kenneth Jefferson, Hugh's father, both joined K&J in the 1930s, becoming directors in 1947. Both served overseas in the war, and neither had an agenda for post-war change. They were, "after all, third generation" and did not understand how much was changing outside K&J.[9] They were "inhibited" and because of the war were "embedded in a certain tradition or way of life" which prevented them from seeing any need for change. Within the firm, there gradually dawned a sense that life under the third generation was not as dynamic as it had once been under their predecessors.[10] Ivan Walker, a 47-year veteran of the company who had joined it in 1932 under the dynamic "Mr. Fred", felt that under his successors' leadership it was no longer clear what its directors actually did.[11]

Hugh Jefferson recalls that neither his father nor Peter Kenrick received much encouragement from K&J's senior directors: the omission of both younger men, executive directors since 1947, from the directors' portrait which was commissioned for the firm's 75th anniversary in 1953 symbolised the older generation's view of the younger.[12] This is not to say that K&J had traditionally been a reactionary company, closed to ideas from outside the controlling families. Before 1940, it is possible to trace the ascent of men like James Reid Adam from newly recruited sales representative to sales director over the course of thirty years.[13] General management and technical leadership were the domains of the Gifford family, who served K&J in senior positions for three generations. Unfortunately the archive holds records on only one of them. Dr. Randolph Gifford, who joined K&J in 1926 as chief engineer and held that position until he retired in 1954, was technically capable, with a D.Sc. from Birmingham University, and played a prominent role in developing

---

7   Paulson, 'Interview Jefferson'.
8   M.J. Daunton, 'Inheritance and Succession in the City of London in the Nineteenth Century', *Business History*, 30.3 (1988), 269–86 (pp. 275, 278).
9   Paulson, 'Interview Jefferson'. In fact Peter Kenrick appears to have been more of a change agent than Hugh Jefferson credited him with being, as we will see below. Criticism of third-generation family managers is in Nicholas.
10   Paulson, 'Interview Jefferson'.
11   David Paulson, 'Interview with Ivan Walker, Former Production Supervisor K&J'.
12   Paulson, 'Interview Jefferson'; The portrait itself and the circumstances of its commissioning by K&J are reviewed in Marie Considine, 'The Social, Political and Economic Determinants of a Modern Portrait Artist: Bernard Fleetwood-Walker (1893–1965)' (unpublished Ph.D. thesis, 2012) <http://etheses.bham.ac.uk/3639/1/Considine12PhD.pdf> [accessed 31 May 2014].
13   Paulson, 'Professionalisation'.

new products and implementing new processes. His personal history can be interpreted positively: while K&J was dominated by its founding families, who sustained its culture of paternalism and emotional engagement with the business, they were not "personal capitalists" who were complacent and insular; they utilised their managers' intellect and energy in the pursuit of growth.

But they did not then invite those managers to join the company's board, to help deliver revolutionary changes. It seems neither the Kenricks nor the Jeffersons were urgently seeking the next management outsider keen to shake up their business. A more sceptical interpretation of their management resourcing approach may therefore be that the employment of three generations of the same family by three generations of two other families reflects the poverty of British management talent in the period, and that their domination of K&J reflects the persistence of barriers to "the flow of human capital (ideas *and* people)" that led to the "backwardness of British management" – at K&J as elsewhere.[14]

Sales to the mid-1950s

In 1958, K&J would remind their customers of what they themselves had believed and practised for over half a century: "Selling is as important and should be as scientific in operation as production ... It is a fact that sufficient care, study and research are not given to the problem of selling by a big percentage of manufacturers."[15] A clear and consistent commitment to professional selling is observable throughout the company's early history. They employed very capable sales leaders, most notably James Reid Adam, who was sales director for over twenty-five years until he retired in 1946, achieving exceptionally high standards and operating a sophisticated sales system. Strong management was complemented by a customer-focused attitude throughout the business.[16] K&J's sales team were the antithesis of stereotypical contemporary salesmen: unlike the Hoover sales force, for example, K&J's men were few in number relative to sales achieved, long-serving, committed to the company, productive, and treated as professionals.[17] In the pre-war period at least, they were one of K&J's distinguishing strengths.

14   Leslie Hannah, 'Scale and Scope: Towards a European Visible Hand?', *Business History*, 33.2 (1991), 297–309 (pp. 301–2); Chandler, *Scale and Scope*, passim. Both Chandler and Hannah's critique of his work are concerned primarily with larger companies than K&J, but their reservations and their negative comparisons of British managerial expertise with that of their German counterparts are a fair benchmark for K&J.
15   Kenrick & Jefferson, 'The K&J Direct Advertising Service' (Kenrick & Jefferson, 1958), Sandwell, BS/KJ/2/2/10.
16   Paulson, 'Professionalisation', pp. 5–14.
17   Peter Scott, 'Managing Door-to-Door Sales of Vacuum Cleaners in Interwar Britain', *Business History Review*, 82 (Winter 2008), 761–88.

Having achieved so much before the war, the sales team's perception of themselves in the post-war period remained positive. But photographs of them taken at contemporary meetings show avuncular figures, many of considerable seniority: two active members of the team each had fifty-two years' service by 1953.[18] It is probable that they achieved a reasonable sales performance (no records remain of individual targets or achievements) and were liked and appreciated by their customers, otherwise they would not have survived Reid Adam's exacting standards. But it is likely that in a period of technological change and increasing competition, K&J's future interests were not going to be best served by a team dominated by elderly gentlemen who had followed the same practices for decades.

Financial Results to the mid-1950s

Despite these concerns, K&J remained financially successful until the mid-1950s. In the year to 30 June 1939, it had returned a trading profit of £45,249 on sales of £454,860. In the corresponding twelve months to 30 June 1950, it had increased its profit and sales to £125,555 and £893,494 respectively. True to their custom, K&J had continued to re-invest profits in productive assets.[19] Financial reports for the year ending 30 June 1955 showed continuing strong performance, albeit with a decline from the booming post-war years. Cash holdings were almost £131,000 and investments of £17,900 in new equipment exceeded depreciation by almost 35%. Profit for the year on the manufacturing and trading account had reached £108,000 on sales of £1.02 million, representing increases of 36% and 12% respectively versus the previous year.[20]

However, the extended Kenrick and Jefferson families were now very large. While dividend returns throughout the post-war period remained attractive by historical standards, despite government efforts to penalise their recipients,[21] the growing number of K&J shareholders increasingly offered an opportunity for conflicting expectations and shareholder unrest.

18   Cartwright, Appendix.
19   'Manufacturing & Trading Account at 30 June 1939', Sandwell, BS/KJ1/3/60/3; 'Notes to Accounts for Year Ending 30 June 1950' (Kenrick & Jefferson, 1950), Sandwell, BS-KJ1/3/80/2.
20   Kenrick & Jefferson, 'Financial Statements for the Year Ending 30 June 1955' (Kenrick & Jefferson, 1955), Sandwell, BS/KJ1/3/90.
21   Neil Rollings, 'The Dividend Prejudice in Postwar Britain' (presented at the Business History Conference, 2014).

Management and Organisation, mid-1950s to late-1960s

In 1955, Edward Jefferson died. In early archival material he is informal and humorous, in later life patrician and remote. It is possible that his own character symbolised the gradual change in K&J's culture. His father Frederick had become very wealthy from K&J and his other business interests. But Frederick Jefferson had started K&J as its only employee, and he and his son Fred, Edward's brother and predecessor as chairman, had been hands-on leaders who had seen the company grow without losing touch with its daily realities. The question was whether K&J had now changed fundamentally, from what might reasonably have been called a British Mittelstand company between the wars, to an organisation whose wealthy directors were increasingly distant from their organisation's needs.

The end of the 1950s marked a low point in K&J's fortunes. In his report to shareholders for the year ended 30 June 1959, Cambridge-educated managing director Wynn Kenrick informed them of the impact of the national printing strike, which had also affected K&J between June and August.[22] How could relations have gone from being so positive to this? Was this situation the consequence of a national decision by the unions of which K&J innocently bore the consequences? Or was its progression at K&J carried out in a way which suggests there were K&J problems too? The K&J archive contains no detailed records of company–union relations, or of the 1959 strike. We know it was a national issue, affecting all of the ten trade unions in the printing industry and its 120,000 workers. By 1959, K&J's workers apparently shared the national demand for a pay rise to be combined with a 40-hour week and what the unions termed "protective practices".[23] Whether or not the strike was expected there, K&J was governed by complex, nationally negotiated wage settlements: the latest filled a 121-page folder marked 'Wages Agreements 1956–1963'.[24] They are complicated and restrictive, and must have required an extraordinary amount of otherwise unnecessary bureaucracy. For example, in the letter on 'Revised Agreements for Bookbinders and Rulers and Semi-Skilled Men and Women Workers', there are 30 unique pay levels just for "Male Learners – Grade 2". Not one of those pay levels is repeated in the matching table for

22   Kenrick & Jefferson, 'Report of the Directors for Year Ended 30 June 1959' (Kenrick & Jefferson, 1959), Sandwell, BS/KJ1/3/96/2.

23   Alf Robens MP in *Hansard*, 'Printing Strike' (House of Commons, 6 July 1959); John Gennard and Peter Bain, *A History of the Society of Graphical and Allied Trades* (London, 1995), pp. 452–57; Demands made at this time built on successes achieved in prewar disputes. See Jonathan Zeitlin, 'Craft Control and the Division of Labour: Engineers and Compositors in Britain 1890–1930', *Cambridge Journal of Economics*, 3.3 (1979), 263–74.

24   Kenrick & Jefferson, 'Wages Agreements 1956–1963' (Kenrick & Jefferson, nd), Sandwell, BS/KJ3/3/3.

"Male Learners – Grade 1".[25] To add to the complications, there were separate instructions from each of the numerous unions representing each of the trades under K&J's roof. These differing interests complicated labour relations and internal administration, and increased costs, while the unions maintained both collective national strength and individual craft identities.[26] Moreover, these detailed documents did not only relate to the literally hundreds of different wage levels affecting the K&J factory. They also set constraints on management action, such as restrictions on overtime, hugely complicating the challenge of running a business like K&J.

The strike was not the only worry for K&J's board: shareholders were unhappy too. In August 1959 K&J sold its 50% stake in office equipment manufacturer Kingfisher, delivering a significant gain.[27] Shareholders now demanded that the proceeds either be returned to them or be reinvested in another undertaking. Directors seemed to have no compelling long-term strategic plan that they were able to sell to the shareholders as the most appropriate and prudent use of their £212,000, and shareholders thought mostly of themselves. In his 1961 review of business, Wynn Kenrick was less confident about the future. Shareholders had demanded, and got, an increase on the normal, generous 15% dividend. Management had made further concessions to unions with little confidence of any reciprocal commitment: "we shall be working a 40 hour week, and with the co-operation of our workpeople we have reason to believe that production will not suffer."[28] Having been a company whose owners had grown it by putting customers first, innovating constantly to meet their needs, and paternalistically looking after the workers who met them, K&J's leaders now had strategy dictated to them by non-contributing shareholders and previously invisible unions.

Wynn Kenrick died unexpectedly in 1963. He was replaced as chairman by his brother Peter, an enthronement without any apparent reference to Peter's qualifications or suitability. Hugh Jefferson's negative view of his father and Peter Kenrick as the proverbially disappointing third generation has been discussed already. Recollections and written records held in the K&J archive suggest an urbane and cultivated man, widely respected as "a gentleman". This implies little of the concentrated dynamic leadership that the company had experienced throughout its history up to 1940 under chairman Fred Jefferson, and needed

25   British Federation of Master Printers, 'Revised Agreements for Bookbinders and Rulers and Semi-Skilled Men and Women Workers', 11 September 1956, Sandwell, BS/KJ3/3/3.
26   F. Mitchell and S.P. Walker, 'Market Pressures and the Development of Costing Practice: The Emergence of Uniform Costing in the UK Printing Industry', *Management Accounting Research*, 8 (1997), 75–101 (p. 80).
27   Kenrick & Jefferson, 'Report of the Directors for Year Ended 30 June 1959'.
28   Kenrick & Jefferson, 'Report of the Directors for Year Ended 30 June 1961' (Kenrick & Jefferson, 1961), Sandwell, BS/KJ1/3/98.

now. In fact Peter Kenrick's tenure during the mid-1960s suggests that he was less patrician than Edward Jefferson had seemed, and more dynamic than Hugh Jefferson suggests. This was a period of extraordinary social change outside the company and within. The pre-war 'K&J Family' was in many respects no more: workers had been on strike; the social club and sports grounds which had been the centre of their employees' lives in the 1930s were no longer valued by staff who had televisions and cars.[29] The company itself had perhaps held on to its patriarchal culture for too long, retaining employees whose length of service meant that their learning had come from a bygone era.[30] In these circumstances, Kenrick faced difficult and fast-changing challenges.

Innovation between 1955 and late 1960s

There were two key challenges during this period, which had the potential to conflict with each other. In addition to managing union demands for different pay rates for different machines, K&J's directors had to worry about the machines themselves within an industry facing constant downward pricing pressures.[31] In October 1959, chairman Wynn and Peter Kenrick and general manager Guthrie Gifford visited the USA, telling shareholders: "We went to investigate new processes and recent printing trends and it is hoped that in due course some applications of what we saw may be introduced here."[32] In the interwar years, K&J had considered themselves to be world leaders, designing and producing relief-stamped (or die-stamped) stationery for corporate customers around the globe. While benchmarking can be seen as the positive action of a strong management team receptive to new thinking, this trip might also have been evidence that they no longer had world-class ideas themselves. To Hugh Jefferson's point, the third generations of neither the owning families nor the Gifford managerial dynasty represented new blood or new thinking.

K&J had continued to innovate during the late 1950s, being granted two US patents – then, as before and afterwards, K&J remained committed to selling in the United States[33] – but in the wider printing industry, K&J's directors

29 'Council May Consider Buying Playground', *Evening Mail* (Sandwell, 2 May 1968), p. 1, Sandwell, 35A/164.

30 F. Jackson, 'Tribute to Bill Blake and Mr Pieters', *K&J News* (23 June 1961), Sandwell, BS/KJ/4/1/22.

31 Mitchell and Walker.

32 Kenrick & Jefferson, 'Report of the Directors for Year Ended 30 June 1960' (Kenrick & Jefferson, 1960), Sandwell, BS/KJ1/3/97/1.

33 James Gibbon, 'Open Window Envelopes', Google Patents (2014) <https://patents.google.com/patent/US2971689?oq=inassignee%3A%22Kenrick+%26+Jefferson+Ltd%22> [accessed 1 June 2014]; James Gibbon, 'Method and Means of Feeding Window Envelopes

were aware that technology was changing fast. In October 1961, Wynn Kenrick noted that: "owing to developments in our own trade it is becoming clear that further re-equipment will be required in both our lithography and composing departments."[34] There is a sense in the following year's accounts of tension between directors, who saw the need to retain profits for investment in the business, and shareholders, who had used an Extraordinary General Meeting to demand that they be distributed.[35] Reinvestment became an ongoing necessity, as Peter Kenrick pointed out to shareholders in October 1964.[36] He delivered it. By 1966, the book value of plant and equipment had risen to £382,000, representing almost £700,000 of investment in new machinery since 1944 and over £250,000 over the previous thirty-six months, with a further £53,000 of capital expenditure already committed.[37] These investments appear to have been well targeted, as 1966 earnings before interest, tax and depreciation (EBITD) represented a return of over 28% on the book value of machinery and plant.[38]

Peter Kenrick saw changes were required to more than machinery. On becoming chairman, he had indicated an awareness of his "responsibilities … at this particular time in the company's history." Having made a £13,000 loss on the year, the board had initiated "a complete reorganisation of the sales force", "a number of major changes in factory management" which had delivered savings of £35,000, and "a complete overhaul" of company administration "with a view to greater efficiency and considerable economy."[39] In 1963, a market research programme was initiated which lasted for four years. By the end of it, Kenrick had delivered "a switch from a production-orientated company to one that is concentrating emphasis on marketing" and growing sales.[40] Significantly, he had also brought Albert Smart onto the board as finance director and its first non-family director, albeit one with 40 years' experience of K&J. Though Smart's longevity was a potential impediment to change, his appointment and the use of "modern marketing and ideas from all levels" heralded the start of a culture shift.[41] That shift would be carried through

---

to a Folding Machine', Google Patents (2014) <https://patents.google.com/patent/US3037432?oq=inassignee:%22Kenrick+%26+Jefferson+Ltd%22> [accessed 1 June 2014].

34   Kenrick & Jefferson, 'Report of the Directors for Year Ended 30 June 1961'.
35   Kenrick & Jefferson, 'Report of the Directors for Year Ended 30 June 1961'.
36   Kenrick & Jefferson, 'Report of the Directors for Year Ended 30 June 1964' (Kenrick & Jefferson, 1964), Sandwell, BS/KJ1/3/101–2.
37   Kenrick & Jefferson, 'Balance Sheet for the Year Ending 30 June 1966' (Kenrick & Jefferson, 1966), Sandwell, BS/KJ1/3/103.
38   Kenrick & Jefferson, 'Consolidated Profit & Loss Account for the Year Ending 30 June 1966' (Kenrick & Jefferson, 1966), Sandwell, BS/KJ1/3/103.
39   Kenrick & Jefferson, 'Report of the Directors for Year Ended 30 June 1963' (Kenrick & Jefferson, 1963), Sandwell, BS/KJ1/3/100.
40   'New Talents', *Birmingham Post*.
41   'New Talents', *Birmingham Post*.

during the following two decades by the second new appointee to the board, Tom Jefferson, appointed joint managing director at the age of thirty-two to replace T. Jefferson Cottrell, retiring after "46½ years service".[42]

Kenrick was personally active himself, for example playing a key part in winning a significant export order to the US.[43] Though by now in his fifties and already a wealthy man (the Kenrick family's business interests included the nearby Kenricks hardware firm and directorships in Lloyds Bank) who presumably had no need to work, Kenrick was and remained clearly focused on the long-term development of K&J.[44] There is no sense in the company's financial record of directors favouring themselves over the company: total board remuneration was a fraction of the annual investment in new machines. And returning to Hugh Jefferson's rather negative evaluation of his father and Peter Kenrick, there is not much indication of what David Landes refers to as "the complacency of third-generation children of affluence going 'through the motions of entrepreneurship'".[45] On the contrary, there is strong evidence of a feeling of responsibility for their legacy and a commitment to modernise it in order to preserve it.

Peter Kenrick also appreciated the challenge of future markets. He had warned shareholders the company would be "moving into more specialised fields and away from the general jobbing printing which has been the mainstay of the Company for so long." This was necessary because of the arrival of "'Do it yourself' installations and the better equipment and techniques available to the smaller printer."[46] With barriers to entry falling away for competitors (and soon for end-users themselves), it was necessary to start moving into new, more specialised markets. Investments in these new areas soon became visible: K&J's developing expertise in computer-related printing, for example, was reflected in the grant of a 1968 US patent for new methods of numbering documents.[47]

---

42   Kenrick & Jefferson, 'Report of the Directors for Year Ended 30 June 1966' (Kenrick & Jefferson, 1966), Sandwell, BS/KJ1/3/103.

43   Anon, 'A Pat on the Back', *K&J News* (December 1966), Sandwell, BS-KJ4–1-27.

44   Church, *Kenrick*.

45   David S. Landes, 'Technological Change and Innovation in Western Europe 1750–1914', in *The Industrial Revolution and After: Incomes, Populations and Technological Change (I)*, ed. by H.J. Habbakuk and M.M. Postan, The Cambridge Economic History of Europe (Cambridge, 1965), VI, pp. 463–64; quoted in Cheffins, p. 223.

46   Kenrick & Jefferson, 'Report of the Directors for Year Ended 30 June 1963'.

47   John F. Elsworth, 'Apparatus for Use in Sequentially Numbering Documents' <https://patents.google.com/patent/US3603251?oq=inassignee:%22Kenrick+%26+Jefferson+Ltd%22> [accessed 1 June 2014].

Sales between 1955 and the late 1960s

K&J began the 1950s with a very large number of salesmen who had seen exceptional lengths of service with the company. Even as new staff arrived, though, products needed to change. K&J was now straddling the dividing line between leadership in old technology and the impending arrival of word processing and computing. To the extent that comprehensiveness was a virtue, K&J must have been distinctive, with their thousands of stationery products and hundreds of envelopes. Their organisation and discipline were admirable: with their 'Price Instruction Sheets' and 'General Instructions', K&J in the 1960s were clearly operating at the levels of control sought by companies who seek accreditation to ISO 9001 and similar quality systems in the twenty-first century.[48] There is little sense that they were one of the firms identified in a 1961 newspaper article which felt that they could "muddle through and that professional sales training [was] something slick and not quite British."[49] But it is difficult to avoid the conclusion that they sold lots of commodity items, humdrum daily products which might have been professionally offered, but which would not hold office automation at bay.

In terms of their printing business, though, K&J still considered that their expertise was of special value. They provided a range of training booklets on 'Selling Print' published during the 1950s and 1960s, which explained how sales staff should seek to provide comprehensive support.[50] The company ethos which distinguished K&J's sales staff in their pre-war heyday is still emphasised, as the reader is urged to take responsibility for any problems which arise, rather than reprehensibly "seek[ing] business on the ground of the company's good points, yet shrink[ing] from accepting responsibility for its shortcomings." At the same time, it was made clear to the sales force that they were there for a purpose: "Persistently implant the thought that the order will be the natural outcome of your talk."[51]

A contemporaneous article addresses some of the issues facing K&J in the management of its sales force in the 1960s and 1970s. Whereas some companies were paying consultants to help them more aggressively inculcate competitiveness through "brainwashing",[52] its author suggested that: "Aggressive sales

48 Kenrick & Jefferson, 'Price Book and Inserts' (Kenrick & Jefferson, 1966), Sandwell, BS/KJ2/2/10.

49 Anon, 'British Salesmen Untrained and Inefficient', *The Guardian* (London, 9 May 1961), p. 17.

50 Kenrick & Jefferson, 'Levels of Selling', Selling Print (West Bromwich: Kenrick & Jefferson).

51 Kenrick & Jefferson, 'Closing the Sale', Selling Print (West Bromwich: Kenrick & Jefferson).

52 Eric Clark, 'Big Sell for Salesmen', *The Observer* (Manchester/London, 7 February 1965).

management techniques may appear to boost short-run profit, but in the light of negative consequences on loyalty, enthusiasm, self-respect, and esprit-de-corps within the sales force, their affect on long-run profit can never be clear and may well be negative."[53] These negative approaches and their consequences seem to have been avoided by K&J's plan for 'Selling Print'. But only sales growth would confirm that plan's effectiveness, which in turn would depend on its competent management by K&J's leadership.

That is not to say that K&J were performing badly. In 1966 they celebrated sales success in several areas, winning prizes from the British Stationery Council and major export orders personally negotiated by Peter Kenrick on his visit to America.[54] The original K&J export markets for print were "dwindling, as the countries to which this kind of commodity was originally exported move[d] into the technological era and [began] to make their own products." But K&J were trying to keep "one step ahead" of developing countries, producing more sophisticated products than those they could yet produce themselves, as well as providing complete corporate branding.[55] They were, however, far behind their German counterparts in their commitment to winning export business.

K&J's directors now claimed a climate of open innovation. According to new joint managing director Tom Jefferson, "Once you get the sort of climate that fosters imaginative thinking then you get a staggering crop of ideas." Learning from their sales force, rather than from third-party market research, was viewed by the directors as a key strength.[56] It remained to be seen whether the new initiatives and reorganisations led by Peter Kenrick and Tom Jefferson would now bring the transformation that K&J appeared to need.

Financial Results between 1955 and late 1960s

The archives hold detailed annual accounts only for the years 1935 to 1959. The lack of detailed accounts for succeeding years is more likely due to a gap in the archive's holdings than to a decision by K&J's management to move from granularity to generality in their financial reviews. But as research is also hampered by the lack of board minutes or intra-board correspondence, none of which survives from any period of the company's history, conclusions on financial strategy must be made with caution in the absence of contemporary commentary or explanation.

53 Leslie M. Dawson, 'Toward a New Concept of Sales Management', *Journal of Marketing*, 34.2 (1970), 33–38.
54 'A Pat on the Back'
55 'When a Single Dot May Prove to Be a Costly Fault', *Evening Mail* (Sandwell, 28 July 1969), Sandwell, 35B/168.
56 'Smooth Reorganisation Gives West Bromwich Printers New Impetus', *Birmingham Post* (Birmingham, 12 April 1967), p. 1, Sandwell, 35A/131.

Surviving details show Peter Kenrick's urgency in reorganising the business was warranted. Performance had steadily declined on most axes since the end of the war. The lack of sales reporting in the archives makes it difficult to tell whether the fall in net sales in real terms (based on 1950) from £1.2 million in 1952 to £873,000 by 1966 was due to the loss of government business (the end of wartime printing, ration cards, military documents) and the reversion to "normal" trading, or whether increasing competition and weakening K&J competitiveness were to blame. For those years in which detailed annual accounts remain, it is evident that sales were not able to keep pace with a concomitant increase in overheads in general and remuneration in particular. In 1950, overheads were 32.3% of sales, and total pay, including production wages, 42.8%. By 1959, these costs had risen to 49.3% and 54.4% respectively – shortly in advance of the national printing strike which would drive wage costs further upwards. The consequence of this inability to match costs to sales was a decline in pre-tax sales margin from 21% in 1950 to 3.8% in 1959.[57] By 1966, the published pre-tax profit appears to equate to only 1.4% of the net sales figure in the manuscript sales day book.[58] This was a very poor result compared to that achieved fifteen years earlier, albeit an improvement from the end of Wynn Kenrick's tenure.

While heavy capital expenditure on new technology was seen by K&J's board as the best means of repositioning the company in competitive markets, a normalised evaluation of capital employed shows that in real terms the company had not actually increased its capital base appreciably. More importantly, it shows that the return on the capital which *was* invested declined progressively during the two decades.

Criticism of the margins, returns and growth achieved during this period do not mean that the directors can be accused more broadly of financial mismanagement or profligacy. As a measure of their prudence, revenue and capital reserves were increased by the board from £327,000 in 1955 to £795,000 in 1965, a real-terms increase of 65%, with a further £151,000 held in cash and short-term deposits in 1965.[59] While the outstanding financial results of the immediate post-war period were now a distant memory, this was a reasonably solid foundation on which to try to establish K&J's market leadership in new areas in the following decade.

---

57   Sandwell, BS/KJ1/3/80/1, BS/KJ1/3/85/3, BS/KJ1/3/90, BS/KJ1/3/96/1, annual accounts for the years shown. All calculations are the author's.

58   Sandwell, BS/KJ1/2/20, Sales Day Book, July 1943 to February 1973; BS/KJ1/3/103, consolidated accounts to 2 July 1966.

59   Reserves figures drawn from published accounts, matching 1955 and 1965 nominal values and rebasing to 1955 via 'Five Ways to Compute the Relative Value of a UK Pound Amount, 1270 to Present' <https://measuringworth.com/calculators/ukcompare> [accessed 7 September 2014].

Organisation and Management from the late 1960s to 1979

In 1967, Cyril Spector published his guide to *Management In The Printing Industry*. Having taught at the London College of Printing (where Tom Jefferson had studied) until in 1966 he became Head of Department at Birmingham College of Commerce, Spector was well placed to advise the industry generally and to understand K&J's operating environment.[60] He found that the industry was "in a state of flux" and that the "technological pressures from within and the social pressures from without [were] producing a managerial revolution overnight", such that the printing industry would "never be the same again".[61] In this environment, K&J was a significant force, one of only sixty printers in Great Britain, out of 6600 firms, which employed more than five hundred workers, and one of only twenty employing over one thousand.[62] While its size may have given it some advantages of scale and scope, it must also have presented a growing management challenge: new technology was becoming more important, but had to be introduced by management to staff whose various unions had already demonstrated increasing national militancy. Although in the view of one Father of the Chapel K&J had a "young and enlightened management" it was also his view that "usually they manage to bring something controversial up", implying that management meetings were not easy.[63] Any changes also had to take account of greater competition from firms which were smaller, nimbler, and hungrier.

An additional challenge was the desire until this point of its two founding families to retain management control. It was clear to objective contemporary observers like Spector that family companies in the printing industry would now require "trained and professional managers to help run a more complex organisation."[64] His comments reinforced those already made in the 1965 report of the National Board for Prices and Incomes on the printing industry, which noted "little evidence of recruitment to the ranks of top management either from the shop floor or from outside the industry." They were also concerned that "opportunities for desirable technical change are being lost by failure to use modern management techniques."[65] We will now see whether changes implemented at K&J were an adequate response to the internal and

---

60 Interview with Hugh Jefferson, July 2013.

61 Cyril Spector, *Management in the Printing Industry* (London, 1967), p. ix.

62 Spector, *Management*, Figure 1.1, page 7, citing *The Printing Industries of Western Europe – The International Bulletin* (June 1964).

63 'Bill's secret of industrial harmony', *K&J Group News* (January 1975), Sandwell, BS/KJ4/1/31.

64 Spector, *Management*, p. 314.

65 Philip Sadler and Bernard Barry, *Organisational Development: Case studies in the printing industry* (London: Longmans, 1970), p. 3.

external pressures identified by contemporary observers, to the demands of its shareholders, and to the constraints of its family-management traditions.

Changes to Financial Structure

To provide context for any review of K&J's management, it makes sense at this point to review the company's financial and governance structures, which were changed frequently over the thirty years following the end of the Second World War, adding substantially to the burden on the company's leaders. From the earliest days of K&J, the guiding principle had been the company's stability and the maintenance of the families' control, with the emphasis on individuals' service and commitment.[66] This focus remained, even as changes to the capital base were implemented between the wars. Some minor changes effected prior to 1950 were designed to maintain stability and family control. It was from 1950 onwards that this stability began to be threatened.

Ross McKibbin has shown how the imposition of punitive tax rates on unearned income affected the wealth of Britain's richest families in the post-war period.[67] It is likely that the prevailing political climate, as well as the pressure from shareholders among the extended families, forced the directors to reconsider the direction and structure of the company. The eventual outcome was the Special Resolution of May 1960, which declared K&J to be an unquoted public company, with the prevailing limitations on the number of shareholders being removed.[68] There is no explanation in the archive of this decision. Up to that point, shareholders had been treated well. Dividends were generous: UK government gilts yielded returns which were significantly lower than anything received by the holders of K&J's ordinary stock in the period.[69] But from the directors' perspective, the longstanding tensions which had recently culminated in arguments with the shareholders over the proceeds of the Kingfisher sale would keep resurfacing, and they would keep needing to worry about managing K&J's financial structure rather than to driving forward new innovations. To an extent, this attitude was understandable: the shareholders were, after all, their relations and themselves. But the large size of each family (twenty-six Jeffersons and thirty-one Kenricks making up the

---

66   Kenrick & Jefferson, 'Memorandum of Association, Kenrick & Jefferson Ltd.' (Kenrick & Jefferson, 1900), Companies House, archive disk 00064701_1.

67   Ross McKibbin, *Classes and Cultures: England 1918–1951* (Oxford, 1998), p. 41.

68   Kenrick & Jefferson, 'Special Resolution of 27 May 1960' (Kenrick & Jefferson, 1960), Companies House, archive disk 00064711_82.

69   UK Government Debt Management Office, 'UK Government Gilt Returns' <http://www.dmo.gov.uk/rpt_parameters.aspx?rptCode=D4I&page=Annual_Yields> [accessed 7 September 2014; site inactive on 9 August 2022].

fourth generation of the founders' descendants) and the dispersed holdings of shares among them suggested difficulties in maintaining shareholder satisfaction.[70] For some shareholders, whose holdings had been passed down to them but who themselves had no interest or involvement in the company itself, the opportunity to create a market for their shares was preferable to staying locked into a K&J suffering the consequences of the national printing strike. Why not therefore offer shareholders the opportunity to cash out if they were dissatisfied with the company's direction, and allow other investors to take their place?

If relations between themselves and other shareholders were part of the directors' motivation, a more general explanation for the attention paid to financial restructuring might be found in Colli et al's argument that changes to the structure and governance of British family businesses were common after the war: "In Britain the inheritance tax fundamentally and permanently altered family firm behaviour", as the increase in death duties to a maximum of 80% and the 1948 Companies Act "helped to shift the balance of power in British business toward finance capital and the business corporation."[71] It seems likely that it was at this point that some family firms, which might hitherto have had some of the internal characteristics of Mittelstand companies, no longer found it viable to remain in that form. K&J were not alone: another West Bromwich company, George Salter, makers of springs and weighing equipment, became a public company in 1953 because of payment of death duties and high taxation;[72] K&J's competitors in security printing, McCorquodale and Co., went public in 1961.[73]

Organisational and Governance Changes

K&J's directors also made significant changes to the company's governance. Until the mid-1960s, there was no director who was neither a Kenrick nor a Jefferson. This contrasted with the experience of their neighbours at Archibald Kenrick. After decades of poor performance, Kenricks had appointed John

---

70 Kenrick & Jefferson, 'Family Tree of F.T. Jefferson' (Kenrick & Jefferson), Sandwell, BS/KJ5/1/12; 'Descendants of Archibald Kenrick (Nov 1760 – 16 Oct 1835)' <http://www.greywall.demon.co.uk/genealogy/wynnhall/archy.html> [accessed 16 January 2014; site inactive on 9 August 2022].

71 Andrea Colli, Paloma Fernandez Perez, and Mary B. Rose, 'National Determinants of Family Firm Development? Family Firms in Britain, Spain, and Italy in the Nineteenth and Twentieth Centuries', *Enterprise & Society*, 4.1 (2003), 28–64 (pp. 28, 64).

72 'Engineers' Placing', *The Times* (18 November 1953), p. 12, The Times Digital Archive, also cited at http://www.gracesguide.co.uk/George_Salter_and_Co.

73 'McCorquodale Shares START Today', *The Times* (13 June 1961), p. 17, The Times Digital Archive, also cited at http://www.gracesguide.co.uk/McCorquodale_and_Co#cite_note-1.

Donkin to their board in 1956 after he had delivered significant improvements since being recruited from GEC as works manager.[74] Both Peter and Wynn Kenrick would have known about the good work being done by Donkin in their other family business, and Peter Kenrick promoted the Special Resolution that "a Director shall not be required to hold any share qualification",[75] enabling Albert Smart to become, in 1966, the first director to be appointed from among the non-family employees.

Real change began after July 1971, when the 37-year old Tom Jefferson was made sole managing director. He was joined on the board by his cousin Hugh, hitherto company secretary and head of finance, who was appointed production director at the age of twenty-nine.[76] In the midst of all the changes to structure and governance, a sense of the way in which family members might still be appointed to positions for which they were not obviously qualified is conveyed in Hugh Jefferson's comment that his appointment "astounded everybody, not least myself", in view of his complete lack of production experience.[77] Thereafter several external directors were appointed, notably the 33-year old Simon Hodgson as marketing director in 1973[78] and Bertie Rose, a chartered accountant and serial director – neither with any experience of printing – in 1976.[79] Rose became the chairman when Peter Kenrick eventually retired in 1978, forty-four years after joining K&J,[80] presiding over the decision not to re-register K&J as a public company in 1981.[81] The performance of some of these individuals is examined below, but it is striking how, over a period of five to ten years, the exclusive domination of the company's leadership positions by members of the Jefferson and Kenrick families was overturned, apparently of their own volition. What counted now would be the extent to which abandoning K&J's century-old controls would be validated by improvements in the company's performance and prospects.

74   Church, *Kenrick*, pp. 242–62.
75   Kenrick & Jefferson, 'Special Resolution of 19 November 1964' (Kenrick & Jefferson, 1964), Companies House, archive disk 00064711_102.
76   Kenrick & Jefferson, 'Notification of Change of Directors Dated 19 July 1971' (Kenrick & Jefferson, 1971), Companies House, archive disk 00064711_120.
77   Paulson, 'Interview Jefferson'.
78   Kenrick & Jefferson, 'Notification of Change of Directors Dated 29 November 1973' (Kenrick & Jefferson, 1973), Companies House, archive disk 00064711_127.
79   Kenrick & Jefferson, 'Notification of Change of Directors Dated 18 May 1976' (Kenrick & Jefferson, 1973), Companies House, archive disk 00064711_131.
80   Kenrick & Jefferson, 'Notification of Change of Directors Dated 11 May 1979' (Kenrick & Jefferson, 1973), Companies House, archive disk 00064711_137.
81   Kenrick & Jefferson, 'Special Resolution of 11 November 1981' (Kenrick & Jefferson, 1960), Companies House, archive disk 00064711_143.

Management During the 1970s

Notwithstanding the appointment of newcomers to senior roles, by far the most significant individual in the development of K&J after 1970 was Tom Jefferson. The grandson of Fred Jefferson, talismanic leader of K&J until 1940, Tom studied at the London College of Printing and was then sent to the United States for work experience. While his cousin Hugh, seven years younger, was learning about finance and administration through a combination of work experience and study at the Staffordshire College of Commerce (after a public school education at Cheltenham College), Tom was developing his understanding of the technical aspects of printing. By the time he became managing director Tom had accumulated considerable technical knowledge – including an appreciation of the developing market in computer-based materials – and was a capable marketer, having led the improvements to K&J's sales and marketing functions during the 1960s. He was also forceful and highly energetic. In these respects, he resembled a Mittelstand leader: hands-on, technically capable, emotionally committed. From the perspective of some on the shop floor, he was a positive force. Ivan Walker, by this time a K&J employee for well over thirty years, became the supervisor of the Greetings Cards division set up by Tom, which produced some two million cards per week for major retailers. In his eyes, Tom was "a non-stop goer", a hands-on leader whom many employees feared. In Walker's view, the company had been "going downhill" before Tom took over, and his vitality was instrumental in "revolutionising" it.[82]

Hugh Jefferson was his closest collaborator at director level. He had a similar perspective to Walker, but was better placed to see weaknesses as well as strengths. Tom was "a threatening person [who] had a lot of presence" and was "a bit of a control freak", the sort of manager who only employs people less capable than himself. On one occasion Peter Kenrick was forced to complain that managers could be found "quaking in their shoes" outside Tom's office door.[83] The evidence from the archives reinforces these impressions of a highly capable, driven leader who was also an autocrat. Paradoxically, it also hints at the Tom with whom future business development director Jeremy Plimmer worked closely: a leader of "terrific charisma", great work ethic, and high intelligence, who was extremely forceful but also showed "unbelievable loyalty" to those who worked with him.[84]

To understand the company's financial situation as Tom Jefferson implemented his plans, we have the benefit of a 1974 study of the top forty British

---

82   Paulson, 'Interview Walker'.
83   Paulson, 'Interview Jefferson'.
84   David Paulson, 'Interview with Jeremy Plimmer, Former Business Development Manager, K&J'.

printers by turnover.[85] It concluded that on average they generated "an entirely acceptable return" on capital employed while paying higher average wages than any other industry surveyed. K&J was ranked 22nd in turnover, 25th in return on capital employed, and 22nd in profitability (at 7.1% of sales). But with 830 people, K&J had the second-largest headcount, underlining its loss in productivity over the years and suggesting the difficulty of implementing new practices. The fact that K&J's average pay was only 29th in the industry suggests that K&J's staff were either competent but underpaid, and therefore unhappy and at risk of leaving; or adequately paid for low skills which might inhibit the productive implementation of new practices and technologies.[86] Whichever it was, K&J was concerned about its ability to attract and retain skilled staff, commissioning a substantial advertising campaign across local media "to enthuse existing employees about the company" and "produce applicants for specific vacancies" in the 1970s.[87]

The company was effectively a pyramid, in which all important decisions were made by the managing director and board. Hugh believed that the divisions should have been staffed by the most competent managers available and then cut free from headquarters, separately located, and run as semi-autonomous strategic business units with the West Bromwich site sold off at a profit. Central coordination would have been achieved by a small corporate centre of perhaps six people, running an effective IT system. True to his character, Tom disagreed, in practice if not in principle, with the idea of greater autonomy. He went ahead with splitting the company into divisions, but archival evidence of his relationships with their leaders reveals the "control freak" of Hugh's description. This was not necessarily due to any character defect; Hugh suggests that Tom may have felt himself to be guided by a covenant, seeing himself as a steward of the families' company only for a period of time, and therefore feeling unable to relinquish control.[88] He also faced an enormous challenge in delivering cultural change. Jeremy Plimmer recalls a company which was "Victorian" when he joined as a commercial apprentice in 1964, where staff were required to call the "very posh, upper class" Peter Kenrick "Mr. Peter" and the Jeffersons "Mr. Hugh" and "Mr. Tom", and the directors were waited on each lunch time in their formal dining room.[89]

---

85   Financial Analysis Group Ltd., *The British Printing Industry - a Financial Survey* (Winnersh, October 1974), Cambridge University Library, West Room.

86   c.f. Chapter 4 above on the low postwar level of employee training at K&J.

87   Kenrick & Jefferson, 'Proposal for Advertising Campaign by Tom C. Gough & Partners' (nd), Sandwell, BS/KJ3/4/6.

88   Paulson, 'Interview Jefferson'. In this respect, though the companies differed in size and industry, Tom seems to have resembled Rolf Walz at Julius Schneider, whose own sense of a covenant was similarly strong.

89   Paulson, 'Interview Plimmer'.

Plimmer worked with Tom Jefferson to develop new business throughout the 1970s. He recalls K&J needing to "put lots of new ideas out" because they were losing business in their traditional markets, and because the "K&J Family's" welfare provisions (which still included the ownership of houses rented out to employees such as sales staff) were so costly.[90] No matter what reservations some might have had at the time about Tom Jefferson's personal style, he pursued change energetically. His challenge was captured in the *K&J Group News* Centenary edition's headline in 1978: "Marrying yesterday's skills with tomorrow's technology."[91] The archive contains correspondence between computer companies and experts and internal memos to "Mr. Tom", containing technical information on coding and numbering during the period 1965 to 1969, showing Jefferson's personal commitment to understanding and developing the new computer-based technology.[92] From our twenty-first century perspective it is easy to forget that these investments of time and money required vision and courage on his part: the *New Statesman* estimated that in 1965 there were still only 948 computer systems in use in the UK, with a potential market of 5000 systems by the mid-1970s.[93] During the mid-1970s, Jefferson also acquired a calendar manufacturer, launched K&J's Greeting Cards Division, bought a computer services company, and launched a market-changing computerised passbook for building societies.[94] Some of the growth achieved was remarkable. Sales of greeting cards grew to £2 million over seven years, with a 29% production increase to 135 million cards in 1977/8 and plans to increase output by a further 50% following an investment in a new press.[95]

This extraordinarily energetic leadership and rapid pace of change concealed potential problems. First, the newly acquired subsidiary Wespac was active in the computer industry. But the intellectual capital was in other companies, to which Wespac was just providing a low-cost consumable refurbishment service. Second, a review of K&J's eighty-eight patents indicates declining innovation.[96] Only twenty-nine were granted between 1946 and 1979, over half for improvements to envelopes, a commodity item which represented only a small part

90   Paulson, 'Interview Plimmer'.
91   'Marrying Yesterday's Skills with Tomorrow's Technology', *K&J News* (1978), Sandwell Archive, BS/KJ4/1/31.
92   Kenrick & Jefferson, 'T. Jefferson, Ring Binder Containing Multiple Letters and Notes 1965–1970' (Kenrick & Jefferson, 1970), Sandwell, BS/KJ2/3/3.
93   Brian Murphy, *New Statesman*, June 1965, quoted in: Spector, *Management*, p. 316.
94   'K&J Help Launch a Revolution', *K&J News* (Easter 1978), Sandwell, BS/KJ4/1/31; 'Centenary Edition', *K&J News* (1978), Sandwell Archive, BS/KJ4/1/31.
95   'Service – the Key to Greeting Cards Success', *K&J News* (1978), Sandwell Archive, BS/KJ4/1/31.
96   'K&J Patents, 1903–2000' <http://worldwide.espacenet.com> [accessed 1 June 2014]: The company was granted 88 patents in the period 1903–2000, 26 of them after 1979.

of K&J's revenues.[97] In the thirty years to 1979, there is little evidence of the inventiveness which broke new ground with free consultancy services in 1914, or office systems in the 1920s, or relief-stamping in the 1930s, all excellent, niche products delivered as part of a focused, long-term, Mittelstand-style differentiation strategy.

Jefferson's hard driving was, on the face of it, clearly bringing results, with nominal sales growth throughout this period exceeding 20% annually. He was making immense personal efforts to boost organic growth wherever possible; Jeremy Plimmer remembers how hard he pushed himself, working late every night and travelling economy class wherever he went to keep costs down.[98] But the third and most dangerous problem is exemplified in Tom's report of his United States trip in 1978.[99] He reports on the growth of the word processing market. He reviews various opportunities. He is clearly extremely energetic and very hands-on ("I always use services of the British Consulates now. They shorten my research time enormously"), but in a way which seems anomalous for a group CEO. It is commendable that he was pushing to get into new markets; but though he had teams of presumably competent people in senior positions,[100] he micromanaged everything. His approach risked making K&J increasingly vulnerable for the future: over-dependent for its ideas, energy, and strategic direction on Tom Jefferson alone. Jeremy Plimmer's recollections to some extent contradict the archival record, as he recalls Jefferson being not only loyal to his staff but also receptive to some of their ideas. But Plimmer also recalls his "overpowering" personality and tendency to "walk all over" his subordinates, which suggests that the free flow of ideas and of challenges to Tom's thinking would have been as limited as the documentary evidence indicates.[101]

The possible consequence of his approach is suggested by developments in the security printing market, a key area for expansion in which Jefferson had a deep interest. In 1986, one company larger than K&J had proposed to merge with an even larger one. K&J were consulted by the Competition Commission and referred to themselves as a minnow confronted by whales.[102]

97   'K&J Manufacturing & Trading Account at 30 June 1959', 1959, Sandwell, BS/KJ1/3/96/1.
98   Paulson, 'Interview Plimmer'.
99   Kenrick & Jefferson, 'T. Jefferson, Notes on USA Visit, October 1978' (Kenrick & Jefferson, 1978), Sandwell, BS/KJ8/2/1.
100   They were also highly regarded by his fellow director: Paulson, 'Interview Jefferson'.
101   Paulson, 'Interview Plimmer'.
102   Competition Commission, *Norton Opax PLC and McCorquodale PLC A Report on the Proposed Merger* (London: Competition Commission, 24 September 1986), para. 6.3 <http://webarchive.nationalarchives.gov.uk/20111203045905/http://www.competition-commission.org.uk//rep_pub/reports/1986/206norton_opax_mccorquodale_plc.htm> [accessed 30 November 2014].

At one time, though, K&J had been much stronger than one of the merger parties, Norton Opax PLC, and as strong as the other. From 1923 until the 1960s, Norton and Wright Ltd. had been a small family firm with no more than thirty staff in a single premises, producing lottery tickets and card games. By 1973, though, the Norton and Wright group was being floated on the Stock Exchange. It then continued to grow organically and by acquisition at home and overseas until by 1986 it had twenty-two companies in four operating areas. Significantly, it had grown by decentralising management to the heads of each operating company, who were free to set up their own incentive schemes and ran their operating business with an autonomous board. A small head office was responsible only for group strategy, marketing and finance.[103] The largest company, McCorquodale PLC, had also grown through a strategy of decentralised management, the sort of small "centre" which Hugh Jefferson had wanted for K&J.[104] It seems that K&J were left behind as "minnows" not because of a failure to make innovations in security printing in the 1980s but because of a failure to make innovations in management and leadership, supported by committed shareholders, in the 1960s and '70s.

Sales in the 1970s

The character and size of K&J's sales force had begun to change during the 1960s. Tom Jefferson had concluded that the team, many of whom by that time had served the same customers for decades, were not developing new business but were simply "order takers". He therefore "took a scythe to about 30% of the sales force" during a "night of the long knives".[105] As a result, by the beginning of the 1970s there were thrity-five representatives, based at their homes, and five managers across four regions, the largest of which was London with seventeen salesmen.[106] Some of their "new" approaches suggested that K&J's competence in marketing had deteriorated over the course of forty years. For example, one meeting called for a "centralised mailing list to be built up to be used for raising additional enquiries to those got by personal calls" as though this was a new idea; in fact, K&J had pioneered the use of mailing lists in the 1920s and '30s and had managed their use brilliantly.[107]

103   Competition Commission, chap. 3, Norton Opax PLC.
104   Competition Commission, chap. 4: McCorquodale PLC.
105   Paulson, 'Interview Jefferson'. The "long knives" description was also used by Jeremy Plimmer, interview, 21 November 2014, suggesting the event had lodged in K&J's folk memory.
106   Kenrick & Jefferson, 'Memorandum: "Sales Organization"' (Kenrick & Jefferson, 1971), Sandwell, BS/KJ2/3/10.
107   Paulson, 'Professionalisation', p. 12.

It is, however, clear that they were not operating in an easy sales environment. The industry's trade body, the British Printing Industries Federation, warned that "competition continues to be fierce in many markets and prices remain too low" relative to the substantial general cost increases in the industry, up 458% between January 1962 and January 1978.[108] Companies struggled to maintain their competitiveness when average annual inflation in the UK in 1977 was 15.89%.[109] In West Germany, in contrast, average inflation in 1977 was 3.74%.[110] In these circumstances, K&J's push into European markets contrasted with the poor performance of other British firms which, according to the Institute of Export, were failing through inertia and incompetence, at a time when colleges were dropping export courses owing to a lack of demand from "apathetic industry".[111] The contrast, in performance and background environment, with Mittelstand exporters was stark.

K&J's progress was more impressive than that of some others. Over three years, exports doubled annually and K&J won a regional export prize.[112] But their market-positioning strategy, explained by export manager Mark Young, seems defective: "We have got to make it as natural in Oslo to regard us as local printers as it would be if we were the printer round the corner."[113] For a company which had prided itself on innovative, value-added selling for the previous sixty years, this seems a limited strategy. If proximity (real or imagined) was supposed to be K&J's greatest differentiator, how would they compete with someone who *was* around the corner? They appeared to be positioning themselves as a commodity supplier which turned orders round quickly, with little sense of any world-leading niche product or unique value proposition. An anecdote from the time serves as an appropriate metaphor for K&J, and indeed for the theme of this whole study. A group of German schoolchildren toured K&J as part of a schools exchange, and Mark Young showed them round, speaking German. In the view of *K&J Group News* this was "a performance that impressed the youngsters as much as the sight of so much German machinery in day-to-day use in the factory." It is an unfortunate reflection on

108   British Printing Industries Federation, 'Editorial', *Printing Industries*, 85 (February 1978), p. 85.
109   'Inflation, Great Britain, 1977', Inflation EU: Worldwide Inflation Data <http://www.inflation.eu/inflation-rates/great-britain/historic-inflation/cpi-inflation-great-britain-1977.aspx> [accessed 15 November 2014].
110   'Inflation, West Germany, 1977', Inflation EU: Worldwide Inflation Data <http://www.inflation.eu/inflation-rates/germany/historic-inflation/cpi-inflation-germany-1977.aspx> [accessed 15 November 2014].
111   'Salesmen "Hampering Exports"', *The Guardian* (Manchester/London, 1 April 1974), p. 13.
112   'K&J Wins Major Export Award', *K&J News* (Easter 1978), Sandwell, BS/KJ4/1/31.
113   'K&J Must Be Europe's Printer Round the Corner', *K&J News* (Summer 1977), Sandwell Archive, BS/KJ4/1/31.

K&J's and Britain's position relative to German businesses that a British export manager speaking his customers' language could be considered extraordinarily talented, while no concern was voiced that a British printer, whose growth strategy largely depended on quickly producing low-value printed commodities in local languages, depended for its existence on high-value machinery produced in Germany.[114]

Ironically, as K&J was expounding its "local printer" thinking and heralding the appointment of an aggressive new sales manager for its commodity calendars,[115] the British Printing Industries Federation was asking its members, "Why don't you have it die-stamped?"[116] Celebrating a resurgence in orders to a current level of twenty million impressions per week, the Federation offered instructions on how to sell the die-stamping work in which K&J had once dominated a world-leading niche position, and for which it had just won an international award. Now, though, the die-stamping group was one of K&J's smallest departments.[117] In the pursuit of volume, it appeared, K&J had failed over time to build upon the inimitable, high-profit skills which had in the interwar years set it apart from national and international competitors – meeting in that period resource-based management theorists' requirement that a company's products must exhibit Value, Rarity, Inimitability and a supporting Organisation to achieve sustainable competitive advantage – and had never yet found others to replace them.[118]

Financial Performance in the 1970s

Throughout the 1970s, K&J's revenues and profits appeared to grow in response to the efforts of Tom Jefferson and his team to develop new products and boost exports. By the end of the financial year 1979/80, record sales of almost £11.1 million showed a seven-fold increase over the period since Tom had become a director in 1966. Profits had grown even more dramatically, rising by over twenty times, and spoilt only by a decline in nominal terms of 26% between 1978/9 and 1979/80. The story appears to be one of continuing success. In reality, K&J's history between 1949 and 1979 was one of minimal sales growth

---

114 'Impressing the Germans', *K&J News* (Summer 1977), Sandwell Archive, BS/KJ4/1/31.
115 'New Supremo at Lockwoods', *K&J News* (Easter 1978), Sandwell, BS/KJ4/1/31.
116 British Printing Industries Federation, 'Why Don't You Have It Die-Stamped?', *Printing Industries*, 85 (September 1978). At K&J, die-stamping was traditionally known by its alternative name, relief-stamping.
117 'Excellence Brings Its Own Great Reward', *K&J News* (Easter 1978), Sandwell, BS/KJ4/1/31.
118 Jay Barney, 'Firm Resources and Sustained Competitive Advantage', *Journal of Management*, 17.1 (1991), 99–120.

and declining profitability in real terms. The company's leadership continually failed to recapture the achievements of the pre- and immediate post-war years, apparently not finding contracts which were of equivalent volume and profitability to those K&J had enjoyed before and through the war and beyond it. None of Tom Jefferson's export growth, nor his new computer and Business Forms product lines, nor his remodelled envelope factory, though all showed nominal gains throughout the 1970s, was sufficient to enable the company to return to its past strengths, let alone to grow to the next level, as companies such as McCorquodale and Norton Opax were doing. In actuality, as Figure 10 shows, both sales and profits had remained flat in real terms over the 30 years since 1949.[119]

This was despite the fact that the company continued to invest in technology and process improvements. During the 1970s, investment in plant continued to outstrip depreciation each year. At almost £2.7 million in 1979, K&J's fixed assets were worth in real terms almost 2.5 times what they had been in 1949, but there was no concomitant real-terms increase in the company's profits.[120]

We have seen how the board of directors were increasingly preoccupied with the concerns of the company's shareholders from 1950 onwards. Jeremy Plimmer recalls that Tom Jefferson was nervous every September in anticipation of "being beaten up" by shareholders at the Annual General Meeting (AGM).[121] We have also seen how, relative to the fortune of holders of Government securities and shareholders generally in the UK, K&J's own shareholders were very well rewarded in the 1950s and 1960s. This continued during the 1970s. Between 1973 and 1980, dividends per £1 share rose each year, from 11.63p to 25.0p. During the last five years of the decade, while the company's bank overdraft rose from nil to £587,000, gross dividends distributed amounted to £252,000 out of total after-tax profits of £1.3 million.[122] It may have been reasonable for its shareholders to contrast unfavourably K&J's performance in 1979 with that in 1949. But it is also reasonable to conclude that shareholders did exceptionally well out of investments, which in most cases they had inherited. More modest demands and a more supportive, less short-term, attitude from shareholders might have permitted Tom Jefferson to deliver greater long-term returns through the focused, long-term, niche products strategy that his grandfather had pursued.

---

119   Compiled by the author from financial data from Sandwell, BS/KJ1/3/ sequence of annual accounts; Companies House files of 1970s accounts; normalised to 1949 based on https://measuringworth.com/calculators/ukcompare/ [accessed 1.12.2014].

120   At £2.693 million versus £154, 437, adjusted by the real price index of 6.98.

121   Paulson, 'Interview Plimmer'.

122   Companies House, 6000 series of K&J annual accounts for the years ending 26/6/76, 2/7/77, 1/7/78, 30/6/79 and 28/6/80.

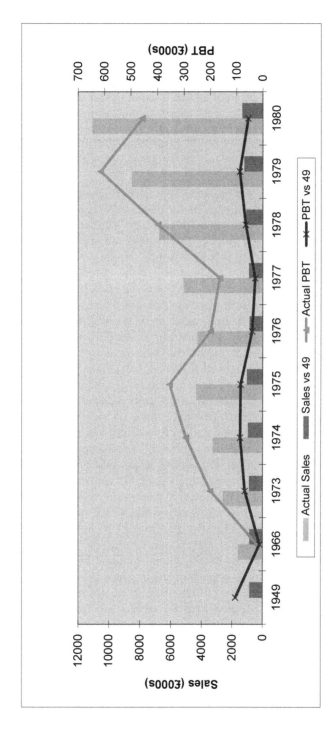

Figure 10 Kenrick & Jefferson Ltd., Nominal vs. Real Growth, 1949–79.

Conclusion: Kenrick and Jefferson, 1949 to 1979

K&J's immediate post-war history reveals a company which maintained many of its traditional virtues. It retained its staff and treated them well, even after paternalism had ceased to be fashionable; it cared deeply about its customers and their needs; it continued to invest in new equipment and to seek ways of working more productively and professionally. But within fifteen years of the war's conclusion, the company's future seemed imperilled, with long-serving staff and apparently uninspired directors failing to generate sufficient ideas or energy, and proliferating shareholders demanding short-term gains. Once the third generation of owners had begun to fight back, however, a leader from the fourth generation took the company by the neck and dragged it forward. Tom Jefferson invested in new technology with an eye to the emerging computer age, purchased companies in new and complementary markets, and drove K&J's exports to extraordinary levels in a short time. Yet while his 1978 end-of-year report shows that the company paid attention to the age and remaining service of its most senior thirty-four managers, marking the eldest "for particular attention", there is no mention anywhere of any succession plan for Tom himself.[123] This was reasonable in as much as he was still in his forties, but it added to K&J's dependency on a figure who seems to have been completely dominant. Though Hugh Jefferson held the position of second-in-command as a senior family member, the archival and anecdotal evidence suggests that the company derived a disproportionate, and therefore highly risky, amount of its energy from one domineering individual: his cousin Tom.

No matter that he was motivated by a sense of moral obligation to his family, as his cousin Hugh claims; and was personally industrious and financially modest, as Jeremy Plimmer suggests; and was compelled to manoeuvre around the excessive short-term demands of greedy shareholders throughout his tenure: Tom was a liability as well as an asset. His refusal to build a team of equals and his insistence on taking personal responsibility for all key initiatives rendered his company vulnerable to his own fallibility. Of course, any historian of the company must risk the accusation that his or her conclusions are shaped by the knowledge of Tom's early death a decade after the end of our period, and the terminal impact caused by the "huge vacuum" he left behind.[124] But by the time that Tom took sole control of the business in 1971, K&J was over thirty years past its best days, and it was not possible for one man, no matter how committed or intelligent or visionary, to reverse its relative decline alone: Tom Jefferson's tireless efforts to do so might, ironically, have hastened the end of K&J.

---

123   T.F. Jefferson Annual Report, Annex K (21 July 1978), Sandwell, BS/KJ8/2/1.
124   Paulson, 'Interview Plimmer'.

7

Julius Schneider GmbH & Co. KG, Ludwigsburg

Julius Schneider Stahlbau und Verglasung (Schneider), based first in Stuttgart then in nearby Ludwigsburg, was a designer, producer and installer of steel-framed buildings and glass roofing. It originated in a one-man technical services bureau started by Julius Schneider in Stuttgart in 1902.[1] He recruited Karl Walz, newly graduated from Stuttgart's Königlich Württembergische Baugewerkschule (building trades school), and in 1910 the company was established as Julius Schneider Eisenkonstruktion und Glasdachbau (ironwork and glazed roof manufacture). After difficult conditions during World War One, when Walz served at the front, they established relationships with firms such as Mercedes and Bosch which remained their customers until the 1970s. After setbacks during the difficult economy of the 1920s, Schneider began to focus on steelworks for buildings; ever larger constructions were manufactured and erected, including turbine halls and a steel-rolling mill. Schneider improved and expanded its plant, albeit still using very primitive tools and machinery: the company history recalls the use of tree boughs as levers for lifting steelwork, the carriage of finished products on handcarts, and the use of city trams for deliveries, all of which created a culture of resilience. Having cut staff from one hundred to six during the recession of the early 1930s, the building industry experienced such a sharp upswing under the Hitler regime's industrial policy that the works was soon overwhelmed.[2] In response, the factory expanded, offices and workshops were updated, and the workforce expanded to 120 men.

From 1 January 1937 the single-owner firm (*Einzelfirma*) became a partnership (*offene Handelsgesellschaft*) between Julius Schneider and the by-now Senior Engineer (*Oberingenieur*) Karl Walz. The elevation of the "trusted colleague",[3] after what was effectively a 28-year apprenticeship, illustrates a preference for expertise and experience over youth and energy

---

1   This section based on Rolf Walz; and W. Zimmermann, 'Kurzer Abriss Der Betriebsgeschichte – Julius Schneider, Stahlbauten, Kittlose Glasdächer' (Julius Schneider GmbH, 1962), WABW B4/Bü3.

2   Tooze, *Wages*, pp. 108–14.

3   IHK Ludwigsburg, 'Die Kammer beglückwünscht', *Mitteilungsblatt der Industrie- und Handelskammer Ludwigsburg* (November 1960), p. 163, WABW B4/Bü3.

in the selection of management, and indeed in some individuals' decisions to seek management responsibility: Christian Wandel chose to start out on his own only at the age of forty-eight, when he was fully confident in his own experience and ability. Walz became the sole owner in 1943 on Schneider's death. Having worked at a relentless pace, he suffered a complete breakdown in autumn 1944 and needed the support of the company's senior engineer to steer the badly bomb-damaged company through the remaining months of the war. The successes in this period up to 1945 were later attributed by his son and successor Rolf Walz to "painstaking attention to detail", the "dogged work" of "undemanding", "industrious, capable workers", and the "daring and capability" of the company's leaders. Rolf's nostalgic views of the early struggles of his father and the company's workers are respectful to the point of uncritical reverence, and he subsequently "rejoice[d] in the fact that we are still a big organisation of craftsmen (*dass wir noch ein handwerklicher Grossbetrieb* [*sind*])".[4] The company's early history reveals the accretion of culture and the accumulation of path dependencies that would shape its future progress.

At the war's end, the imposition of denazification programmes meant a return to business leadership positions was delayed, in some cases for several years, across the western occupied zones of Germany.[5] By December 1945, Karl Walz had himself still not been permitted to regain his former role at Julius Schneider.[6] Notwithstanding subsequent endeavours to distance himself from Party matters, the archive reveals that under Walz's direction, Julius Schneider had been an active contributor to the war effort, despite having suffered on numerous occasions from bomb damage.[7] A 1953 claim by Walz for compensation shows that turnover had been RM960,000 in 1943, admittedly a decline from its high point of RM1.4 million in 1941. But with eighty-seven staff in 1944 (the number of whom were slave labourers, perhaps a contributing factor in Walz's exile from the company after 1945, is unknown), the company had remained busy.[8] Karl Walz's conduct during the war suggests a determination to persist with pre-war business etiquette to an extent which is surprising given the context; it also makes comprehensible the speed with which his business (and others in similar wartime and post-war situations) recovered despite the

---

4   Rolf Walz.
5   Richard Bessel, *Germany 1945: From War to Peace* (London, 2012), pp. 361–69.
6   The company history recalls that he had been barred since the introduction of Law No. 8 in September 1945. See Hege, 'Geschichte', p. 34.
7   Karl Walz, 'To: Kriegschädenamt, Stuttgart and Städt. Wohnungs-u. Siedlungsamt, Stuttgart' (29 January 1945), WABW B4/Bü15.
8   Karl Walz, 'Schäden und Verluste an Betriebsvermögen' (1953), WABW B4/Bü16. This total differs from the 55 staff later recorded in the company's history, suggesting either that the situation deteriorated as 1944 went on, or that Walz might have deliberately overstated his losses - or perhaps that he counted wartime slave labour as part of his total headcount. c.f. Hege, p. 32.

post-conflict devastation. Three weeks before French troops occupied Stuttgart,[9] Walz was invoicing architects for a cancelled project for Messerschmitt, including overtime pay for on-site labour.[10] It is difficult to understand whether Walz was determined to display a blithe indifference to reality or whether his behaviour was a manifestation of the apparent determination of both the Nazi Party and many individual Germans to continue with daily life as though there were no likelihood of defeat or any change in local circumstances.[11]

It seems from the limited archival evidence that Walz and his staff adeptly navigated their way through what must have been extraordinarily trying circumstances at the war's end. Walz's ban on rejoining Schneider did not prevent him from positioning the company, through his nominated stand-in, as a very capable supplier to the American forces of replacement bridges and other steel structures, while energetically pursuing claims for non-payment of his war work.[12] His strength of character, punctiliousness, and energy all seem evident from the archival material pertaining to the months before and just after the war ended. The question now would be how he would rebuild the business for the challenges of peacetime.

He seems to have begun by demanding detailed reports on the weekly condition of the business from Hermann Maier, his finance manager, who was given operational responsibility for the business as its custodian (*Treuhänder*) by the American authorities. Walz was only allowed back into the managing directorship of Julius Schneider in January 1948.[13] The extended period under which the company was subjected to the so-called *Vermögenskontrolle* suggests that the Americans considered Walz to have been an active supporter of the Nazi regime.[14] But the tight financial supervision under which the company was placed, the Americans requiring monthly management accounts which even in the "brief report" (*Kurzbericht*) form required them to account for amounts as small as RM12, must have ensured that Schneider and other companies were carefully administered. And while the economic situation was undoubtedly challenging and would remain so until after the currency was reformed a year later, the detail in the March 1947 *Kurzbericht* might in retrospect be said to have promised a positive future: turnover was RM141,900 for a total wage outlay

9   Frank Roy Willis, *The French in Germany, 1945–1949* (Stanford University Press, 1962), p. 18.
10   Karl Walz, 'Invoice to Herren Architekten Lambrecht und Osthus (14) Leonberg, Bauleitung' (31 March 1945), WABW B4/Bü37.
11   Kershaw passim; Bessel passim.
12   Karl Walz, 'Letter to Abrechnungstelle der früheren O.T., Heidelberg' (11 September 1945), WABW B4/Bü37.
13   Hege, 'Geschichte', pp. 34–35.
14   A file was held on him by US military authorities: Department of Defense, Office of Military Government for Germany, 'Record of File on Karl Walz' (2016) <https://catalog. archives.gov/id/7569400> [accessed 31 March 2016].

of RM20,330, cash holdings stood at almost RM151,000, and total output was only 60% of actual productive capacity.[15] As at nearby Karosseriewerk Reutter, this was a troubled period during which business was nevertheless found, premises and workforces restored, and cash safeguarded. This brief review of Schneider's experience, during and immediately after the war, shows that despite bomb damage and Allied occupation, the company was scrupulously managed in a reasonable financial condition, and able after denazification and currency reform to power ahead with rebuilding and the consumer boom.

Post-war Business Activity to 1954

The archival holdings of Julius Schneider's sales records are incomplete, but give some indication of activity levels before, during, and after the war. The sales ledger for the period up to 25 July 1938 was one of the few original documents to survive the air raids of 1944. Though it has been damaged by fire and water, it is possible to see that the company was busy throughout the pre-war period, averaging 11.6 sales orders or contracts per week.[16] We have already seen examples from correspondence files of the company's sales activity during the war. Details of them are also held in the next remaining sales ledger, running from 1943 to December 1948, which shows a decline in the number of orders to 7.8 per week.[17] Subsequent ledgers contain fewer months' worth of orders, as Julius Schneider became busier.

A review of the extant post-war ledgers at six-monthly intervals shows that the company managed its order book in detail. Entries are neatly written in fountain pen (not typed), showing the order number, date, customer name and, where relevant, the commissioning architect's name. Prices are usually shown for steelwork in Marks per tonne, with the total calculations completed on a per-tonne basis; for glasswork, however, orders were normally priced per item. The persistence of entrepreneurs like Walz in this period is notable, given that, as his employee Kurt Hege subsequently recalled, it was possible to make as much money selling a few cartons of cigarettes as it was building steel structures, without any of the associated personal difficulties and responsibility. But "all this changed completely with the currency reform ... Money was indeed scarce, but it had a value again, and it was worthwhile working and producing" once

15 'Monatlicher Kurzbericht für März 1947 der Firma Julius Schneider Stahlbauten, Serial Nr. X.C. 1503–547' (Amt für Vermögenskontrolle Stuttgart, 1947), WABW B4/Bü47. Signed by Hermann Maier, Treuhänder.

16 Julius Schneider GmbH, 'Auftragsbuch Nr. 8 vom 11. Juni 1935 bis 25. Juli 1938' (1938), WABW B4/Bü29.

17 Julius Schneider GmbH, 'Auftragsbuch vom 24. Oktober 1943 bis 31. Dezember 1948' (1948), WABW B4/Bü30, all calculations by the author.

more.[18] While there have been differing interpretations of the impact of the 20 June 1948 currency reform on the production of capital goods,[19] the effect on Julius Schneider's order book was immediate and significant, as it was at Reutter: total tonnage sold increased by 3.4 times between the first and second half of 1948.[20] Though business volumes increased overall, however, it is clear that winning work remained a challenge. A detailed examination of the 1949 ledger shows that orders varied greatly in size and came from both the private and public sectors.[21] Examples include:

- DM54 (handrail for ramp).
- DM47,034 approximately (steelworks for work hall for Stuttgart Strassenbahn, 78 tonnes @ DM603 per tonne, fully assembled, delivery time three months).
- DM13,800 (various roof light assemblies, with installation, for Salamander AG shoe factory, Kornwestheim).
- DM510 (steelwork for a roof 3.0m x 11.9m, Stuttgart Strassenbahn).
- DM113,718 + DM3879 delivery and assembly (Werner & Pfleiderer, Stuttgart-Feuerbach, planned rebuilding and steelwork, total weight 206,012kg@DM552).

Orders are predominantly local or regional, but include major enterprises, indicating that Schneider must have been held in some esteem despite its relatively small size. There is no differentiation within the ledger: equivalent attention seems to have been given to every order in the book; even for very small orders there is sometimes a large amount of detail. The variance in order value and complexity suggests that in the period up to and following currency reform, Karl Walz was trying to find work wherever he could while he rebuilt the business. It is clear that the company was capable of handling larger, more complex orders, with elements of design and project management within them. But it is equally clear that in still straitened times, Walz had no desire to turn down any work, no matter how low the value. No doubt Schneider's competitors were also active, adding urgency to the search for work.

Over the course of two years, however, it appears the company's prospects began to stabilise. The archival evidence shows that the quantity of orders in the sales ledgers decreased; one explanation for this could be that the reduction was a result of increased competition. But the increase in their average value suggests that as time went on and the economy strengthened, the company was able to

---

18 Hege, 'Geschichte', p. 35.
19 See, for example, the analysis in Alan Kramer, *The West German Economy, 1945–1955* (New York and Oxford, 1991), pp. 134–40.
20 Hege, 'Geschichte', p. 35.
21 Julius Schneider GmbH, 'Auftragsbuch vom 1. Januar 1949 bis 16. Oktober 1950', 1950, WABW B4/Bü31.

rely with greater confidence on its ability to win fewer, larger orders, which Walz was satisfied would enable Schneider to increase its profits. Moreover, a focus on more demanding projects would better highlight its experience and competencies.

The order books also hint at Walz's personal identification with the company. For example, order 14078 of 12 April 1951 to Hanke & Kurtz, Stuttgart, is shown to have been delivered "from my factory" (*ab meinem Werk*).[22] As the health of this very driven entrepreneur began to deteriorate in that same year, the effective direction of the business would become a concern; his management style, which appears from archival evidence to have been rather more autocratic than paternalistic, left little room for other managerial talent to emerge. The leadership of the company was held in a small group of five managers, including Walz, plus two *Meister* who were responsible for the works. Given the size and complexity of their orders (including the technically demanding reconstruction of damaged churches), this suggests a high level of efficiency, but also a high degree of individual dominance by Walz, and a small pool of talent to enable future growth.[23]

Material Supply Problems

One immediate and enduring challenge for Schneider, before and after Karl Walz's return, was the difficulty in obtaining scarce raw materials. There was an obvious and ubiquitous demand for steelwork, and problems of supply were expected, as evidenced by the American forces' appropriation of Schneider stocks. Years of bombing had affected the Ruhr's productive capacity. Available output could not possibly meet the demand: not only were normal industrial requirements to be met (among them the day-to-day work of Julius Schneider), but also the long-neglected "housekeeping" of the ordinary German population, not to mention the repair of war damage and the need to replace industrial plants that had been broken down and shipped to the Russian zone.[24] In fact, subsequent analysis shows that in 1949 only 8.8 million tons of crude steel and 7.0 million tons of pig iron were produced in the bizonal area; this represented an increase of 59% over 1948's output, but was still only 59.2% of 1936 production, a crippling shortfall even without the requirement to repair war damage.[25] In Berlin, neither bomb damage, the removal and shipment to the

22   Julius Schneider GmbH, 'Auftragsbuch vom 17. Oktober 1950 bis 30. Dezember 1952.' (1952), WABW B4/Bü32.
23   Hege, 'Geschichte', p. 38.
24   Werner Bührer, *Ruhrstahl und Europa: Die Wirtschaftsvereinigung Eisen- und Stahlindustrie und die Anfänge der europäischen Integration 1945–1952* (München: Oldenbourg Wissenschaftsverlag, 2010), pp. 65–66 <https://doi.org/10.1524/9783486703276> [accessed 7 August 2022].
25   Kramer, p. 102 Table 4.4.

USSR of industrial plant, nor prevailing personnel shortages were considered by city authorities to be the most significant factor in the region's inability to return to pre-war productivity levels; the critical issue was in fact the shortage of materials, with industry receiving only 10,500 tonnes of steel in 1947 compared to 1,026,000 tonnes in 1936.[26]

In the immediate aftermath of the war, a "unified, integrated German economy appeared to be a thing of the past", with inter-zonal trade difficulties precluding the continuation of long-established trading relationships, such as those between the Ruhr and Württemberg.[27] Schneider's own ability to obtain materials was hampered in this way, being particularly complicated by the fact that it had previously purchased its steel from producers in the Saar. Now that the French occupation made that impossible, the company was forced to seek new sources of supply, especially from Rhineland producers. It mitigated its difficulties by developing such good relationships with two local steel stockholders that in its own estimation "the Schneider company came out of this period in better shape than its competitors." Even so, it was necessary to supplement supplies by buying up scrap girders and beams from bomb sites in Berlin and other major cities.[28]

The company's difficulties in obtaining raw materials were recollected as a major challenge during its 50th birthday celebrations in 1960.[29] The freshness of the memory is explained not only by the problems in the immediate post-war years, but also by their continuation into the early 1950s: when Schneider's *Prokurist* Herr Epple travelled round the Rhineland looking for sources of steel supply in May 1951, he found that suppliers there were "giving the cold shoulder" to south-German buyers, magnifying the difficulties Schneider faced.[30] As Schneider spent DM1.92 million on metals in 1952, the scale of the ongoing challenge can be imagined.[31] The purchasing of steel may have been made more difficult by the "steel boom" which happened in response to the Korean war.[32] It would also have been made acute by demands such as the huge quantity of repairs to railway bridges, just one example of the rebuilding work necessary across West Germany: at the war's end, 2472 were unusable, and by the end of 1950 only 1181 had been permanently restored, leaving 322 in

---

26   Renate Schwärzel, 'Die Berliner Elektroindustrie Nach Dem Zweiten Weltkrieg. Eine Bestandsaufnahme', in *Unternehmen Zwischen Markt Und Macht. Aspekte Deutscher Unternehmens- Und Industriegeschichte Im 20. Jahrhundert*, ed. by Werner Plumpe and Christian Kleinschmidt, Bochumer Schriften Zur Unternehmens- Und Industriegeschichte (Essen, 1992), I, 167–78 (pp. 174–76).

27   Bessel, p. 370.

28   Hege, 'Geschichte', pp. 35–36.

29   Zimmermann, p. 3.

30   M. Epple, 'Reise vom 23.5 – 26.5.51.' (1951), WABW B4/Bü20.

31   Julius Schneider GmbH, 'Eisenhändler – Umsätze im Jahre 1952' (nd), WABW B4/Bü19.

32   Bührer, p. 185.

the Stuttgart region alone still to be repaired.[33] This massive restoration project clearly provided attractive sales opportunities for firms like Schneider, but also added further to the difficulties they and their competitors had in finding materials to do the work, even when they made personal purchasing visits.[34] No matter whether their difficulty in procuring supplies was a general shortage driven by the Korean armaments boom or by European rebuilding plans funded by Marshall Aid, or, indeed, by cultural or political differences within West Germany, sourcing appears to have been an ongoing problem for Schneider for a decade after the war's end. As such, it underscores another aspect of the Mittelstand's challenge: for struggling businesses, the *Wirtschaftswunder* was frequently anything but wonderful as a daily experience.

Management and Operational Changes 1954 to 1960

The archive contains no sales ledgers from the period after 30 December 1952, but Hege's company history, supported by a collection of photographs, shows that Schneider completed significant projects from the early 1950s until 1974. They included work with major companies such as Mercedes-Benz and AEG, several churches, Stuttgart University, public transport works, power stations, and public spaces such as a cinema and a concert hall.[35] In order to achieve these successes, Schneider had to manage significant leadership and operational challenges. For an understanding of how it did so, we rely on the company history written after its demise in 1977, and on material created for its 50th anniversary celebrations in 1960.

Karl Walz died in April 1954 after a prolonged illness during which he had nevertheless "shared in the fortunes of the business from his home until his dying day" – an emotional, and controlling, bond with the workplace that would later be recalled by his staff.[36] The company published the customary death notice, praising his "outstanding knowledge and capabilities" and his concern for the wellbeing of his staff. The extent to which Walz and his "tireless creativity" were felt to have been the sources of the company's "present size and significance" is striking: in honouring his memory, his family presented him as a man on a personal forty-year crusade. But the reassurance to readers that the business would continue to be run "in his way and following his example"

---

33 Eugen Ernst, 'Der Brückenbau der Deutschen Bundesbahn im Jahre 1950', *Die Bautechnik* (March 1951), 49–53 (p. 50).
34 M. Epple.
35 'Wirtschaftsarchiv Baden-Württemberg. Bestand B4, J. Schneider GmbH & Co. KG. Findbuch: 10.1, Fotos, "Ausgeführte Aufträge"' (Wirtschaftsarchiv Baden-Württemberg, 1982), WABW B4/Bü51–118; See also Hege, 'Geschichte' passim.
36 Hege, 'Geschichte', p. 38.

might be viewed as a commitment to a way of working which was by then forty years old, and which required a single, all-dominating leader to take all the decisions.[37] It is also reasonable to wonder whether Karl Walz's overweening presence and insistence on control had stifled the company's development, particularly in relation to the incubation of future leadership talent. Instead of being invited to join him in the workplace as a co-director when he was released from Soviet captivity in 1950, Rolf Walz returned at the age of thirty-one – presumably with his father's encouragement – to the university course he had left when he was conscripted. In consequence, though his father had been seriously ill for three years before his death and presumably aware of the need to guide his successor, Rolf felt very much unprepared to assume control of the company when he died.

Nevertheless, on his father's death, he immediately assumed the position of sole leader. Terminating his studies, he took overtly personal responsibility for the company, changing its legal form to a "family partnership" (*Familien-KG*), in 1954, and pronouncing himself its "sole authorised representative [and] personally liable shareholder" (*allein zur Vertretung befugter persönlich haftender Gesellschafter*).[38] In doing so, he declared himself to be committed in a completely different way from his counterparts at Braithwaites in the UK. As we will see, their governance model was based on one family dominating a public company by owning the largest single block of shares and ensuring that each son succeeded his father as controlling chairman. Each had significant power, but none accepted the personal accountability and financial liability that Walz (or Ulrich Putsch or the Wandels) actively sought.

Rolf found the business constrained by manpower shortages and poor facilities, which dissuaded younger people from joining the firm (and suggests that his father had either lost touch with current views, or had determined that what had been good enough for his generation should be accepted by the present one). Against the wishes of the city authorities, which owned the Schneider site, Walz built roofed areas where previously the work had been done in the open air, and built a separate sales office which allowed engineers to be added to the technical office, so that by 1955 there were ten staff supported by eight site foremen ("master craftsmen" or *Meister*).[39] Two things are noteworthy in Hege's recollections of this period: that working conditions were "primitive" and that city authorities could be obstructive, suggesting that latter-day conceptions of an economic miracle being achieved from pristine premises with the support of growth-minded local governments do not necessarily reflect

---

37 'Death notice for Karl Walz, 24.4.1954' (Julius Schneider GmbH, 1954), WABW B4/Bu50.

38 IHK Ludwigsburg.

39 Hege, 'Geschichte', pp. 44–45.

contemporary reality; though most of the wartime rubble had been cleared, German businesses still faced a hard slog.

Having achieved only a temporary respite from his capacity constraints, Walz bought land in a new industrial area from the city of Ludwigsburg, 17km away from the existing Schneider site. The deal included thirty houses for long-serving workers, a reflection of both the prevailing manpower constraints and the Walz family's paternalism. Walz and his management team decided that "in view of the prospects for the steel industry and especially for Schneider at that time" they should build ambitiously, eventually erecting 90m-long fabrication sheds.[40] All of the layout and most of the building design was done by Rolf Walz himself. Of more consequence, perhaps, was his decision in this same period to turn down a request from his senior engineer, Zimmermann, to acquire a shareholding in the business. Zimmermann had joined the company after the war, and therefore had by this time ten years' experience as the head of Karl Walz's technical office. He was remembered by Hege as "a very good engineer, who committed himself to an extraordinary extent to the firm and its interests. He knew how to develop relationships with new customers and how to win new contracts from them."[41] No other evidence exists which might offer a contradictory appraisal to Hege's, and therefore explain why Rolf Walz turned Zimmermann down. Assuming therefore that Hege was correct, it seems to have been a misjudgement which would be to the long-term detriment of the company. It is evident that the emotion which suffused Karl Walz's relationship with Schneider was shared by his son, and deepened by the son's admiration for his father, and it therefore seems likely that the refusal to accept an experienced partner was motivated less by the head than by the heart: Schneider was Rolf's, and only he could be responsible for its destiny.

In the short term, however, Walz's developmental work had an immediately beneficial effect. Once the official move to Ludwigsburg was completed in November 1958, Schneider was immediately able to boost its engineering staff to thirteen, with eight in the new commercial office. By 1959, staff numbers reached twenty-nine, with 121 workers, and "between 1960 and 1966 output and turnover rose in step with each other."[42] The increase in sales up to 1958 had come both from longstanding clients who were repairing war damage and from new customers. With the new premises and additional staff, work with both new and old customers increased: turnover grew, and larger contracts were won; orders for one hundred to five hundred tonnes were no longer a rarity, and an increasing number of one thousand-tonne contracts were executed. As

---

40   Hege, 'Geschichte', pp. 51–52.
41   Hege, 'Geschichte', pp. 38, 50.
42   Hege, 'Geschichte', p. 56.

Figure 11 illustrates, revenue growth gradually outstripped tonnage growth as more value-added work was produced.[43]

While the new workload encompassed a range of building types, indicating that Schneider was not over-reliant on a single industry, there was evidently little effort to achieve any geographic diversification to mitigate future economic risk: the list of clients shows that Schneider was largely dependent on local firms, apart from the occasional contract in more distant locations such as Cologne. It was in this respect that Schneider most obviously differed from Braithwaites, which offered similar products and skills but had cultivated an international customer base since its foundation. Schneider also differed in this regard from Mittelstand companies like Wandel and RECARO, both of which were internationally active. It continued to resemble them, however, in its attachment to the Stuttgart region, the commitment of a single family owner to his staff, and a focused, long-term strategy on excellent products. Whether those products were sufficiently niche was, however, an additional potential risk in a competitive market.

Fiftieth Anniversary Celebrations, 1960

Schneider's anniversary celebration, which happened soon after the move to the new premises in Ludwigsburg, warrants a detailed examination, because the occasion was used to state publicly the company's values and, more significantly, to explore what it meant to be an entrepreneur (*Unternehmer*) in a Mittelstand family business in this period.[44] Like many Mittelstand companies, Schneider laid great store by its culture and history, and archival materials reveal the considerable emotional investment in the company which was manifested in the anniversary celebrations. In its own acknowledgement of Schneider's achievements, the Chamber of Commerce (represented here as at other company celebrations, demonstrating its close engagement with its member businesses) praised the firm's accomplishments and remarked that "a positive social climate, made possible by the special traditions of a family business, [had] had a significant impact on the company's capabilities and on its growth."[45] What were those special traditions? In his own speech, Rolf Walz lauds traditional craft skills and the commitment of the company's "industrious and capable men (*fleissige und tüchtige Männer*), who think for themselves, know how to help themselves" and are more important than any

---

43 Compiled by the author from WABW B4/Bü1, pp. 36, 56. Sales data for 1958 and 1959 are omitted from the source.

44 Also reviewed in Paulson, 'Memory', pp. 15–16.

45 IHK Ludwigsburg.

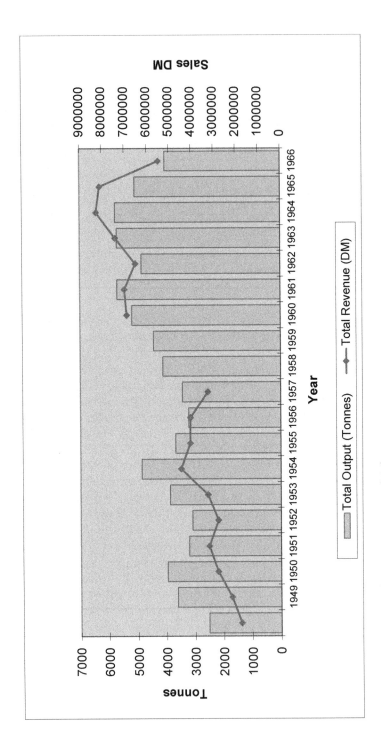

Figure 11 Julius Schneider KG, Output and Sales, 1949–67.

machines.[46] It is not clear whether Walz was honouring the workers before him, or abjuring the modern; a nostalgic admiration for the working man (chief among them his own father) that might have blinded him to the need to invest in evolving techniques and technologies. Quoting Goethe, he invokes the image of a chain, in which every link is free to move but on which every other link is dependent, to describe himself and all his colleagues in the business. In his own speech, the company's deputy leader (*Prokurist*) and future managing director and historian Kurt Hege restates the importance of each individual: "Without human strength, spiritual or physical, there would be no continuation and no jubilee to celebrate."[47] And it is this "strength" that Walz emphasises, railing against the ignorance of contemporary youth who showed no respect for their predecessors.[48] Had the latter not "worked under great privations to lay down the foundations of today" it would be young people themselves who would have to bear this burden. Everyone would need to play their part in the future and hope that it would "preserve them from years like 1914–18, 1921–23, 1928–33, 1939–48".[49] Walz is constantly mindful of the past, perhaps because his own past contained considerable hardship on the Eastern Front and then in the Gulag, and of the sacrifices made by his father and the older workers. His emotions were apparently shared by others. Hege speaks of the need to appreciate one's good fortune, and hints at the mixed emotions some felt in the post-war world: "In this era of materialism, we should all take the trouble to hold on to a few ideals. We should try to be as happy as our elders were in the past and are today" with the gift of fulfilling work.[50]

Walz tells the audience of the foundation he has set up in his father's memory to look after sick and retired colleagues. He restates his own paternalistic ethos, "always committed to improving the workplace and working conditions", but reminds them that he can "only do all of that if every person connected with the business fulfils his duty with industry and personal commitment." Strikingly, Walz personalises the company's efforts to improve conditions; it is *his* commitment. But he also does not hesitate, even in this celebration, to demand they do *their* duty. He closes his speech on an emotional note that is almost existential, reminding every person there that "they too are a link in the chain, which ties us all together and links us, as members of a company, as citizens of a state, to the protection of our greatest good, our freedom."[51] This

46   Rolf Walz.
47   Herbert Epple, 'Welcome speech by Herr Prokurist Epple' (1960), WABW B4/Bü3.
48   As Kenrick & Jefferson had recently railed against 'irresponsible juniors': Kenrick & Jefferson, 'A Contribution to Office Efficiency by Britain's Business Equippers' (Kenrick & Jefferson, 1952), Sandwell, BS/KJ/2/3/10.
49   Rolf Walz.
50   Kurt Hege, 'Speech by Herr Hege' (1960), WABW B4/Bü3.
51   Rolf Walz.

is a strange juxtaposition of "duty" and freedom, though Armin Grünbacher's evocation of the "authoritarian-patriarchal" management style prevalent at the time in West Germany suggests one interpretation of Walz's standpoint.[52] It seems possible that for Schneider's leadership and older employees, there was an emotional engagement with the company that was founded in something much more fundamental – a consciousness of their good fortune in surviving the war, and of the potential threat posed by the Cold War – than a simple desire to make a living.

As well as honouring the service of others to the business and reminding its present staff of what united him and them, Walz talks at length about what it means to be the company's leader. In a striking section of his speech, he refers to his own position:

> I see my duty as an entrepreneur (*Unternehmer*) as an office which has been entrusted to me by my father, by Fate. Continuity in the succession of bearers of this office must be preserved, and I see myself as but one link in a chain, motivated by the highest consciousness of my responsibility but also by modesty and humility ... the highest duty of the entrepreneur is to guarantee the care of human ties and linkages and entanglements within and without the enterprise.[53]

Walz admitted to his audience that he had not found the assumption of his responsibilities easy on the death of his father. "Breaking off my studies I immediately took on the leadership of the business, but found it difficult to appreciate the overall picture. However I soon managed to get hold of the most significant aspects of it, and in Senior Engineer (*Oberingenieur*) Kurt Hege I found a true and valuable colleague."[54] Rolf Walz's explanation of his inner motivation is borne out in the description of both him and his father by Kurt Hege in his own speech. Speaking of Karl Walz, he recalled a man whose human qualities and abilities as an engineer were respected by all, who possessed

> an enormous energy for work and gave it fully and without limitation to the service of the company ... throughout his working life he never once asked when it was time to stop work, but just carried on until he had finished his task. And for such a man, work really never ends. Such a commitment to work is only really possible at the expense of one's family ... That is the contribution of the entire Walz family.[55]

---

52 Grünbacher, *West German Industrialists and the Making of the Economic Miracle*, p. 106.
53 Rolf Walz.
54 Rolf Walz.
55 Hege, 'Speech by Herr Hege'.

Hege goes on to praise Rolf Walz, who came back from the war with his nerves and health affected, yet had to take on responsibility for the firm without any real preparation for the job, then being immediately faced with the demand to vacate their premises:

> In those days and weeks he showed us all what an entrepreneur is. He took on the entire risk, bought the place in Ludwigsburg, staked his entire fortune, and created this new workplace that we see here today. ... and which, let's be honest, none us ever thought we would see. We can thank his courage, his entrepreneurial spirit and his architectural flair for the clean, bright offices and workshops that we can now work in.[56]

It is possible to discount Hege's admiring words as sycophancy, and Walz's public expression of his own sentiments as self-indulgence. But it is noticeable that at no part of the archive is there any mention of financial motivation, or of a desire to avoid one's obligations. For Rolf Walz himself, there appears to have been a special level of emotional devotion to the workplace. Christel Lane describes "the feeling of common purpose, generated in a professional community" within German firms. Where her analysis appears to differ from Walz's very personal conception is in the sense that while "workers, technical, supervisory and managerial staff see themselves as a professional community, united around particular work tasks and committed to common standards of achievement", it is because they are pragmatically self-interested; it is sensible to co-operate to assure one's own wellbeing, not because one has Walz's sense of a covenant.[57] Yet Lane wrote these words in 1989, and it is possible that they convey the sentiments of the new West Germany of younger employees born since the war more accurately than those of Walz and his staff: younger workers were committed and professional, but did not themselves appreciate the post-war workplace as a haven from earlier suffering or feel, as Walz and entrepreneurs like him did, the need to give one's total emotional engagement.

Company Management up to the death of Rolf Walz in 1967

As well as honouring tradition, Walz appears to have taken positive steps to propel the business forwards. It is appropriate at this point to say something about the company's organisational structure: its legal form, its staffing and

56   Hege, 'Speech by Herr Hege'; Christel Lane comments on the persistence of the term 'Unternehmer' 'with its connotations of risk-taking and creativity' in *Management and Labour in Europe: The Industrial Enterprise in Germany, Britain and France*, p. 88.
57   Lane, *Management and Labour in Europe: The Industrial Enterprise in Germany, Britain and France*, p. 53.

hierarchy, and its management and supervisory arrangements. While the limited-liability company, the *Gesellschaft mit beschrankter Haftung* (GmbH), has been regarded as Germany's "most important legal export" to other countries following its adoption in Germany in the 1890s, it fell out of favour under the Nazis as a desire to limit one's liability was seen to be inimical to the Nazi world-view.[58] Having chosen not to seek any limitation of his own liability, Karl Walz apparently inspired his son to follow suit, adopting in 1954 the *Kommanditgesellschaft* structure, in this case as a Familien-KG, in which the family members' liability was limited to the value of their shareholding, whereas Rolf's own liability was unlimited. The KG legal form dated back to medieval merchant venturers on the Mediterranean: ships' captains whose personal risk was by definition unlimited as they set sail to dangerous places, and who were rewarded with a quarter of all the proceeds if they survived, funded by investors whose own losses would be limited to the amount they had invested in that voyage; the concept is said to have passed from Northern Italy into Southern Germany.[59] Whether Rolf was aware of this history and saw himself as the captain of the Schneider ship, or whether he shared what seemed to be his father's view, that the avoidance of personal liability was somehow dishonourable, is not clear. But it was clear to his staff that Rolf had put literally all he had into the firm, for example betting his "entire fortune" on the success of the new factory in Ludwigsburg.[60]

Rolf Walz also put his trust in the people who worked for him. He changed the company's legal status again in April 1962, for reasons which are not recorded, renaming it J. Schneider KG and continuing in his own role as *Geschäftsführer* and *Komplementär* (the fully liable partner in a limited partnership). He promoted *Oberingenieur* Kurt Hege to *Prokurist* and technical leader. In this capacity, Hege was presumably like other technical directors in German firms, seen by Christel Lane as "invariably more powerful than the commercial director, highlighting the central importance of production in the German enterprise."[61] She shows that the typical German firm had a much flatter hierarchy than its counterparts in Britain and especially in France: on average up to 1980, German companies' ratio of workers to managers and office/technical staff was 71.8%.[62] Only in 1975, its penultimate year, did the ratio at Julius Schneider fall below 80%.[63] Hege's history mentions the

58   Prof Dr Albrecht Cordes et al, *Handwörterbuch zur deutschen Rechtsgeschichte (HRG) - gebundene Ausgabe Band II: Geistliche Gerichtsbarkeit - Konfiskation*, 2nd edn (Berlin: Erich Schmidt Verlag GmbH & Co, 2012), pp. 286–87.

59   Cordes et al, pp. 1966–70.

60   Hege, 'Speech by Herr Hege'.

61   Lane, *Management and Labour*, p. 58.

62   Lane, *Management and Labour*, p. 41.

63   Hege, 'Geschichte', p. 56.

company's *Meister* in several places, and it is to the presence of these highly qualified individuals that Lane and others attribute the flatter hierarchies and smaller workforces of German industrial businesses. With formal education and training for the role, over and above their training in their trade and years of experience, the *Meister* were much more than foremen; responsible for the training of apprentices, for production coordination, and for expert input into technical issues.[64] In these respects, Walz's high regard for his most experienced members of staff was warranted.

Walz also invested in Schneider's facilities, which enabled sales growth, which in turn required additions to the workforce. In 1959, there had been 150 employees in total, twenty-nine of them in staff positions. By 1966, total numbers had grown to 203, with all but six of the additions in the revenue-earning workforce: further evidence of a flat hierarchy and a sensible control of non-earning overheads. The growing workforce delivered steadily increasing sales, which grew from DM6.9 million in 1961 to DM8.2 million in 1965.[65] The search for new, larger contracts inevitably led to the need to invest in facilities which would enable competitive differentiation. Having continued to improve the new buildings, Schneider implemented a new sandblasting facility in 1966 which was "one of the most advanced in southern Germany" to overcome the problem of rusting components being delivered to site. Rolf Walz had come very far, very quickly from the "primitive" conditions of the old Stuttgart yard. But Hege's recollection of this period conveys the pressures which the business, ostensibly in an increasingly fortunate position, now faced: in its new factory, it had the equipment to produce rust-free parts, but immediately had to add roofing to keep the sandblasting material dry. Then, to handle the larger structures in the bigger new contracts they were now winning, the business had to invest in new cranes which would enable them to be moved around the factory. And having spent all of this money, Schneider's management then saw the entire facility become outmoded and have to be replaced by a whole, new automated production line within five years.[66]

Having made these investments and seen its situation improve accordingly, Schneider was hit first by difficulties, then by catastrophe. Several of the *Richtmeister*, the installation foremen, had to retire owing to their age, but the company was able to replace them with "particularly capable riggers". The business managed to achieve a profit of almost DM0.4 million in 1966, representing an after-tax return of 4.8% on sales of almost DM8.1 million. In comparison with their peers, Schneider's performance appears to have been good: while it is not possible to obtain discrete data for the steelwork branch

64 Lane, *Management and Labour*, pp. 42–48. For an appraisal of Meister and their training, see chapter 4 above.
65 Hege, 'Geschichte', p. 56.
66 Hege, 'Geschichte', p. 62.

of the building industry, Schneider's sales of DM40,000 for each of its 203 employees compared favourably with the overall building industry average of DM31,000 (for firms with 100–199 employees) or DM34,000 (200–499 employees), and even more favourably with firms specialising in engineered buildings which averaged DM29,000 and DM34,000 respectively.[67] But recession was already starting to bite, and sales dropped alarmingly to DM5.7 million in 1967, with output tonnage declining by 30%. Financial disaster was only averted thanks to stable personnel costs and the drop in raw material prices, cut by the rolling mills and steel stockholders who were themselves badly hit by the recession, allowing Schneider still to make a very small profit.[68]

Commercial difficulty then turned to catastrophe when, in December 1967, Rolf Walz died at the age of forty-eight after years of precarious health caused by his time in the Gulag.[69] It is not surprising that he was affected by his suffering in Russia: for one prisoner, who returned to Germany two years before him, the "spiritual martyrdom" he suffered would change the remainder of his life.[70] For returnees generally, there was widespread national sympathy, and a consensus in the medical profession that many were suffering from "dystrophy", a pathological condition caused by their experiences in Russia which had led to "the extreme reduction or even complete extinction of physical and psychological capacities."[71] His death could not have happened at a worse time for the recession-stricken business. A change of leadership was necessary, but not straightforward. In the spirit of his sense of covenant, Walz's will specified that one of his children should take over the running of the business, provided that they had completed their commercial or technical training. If they had not, Hege was to take over. As the eldest son was still only fifteen, Hege duly took control and the governance structure of the company was amended; whereas Walz had held personal liability within the family partnership, his position was replaced by a newly formed limited company of which Hege was the sole director: the KG became a GmbH & Co. KG.[72] Other governance changes were made by direction of the county court, holder of the trade register, an

67   Statistisches Bundesamt, 'Baugewerbe', in *Statistisches Jahrbuch Für Die Bundesrepublik Deutschland 1970* (Stuttgart, 1971), pp. 224–30 (p. 227) <http://www.digizeitschriften.de/dms/img/?PID=PPN514402342_1970%7Clog48> [accessed 22 December 2016].

68   Hege, 'Geschichte', pp. 66–67.

69   'Sterbebuch für das Jahr 1967, Band 2, Nr. 551 bis Nr. 1100' (Stadt Ludwigsburg, 1967), Stadtarchiv Ludwigsburg L34/5.

70   Heinz Höhner, *Kriegsgefangen in Sibirien: Erinnerungen eines deutschen Kriegsgefangenen in Russland* (Aachen, 1994), p. 2.

71   Frank Biess, 'Survivors of Totalitarianism: Returning POWs and the Reconstruction of Masculine Citizenship in West Germany, 1945–1955', in *The Miracle Years*, ed. by Hanna Schissler (Princeton and Oxford, 2001), pp. 57–82 (p. 62).

72   'Verfügung Vom 20.12.1968, J. Schneider KG' (Amstgerichts Ludwigsburg, 1968), Staatsarchiv Baden-Württemberg, Ludwigsburg, FL300–31 V / Bü 227.

intervention which demonstrates the strong corporate governance framework within which Mittelstand companies were required to operate.[73]

Investment and growth following recession, 1967 to 1972

As in the past, the company proved resilient, even though it was now without Walz's leadership. As the recession drew to a close, output rose considerably, increasing by 63% to almost 7000 tonnes by the end of 1968 (Schneider's business appears to have fallen further and risen higher than that of the wider industrial-building trade, which first declined by 28% and then rebounded by 57%).[74] With attractive new contracts – Hege gives the example of a 1500 tonne job to build three new halls for Mercedes Benz – the business should now have been able to continue growing.[75] But instead it faced a new difficulty, shared by other companies in the region, and indeed across West Germany and in the UK: a growing shortage of skilled workers. After the fifteen years to 1965 in which per capita output had grown by 5.6% annually in West Germany (versus 2.3% in Great Britain), the economy slowed, but still continued at an average growth rate, even taking into account the recession of 1966–67 and the oil-price induced crisis of 1973–75, of 3.9% per head (versus 2.0% in Great Britain) between 1965 and 1980.[76] As early as 1955, Baden-Württemberg "was particularly pinched by a shortage of labour" as unemployment fell to 2.2%.[77] By 1970, West German unemployment was only 149,000 in a working population of 26.6 million, necessitating the employment of over two million foreign workers.[78] As Schneider's order book grew rapidly – and as the economy as a whole recovered from the short recession to regain growth rates previously seen in the 1950s[79] – every member of Schneider's workforce was required to work extraordinary levels of overtime, leading the company to build a dormitory on the site and recruit twelve Yugoslav workers in 1970.[80] This did not help. Though Stuttgart had the highest proportion of foreign workers of all Germany's major cities, and though

---

73 Amstgerichts Ludwigsburg, Justizoberinspector, 'Registergericht, Form HRA 563, J. Schneider KG' (Amstgerichts Ludwigsburg, 1969), Staatsarchiv Baden-Württemberg, Ludwigsburg, FL300–31 V / Bü 227.

74 Statistisches Bundesamt, p. 229.

75 Hege, 'Geschichte', p. 67.

76 Abelshauser, *Deutsche Wirtschaftsgeschichte*, p. 301 table 14.

77 Mark E. Spicka, 'City Policy and Guest Workers in Stuttgart, 1955–1973.', *German History*, 31.3 (2013), 345–65 (p. 347).

78 Abelshauser, *Deutsche Wirtschaftsgeschichte*, p. 297 table 13.

79 Abelshauser, *Deutsche Wirtschaftsgeschichte*, p. 298.

80 Hege, 'Geschichte', p. 68.

the Yugoslavs were the largest group among them,[81] Hege found them to be of only limited use to the company as it was so difficult to bring any of them up to the required standard of work.[82] There is no archival record of employment-related processes. But the difficulty in achieving a particular standard with the foreign workers suggests not that such individuals necessarily lacked capability – for if they did, how could they have made such significant contributions to other Baden-Württemberg industries, such as machine-building?[83] – but perhaps that they failed to meet the requirements of a managing director who still saw his company is a craft-shop and had perhaps failed to de-skill where it would have been economically sensible, if emotionally undesirable, to do so. Of course, it might also indicate a degree of xenophobia: certainly, Hege seems to have been more committed to young German workers. Though adding apprentices was impossible until 1972 because no young people were willing at a time of full employment to become steel riggers, by 1975 there were six apprentices in the works, joined each year by six to eight interns from technical universities and colleges. In Hege's view, the apprentices "were a very valuable resource in the works and guaranteed the supply of new blood into the skilled workforce."[84]

Despite challenging circumstances and his failure to integrate potentially useful foreign *Gastarbeiter*, then, Julius Schneider apparently continued to prosper under Hege's leadership. Although the most wonderful years of the *Wirtschaftswunder* were now behind them, the West German economy continued to grow at a tempo which in later years would look very attractive: down from 8.8% and 7.2% growth in the 1950 to 1954 and 1955 to 1958 economic cycles respectively, it still attained 3.6%, despite the recession, in 1964 to 1967 and 3.8% between 1968 and 1975; by the late 1990s it was growing at only 1.6%.[85]

As Figure 12 shows, sales and output both grew after Walz's death.[86] But the slowing of economic growth became a concern which would worsen sharply after the oil-price crisis of 1973. Though the company had invested in new lifting equipment, delivery lead times to customers grew from 3–5 to 9–10 months on average between 1969 and 1972. Hege attributes this to the scarcity of steel and the concomitant sharp increase in its cost up to 1971, up by 33%

81   Spicka, 'City Policy', p. 348.
82   Hege, 'Geschichte', p. 68.
83   In Stuttgart/Ludwigsburg and the surrounding area, 'Gastarbeiter' were 45.2% of metalwork-related and 17.8% of building employees in 1969: Reinhold Grotz, *Entwicklung, Struktur und Dynamik der Industrie im Wirtschaftsraum Stuttgart - eine Industriegeographische Unterstutzung*, Stuttgarter Geographische Studien (Stuttgart, 1971), LXXXII, p. 58, table 1.
84   Hege, 'Geschichte', p. 68.
85   Abelshauser, *Deutsche Wirtschaftsgeschichte*, p. 305, Table 15.
86   Compiled by the author from WABW B4/Büı, pp. 66–81.

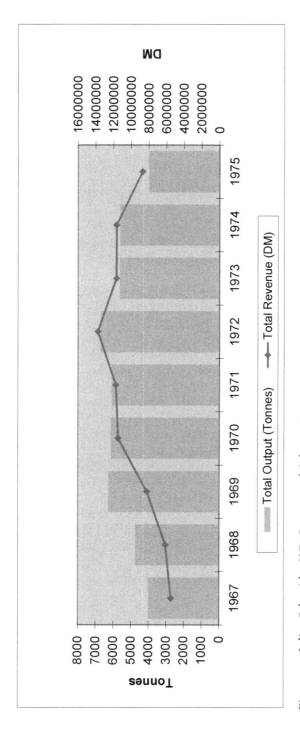

Figure 12 Julius Schneider KG, Output and Sales, 1967–75.

over two years, problems also faced by Braithwaites.[87] Nevertheless, "despite all these difficulties, the years 1969 to 1972 were the best at Schneider since the Second World War." The firm had almost DM850,000 in its deposit accounts and most of its debt, taken on to pay for its new mobile cranes, had been paid back. But it was at this point, according to Hege, that "the good times in the steelwork industry came to an end, and the long shadow of economic crisis began to loom", with the company's ability to fight back compromised by structural issues over and above its recruitment frustrations.[88]

Continuing challenges after 1972 to 1973

In his own analysis of the company's financial evolution, Hege claims that rising costs, particularly in respect to labour, increasingly hampered its ability to increase profits. He depicted the changing relationships between turnover (*Umsatz*), employee costs (*Personalkosten*), materials (*Materialeinsatz*), and overheads (*Gemeinkosten*), as the illustration he produced for his personal history of the company shows in Figure 13.[89]

The graph appears to indicate, though, that neither material costs nor employee costs were terminally destructive: until business began to fall away during the 1974 recession, in fact, the rate of increase in turnover appears to have exceeded that in any cost area, suggesting either that the employees were exceptionally productive or that rising costs were universally recognised within Germany industry, and compensatory price increases were therefore accepted.

In fact, sales growth was achieved at almost all points in the company's history where external economic downturns did not also impact Schneider, as Hege shows in a further analysis in Figure 14.[90]

Production output, which Hege also included in his report, appears to have been more variable than turnover, and is shown in Figure 15. It increased less rapidly from the mid-1950s, suggesting the possibility that Schneider were able to increase the perceived value of their products and command a higher price per tonne of production.[91] The company benefited from the general boom in the building industry, but historian Willi Boelcke's suggestion that overstaffed building firms sought ever-increasing turnover to allay their rising costs offers another interpretation of Schneider's situation.[92]

---

87   Hege, 'Geschichte', p. 71.
88   Hege, 'Geschichte', p. 72.
89   Hege, *Progression of Turnover, Personnel Costs, Materials, Overheads, 1966–75*, in Appendix, 'Geschichte'.
90   Hege, *Sales Turnover, 1910–18, 1931–75*, in Appendix, 'Geschichte'.
91   Hege, *Production Output, 1929–75*, in Appendix, 'Geschichte'.
92   Willi A. Boelcke, *125 Jahre*, pp. 532–33.

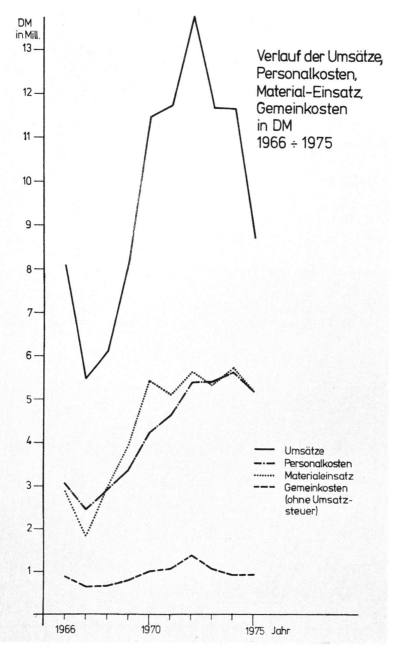

Figure 13 Julius Schneider KG, Progression of Turnover, Personnel Costs, Materials, Overheads, 1966–75. Wirtschaftsarchiv Baden-Württemberg, Stuttgart-Hohenheim (WABW), Bestand B4/Bü1.

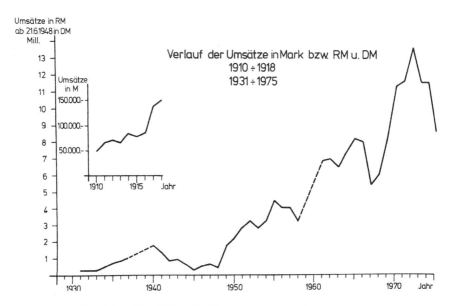

Figure 14 Julius Schneider KG, Sales Turnover, 1910–18, 1931–75.
Wirtschaftsarchiv Baden-Württemberg, Stuttgart-Hohenheim (WABW), Bestand
B4/Bü1.

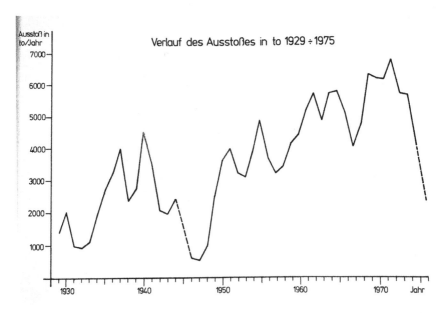

Figure 15 Julius Schneider KG, Production Output, 1929–75. Wirtschaftsarchiv
Baden-Württemberg, Stuttgart-Hohenheim (WABW), Bestand B4/Bü1.

Given rising sales, rising output, and apparently manageable cost increases over two decades, why was the decision taken to close the business in 1976? In an article in the local newspaper in March 1976 entitled "Respected Steelwork Company Will Go Into Voluntary Liquidation in Autumn – Ruinous Competition in its Industry – No Profits for Two Years", much of whose content was subsequently repeated in Hege's company history, it was reported that in 1972 Schneider had had 210 staff, but now had 160; sales had reduced from DM14.5 million to barely DM10 million.[93] Now sixty-one years old and the sole leader of the business (another failure of succession planning), Hege was reported as seeing no further opportunities for the firm, owing to the "murderous competition" which in two years would bring them to bankruptcy unless immediate action were taken. This was an outcome for which Hege was unwilling to be responsible, either to the Walz family or to the firm's staff. He had apparently explained to the family that the industry had 30% too much capacity and many firms had already gone to the wall. Better in these circumstances to close while there was still value in the company, honouring its pension commitments and implementing a redundancy programme for all members of staff.

According to Hege, the problem lay in the general economic situation. Since 1975 there had been a reduction of 50% in factory-building work (*Hallenbau*). Post-war rebuilding was finished, companies were not investing in new buildings, and demand had fallen ruinously. For that reason, all remaining contracts were being fought over by every means possible, and pricing had not covered costs for a long time (as Braithwaites were finding in this same period in Britain). There would be no improvement even if there was a reduction in interest rates, because manufacturers had too much capacity already and so did not need any new buildings. Competition had come not only from within the steel-buildings sector, but also from other sectors and particularly from reinforced concrete companies in response to new fire-prevention regulations, a point he repeated in his subsequent company history. It should be noted, however, that steel-reinforced concrete was not a new arrival – its producers had been represented in the German market by a professional association since 1907,[94] and it is credited by historian Willi Boelcke as being the reason that the region gave priority to completely new buildings rather than the slower renovation of war-damaged stock.[95] It must therefore have been visible as both a threat and a potential means of product diversification for some time before it began to take business away from Schneider. For reasons which are not clear, neither Hege

93 'Angesehene Stahlbaufirma wird im Herbst freiwillig liquidieren', *Ludwigsburger Kreiszeitung* (Ludwigsburg, 24 March 1976), 74 edition, Stadt Ludw SK4.4.2.
94 'DAfStb - Deutscher Ausschuss Für Stahlbeton e. V. – 'Leitbild', *Dafstb* (2022) <http://www.dafstb.de/leitbild.html> [accessed 2 August 2022].
95 Willi A. Boelcke, *125 Jahre*, p. 533.

nor Walz appears to have taken any steps either to adopt reinforced concrete as a new product, or to develop a business relationship with a potential partner which specialised in the competing material.

Although in the newspaper interview he extols Schneider's capabilities, presumably aiming to find a partner willing to take it forward as a going concern, Hege had apparently already found that there was no interest. Rather strangely in such a public statement, he goes on to argue that "as the firm has a completely unique workforce (*einen volkommen anderen Arbeitskräftestamm hat*), the employees, some of whom have been there for thirty years, will not be able to be taken on by anyone else."[96] His meaning in relation to the workforce is not clear: he seems to be saying that as they have their own particular way of working, his workforce are unemployable elsewhere, a limitation which on the face of it says little about his encouragement of flexible skills. He may simply have meant that jobs in their own area of specialism were unavailable. In fact, in relation both to his workforce's employability and to his company's ability to compete, Hege seems to have been too pessimistic. An examination of the city of Ludwigsburg's monthly employment reports reveals that in April 1976, when he announced the need to close the business, there were indeed 6504 unemployed persons in Ludwigsburg, 3.6 per cent of the workforce. However, there were also open vacancies for 350 metal workers and 334 building workers.[97] By September 1976, the steelwork industry was "predominantly satisfied" with workloads. Their only difficulty was their inability to recruit qualified fitters and welders, none of whom could be found amongst the ranks of the currently unemployed.[98] By the end of October, the unemployment rate had fallen to 2.8 per cent and there were over 700 vacancies in the building trade.[99] Within the construction industry nationwide, the short-term difficulties of 1975–76 were quickly alleviated by a "genuine boom" in the building trade, which grew by 25% between mid-1977 and mid-1978. There was significant growth in public-sector building, traditionally an area of strength for Schneider, following the Schmidt government's $8 billion medium-term investment programme: hanging on for twelve to eighteen months might therefore have brought a turnaround in the company's fortunes.[100]

96 'Angesehene Stahlbaufirma wird im Herbst freiwillig liquidieren'.
97 'Der Arbeitsmarkt im Arbeitsamtbezirk Ludwigsburg, April 1976' (Stadt Ludwigsburg, 1976), pp. 2, 4, Stadtarchiv Ludwigsburg, Stadt Ludw L55.
98 'Der Arbeitsmarkt im Arbeitsamtbezirk Ludwigsburg, September 1976' (Stadt Ludwigsburg, 1976), p. 2, Stadtarchiv Ludwigsburg, Stadt Ludw L55.
99 'Der Arbeitsmarkt im Arbeitsamtbezirk Ludwigsburg, Oktober 1976' (Stadt Ludwigsburg, 1976), p. 4, Stadtarchiv Ludwigsburg, Stadt Ludw L55.
100 'West Germany: Construction Boom', *The Economist* (23 September) 1978, p. 97, The Economist Historical Archive.

How did Schneider's competitors fare in this period? A simple contemporary web search carried out in December 2016 found Mittelstand steelwork companies around Stuttgart which were apparently thriving and which grew during the period when Hege declared that it was impossible to continue.[101] A survey of a representative sample of steelwork companies listed in the Baden-Württemberg trade register in December 2016 revealed there had been a total of 387 companies in 1976, 168 of which were still active forty years later. The disappearance of 219 firms from the register suggests that theirs was not an easy industry in which to maintain sustainable profitable performance over an extended period, and that Hege's claims of over-capacity were justified – although it is possible that companies disappeared for positive reasons, including voluntary closure on retirement or amalgamation. However, of the fifty firms still extant in the Stuttgart region, nine had entered the register before Schneider's demise and were still active in late 2016, suggesting that survival may have been challenging, as Hege suggests in his history, but would not have been impossible. Of those nine, six were KGs, but only five other KGs have been registered in the period since 1976. However, of the fifty extant steelwork firms in the Stuttgart region at the time that this analysis was undertaken, thirty-five were limited liability companies (GmbH) formed since the closure of Schneider, suggesting that Rolf Walz's determination to maintain full personal liability was becoming unfashionable during his lifetime and was considered to be unattractively risky by the vast majority of steelwork entrepreneurs who have succeeded him.[102]

Closure, 1976

Despite the theoretical possibility of continuing, Julius Schneider closed in 1976. The filter manufacturer Mann + Hummel GmbH, a longstanding customer and Schneider's next-door neighbour in Ludwigsburg, was constrained by a shortage of space and skilled workers. Schneider's factory offered the required space. Hege's pessimism regarding the employability of his staff turned out to be doubly inappropriate: the building and steelwork trades actually needed their skills, as evidenced in the city's employment data archives, and Mann +

101   See, for example, 'Unternehmen - Stahlbau OTT Kirchheim Unter Teck' <http://www.stahlbau-ott.de/unternehmen/> [accessed 31 December 2016]; 'Daten & Fakten' (2016) <http://schreiberstahlbau.de/de/unternehmen/daten-fakten.html> [accessed 31 December 2016]; 'Unternehmen | Stahlbau Nägele' <http://stahlbau-naegele.de/unternehmen/> [accessed 31 December 2016].
102   Survey conducted by the author of 'Currently or Previously Registered Companies Whose Name Includes "Stahlbau" in Baden-Wuerttemberg', Common Register Portal of the German Federal States (2016) < https://www.handelsregister.de/rp_web/welcome.xhtml> [accessed 29 December 2016].

Hummel also took one hundred Schneider employees onto their own payroll with seniority from the start of their employment with Schneider.[103]

It is easy to be critical of Hege with the benefit of hindsight. Though the analysis he presented in his company history seems to indicate that the company's financial situation was on average improving between 1966 and 1973, during 1974/5 it had begun to deteriorate dramatically and in reality was rather worse than he had conveyed in the newspaper interview. Expenses increased in all areas, especially employee costs: whereas turnover increased by 44%, average price per ton by 35.9%, and average material costs by 54.9%, the annual average cost per employee rose by almost 120%. Schneider's payroll had grown from 203 employees in 1966 costing just under DM15,000 each to 171 employees costing almost DM33,000 each by 1974, with an increase of almost DM3300 or 11% between 1973 and 1974 alone.[104] This aggressive increase was reflective of the situation across West Germany as a whole: although firms' payrolls had grown in the past, their employees' wages had increased roughly in line with the growth in the income of self-employed people. Between 1970 and 1977, though, the income of self-employed workers grew by 78.5% – a sharp enough rise in itself, but for the first time significantly different from the 93% increase in the wages of employees, whose changing situation reflected the shift in relations between employee and employer and the increasing strength of organised labour.[105] Unfortunately we have almost no archival records of union activity at Schneider, but it is inconceivable that in a tight labour market pay demands within the business were not adversely affected by the soaring wage rates beyond its gates.

Although Hege and his team seem to have continued to fight hard, they were in a losing battle: almost all of the fifteen new contracts for important customers – each over one hundred tonnes, each technically interesting, each further securing the good reputation of Schneider – were loss-making.[106] In early 1975, Hege cut headcount in a bid to reduce employment costs and put his staff onto short-time working for six weeks, "but there were simply no longer any contracts available which could be won at prices that covered [the company's] costs." Much more fundamentally, by December 1975 Schneider's two banks, both local, "were no longer willing to offer long-term support and suggested that we liquidate the firm while there was still value in its assets",

103   Gerd Heimisch, *75 Years of Mann + Hummel / 1941–2016* (Ludwigsburg: Mann + Hummel GmbH, 2015), p. 109 <https://www.mann-hummel.com/content/dam/mann-hummel-group/communication-media/historical/Chronicle%20MANN+HUMMEL_EN_2015.pdf> [accessed 15 November 2016].
104   Hege, 'Geschichte', p. 76.
105   Abelshauser, *Deutsche Wirtschaftsgeschichte*, pp. 344–45.
106   Hege, 'Geschichte', p. 77.

though the "house bank", the *Stuttgarter Volksbank*, did offer its support during the winding-up period.[107]

Having agreed with the Walz family that the business could not be saved, Hege worked with the directors of Mann + Hummel to create an employee-transfer plan within the framework of an asset takeover. He then worked with the IG Metall representatives (unlike Braithwaite, Schneider had only one union) and an official of the Metal Industry Association (*Verband der Metallindustrie*) (both demonstrating the ongoing support of institutions to businesses in their industry, but neither mentioned at other points in the archival records) to formulate a social plan which paid up to DM13,000 in redundancy and which, with the support of the Walz Foundation, guaranteed all existing and impending company pensions. Strikingly, he chose to honour all outstanding contracts and to keep the employees busy for the whole of their six-month notice period, a joint commitment which was recognised by the award of large contracts in the company's final few months by several sympathetic, longstanding major customers, including Daimler-Benz and Miele, totalling over DM2 million.[108] In what might be seen as the ultimate irony, weeks after its closure Schneider was awarded a national prize for Germany's outstanding steel-framed building.

Faced at the time with the challenges posed by his own age and approaching retirement – by depressed contract prices caused by supplier over-capacity and customer retrenchment; by constantly rising wage costs; by the end of the *Wirtschaftswunder* and recent economic difficulties – Hege concluded that in both its dying days and its earlier life, "the company had made a good name for itself throughout its industry and across its customer base thanks to its tidy and scrupulous work and its respectable and serious leadership."[109] Thus his own legacy as an engineer and as Schneider's final leader was secured. For observers who consider longevity to be ultimate determinant of a company's success, Schneider's closure must be viewed as a negative outcome. Hege had failed to foresee and deflect the threat of new materials. The building trade and economy both soon grew again, as the motor industry had grown again following precipitate mismanagement by RECARO's leaders. Though a vacuum had been caused by the premature death of Schneider's owner, that had been nine years earlier. There should have been time enough to prepare appropriate candidates for management succession even if Andreas Walz, now aged twenty-four, or his siblings were uninterested in the family legacy.

Others might conclude that the company's demise was as skilfully managed as its operations had been throughout its 66-year history. Having survived two world wars, Julius Schneider's owners and managers had adroitly managed

---

107 Hege, 'Geschichte', pp. 81–82.
108 Hege, 'Geschichte', pp. 83–88.
109 Hege, 'Geschichte', p. 88.

its successful growth during the *Wirtschaftswunder* decades, creating and maintaining a reputation for product excellence. The decision to close the company was arrived at rationally, its external relationships managed respectfully, and its employees treated compassionately, the majority of them transitioning into employment at a highly reputable company with no loss to themselves and the remainder being given generous redundancy packages. In its termination as in its life, Julius Schneider was managed in a way that was consistent with Mittelstand values of respect for all its stakeholders.

8

Braithwaite & Co. (Engineers) Ltd., West Bromwich

Company Origins and Pre-1945 History

Braithwaite & Co. (Engineers) Ltd. (hereafter, Braithwaites) was established in 1884 in West Bromwich. It was eventually run from head offices in London, then Surrey, with staff there and at factories in Newport (making water tanks and supporting towers) and West Bromwich (for steel structures and associated construction work), selling at home and overseas. The West Bromwich site was closed in 1979, and the group radically transformed in the 1980s. This chapter deals primarily with West Bromwich and the group's management in the period between the end of the Second World War and the site's closure in 1979. But it begins with a discussion of its interwar activities, firstly because they set the pattern for its post-war culture, and secondly because the same man led the business in both periods.

Braithwaites was originally a local Black Country engineering company. Although his son and grandson, his successors as the company's chairmen, based themselves in London, James Hulse Humphryes was a Black Country native. Born in Wednesbury in 1869, Humphryes appears to have been a self-made man of exceptional ability, like his near-contemporary Frederick Jefferson of Kenrick & Jefferson. Humphryes attended a local grammar school and the Technical Schools in West Bromwich and Manchester. After an apprenticeship at Braithwaites, he progressed from draughtsman to director of a Manchester engineering business before he returned to Braithwaites as a partner in 1912. He was committed to workplace innovation, presenting a paper on workshop productivity improvements to the Manchester Association of Engineers in 1902.[1] While running Braithwaites, he was granted ten patents and became a council member of both the Federation of British Industry and the British Engineers Association.[2]

---

1 'Manchester Association of Engineers', *The Manchester Guardian* (Manchester, 8 December 1902), p. 3.
2 Espacenet, accessed 9 November 2015.

After successes, especially in India, over several years, Humphryes separated from his partner to take Braithwaites forward on his own in 1921. He constructed the deal cleverly,[3] with the much larger steel and fabrications company Dorman, Long as principal investor and Sir Arthur Dorman, KBE, as chairman.[4] Their presence, and quick departure, showed how astute Humphryes was: he took on the new business with a financially strong partner whose reputation enhanced his own, and with which he needed amicable relations over the long term.[5] After their departure, he secured his position at the head of the new company,[6] retaining it after floating Braithwaites as a public company in 1927.[7] In doing so, he epitomised the prevailing thinking that "families making flotations ensured that they held equity, with its attendant voting rights, so the extent to which ownership and control was divorced, even in public companies, was distinctly limited."[8]

Despite this clever financial practice, it is notable that the new "public" company's directors – who included Humphryes' son – were all listed as engineers;[9] though Humphryes had moved away from his Black Country roots, this was not to be a financial holding company but an engineering business, with numerous impressive projects done and in hand and a combined works capacity of 50,000 tons a year.[10] James Hulse Humphryes died unexpectedly in May 1927.[11] As the Institution of Mechanical Engineers' obituary writer said, Humphryes' "eminent position was gained after a thorough engineering

3 'Agreement for Sale of Business – James Hulse Humphries to Braithwaite & Co. Engineers Ltd.' (1921), Companies House, archive disk 00175912–02.

4 Braithwaite & Co. Engineers Limited, 'Memorandum of Association, Braithwaite & Co. Engineers Limited' (Braithwaite & Co. Engineers Limited, 1921), Companies House, archive disk 00175912–01.

5 'Dorman, Long & Co', *The Times* (London, England, 11 December 1924), p. 24, The Times Digital Archive.

6 'Special Resolution of Braithwaite & Co. Engineers, 19/11/1924' (Companies House, 1924), Companies House, archive disk 00175912–02; 'Special Resolution of Braithwaite & Co. Engineers, 8/5/1925' (Companies House, 1925), Companies House, archive disk 00175912–02.

7 'Revised Articles of Association' (Companies House, 1927), Companies House, archive disk 00175912–02.

8 Andrea Colli and Mary B. Rose, 'Families and Firms: The Culture and Evolution of Family Firms in Britain and Italy in the Nineteenth and Twentieth Centuries', *Scandinavian Economic History Review*, 47.1 (1999), 24–47 (p. 37).

9 Listed in Braithwaite & Co. Engineers Limited, 'Prospectus: Issue of 150,000 7 1/2 per Cent. Cumulative Preference Shares of £1 Each, at Par.' (Braithwaite & Co. Engineers Limited, 1927), Companies House, archive disk 00175912–03.

10 Braithwaite & Co. Engineers Limited, 'Prospectus Issue of 150,000 7 1/2 per Cent. Cumulative Preference Shares'.

11 'Deaths - James Hulse Humphryes.', *The Times* (London, England, 26 May 1927), p. 1, The Times Digital Archive.

experience."[12] He was a forward-thinking, creative and ambitious engineer, whose technical understanding was matched by his commercial astuteness. He was also well-rewarded for his expertise, leaving £212,000 (some £12 million in 2018 values) at his death.[13]

The chairman of the new public company was his son James Harvey Humphryes who, having only just reached the age of twenty-nine, clearly faced a considerable challenge.[14] But he was confident. In the 1930 publication *Britain's Message to the Empire from the Air*, the company assured readers that "Braithwaites will go anywhere and do anything that has Structural Engineering connected with it." Its successes to that point make impressive reading even now: a 110-mile pipeline in India, for which they had built a works on a green-field site to save on shipping costs; 20,000 tons of steel plates shipped from Newport to Sao Paolo for its new aqueduct, assembled in a purpose-built factory that was then levelled and returned to nature; five deep-water wharves at Calcutta.[15]

The inevitable question regarding Braithwaites' export performance was whether it depended on Imperial preference rather than on the genuine international competitiveness that was required of its German and other international competitors. Many of the contracts awarded prior to World War Two *were* won in countries of the Empire – although they could also point to contract wins in Iraq and Argentina.[16] But the projects they and others completed were, irrespective of the geo-political-commercial influences involved, innovative and brilliantly executed. Humphryes urged co-industrialists that for "their own contribution to recovery they must continue to critically examine and investigate every field for the expansion of the new uses of steel."[17] This, it turned out, would not be straightforward: two years later, Humphryes had reason to deplore the failure of the steel manufacturing industry to "set its house in

12   'James Hulse Humphryes - Obituary', *Institution of Mechanical Engineers – Obituaries* (May 1927), p. 583 <http://www.gracesguide.co.uk/James_Hulse_Humphryes> [accessed 9 November 2015].
13   'RECENT WILLS - James Hulse Humphryes'; <https://measuringworth.com/calcu-lators/ukcompare> [accessed 9.1.2019].
14   Braithwaite & Co. Engineers Limited, 'Form 9, Particulars of Directors and Secretaries' (Braithwaite & Co. Engineers Limited, 1948), Companies House, archive disk 00175912–03.
15   Air League of the British Empire, '1930 Industrial Britain: Braithwaite and Co. Engineers', in *Industrial Britain. Britain's Message to the Empire from the Air* (London: Albion Publishing Co. Ltd., 1930), 1: ENGINEERING, MOTOR AND AIRCRAFT INDUSTRIES <http://www.gracesguide.co.uk/1930_Industrial_Britain:_Braithwaite_and_Co_Engineers> [accessed 3 November 2015].
16   'Braithwaite & Co., Engineers, Limited: Report on 1934 AGM', *The Times* (London, England, 3 October 1934), p. 19, *The Times* Digital Archive.
17   'Progress In Steel Construction', *The Times* (London, England, 5 November 1932), p. 6, The Times Digital Archive.

order", as manufacturers of steel structures were hindered by high raw material prices and deriving no benefit themselves from reformed tariffs.[18] Braithwaites would continue to suffer from failings in Britain's steel industry for the next forty years.

As chairman of the British Steelwork Association and in other appointments, Humphryes displayed remarkable maturity for a young man barely thirty years old.[19] In his public speeches, he embodied a commitment to industry growth which characterised his direction of his own business. His leadership was tested in 1930s, as Braithwaites' situation was affected by prevailing economic conditions. During 1931, board minutes reveal, work was lost despite specially low pricing,[20] and closure plans were discussed.[21] By May 1935, the company's overdraft was up to £80,000 against a limit of £75,000. However, "a letter from the Manager of the Bank was read, in which he anticipated no difficulty in obtaining sanction for an increased limit up to £90,000." No doubt his decision was guided by his faith in the company and its prospects; the preceding item in the minutes, recording that "a canteen of cutlery had been presented to Mr. Robinson on behalf of the Company on his retirement from the post of Manager of Lloyds Bank, West Bromwich", seems to have been mentioned without any sense of irony or embarrassment.[22] It appeared that no matter how straitened the circumstances, Braithwaites would courteously preserve relationships, and would continue fighting hard to win new business. In the board meeting of 13 July 1938, for example, with their highest-ever overdraft looming, he and his directors approved twenty-seven tenders for UK and overseas work, and reviewed another eighteen papers, mostly relating to overseas contracts.[23]

Another interpretation of their performance in this period suggests itself in the archives of Dorman, Long: that Braithwaites' board managed the

18 'Braithwaite & Co., Engineers, Ltd.', *The Times* (3 October 1934), p. 19.

19 Department of Scientific and Industrial Research, *Steel Structures Research; Verbatim Proceedings of a Conference Presided over by Sir Clement Hindley, on 16th October, 1930.* (London: HMSO, 1930) <http://babel.hathitrust.org/cgi/pt?id=coo.31924004638007;view=1up;seq=7> [accessed 14 October 2015].

20 Minutes of 12 February 1931 meeting. Braithwaite & Co. Engineers Limited, 'Board of Directors' Meetings, 9 October 1930 to 17 March 1932.' (Braithwaite & Co. Engineers Limited, 1932), Sandwell, BS-B1/1/1.

21 Minutes for 1 October 1931 meeting. Braithwaite & Co. Engineers Limited, 'Board of Directors' Meetings, 9 October 1930 to 17 March 1932.'

22 Minute for the meeting of 24 May 1935. Braithwaite & Co. Engineers Limited, 'Board of Directors' Meetings, April 1932 to August 1936.' (Braithwaite & Co. Engineers Limited, 1936), Sandwell, BS-B1/1/2.

23 Minutes for 13 July 1938 meeting. Braithwaite & Co. Engineers Limited, 'Board of Directors' Meetings, September 1936 to April 1940.' (Braithwaite & Co. Engineers Limited, 1940), Sandwell, BS-B1/1/4.

company's relationships in a way which might later make them vulnerable. Braithwaites are shown to have approached the South Durham Iron and Steel Company with an offer to "protect" their prices on a contract, in exchange for a £5000 payment which would be shared between Braithwaite, Dorman, Long and another company.[24] In other correspondence, Dorman, Long were told that Braithwaites underbid them in Argentina, whose government was willing to favour British firms to foster links with the UK.[25] These situations suggest either that Braithwaites were alive to international opportunities, sharp-witted, and more nimble than the larger, more bureaucratic Dorman, Long; or that they were shielded from true international competition by geopolitical factors, were unwisely aggressive in their international pricing, and would resort to price-fixing if necessary. The latter approach portended problems in a changing post-war world.

Post-war Business Activity 1945 to 1979

Introduction: Company Chairmen
Given the Humphryes family's domination of Braithwaites, it makes sense to divide the review of post-war activities into the two periods they controlled as its chairmen. The first ends with the retirement of James Harvey Humphryes (James) in 1971. The second covers the accession of his son James Anthony (Tony) to the chairmanship until the closure of the West Bromwich works in late 1979. As we have seen above, James Harvey Humphryes was, by the age of forty, an experienced and dynamic chairman who had led Braithwaites through difficult pre-war circumstances. He went on to manage its wartime work building tank hulls and Bailey bridges, and then progressed into a successful post-war business career. Thereafter, he continued winning. Little can be discovered of his personal life or background from the archive or other sources, other than that he was a member of two professional engineering bodies. He had a public school education at Dulwich College, demonstrating his father's desire to move upwards socially, and had served in the First World War.[26] He remained chairman until 1971, and the minutes reveal a man who was intelligent, decisive, orderly, technically proficient, not afraid to be confrontational, but who also looked after his staff. Alternative perspectives on his

24 'Correspondence Relating to North Wales Power Co. Dolgarrog Extension' (Dorman, Long & Co. Ltd., 1935), Teesside Archives, Middlesbrough, BS.DL/3/2/1/5/30.
25 'File Relating to Contract for Riachuelo Bridge, Argentina' (Dorman, Long & Co. Ltd., 1935), Teesside Archives, Middlesbrough, BS.DL/3/2/1/5/30.
26 'Who's Who In Engineering: Name H', Who's Who In Engineering 1939 (1939) <https://www.gracesguide.co.uk/1939_Who%27s_Who_In_Engineering:_Name_H> [accessed 10 January 2019].

personality and performance are not available. Unlike his father, he did not die a very rich man as a result of his five decades at Braithwaite: at £144,693, his 1981 estate was worth no more than £1 million in 2018 values.[27]

A dynamic second-generation leader following the founding father often does well and can take a business to the next level of success. Conversely, received wisdom suggests that as the third-generation leader, James Anthony (Tony) Humphryes, born in 1927, would be most likely to waste his predecessors' achievements. In fact, he appeared from an early age to have shared his father's and grandfather's intelligence and drive, and their desire to retain command of the family firm. His father apparently used the wealth generated by the company to further distance his family from their Black Country roots, sending Tony to Harrow.[28] But his performance there suggested that James Hulse's qualities had reached the third generation: Tony showed leadership qualities, as Head of School, and captain of Rugby and shooting. He was also bright, a Rothschild Scholar who went to Pembroke College, Cambridge,[29] graduating with a BA in Engineering in 1950 after service as an officer in the Coldstream Guards.[30] In his university file, a letter from his Harrow housemaster describes him as "a very good fellow and a good citizen" whose "ultimate destination is probably the family business." His comment that Humphryes was "competent at his work without being a scholar" is apparently contradicted by a supplementary note which describes him as "alpha + or at any rate a good alpha."[31] Tony seems to have thought ahead for Braithwaites' benefit, taking papers in Civil Structures, Surveying and Geology, and Hydraulics.[32] A year after graduating, he was also awarded a certificate of proficiency in engineering studies by the university.[33]

27 'Probate: James Harvey Humphryes', *Find a Will* <https://probatesearch.service.gov.uk> [accessed 4 December 2015] and <https://measuringworth.com/calculators/ukcompare>. It is of course possible that he gave away more of his wealth before his death.

28 With the other former pupils of Eton, Rugby or Harrow who made up 21% of British industrialists in the period 1960–70, according to Isabelle Lescent-Giles, 'Les Elites Industrielles Britanniques: 1880–1970', *Historie, Economie et Societe*, 17.1 (1998), 157–88 (p. 171).

29 'News in Brief - Harrow School', *The Times* (London, England, 26 September 1945), p. 7, The Times Digital Archive; 'News in Brief - Harrow Speech Day', *The Times* (London, England, 28 June 1946), p. 6, The Times Digital Archive; email to David Paulson from Harrow School Archivist, 'RE: Enquiry Re Old Harrovian', 17 November 2015.

30 'Foot Guards', *Supplement to the London Gazette* (London, England, 7 November 1947), p. 5240 <https://www.thegazette.co.uk/London/issue/38117/supplement/5240/data.pdf> [accessed 1 November 2015].

31 Email to David Paulson from Hon. Archivist, Pembroke College, Cambridge, J.S. Ringrose, 'J.A. Humphryes', 24 November 2015. By permission of the Master and Fellows of Pembroke College, Cambridge.

32 'Examination in Engineering Studies, Michaelmas Term 1951 - Section II', in *Cambridge University Reporter* (Cambridge: Cambridge University Press, 1951), MMMDCCLX, 218.

33 Ringrose.

It was clear that James Hulse Humphryes had made possible a significant achievement of social mobility, moving his family's aspirations from an apprenticeship in Wednesbury to Harrow, Cambridge and the Brigade of Guards in little over fifty years. The social "achievement" (for those who see it that way) seems unquestionable. The question in due course would be, as his career progressed, whether Tony's performance in the family firm would substantiate Tom Nicholas's finding that "an education in the upper echelons of the British system – at a Clarendon school or an Oxbridge college – was associated with negative rates of return to entrepreneurship"[34] or instead would reflect Hartmut Berghoff's contention, in relation to his grandfather's generation, that "entrepreneurs who had been to public school were very likely to enlarge their families' fortunes."[35] His succession exemplified criticism which was aired by A.P. Young in his 1949 speech, referred to in Chapter 4 above, made close to Braithwaites' West Bromwich works: "Unfortunately, in British industry ... top management is cluttered up by the owner-manager complex, where the owner of the business is so often the manager; and sons and grandsons rise to the top in apostolic succession, often regardless of whether they have either the ability or the desire to manage the business."[36] The post-war years would reveal whether Tony – and indeed his father – had either.

Business Performance, 1945 to 1971

Operational Management

Braithwaites performed effectively throughout the 1950s. In the period 1954 to 1959, pre-tax profits averaged £143,000 in contemporary values.[37] But by December 1959 the Group was experiencing economic strain, despite winning substantial contracts such as the Tasman Bridge in Hobart, in which it was a

34   Nicholas, p. 707.

35   Hartmut Berghoff, 'Public Schools and the Decline of the British Economy 1870–1914', *Past & Present*, 129.1 (1990), 148–67, p. 166.

36   Young, '"The Foreman and Works Management": Speech to the Institute of Works Managers, Smethwick'.

37   Data extracted from annual reports recorded in the following pages (on which Braithwaite was not always the headline report): 'Braithwaite & Co. Engineers Ltd.', *The Economist* (London, 6 October 1956), p. 94, The Economist Historical Archive; 'Braithwaite & Co. Engineers Ltd.', *The Economist* (London, 5 October 1957), p. 83, The Economist Historical Archive; 'Anglo-Ceylon & General Estates - Braithwaite & Company Engineers Limited - Wm. Cory & Son Limited.', *The Economist* (London, 3 October 1959), p. 82, The Economist Historical Archive; 'Volkswagenwerk G.m.b.H. - The Calico Printers' Association Ltd. - A.C. Cossor - The Tor Investment Trust Limited - Gold Mines of Kalgoorlie - Braithwaite & Co. Engineers Ltd. - Hecht, Levis & Kahn - Pye Ltd. - British Homophone', *The Economist* (London, 4 October 1958), p. 91ff., The Economist Historical Archive.

44% partner, and submitting a £400,000 tender bid for steelwork for the Thorpe Marsh power station in 1961/2. Their expectation of profits for the current year was £40,000, with the possibility that this would increase by £10,000 to £20,000: enquiries were increasing in number and prices were hardening.[38] Characteristically, Humphryes did not let the business accept the status quo. Two directors were examining ways in which overhead could be reduced at the Surrey office and at both manufacturing plants, and the company, whose accounts were £88,000 overdrawn, had got the support of Lloyds Bank, which had offered to back its Hobart project.[39]

As it turned out, matters did not quickly get better. In his address to the 1962 AGM, Humphryes offered a picture of a difficult trading environment, in which Braithwaites seems to have been as well managed as it could have been in the circumstances.[40] He and his managers appear to have managed the international business effectively. In Tasmania and Ireland, projects including the technically challenging Hobart Bridge were progressing well.[41] Projects in India and Turkey were also reviewed. Growth was a priority: to pursue more export business, the company was to send executives abroad to meet agents and customers. Domestically, business was more difficult. In 1960, low margins and a dearth of work had forced them to accept unattractive margins to retain skilled labour, though they had supplemented pensions at both works.[42] In 1961, a recession in the steel industry had resulted in a reduced order book and forced Braithwaites to accept contracts at low prices. In response, Humphryes reported to shareholders, management had reorganised, made economies in all areas, and instituted a planned early retirement programme. Combined with improved trading conditions, including work on Sizewell B and West Burton power stations, this had allowed them to get back into profit. He was anxious to avoid making further reductions in the labour force, as the company had done in 1959/60 during another difficult period, with consequent losses in labour efficiency.[43]

Given these general concerns, and the problems with specific issues which are reviewed separately below, management in the 1960s, despite the measured

---

38   Minutes for meeting of 18 December 1959. Braithwaite & Co. Engineers Limited, 'Board of Directors' Meetings, 4 September 1963 to 29 May 1968.' (Braithwaite & Co. Engineers Limited, 1968), Sandwell, BS-B1/1/9.

39   Minutes for meeting of 2 December 1959. Braithwaite & Co. Engineers Limited, 'Board of Directors' Meetings, 4 September 1963 to 29 May 1968.'

40   'Braithwaite & Co. Engineers Limited: Report on 1962 AGM', *The Times* (London, England, 28 September 1962), p. 21, The Times Digital Archive.

41   Anon, 'Hobart Bridge, Tasmania', *The Engineer* (15 January 1960), 102 <http://www.gracesguide.co.uk/images/b/be/Er19600115.pdf> [accessed 19 October 2015].

42   'Braithwaite & Co. Engineers Limited. Mr. J. Harvey Humphryes's Review of Activities', *The Times* (London, England, 23 September 1960), p. 25, The Times Digital Archive.

43   'Braithwaite & Co. Engineers Limited: Report on 1962 AGM'.

tones of the Board's Minute Book, must have frequently been a test of nerve. A review of events during and after 1963 gives a sense of the challenges faced in managing a British engineering company during this period. At the 1963 AGM, Humphryes announced that the outlook was better but still not good. Improvements discussed the previous year had been achieved, and the order book was improving, with a 6000-ton order for transmission towers. However, "the current year's results were likely to be affected by the necessity of accepting orders at unusually low prices."[44] Orders for 1000 tons of steelwork had been booked in a six-week period in July and August 1963, but "at cut prices in order to assist in filling the gap in production." For the following months, the outlook "was not very bright and work was badly needed", but the company was having to wait for the start of the Fiddlers Ferry and Aberthaw power station contracts, as well as for more transmission line tower orders. These commercial uncertainties created a cash book deficit which was projected to reach or exceed the £600,000 overdraft facility several times over the next six months.[45]

Though Humphryes adopted a positive tone in his 1963 AGM speech, he admitted that orders had been won at "prices which in normal times would not [have been] contemplated" and which would colour the company's performance during the year to come.[46] The situation seemed to improve over the next two years, however. In the Board meeting of 18 November 1965, directors were told that the "West Bromwich fabrication programme provided full production over the period up to the end of January 1967 at which date there would be approximately 10,000 tons of steel to be fabricated, i.e. 7000 tons for Pembroke Power Station and 3000 for Dungeness Power Station." Regrettably, the "labour position had improved somewhat in October but had become more difficult again in November."[47] The minutes do not tell us what the "labour position" was, but several problems had presented themselves in recent years, from labour shortages at West Bromwich through to union-led militancy and poor productivity on power station construction sites. Any of these must have presented a challenge. Nevertheless, in the September 1966 AGM, Humphryes was able to report "that the trading profit achieved for the year ended March 31, 1966 was the highest achieved in the company's history", and that he "looked forward

44   Anon, 'Braithwaite & Co.: Statement of 1963 Results', *The Times* (London, England, 3 September 1963), p. 17, The Times Digital Archive.
45   Minutes of 23 October 1963 meeting. Braithwaite & Co. Engineers Limited, 'Board of Directors' Meetings, 4 September 1963 to 29 May 1968.'
46   'BRAITHWAITE & CO. ENGINEERS LIMITED: Annual General Meeting', *The Guardian (1959–2003)* (Manchester, London, 27 September 1963), p. 17.
47   Braithwaite & Co. Engineers Limited, 'Board of Directors' Meetings, 4 September 1963 to 29 May 1968.'

to this level of profitability being maintained in the current financial year."[48] The business had won "considerable tonnages" for Fiddlers' Ferry and Cottam power stations, and for another in India. But Humphryes raised a note of caution in relation to the Government's prevailing prices and incomes standstill: "Any cut-back or postponement in placing orders for capital equipment may well affect the Company's trading in the long term. This [would] be particularly disappointing after the great efforts that had been made to recover from the effects of the 1960, 1961 recession in the steel fabricating industry."[49]

As the decade ended, Braithwaites were able to report another record year for profits at the 48th AGM. Orders for "substantial tonnages" of motorway bridgework had been won; there was ongoing volume of orders for pressed steel tanks; they had won an export order for steelwork for a US aluminium plant. Humphryes anticipated in his 1969 chairman's statement that the output of bridgework and other construction-related material would be maintained, though "the future of the industry remained uncertain."[50] A year later, he welcomed "the resumption in the Central Electricity Generating Board's power station programme and looked forward to being able to renew participation in that class of work."[51] On the face of it, his company had prospered reasonably well during the 1960s, in several years achieving its highest-ever profits. He had continued to win orders overseas, and had taken the business into Britain's motorway- and power station-building programmes with apparent success. His shareholders had received an annual dividend of at least 8.28% since 1964, on two occasions receiving 12%.[52] Yet at each annual meeting he seemed at pains to express a closing note of pessimism. The following review of some of the particular challenges Braithwaites faced will help us to appreciate whether his pessimism was justified.

48   Neither the Minutes, nor the press, nor the Companies House archive reveals the actual profit figure.
49   'BRAITHWAITE & CO. ENGINEERS LIMITED: Annual General Meeting - ProQuest', *The Guardian (1959–2003)* (Manchester, London, 22 September 1966), p. 13; 'Boardroom News - Braithwaite Engineers', *The Guardian (1959–2003)* (Manchester, London, 30 August 1966), p. 11; *The Times* (London, England, 22 September 1966), p. 18, The Times Digital Archive.
50   'Company Meeting', *The Times* (London, England, 26 September 1969), p. 23, The Times Digital Archive.
51   'Company Meeting', *The Times* (London, England, 25 September 1970), p. 25, The Times Digital Archive.
52   *The Stock Exchange Official Year-Book 1979–80*, ed. by Jeffrey Russell Knight (East Grinstead, 1979), p. 767.

Personnel Challenges

Recruitment and Retention

In the absence of personnel records other than individual workers' index cards, it is difficult to understand the detail of Braithwaites' recruitment and retention activities. Given the complexity of some of their engineering work, investing in staff at all levels was clearly important and we know that like other companies in both the West Midlands and Baden-Württemberg, Braithwaites struggled throughout this period to overcome skill shortages. But we will see that in their approach to the recruitment and support of engineers, Braithwaites contradicted the view that engineering in Britain was "a Cinderella profession", and that formal engineering training was not a prerequisite for advancement into management, as it was in West Germany.[53]

Problems began soon after the Second World War. In reports to the joint general managers of the Structural division in 1949, managers complained of an ongoing staff shortage, despite increasing wages and offering more overtime,[54] and in 1950 the management committee had apprenticeship brochures sent into local schools as a matter of urgency.[55] By then the company was already supporting employees who wished to study engineering at Birmingham University. The two staff members who were students in 1950 were "making very good progress", and the management team were keen to draw the attention of all West Bromwich staff "to the provision of the facility for Employees of the Company to obtain scholarships to Birmingham University."[56] The company seems to have had an enlightened attitude and openness to others' ideas, as well as a commitment to professional qualifications and memberships. In 1958, the management committee reviewed plans to recruit staff at three levels: works trainees, drawing office trainees, and graduates. They intended to recruit "good quality graduate staff", visiting Cambridge University and offering training to two engineering graduates, as well as committing to future participation in a post-graduate scheme at Imperial College. Despite Braithwaites' commitment,

---

53   Robert Millward, 'Industrial and Commercial Performance since 1950', in *The Economic History of Britain Since 1700. Volume 3: 1939–1992*, ed. by Roderick Floud and Deirdre McCloskey (Cambridge, 1994), pp. 123–67 (pp. 149–50).

54   Reports of 29 August and 28 September 1949, appended to JGM meeting minutes. Braithwaite & Co. Engineers Limited, 'Minutes of Joint General Managers'' Meetings, 21 January 1949 to 13 May 1952.'

55   Minutes of 14 June 1950 meeting. Braithwaite & Co. Engineers Limited, 'Minutes of Joint General Managers'' Meetings, 21 January 1949 to 13 May 1952.'

56   Minutes of 10 August 1950 meeting. Braithwaite & Co. Engineers Limited, 'Minutes of Joint General Managers'' Meetings, 21 January 1949 to 13 May 1952.'

graduate engineers proved difficult to find. Headhunters had been engaged after the company failed to recruit a chief designer, but they also failed.[57]

Ironically, but unavoidably given a downturn in business and all prices being "too thin", these recruitment discussions came at a time when managers were also having to cut headcount to save money. Even without short-term financial constraints, staffing seems to have remained a perennial problem throughout the post-war period. In his annual statement reviewing the 1965/6 financial year, James Humphryes said "the limiting factor preventing higher output [was] still the shortage of skilled and semi-skilled men."[58] Board minutes in 1970 recorded that recruiting and retention for the drawing office was a major challenge, with only six of the twenty-six apprentices they had trained still in the company, a difficulty faced by other businesses hoping to hang on to the apprentices they had trained, as we saw in Chapter 4 above. Shortages of skilled labour were reviewed at other board meetings in this period as a damaging constraint.[59] The training and retention of those who might make a career in the company therefore remained important. The formal apprenticeship programme in civil engineering still attracted staff members who wanted to join a programme sponsored by the Institution of Civil Engineers, and the company continued to sponsor employees on degree programmes.[60] Several were on sandwich programmes at Aston University in 1970.[61] Merit and potential to make a difference to the company's technical capacity and performance, rather than any class-conscious sense of university being appropriate only for a certain type of person, seem to have motivated Braithwaites' decisions: both of the sponsored students holding Braithwaite Scholarships in 1960 were originally apprentice draughtsmen.[62] The commitment to merit also appears to have been followed with senior management. Professionally qualified engineers dominated the company's board in the 1970s, and it is evident that experienced managers were offered a path onto it: Geoffrey Instone and James Leggett joined as

57   Meetings between 21/4/1958 and 21/12/1958 in Braithwaite & Co. Engineers Limited, 'Minutes of Joint General Managers' Meetings, 17/3/1958 to 21/11/1960' (Braithwaite & Co. Engineers Limited, 1960), Sandwell Archive, BS-B1/1/7.
58   'Boardroom News - Braithwaite Engineers'.
59   Minutes of 28/5/1970, 24/9/1970, 16/2/1971 meetings in Braithwaite & Co. Engineers Limited, 'Board of Directors' Meetings, 10 July 1968 to 11 December 1974'.
60   Minutes of 26 September 1963 meeting. Braithwaite & Co. Engineers Limited, 'Board of Directors' Meetings, 4 September 1963 to 29 May 1968.'
61   Meeting of 8/7/1970 in Braithwaite & Co. Engineers Limited, 'Board of Directors' Meetings, 10 July 1968 to 11 December 1974'. Braithwaites signed a 7-year covenant to support the Aston programme.
62   Minutes for meeting of 12 January 1960. Braithwaite & Co. Engineers Limited, 'Board of Directors' Meetings, 4 September 1963 to 29 May 1968.'

engineers in 1963, both eventually becoming statutory directors.[63] Despite the constraints imposed by the limited availability of skills within the British economy, in summary, Braithwaites demonstrated a commitment to finding engineering talent, investing in it, and giving it a path to senior management that belies conventional criticisms of British businesses' failure to do any of these things.

But although it was apparently successful in retaining many workers – analysis of two decades of the workforce's records, summarised below, reveals that Braithwaites managed to retain a similar percentage of its most experienced staff – it faced challenges finding capable manual workers. As Schneider, Wandel, and many other West German businesses had found, one solution to the shortage of suitably skilled labour in the 1970s was the employment of immigrant staff. Of the 145 manual workers employed by Braithwaites in West Bromwich on 1 January 1978 whose records are available, eighteen had family names which suggest they were from the high numbers of immigrants from the Indian subcontinent who had taken on factory and foundry work in the Black Country.[64] None of them were employed as unskilled workers.[65] But job titles suggest that the company may have had employees who were practised in their roles, but who did not offer skills levels that would have allowed the company to differentiate itself by any difficult-to-replicate expertise, as Figure 16 indicates.[66]

Paternalism

In reading through its archives and public announcements, there is always a sense that the company was conscious of the value of its staff. Each chairman unfailingly paid tribute to the work of all staff members at the close of each AGM; this was not necessarily just formulaic, as the board's actions in relation to individuals throughout its history show. Management seem to have continued to try to combat skill shortages through generous benefits, going back to the payment of extended sick pay and the rental of company-owned housing to employees in the 1950s.[67] For example, they voted to pay a pension of £600 per annum to a former employee who had lost his job with a later employer, on the

63 Minutes for 23 October 1963 meeting. Braithwaite & Co. Engineers Limited, 'Board of Directors' Meetings, 4 September 1963 to 29 May 1968.'
64 'Facing Up To Colour'.
65 Braithwaite & Co. Engineers Ltd., 'Employee Record Cards': Author's own calculations.
66 Individual reviews of 190 employee details: calculated by author from BS/B/1/1/7, minutes 17/10/1960 ; BS/B/3/2/1 employee record cards. Skills levels assigned by author.
67 For an example of both see the minutes of 29 April 1957 meeting. Braithwaite & Co. Engineers Limited, 'Minutes of Joint General Managers'' Meetings, Braithwaite & Co. Structural Limited, 8 April 1957 to 5 December 1960' (Braithwaite & Co. Engineers Limited, 1960), Sandwell, BS//3/1/2.

Years of Service	Total Workforce (Group) in 1960	% of 1960 Group Workforce	Total Workforce (West Bromwich) in 1978	% of 1978 West Bromwich Workforce
< 10 years	237	61%	74	51%
10–15 years	32	8%	26	18%
> 15 years	117	30%	45	31%
Total Workforce	386	100%	145	100%

Skill Level	Rating	Example Job	Total at Level	Immigrants as % of Skill Group
0	Unskilled	Sweeper-up	10	0%
1	Low-Skilled	Slinger; helper	45	4%
2	Semi-Skilled	Crane driver; plater	64	20%
3	Skilled	Welder	26	12%
Total Workforce (West Bromwich), 1978			145	

Figure 16 Braithwaite & Co. Engineers Ltd., Workforce Composition.

strength of his having "previously given many years valuable service both in India and also as Branch Manager, West Bromwich works." Other individuals were given company loans to help them buy a house.[68]

Wages
In addition to this paternalistic approach to benefits, Braithwaites found itself having to pay increasingly high wages. For them and for all their UK competitors, an ever-increasing wage bill was a problem which worsened over time. It was not confined to Braithwaites' own payroll, as we will see in the history of Jensen Motors. As *The Economist* reported in 1970, steeply rising wages were also a critical element in the ever-increasing cost of steel and other products, as shown in Figure 17.[69]

68   Minutes of meeting on 12 January 1960. Braithwaite & Co. Engineers Ltd., 'Board of Directors' Meetings, 4 September 1963 to 29 May 1968.'
69   'The Price Rocket', *The Economist* (25 April 1970), p. 68, The Economist Historical Archive.

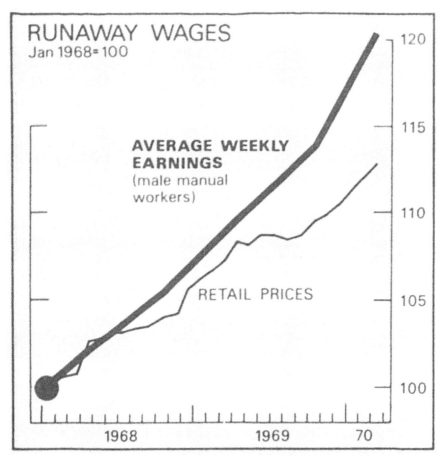

Figure 17 Rates of Wage Increase, Britain, 1968–70.

Braithwaites naturally had to suffer the consequences of ever-increasing wages in other areas of the supply chain too, not to mention the growing burden on their own payroll. Insufficient source material is available for a full analysis, but pay cards show, for example, two individuals receiving thirty-nine and forty-five pay increases respectively over a 26-year tenure at Braithwaites during which they were not apparently given any promotion or increased responsibility, indicating the difficulty for management of maintaining profitable, consistent contract pricing.[70]

70   Braithwaite & Co. Engineers Ltd., 'Employee Record Cards'.

Market Opportunities and Constraints

While we have no separate records of sales and marketing activity, we know that Braithwaites actively pursued business growth. Overseas efforts were ongoing, and all board meeting minutes contain reviews of sales activity. In many board meetings, a director is either away on a sales visit or has recently returned from one. Advertising was also important, though its value and impact cannot be determined and it declined over time: between 1930 and 1959, 308 advertisements (some, admittedly, shareholder announcements) were posted in *The Times*.[71] Yet despite the obvious sales successes, and for all his positive comments on the company's own efforts, James Humphryes was characteristically blunt on the external problems which continued to hurt the company, not least the Government's "present economic policy which [was] stultifying development work".[72] The key challenges facing the business within the UK related both to inputs, principally of steel, and outputs, especially in government work on the motorway and power generation projects which should have been a boon for Braithwaites. Each merits a separate comment below.

Motorways
In 1956, the many academics, members of various institutions, and expert representatives of foreign transport ministries who attended the British Road Federation's conference on urban motorways, were told that they "should be regarded as part and parcel of our nation's industrial equipment."[73] We do not know whether representatives from Braithwaites attended, but they must have been aware of the motorway programme and its putative benefits for the company. The conference report shows that enthusiastic British delegates were keen to learn from their foreign counterparts; a three-page presentation on the plans for an urban motorway into the centre of Stuttgart, one of nineteen foreign cities invited to participate, showed how relatively advanced the progress of German cities was, even so soon after the war.[74] Delegates passed unanimously "the opinion that: the economic needs and traffic problems of large cities demand the construction of Urban Motorways" in Britain, and they demanded immediate plans to extend the motorways currently being planned into urban areas where transportation was particularly challenging.[75]

   A company like Braithwaites, with expertise in building bridges, should have been looking forward to a period of prolonged prosperity as Britain's

71   *The Times* Digital Archive <https://www.gale.com> Search date: 10/1/2019. Search term: "Braithwaite & Co. > between 1/1/1927 and 31/12/1979 >" in "Advertising".
72   'Braithwaite & Co. Engineers Limited: Report on 1962 AGM'.
73   British Road Federation, *Urban Motorways: Report of the Conference Organised by the British Road Federation, 1956* (London: British Road Federation, September 1957), p. 12.
74   British Road Federation, pp. 128–31.
75   British Road Federation, p. 5.

motorway building programme took off. Yet three years after the conference, the motorway programme's progress was a cause for concern. In 1959 *The Economist* reported that it had been described by Parliament's Select Committee on Estimates as "inadequately prepared, to some extent out of proportion, and not ideally organised". Particular concerns were raised about the paucity of research into materials and traffic management and the implementation of that research only after construction had begun.[76] Though participants in the 1956 conference must have been disappointed by the slow progress made by the time of *The Economist's* 1959 article, it may not have come as a surprise to those who recalled the conference speech by the Minister of Transport and Civil Aviation, the Rt Hon. Harold Wilkinson, MP: "When we have achieved this new road plan", he had told them, "We shall slowly have to bring it into effect."[77] If conference attendees hoping for Government decisiveness and energy were perturbed by the Minister's views on the speed of development, they must have despaired as they listened to his peroration: "So that is my policy, and the policy of my Ministry, which is responsible for all these forms of transport, and if we can make a success of this, as I believe we shall, we might even one day be able to go where we want and when we want as quickly as we want, and that, I suppose, is really the objective of us all."[78]

In spite of Mr. Wilkinson's leadership, the programme continued until, by 1961, there were forty miles, and by 1966, 340 miles, of motorway completed.[79] In his celebration of this achievement, which had risen to 715 miles by the time of the Institution of Civil Engineers' 1971 conference on motorways, the Minister for Local Government neglected to remember that Britain's Institution of Highway Engineers had proposed a 2826-mile motorway network as long ago as 1936.[80] Any work for Schneider and other West German counterparts was, in contrast, on an Autobahn network which grew from 2186 kilometres (1355 miles) in 1955 to 4460 kilometres (2765) miles by 1971, worthy of the aspirations of Britain's Highway Engineers thirty-five years earlier, but a vastly greater achievement than that delivered in practice in the UK.[81] No matter what the final outcome, engagement in the motorways programme was difficult.

---

76 'Mistakes on the Motorways', *The Economist* (London, 25 July 1959), p. 236, The Economist Historical Archive.
77 British Road Federation, p. 3.
78 British Road Federation, p. 3.
79 The Institution of Civil Engineers, *Motorways in Britain, Today and Tomorrow. Proceedings of the Conference Organized by the Institution of Civil Engineers Held in London 26–28 April 1971* (London, 1971), pp. 1–3.
80 The Institution of Civil Engineers, *20 Years of British Motorways. Proceedings of the Conference Held in London 27–28 February, 1980* (London, 1980), p. 5.
81 'Längenentwicklung Der Bundesautobahnen Seit 1950', Autobahn-Online.de - Autobahnen in Deutschland (2021) <https://www.autobahn-online.de/geschichte.html> [accessed 12 December 2021].

Its slow start and subsequent difficult progress augured badly for a company like Braithwaites, which should have been expecting to build bridges, manage difficult foundations projects, and contribute to best-practice research on each for the foreseeable future. Nevertheless, they appear to have responded well to the challenge: a 1961 Braithwaites' advertisement in *The Times* for the Doncaster bypass shows the scale of work delivered and hints at the depth of expertise available within the company.[82]

Power Generation

Plans for power station construction offered the other major market for domestic growth. But by 1965 there was scepticism about the Government's predictions of future power use and the fuels which would enable electricity production. Government fuel policy had been, *The Economist* found, simply "an array of *ad hoc* measures taken to influence the British fuel industries at different times to meet different circumstances."[83] As these judgements might have foreshadowed, the power station construction programme was ambitious in its scope, but problematic in its execution.[84] One internal civil service memo judged the building programme a "microcosm of the mediocrity of British industrial performance and managerial quality".[85] A Parliamentary Committee of Enquiry into commissioning delays blamed them on failures of planning and managerial incompetence, at both the Central Electricity Generating Board (CEGB) and contractors.[86] Several of those coal-fired and nuclear stations which were built were soon afflicted by mechanical failures, occasioning a further Parliamentary enquiry which lamented inadequate attention to, and sometimes a "lack of competence" in, design engineering.[87] It is not known which, if any, of these failings were shared by Braithwaites. But it is clear from the directors' minutes that the delays and inconsistencies of the power station programme caused the company serious difficulties, not of its own making, during the 1960s and into the 1970s.

82 'Braithwaite & Co. Engineers: Advertisement for Doncaster Bypass, 1961', *The Times* (London, England, 1 August 1961), p. 7, The Times Digital Archive.
83 'Cold Comfort for Coal?', *The Economist* (London, 23 October 1965), p. 415, The Economist Historical Archive.
84 I am indebted to Dr. Tae-Hoon Kim for his advice on sources for the remainder of this paragraph.
85 TNA, T 319/834, 'Brief for Permanent Under Secretaries of State', 11 March 1968, p. 2: cited by Dr. Tae-Hoon Kim in an unpublished paper dated 15 October 2015.
86 'Report of the Committee of Enquiry into Delays in Commissioning CEGB Power Stations' (London: House of Commons, March 1969), paras 132, 134.
87 'First Report from the Select Committee on Science and Technology. Generating Plant Breakdowns: Winter 1969–70' (London: House of Commons, 13 April 1970), para. 9 <http://gateway.proquest.com/openurl?url_ver=Z39.88–2004&res_dat=xri:hcpp&rft_dat=xri:hcpp:rec:1969–058351> [accessed 9 January 2019].

Steel

As though its customers' failings were not challenging enough, Braithwaites had problems obtaining appropriate quantities of steel, of the right quality, when they needed it. The Iron and Steel Board (ISB) was tasked with "promoting the efficient, economic and adequate supply under competitive conditions of iron and steel products". But over the fourteen years between its creation in 1953 and its disappearance after nationalisation in 1967, it exhibited powers of only "a negative and passive character", disagreeing with the British Iron and Steel Federation on demand forecasting.[88] Differences of a million tons per year in each group's forecasts of capacity by 1962, and the continuation of the ISB's policy of requiring all producers to sell at a predetermined maximum price even in times of recession, caused problems in Braithwaites' supply chain.[89] Reliable deliveries and consistent pricing were both critical to sustainable operations. Neither usually applied. As the steel industry struggled with nationalisation, then privatisation, then in 1967 nationalisation again, customers like Braithwaites were more often its victims than its beneficiaries. To be fair to the British Steel Corporation (BSC), other countries' steel industries were also challenged by the vicissitudes of the global market – including that in West Germany, notwithstanding a successful rationalisation programme – and German customers experienced frustrations in turn.[90] Julius Schneider, for example, suffered a 54% price increase between 1968 and 1974, as well as some delivery problems in 1970 and 1971, but Braithwaites' situation was much worse.[91] As Figure 18 shows, *The Economist* reported an 11% increase in BSC prices in January 1970 on top of those imposed since nationalisation.[92]

Six months later, more increases were threatened,[93] followed by BSC's request for a further 15% nine months after that.[94] Justification for further increases was reviewed in March 1973.[95] Actual price uplifts happened more frequently: British Steel's prices were 35% higher in 1970 than in 1960, and then rose by a further 75% to 1974. Between 1975 and 1978, they rose by an additional 54%. Average

88   Keith Ovenden, *The Politics of Steel*, Studies in Policy-Making (London: Macmillan, 1978), p. 17.

89   'Whose Responsibility?', *The Economist* (London, 25 July 1959), p. 236, The Economist Historical Archive.

90   Gary Herrigel, *Industrial Constructions: The Sources of German Industrial Power*, pp. 220–21.

91   Hege, 'Geschichte der Firma J. Schneider GmbH & Co. KG, Ludwigsburg', p. 71.

92   'Steel: Adding £200 Million to the Bill', *The Economist* (10 January 1970), p. 55, The Economist Historical Archive.

93   'Steel: Yet Another Price Rise Coming?', *The Economist* (6 June 1970), p. 60.

94   'Is British Steel Really Worth an Investment of £3 Billion?', *The Economist* (13 March 1971), p. 69.

95   '£250m on the Bill', *The Economist* (24 March 1973), p. 79.

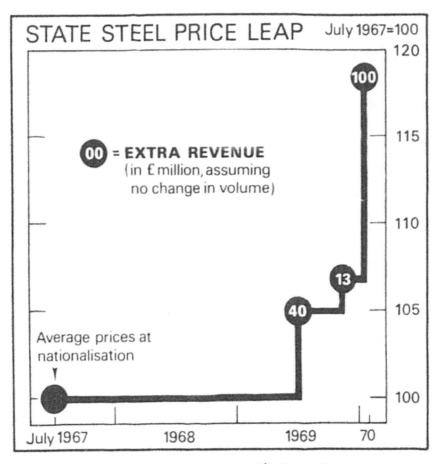

Figure 18 State Steel Price Increases, 1967–70 (*The Economist*).

weekly deliveries to the civil engineering sector varied greatly throughout these periods.[96] In April 1974, having suffered "disruption to production planning

---

96   Iron and Steel Board and British Iron and Steel Federation, 'Iron and Steel Monthly Statistics', Iron and Steel Monthly Statistics, 5.12 (1960); Iron and Steel Board and British Iron and Steel Federation, 'Iron and Steel Monthly Statistics', Iron and Steel Monthly Statistics, 10.12 (1965); Iron and Steel Board and British Iron and Steel Federation, 'Iron and Steel Monthly Statistics', Iron and Steel Monthly Statistics, 15.12 (1970); Iron and Steel Board and British Iron and Steel Federation, 'Iron and Steel Monthly Statistics', Iron and Steel Monthly Statistics, 20.12 (1975); Iron and Steel Board and British Iron and Steel Federation, 'Iron and Steel Monthly Statistics', Iron and Steel Monthly Statistics, 24.12 (1979).

throughout the year", Tony Humphryes met senior BSC managers in London.[97] Finding that it "was clear from these discussions that BSC were not in a position to make any definite promises regarding steel supplies and that the position for at least the next six months would be difficult", he concluded that Braithwaites might have to buy up to two hundred tons of steel per quarter from foreign suppliers.[98] To have suffered with this combination of relentlessly increasing cost from a hopelessly unreliable, all-dominant supplier must have made the job of management extraordinarily difficult, and placed severe limitations on company growth and profitability.

Innovation

Braithwaites' board minutes say little about technological advances, though they refer in 1968 to a research committee which appears to have been active in both product R&D and market development. The company had continued success with their pressed steel water tanks for decades.[99] Perhaps conscious of forthcoming reductions in their traditional markets for bridgework and building steels, a "Sub-Committee had been set up to investigate and report on the possibility of extending the Company's activities beyond those of normal structural steelwork to work which could be carried out within the scope of the Company's existing plant, premises and organisation."[100] Braithwaites' patent portfolio shows R&D was being carried out throughout this period. James Hulse Humphreys had registered numerous patents during his chairmanship, and his son and grandson did the same, registering six patents on roof building and load handling between 1958 and 1976.[101] It might reasonably

---

97   'Statement by the Chairman', Braithwaite & Co. Engineers Ltd., 'Report and Accounts for the Year Ended 31 March 1974' (Braithwaite & Co. Engineers Ltd., 22 August 1974), Companies House, archive disk 00175912–21.
98   Minutes for 24 April 1974: Braithwaite & Co. Engineers Limited, 'Board of Directors' Meetings, 10 July 1968 to 11 December 1974'.
99   Braithwaite & Co. Engineers Ltd., 'Pressed Steel Tanks' (Braithwaite & Co. Engineers Ltd., 1957) <http://www.gracesguide.co.uk/images/1/15/Im1957v203-p770ca.jpg> [accessed 3 November 2015].
100   Minutes of 29 May 1968 meeting. Braithwaite & Co. Engineers Limited, 'Board of Directors' Meetings, 4 September 1963 to 29 May 1968.'
101   J. Humphryes, 'A Method of Applying Distinguishing Markings to Metal Articles', Espacenet (1976) <https://worldwide.espacenet.com/publicationDetails/biblio?DB=&ND=5&locale=en_EP&FT=D&date=19760325&CC=ZA&NR=755847B&KC=B> [accessed 9 November 2015]; James Anthony Humphryes, 'Containers', Espacenet (1968) <http://worldwide.espacenet.com/publicationDetails/biblio?FT=D&date=19680828&DB=worldwide.espacenet.com&locale=en_EP&CC=GB&NR=1125001A&KC=A&ND=4> [accessed 10 November 2015];

be argued that a company like Braithwaites, financially sound and supposedly an international leader in its specialist area, should have been much more active in creating new intellectual property for exploitation. Unfortunately, the archive does not contain any more detail on development work to counter this argument, although by 1978 one of Braithwaite Structural's board was separately identified as its research manager.[102] But the business could have invested consistently and extensively in both new product development and productivity efforts without applying for patents; and in any case, Braithwaites' rival, Cleveland Bridge & Engineering, only registered four patents itself during the same period.[103] Neither of the British firms' intellectual activity in their area of expertise, unfortunately, came close to that of Germany's leading bridge-engineering specialist, Professor Fritz Leonhardt of Stuttgart University,[104] who personally registered thirty-seven bridge-related patents in the post-World War Two period.[105] It is possible that Braithwaites were alert to the work of thinkers like Leonhardt and developed academics' innovations as elements of their own best practice, but their approach to patentable innovation is clearly different from Reutter and RECARO.

Braithwaites should have benefited from the need for innovation in bridge-building within the motorway programme. For bridge designers this was,

James Anthony Humphryes and Alfred William Pond, 'Improvements in and Relating to Grabs', Espacenet (1959) <http://worldwide.espacenet.com/publicationDe-tails/biblio?FT=D&date=19590708&DB=worldwide.espacenet.com&locale=en_EP&CC=GB&NR=816175A&KC=A&ND=4> [accessed 10 November 2015]; James Anthony Humphryes, 'Improvements in and Relating to Load Lowering and Lifting', Espacenet, (1958) <http://worldwide.espacenet.com/publicationDe-tails/biblio?FT=D&date=19580709&DB=worldwide.espacenet.com&locale=en_EP&CC=GB&NR=797839A&KC=A&ND=4> [accessed 10 November 2015]; James Anthony Humphryes, 'Improvements in and Relating to the Strengthening, Preservation and Repair of Roofs', Espacenet (1969) <http://worldwide.espacenet.com/publication-Details/biblio?FT=D&date=19690806&DB=worldwide.espacenet.com&locale=en_EP&CC=GB&NR=1160570A&KC=A&ND=4> [accessed 10 November 2015].

102   Companies House, 'Form 6A, Annual Return of a Company Having Share Capital, Braithwaite Structural Ltd., 1978.' (Companies House, 1978), Companies House, archive disk 00418563–07.

103   'Patents List - Cleveland Bridge', Espacenet (2015) <http://worldwide.espacenet.com/searchResults?ST=singleline&locale=en_EP&submitted=true&DB=worldwide.espacenet.com&query=%22cleveland+bridge%22> [accessed 22 November 2015].

104   Ben Gerwick, 'FRITZ LEONHARDT 1909–1999', in Memorial Tributes: National Academy of Engineering, Volume 9 (Washington, DC, 2001), pp. 199–202 <https://nae.edu/188253/FRITZ-LEONHARDT-19091999> [accessed 12 December 2021].

105   'Patents List - Fritz Leonhardt', Espacenet (2015) <http://worldwide.espacenet.com/searchResults?page=0&compact=false&ST=singleline&sortField=prd&query=%22fritz+leonhardt%22&locale=en_EP&DB=worldwide.espacenet.com&ascending=false> [accessed 22 November 2015].

in principle, a seller's market: the deputy chief highway engineer of the Department of Transport concluded, when reviewing the previous twenty-five years of the motorway programme in 1980, that bridges, viaducts and retaining walls represented 20–30% of the design effort on inter-urban motorways and 80% on urban motorways. But on the first fifty-five mile section of M1, 132 bridges had had to be designed in twenty-four months and constructed in nineteen months between 1956 and 1959, a rush of work that was evidence, perhaps, of a lack of long-range planning by Government and the civil service. "Some 4000" bridges and viaducts had been designed and constructed on the motorway network since then. The majority were large structures "and, in spite of similarities in some respects, each in respect of foundation, geometry and span require]d] individual design."[106] As the programme had evolved, bridge-works had remained challenging, though builders and fabricators of bridges had made technical advances during the 1960s.[107] In principle, this would appear to have been a market for Mittelstand-style niche expertise, in which each bridge required the sort of special capabilities Braithwaites had been developing for decades. In practice, however, the Government's approach to programme management and serious technical difficulties with some kinds of bridge must, despite the welcome volume of work, have been more a frustrating burden for Braithwaites than an exciting period of growth.[108]

Banking and Shareholder Relationships

We have already considered the financial challenges of the 1930s and the ensuing need for bank support. As the 1960s progressed, the requirement for an understanding bank increased. By October 1963 the Group's accounts were £454,538 in deficit; within another six weeks this figure was £535,668. Nevertheless, the board were told that "Lloyds Bank Limited, Head Office, had agreed to the renewal of the company's overdraft limit of £600,000 for a further twelve months."[109] By the nature of the company's business, cash flow was bound to be difficult. No correspondence or commercial contracts remain in the archive, but any international bridge project must have necessitated outflows for the procurement and shipment of steel to West Bromwich: for the wages and overheads incurred in its fabrication, for international shipment, seldom to a European country, and for all the stages of bridge erection for which Braithwaites were responsible. Against this there were compensating inflows

106 The Institution of Civil Engineers, *20 Years of British Motorways*, p. 46.
107 The Institution of Civil Engineers, *Motorways in Britain, Today and Tomorrow*, p. 61.
108 The Institution of Civil Engineers, *20 Years of British Motorways*, pp. 11–12.
109 Minutes for meetings of 23 October and 20 November 1963. Braithwaite & Co. Engineers Limited, 'Board of Directors' Meetings, 4 September 1963 to 29 May 1968.'

of stage payments which are referred to in the company's accounts, and in the vast majority of years the company made a profit, suggesting that the contracts were ultimately beneficial. But in the very extended period between winning a contract (with all the associated sales visit, survey, and detailed design costs which preceded all of the product-engineering costs mentioned above) and completing it, Braithwaites could not have managed without the support of their bankers. These financial tensions may have made day-to-day investment challenging. Isabelle Lescent-Giles insists that British industrialists in this period were guilty of pursuing an all-pervading mantra of growth at all costs, at the expense of "notoriously insufficient" investment in research and development and tooling.[110] Though we have observed the lack of much patented innovation, it seems unfair to include Braithwaites in this criticism, as fixed assets increased from £1.02 million in 1972 to £2.9 million by 1979 and its work, by definition, required the development and application of deep specialist knowledge.[111]

During these difficult operational years, Humphryes ensured that shareholders benefited from the company's progress, capitalising £150,000 of its profits and distributing them to all shareholders in 1965, then in 1967 enlarging its share capital by capitalising £300,000 of existing profits to increase it to £1,050,000, distributing the new shares to existing shareholders.[112] Though he and those of his fellow directors who were also shareholders certainly benefited from the profit distribution, it is important to note that the directors paid themselves only £500 per annum (£750 for the chairman) by a special resolution passed in 1963: there is little sense of them feathering their own nests in this period.[113] It is also important to note that, although by this time the group had been a public company for over forty years, there is absolutely no indication during the 1960s of its directors becoming any less active in daily management. At many board meetings, one of the board is absent on a foreign sales visit. At every meeting, current major contracts are reviewed and developing opportunities discussed. According to the minutes up to 1974, at least, these men are financially prudent and conscious of their margins and their cash position, but

---

110   Lescent-Giles, p. 186.
111   Five-year summaries, in: Braithwaite & Co. Engineers Ltd., 'Report and Accounts for the Year Ended 31 March 1981' (Braithwaite & Co. Engineers Ltd., August 1981), Companies House, archive disk 00175912–25; Braithwaite & Co. Engineers Ltd., 'Report and Accounts for the Year Ended 31 March 1976' (Braithwaite & Co. Engineers Ltd., August 1976), Companies House, archive disk 00175912–22.
112   'Ordinary Resolutions of Braithwaite & Co. Engineers' (Companies House, 30 November 1967), Companies House, archive disk 00175912–04.
113   'Special Resolution of Braithwaite & Co. Engineers' (Companies House, 1963), Companies House, archive disk 00175912–04.

they are operating engineers first and foremost, and emphatically not financial manipulators or stock watchers.

Business Activity 1971 to 1979

Governance: Succession

In October 1971, "The chairman reported that for medical and other reasons he had decided to retire at the end of the present calendar year." The board accepted his resignation "with very great regret" after fifty-two years' service with the company,[114] and in the subsequent board meeting he was replaced by his son Tony, who would now relinquish all executive responsibilities.[115] It seems reasonable to ask two questions of this situation. First, whether forty-four unchallenged years as the chairman was simply too long for effective, innovative leadership. Notwithstanding the successes achieved under James Humphryes' command, it is conceivable that an earlier change of leader might have enabled Braithwaite to seek opportunities in new technologies and markets, or as part of a larger group with greater leverage in structural engineering.

The second question is whether the automatic elevation of the third-generation Humphryes represented good governance – with or without the minuted board vote of approval – or nepotism. Tony had been educated as an engineer and had committed his life to the business. In Board meetings leading up to his appointment, the minutes show him to have been playing an active role in strategic selling.[116] The Humphryes family remained the largest single shareholders in the company. Yet his decision to withdraw from executive responsibilities was a further distinction between Braithwaites' management team and that of similar German companies. Not only had an important part of the shareholding been released from family control following Tony's partial divestment in 1974, Braithwaites' new leader chose to continue to base himself and his senior executives two hours' drive away from either factory and, despite being an engineer, to leave hands-on leadership to others. In fact, the remainder of the decade would reveal that this approach, very different from that at the admittedly smaller Schneider, appears nevertheless to have delivered success.

The key concern about Tony's appointment, that it might have prevented the inclusion of new talent with new ideas in the business, remains valid. But the company was not averse to promoting capable men from within, as we have

114   Minutes of 23 September 1971 meeting. Braithwaite & Co. Engineers Limited, 'Board of Directors' Meetings, 10 July 1968 to 11 December 1974'.
115   Minutes of 27 October 1971 meeting. Braithwaite & Co. Engineers Limited, 'Board of Directors' Meetings, 10 July 1968 to 11 December 1974'.
116   Braithwaite & Co. Engineers Limited, 'Board of Directors' Meetings, 10 July 1968 to 11 December 1974', passim.

seen, or importing senior talent. Alfred Vickers, one-time managing director of Jensen Motors, was on Braithwaites' board in 1974.[117] In 1975, Lord Tanlaw, formerly Simon Brooke Mackay, was appointed as a director.[118] Aged thirty-eight, he had been chairman of his family's business, Inchcape, and was also a director of a merchant bank and eight other companies. By 1981 he was the owner of 85,000 Braithwaites shares, almost as many as Tony Humphryes and 75,000 more than the next largest board shareholder, suggesting that Tony had invited him to buy some of his own shares, or to make an investment of cash that the business could use to grow.[119] It is not clear how he and Braithwaites became connected, but his business track record and Inchape's involvement in Asian trade were distinctive. Tanlaw also offered corporate, public company experience. His willingness to speak in the House of Lords on the need for a new government energy policy, and for investment in the Scottish oil industry, was perhaps seen as a means of encouraging structural investment in power plants and pipelines that might benefit Braithwaites.[120] In the absence of minutes after 1974 or references to his Braithwaites work in any other sources, Tanfield's contribution cannot be judged.[121] But the evolution of events during the 1970s and early 1980s suggest that his recruitment was as a contributor, rather than as a social asset, and was astute.

Other directors were drawn up from the ranks, as Geoffrey Instone's appointment as managing director showed.[122] The Newport works manager was also made a director in 1974.[123] A tradition of engagement within the wider industry was maintained, for its and for Braithwaites' benefit. James Hulse

---

117   Braithwaite & Co. Engineers Ltd., 'Accounts for the Year Ended 31 March 1974' (Braithwaite & Co. Engineers Ltd., August 1974), Companies House, archive disk 00175912–21.

118   'Business Appointments', *The Times* (London, England, 29 July 1975), p. 18, The Times Digital Archive; 'Business Diary: Moneychanger in the Temple · Bermuda Triangle', *The Times* (London, England, 23 March 1977), p. 21, The Times Digital Archive; Braithwaite & Co. Engineers Limited, 'Form 9A, Notification of Change of Directors or Secretary or in Their Particulars' (Braithwaite & Co. Engineers Limited, 1972), Companies House, archive disk 00175912–06.

119   Companies House, 'Form 6A, Annual Return of a Company Having Share Capital, Braithwaite & Co. Engineers Ltd.' (Companies House, 1981), Companies House, archive disk 00175912–25.

120   'Demand for Energy Policy Linked to EEC', *The Times* (London, England, 1 March 1973), p. 12, The Times Digital Archive; 'Oil Firms to Be Asked Why They Buy Abroad', *The Times* (London, England, 14 December 1972), p. 6, The Times Digital Archive.

121   He also did not reply to a letter from the author.

122   Minutes for 23 October 1963 meeting. Braithwaite & Co. Engineers Limited, 'Board of Directors' Meetings, 4 September 1963 to 29 May 1968'.

123   Companies House, 'Form 9A, Notofication of Appointment of Director, Braithwaite & Co. Engineers Ltd., 1974.' (Companies House, 1974), Companies House, archive disk 00175912–05.

Humphryes had applied in October 1908 to join the Institution of Mechanical Engineers, and father, son, grandson, and colleagues participated in professional organisations throughout their careers.[124] Engagement included roles in both national and international industry bodies. In the interwar years, for example, the company was represented in the Institution of Welding by James Bickley, a director of Braithwaite Structural, presumably both to learn and to show his peers that Braithwaites were engaged with best practice.[125] Forty years later, Tony Humphryes was chairman of the British Constructional Steelwork Association and was then elected chairman of the executive board of the European Convention for Constructional Steelwork,[126] later winning its Silver Medal for 1983,[127] reflecting the esteem in which he and Braithwaites must have been held. Others also participated in technical organisations: six out of nine Structural directors were members of professional engineering institutions. In all of this activity, reaching back to James Humphryes' committee work in the 1930s, Braithwaites' staff were behaving in a way which resembled German traditions of networking and professional development through industry organisations.

Operations: 1977 to West Bromwich Closure

For all the challenges of its operating environments, Braithwaites achieved impressive financial results – though they were less impressive when inflation was taken into account – for most of Tony Humphryes' tenure as chairman, as shown in Figure 19.[128]

124 *Institution of Mechanical Engineers*, 'Institution of Mechanical Engineers - Membership Proposal Forms' (2015) <https://archivecat.imeche.org/search/all:records/o_50/all/score_desc/%20James%20Humphryes> [accessed 21 November 2015].
125 Institution of Welding Engineers, *Tenth Annual Report* (London: Institution of Welding Engineers, 1933), The Welding Institute <https://www.twi-global.com/pdfs/PDFs-Public/IWE-Annual-Report-10-1933.pdf> [accessed 2 August 2022].
126 'Business Appointments', *The Times* (London, England, 31 October 1977), p. 18, The Times Digital Archive.
127 'The European Convention for Constructional Steelwork: History and Achievements 1955 – 2015' (The European Convention for Constructional Steelwork, 2015), p. 83 <https://www.tucsa.org/images/haber/606/606_2_3_15012016141359.pdf> [accessed 12 January 2019].
128 Table compiled by author from: Braithwaite & Co. Engineers Ltd., 'Accounts for the Year Ended 31 March 1975' (Braithwaite & Co. Engineers Ltd., August 1975), Companies House, archive disk 00175912–21; Braithwaite & Co. Engineers Ltd., 'Report and Accounts for the Year Ended 31 March 1976' (Braithwaite & Co. Engineers Ltd., August 1976) Companies House, archive disk 00175912-22; Braithwaite & Co. Engineers Ltd., 'Report and Accounts for the Year Ended 31 March 1977' (Braithwaite & Co. Engineers Ltd., August

	1972	1973	1974	1975	1976	1977	1978	1979	1980	1981
Sales (£)	4,936,000	4,780,000	4,978,000	6,862,000	9,621,000	13,006,000	11,786,000	10,466,000	8,793,000	8,299,000
of which exports	714,000	578,000	800,000	1,367,000	2,944,700	5,328,000	7,180,000	6,705,000	6,396,000	4,001,000
% exported	14%	12%	16%	20%	31%	41%	61%	64%	73%	48%
Profit Before Tax (£)	383,946	402,551	326,595	452,531	846,194	1,923,860	1,019,893	526,712	976,627	808,569
PBT as % of sales	7.70%	8.40%	6.60%	6.60%	9.40%	14.80%	8.70%	5.00%	11.10%	9.70%
Total Employees			827	828	832	768	758	693		394
Aggregrate Remuneration (£)			1,623,575	1,916,537	2,438,704	2,685,467	2,904,686	2,772,000		2,160,000
Avg Remun per Employee (£)			1,963	2,315	2,931	3,497	3,832	4,000		
Remuneration as % of Sales			32.6%	27.9%	25.3%	20.6%	24.6%	26.5%		
Balance Sheet Value (£)	2,559,253	2,679,357	2,746,950	2,835,471	3,442,297	4,245,935	4,612,964	4,429,184	5,083,731	5,595,399
Payments to Shareholders (£)	73,041	82,333	89,002	93,910	101,443	111,730	123,865	139,435		
Taxation	157,500	160,500	170,000	236,500	449,000	1,008,500	529,000	235,500	494,000	-580,000
PAT	187,988	255,351	156,595	182,431	337,194	915,369	490,893	-44,315	851,422	1,388,569

Figure 19 Braithwaite & Co. Engineers Ltd., Financial Performance in Nominal Terms, 1972–81.

He and his staff were able to push sales upwards each year, despite the rising cost of steel and, particularly, of wages. In particular, they anticipated a decline in the UK market, like the one Schneider was experiencing in West Germany at the same time, and in response grew export sales by 115% in 1976 and by more in later years. Publicly, he attributed this growth "to the determined efforts of our salesforce and the support they receive from our Works' performance."[129] Export markets themselves were becoming more competitive, though, so Braithwaites invested in enabling quicker delivery from the works and in onsite erection teams in various countries, helping to compensate for "severe cutbacks in Government expenditure and a continuing lack of major expenditure from private industry" in the UK.[130] Despite these domestic problems, sales were driven up by 2.6 times and pre-tax profit by five times between 1972 and 1977, with export sales in 1978 marking a ten-fold increase over seven years and earning Braithwaites the Queen's Award for Export Achievement.[131]

Despite these successes, Humphryes' frustrations were apparent, in several areas. On the subject of pay-restriction legislation he protested, "I cannot accept that the current system is fair when hard-earned rewards cannot be shared to a greater extent with all our employees."[132] Despite it, the company launched a profit-sharing scheme for all staff which paid out 10% of pre-tax profit,[133] and a share-option scheme for directors.[134] But as conditions were "generally as bad as any experienced in the constructional steelwork industry since the 1930s" the company continued to look for diversification opportunities which were – prudently – "within the scope of our existing managerial

1977), Companies House, archive disk 00175912–22; Braithwaite & Co. Engineers Ltd., 'Report and Accounts for the Year Ended 31 March 1978' (Braithwaite & Co. Engineers Ltd., August 1978), Companies House, archive disk 00175912–23; Braithwaite & Co. Engineers Ltd., 'Report and Accounts for the Year Ended 31 March 1979' (Braithwaite & Co. Engineers Ltd., August 1979), Companies House, archive disk 00175912–23.

129 'Statement by the Chairman', in Braithwaite & Co. Engineers Ltd., 'Report and Accounts for the Year Ended 31 March 1976'.

130 'Statement by the Chairman', in Braithwaite & Co. Engineers Ltd., 'Report and Accounts for the Year Ended 31 March 1977'.

131 'Braithwaite & Co. Engineers Ltd.: Statement of 1978 Results', *The Times* (15 September 1978), p. 19, The Times Digital Archive.

132 'Statement by the Chairman', in Braithwaite & Co. Engineers Ltd., 'Report and Accounts for the Year Ended 31 March 1977', a year of record profits for the company.

133 Braithwaite & Co. Engineers Ltd., 'Report and Accounts for the Year Ended 31 March 1978'.

134 Companies House, 'Annual Accounts, Braithwaite Structural Ltd., 31/3/1979.' (Companies House, 1979), p. 3, Companies House, archive disk 00418563–07. It is not known whether this scheme was extended to other employees, as the accounts are required only to show it for directors.

expertise."[135] In 1978 it took its first steps into a new industry, showing in its acquisition of a small plastics recycling company that it was anticipating future market developments.

At home, the motorway-building programme was reaching an end, and it was predicted that "it is most unlikely that there will be anything approaching the intense activity on the construction of inter-urban routes of the past 20 years."[136] This was another sign that returns would continue to diminish, and presumably among the reasons that the company made seventy-two West Bromwich staff redundant early in 1978. The local press reported that management and the Transport and General Workers Union (TGWU) had agreed redundancy payments, giving some workers payments of more than £4600, but with a promise "that the men would get first offer of their jobs back if work picked up by the end of 1978."[137] The comment of a TGWU chief shop steward suggests a positive working environment and a sense of shared destiny: "It was a real wrench for the firm to let the men go as the men were highly skilled top class welders. Nothing would please the bosses more than to get them back and we are all keeping our fingers crossed." The journalist commented that "Braithwaites are one of a number of heavy steel firms hit by the recession. Unions and managements are blaming cuts in Government spending and the old row is raging that nationalised firms are getting the pick of public contracts."[138]

The board's initial thoughts on the prospect of losing West Bromwich works are not available to us. While government funding support for short-time working as a means of protecting skills had been in use on West Germany in one form or another for decades by this time, it was not available to Braithwaites.[139] In April 1979, the decision to close the West Bromwich site permanently was announced. The TGWU's divisional officer argued that there was no logic in closing the site and the local MP demanded that "Every effort must be made to stop this company from closing and keep these jobs in an area where unemployment is too high already." But while Braithwaites' managing director, William Mair, "said he was anxious about the social effect on the area which

135   'Statement by the Chairman', in Braithwaite & Co. Engineers Ltd., 'Report and Accounts for the Year Ended 31 March 1978'.

136   The Institution of Civil Engineers, *20 Years of British Motorways*, p. 12.

137   Andrew Parker, 'Paid-off Men May Be Returning to Old Firm', *Sandwell Evening News* (Sandwell, 25 August 1978), Sandwell Archive, 63/8.

138   Parker.

139   Henner Will, 'Kurzarbeit - makroökonom(etr)ische Erkenntnisse über einen klassischen allrounder' (presented at the Seventh IWH/IAB-Workshops zur Arbeitsmarktpolitik "Lohnpolitik nach der Krise", Halle, 2010), p. 19 <https://www.iwh-halle.de/fileadmin/user_upload/events/workshops/former/20101021/PDF/2/Henner%20Will.pdf>; see also Karl Brenke, Ulf Rinne, and Klaus F Zimmermann, *Kurzarbeit: Nützlich in der Krise, aber nun den Ausstieg einleiten*, Wochenbericht des DIW Berlin, 21 (April 2010), p. 13.

the closure will bring"[140] the company said it had lost over £600,000 at West Bromwich in the preceding year (though this is not apparent in its published accounts) with a "continuing lack of demand worldwide and over-capacity in the industry".[141] Moreover, despite positive recent financial results, Braithwaites also had a deferred tax bill which, having been £44,000 in 1975/6, would rise to £1.8 million by 1979/80.[142]

It is not clear whether Tony Humphryes had emotional bonds to the site given his family's history. He regretted publicly "that so many hardworking and loyal members of the staff and workforce have had to face redundancy" and reached "mutual agreement" with unions and staff.[143] The redundancy terms seem to have been both generous and pragmatic. Workers received redundancy and payment in lieu of notice, and additional bonuses were paid to expedite the closure of the plant. Redundancy payments ranged from £1500 to – for the best-paid workers – £7500, twice the average annual remuneration per worker.[144] But while the total cost of closure exceeded £860,000, the company benefited immediately from tax refunds, the transfer of West Bromwich's best equipment to its Newport operation, which was continuing, and the rapid sale of the site for £1.3 million, 178% of its book value.[145] The prospect of new local jobs was offered by Subaru, which purchased the site as its new UK base.[146]

Humphryes' reflection in the following year's report is worth quoting as an indication of the economic climate prevailing in Britain in 1979/80, against which his and any other British management team's actions and performance must be judged:

> The year under review has been one of the most eventful in the Company's history. Not only was the planned closure of the West Bromwich works brought to a successful conclusion, but the effects of three major national strikes in the transport, engineering and steel industries had to be weathered. In addition, there has been the deepening recession, an alarming escalation in

140 'Sacked Steel Men Battle for Jobs', *Sandwell Evening News* (Sandwell, 12 April 1979), Sandwell Archive, 63/126.

141 'Statement by the Chairman', in Braithwaite & Co. Engineers Ltd., 'Report and Accounts for the Year Ended 31 March 1979'; 'Braithwaite Works Losses', *Evening Standard* 26 July 1979, Sandwell Archive, 63/190.

142 *The Stock Exchange Official Year-Book 1975–76*, ed. by Jeffrey Russell Knight (Croydon, 1975); Russell Knight, *The Stock Exchange Official Year-Book 1979–80* (East Grinstead, 1979); *The Stock Exchange Official Year-Book 1980–81*, ed. by Jeffrey Russell Knight (London and Basingstoke, 1980).

143 'Statement by the Chairman', in Braithwaite & Co. Engineers Ltd., 'Report and Accounts for the Year Ended 31 March 1979'.

144 'Golden Pay-Off for Workers at Doomed Factory'', *Sandwell Evening News* (Sandwell, 30 June 1979), Sandwell Archive, 63/175.

145 'Contract for Site Sale', *Evening Standard* (26 July 1979), Sandwell Archive, 63/249.

146 'New-Look Car Firm Lines Up Big Jobs Boost'.

the rate of inflation and, latterly, the highest interest rates on record. Against such a background, to be able to report a Trading Profit of £976,627 before tax gives me the greatest pleasure.[147]

Moreover, his confirmation that the Plastic Recycling Ltd. subsidiary had been growing was reinforced the following year, when he also revealed the establishment of Braithwaite Investments Ltd., which had begun to invest in industrial property.[148] Different perspectives on the nature of capitalism can be drawn from the decision to close the West Bromwich works. While 270 workers had lost their jobs, directors and investors had profited: the 1980 accounts showed a 42% increase in pay for the highest-paid director, presumably Humphryes, who had also sold 18,000 shares. Aggregate directors' compensation rose by 44%.[149] Gross dividends were £73,000 or 59% higher in 1980 than in 1978. Shareholders continued to prosper, as their successors still do.[150] It seems reasonable to contrast this outcome with that at Schneider in Ludwigsburg: though Braithwaites paid generous redundancy settlements, there was not the same commitment to retaining skills within the community, and the financial wellbeing of Braithwaites' directors and shareholders might have been a more influential factor in the company's decision-making in relation to its workers than it was in the Walz family.

The annual report for the year to 31 March 1983 showed that the group had moved on from the disappointments of the late 1970s. In his chairman's statement, Tony Humphryes announced a 10% increase in profits to £1.02 million, passed on to shareholders as a 12% increase in dividend. Although margins in structural steelwork remained "dangerously thin", the Newport works had won export orders for both structural work and pressed steel tanks. After researching diversification opportunities, the group would now be manufacturing air conditioning filtration units at Newport. Further diversification had come in the acquisition of an engineering company in April 1982, and there had been a "further substantial expansion in sales" at Plastic Recycling Ltd. The industrial properties bought by the newly established Braithwaite Investments Ltd. were all occupied, and had appreciated in value.

147 'Statement by the Chairman', in Braithwaite & Co. Engineers Ltd., 'Report and Accounts for the Year Ended 31 March 1980' (Braithwaite & Co. Engineers Ltd., August 1980), Companies House, archive disk 00175912–24.

148 'Statement by the Chairman', in Braithwaite & Co. Engineers Ltd., 'Report and Accounts for the Year Ended 31 March 1981'.

149 Companies House, 'Braithwaite Structural Ltd., Report of the Directors to Be Presented to the 34th AGM of the Company, with Accounts for the Year Ended 31 March 1980' (Companies House, 1980), Companies House, archive disk 00418563–07.

150 'About Us - Andrews Sykes' <https://www.andrews-sykes.com/info/about-us/#t1> [accessed 31 January 2019].

Although his family had achieved considerable success in one industry over almost one hundred years, Humphryes was rational and committed to change: "We shall continue to look for suitable companies where our experience and skills can contribute and help the Group to widen its activities and reduce its dependence on structural engineering." He was also unsentimental about his own role, announcing that he was stepping down as chairman of Braithwaite Structural as part of a planned devolution of autonomy to local managers within the group and urging shareholders to support the widening of share ownership among employees as a means of strengthening the Group.[151] This was a business whose strategy would no longer be the engineering of steel structures around the world – the Newport works would soon also be sold – but financial engineering close to home.

151 Braithwaite & Co. Engineers Ltd., 'Report and Accounts for the Year Ended 31 March 1983' (Braithwaite & Co. Engineers Ltd., August 1983), Companies House, archive disk 00175912–26.

9

RECARO GmbH & Co., Stuttgart

RECARO Aircraft Seating is a world leader in its market. Consistently innovative, its annual sales exceeded €500 million for the first time in 2018.[1] In 2020 its Economy seating product was awarded the Gold Award of the German Design Council, one of numerous awards won by the company.[2] It belongs to a family business group whose origins date back to 1906 and the foundation of the Stuttgarter Karosseriewerk Reutter. As we will see, business values have been consistent since then, even after one family acquired the business of another.[3] During that period the respective families' companies have sometimes been very large, with international manufacturing operations. But the commitment to Mittelstand values has remained, and as we will see those values are evident at all points of the history which follows, demonstrating that dynamism and growth are not inconsistent with long-term thinking and humane management.

---

1   'Turnover Rises to over 500 Million Euros for the First Time - RECARO Aircraft Seating' (2018) <https://www.RECARO-as.com/en/press/press-releases/details/turnover-rises-to-over-500-million-euros-for-the-first-time.html> [accessed 5 December 2018].
2   German Design Council, 'SLEEPING COMFORT ABOVE THE CLOUDS – Holistic Approach for the Economy Class Long Range: German Design Award Gold 2020', *German Design Award* (2020) <https://www.german-design-award.com/en/the-winners/gallery/detail/27167-sleeping-comfort-above-the-clouds-holistic-approach-for-the-economy-class-long-range.html> [accessed 19 September 2020].
3   'Guiding Principles of the RECARO Group - RECARO' < https://www.recaro.com/recaro-group/guiding-principles-of-the-recaro-group.html > [accessed 18 December 2021]; The history of the Reutter family's businesses is told in: Uta Jung and Helmut Jung, *Stuttgarter Karosseriewerk Reutter: Von Der Reform-Karosserie Zum Porsche 356* (Bielefeld, 2006): Uta Jung is the granddaugher of interwar shareholder and business leader Albert Reutter and the daughter of joint managing director Theodor Koch; Frank Jung, *Porsche 356 Made by Reutter* (Bielefeld, 2011): Frank Jung is the great-grandson of Albert Reutter, and the former Head of Tradition for RECARO Holding GmbH; the history of Keiper, which acquired and still owns RECARO, is told in: Ulrich Putsch and Martin Putsch, *In Bewegung. Der Automobilzulieferer Keiper: Geschichte und Geschichten aus den Jahren 1920 Bis 2011* (Kaiserslautern, 2011); Ulrich Putsch was the business owner at the time of the RECARO acquisition, and his son Martin Putsch is the current business owner of RECARO Holding GmbH.

Company Development, 1906 to 1945

The Stuttgarter Karosseriewerk Reutter & Co. was founded by Wilhelm Reutter, until then a *Meister* (foreman) in a wagon works, in 1906. In a sign of his intent, the twenty members of staff he had recruited by 1908 "were all specialists: wagon-maker, smith, mechanic, tinsmith and painter." Wilhelm Reutter's brother Albert joined in 1909 as commercial leader, and their shared product philosophy was "the highest quality, happy customers, and strongly motivated colleagues."[4] Both men were Pietists, and their religious values permeated the business.[5] Bills were paid on time. Commitments were honoured unfailingly. Hard work was expected of, and delivered by, every member of staff. Employees were of good character and were well looked after.[6] They were also innovative: their *Reform-Karosserie*, patented in 1909, was the first convertible roof which would allow contemporary limousines to function as both a summer and winter car. It brought Reutter into partnership with well-known automakers in Germany and internationally.[7] During the 1920s Reutter held production licences from foreign makers of limousines as well as producing its own designs. Then, as later, Reutter had to prove itself flexible and adaptive to changing circumstances. While the economy was stagnant they had their carpenters and painters making kitchen cabinets rather than dismissing them and losing their skills. And when it picked up, Reutter's engineers had to completely relearn their trade and restructure their working environment, as car body construction gradually changed from wood to steel. Although it was committed to craft excellence, Reutter was also able to grow and reshape its operations to meet new opportunities, moving from custom-built vehicles for individual customers to series production for emerging mass producers such as Daimler-Benz and Wanderer.[8] In the 1930s, business with Wanderer increased, eventually employing six hundred workers who were also engaged in special constructions for other manufacturers.[9] Albert Reutter established a second factory at Zuffenhausen, a suburb of Stuttgart, enabling an increase to eight hundred staff to cope with rising demand. Innovation continued. Reutter developed numerous patents of its own and obtained a licence for the British "Leveroll" mechanism, which enabled seats to slide backwards and forwards. It also began to cooperate with a new engineering consultancy in

---

4   Jung, *Porsche 356 Made by Reutter*, p. 12.
5   See Chapter 2 for an exploration of Pietist values and their application at Reutter.
6   Friedrich Greger, 'Chronik der Firma RECARO GmbH & Co.' (1977), pp. 2–5, Jung Family Archive.
7   Jung, *Porsche 356 Made by Reutter*, pp. 13–14.
8   Jung, *Porsche 356 Made by Reutter*, pp. 15–21.
9   Jung and Jung, pp. 79–100.

Stuttgart, established by Ferdinand Porsche in 1931,[10] delivering the first bodies for Porsche's new Volkswagen in 1938[11] and working with Porsche throughout the Second World War.[12]

By 1939, Albert Reutter and his son-in-law, Theodor Koch, had established an operation which was producing internal and external coachwork of the highest quality for both individual and series-produced vehicles with their staff of 850, achieving annual sales of RM7 million. Within a year, however, staff numbers had fallen to 350 and revenue to RM4 million as the firm moved onto war work.[13] While that work continued without recorded difficulty, Reutter's situation became precarious when, having already lost technical manager Otto Reutter, killed at Stalingrad in 1942,[14] "in a single blow it lost its entire management on 9 December 1944": Albert Reutter and his son-in-law and joint managing director Theodor Koch were killed when inspecting bomb damage from the air raid that had just killed their sales director.[15] In their place, the finance manager Ernst Körner was appointed *Geschäftsführer* (managing director) on 5 January 1945.[16] Though Körner was criticised at the time for *not* embodying the desired qualities of a Mittelstand business leader – tough, visionary, aware of the need to invest – his own Pietist values ensured he kept the business on a steady course in very difficult post-war circumstances.[17]

Post-war Operations, 1945 to 1948

In his business report for 1945,[18] Körner reviewed the closing months of the war. Under occupation, work was barely halted; the Stuttgart factory was quickly required to service French military vehicles and build replacement city trams. Reutter appears to have responded pragmatically to the dramatically changed circumstances. Despite losing several senior members of staff who were barred from continued employment following denazification and the objections

---

10   Ferry Porsche and Günther Molter, *Ferry Porsche: Ein Leben für das Auto, eine Autobiographie* (Stuttgart, 1989), p. 49ff.

11   Jung, *Porsche 356 Made by Reutter*, pp. 22–26.

12   Jung and Jung, pp. 114–27.

13   Jung and Jung, pp. 131–32.

14   Jung and Jung, p. 306.

15   Jung and Jung, p. 135.

16   Schwäbische Treuhand AG Wirtschaftsprufungsgesellschaft, 'Bericht Über Die Prüfung Des Vorläufigen Reichsmarkabschlusses Der Stuttgarter Karosseriewerk Reutter & Co. G.m.b.H. Stuttgart Zum 20. Juni 1948' (Schwäbische Treuhand – Aktiengesellschaft, 1949), p. 4, RECARO Holding GmbH archives.

17   Jung and Jung, pp. 135–47.

18   'Geschäftsbericht 1945' (Stuttgarter Karosseriewerk Reutter & Co. G.m.b.H., 1946), RECARO Holding GmbH archives.

of the firm's works council,[19] relations between workers and employers and their respective committees were "extraordinarily cooperative."[20] The company managed a turnover of RM1.2 million and a profit of RM91,000.[21] Reserves of over RM1.3 million on the balance sheet for factory renovation and war-damage repairs showed the extent to which the war had impacted the business and the amount of recovery required.[22] But as at Schneider, those reserves also hinted at the business's fundamental residual strength. The staffing situation was clearly difficult, but the disposition of employees is noteworthy and suggests why it was possible for the business to respond so readily to the varying challenges it now faced: of 162 members of staff on 31 December 1945, only twelve were classified as unskilled, and only nineteen were office staff, whereas 122 are recorded as being skilled workers.[23]

There were continued difficulties in 1946 and 1947. Reutter won repair and new-build contracts for trams and trains, yet had no opportunities to return to pre-war commercial work. Factory repairs continued (they were still repairing windows as late as 1947), the Price Control Bureau (*Preisprüfungsstelle*) continued to impose restrictions, and "the shortage of materials became ever greater and we could only obtain necessary raw materials with the help of our customers, with bartering and favours in kind (*Kompensationen*)."[24] Staffing increasingly became a problem: many of the 181 employees in 1947 worked only irregular hours, and a shortage of skilled workers continued. In these difficult circumstances, turnover had fallen to RM836,268 with "extraordinarily high" costs.[25]

Though frustrations are evident in the measured tones of the annual reports, the general impression is of pragmatism and resilience. The changes to company and city were difficult to manage, but new staff were employed and each challenge taken on and surmounted. But even this resilience was challenged in 1948.[26] In the first half of the year, the procurement of raw materials became practically impossible unless some service was offered in return. In the run-up to the 20 June currency reform, there were so many demands for vehicle repairs

---

19   Stuttgarter Karosseriewerk Reutter & Co. G.m.b.H., 'Geschäftsbericht 1947' (Stuttgarter Karosseriewerk Reutter & Co. G.m.b.H., 1948), RECARO Holding GmbH archives.
20   Jung and Jung, p. 149.
21   'Gewinn- Und Verlustrechnung Auf 31.12.1945' (Stuttgarter Karosseriewerk Reutter & Co. G.m.b.H., 1946), RECARO Holding GmbH archives.
22   'Bilanz Auf 31.Dezember1945' (Stuttgarter Karosseriewerk Reutter & Co. G.m.b.H., 1946), RECARO Holding GmbH archives.
23   Jung and Jung, p. 144, table.
24   Stuttgarter Karosseriewerk Reutter & Co. G.m.b.H., 'Geschäftsbericht 1947'.
25   Stuttgarter Karosseriewerk Reutter & Co. G.m.b.H., 'Geschäftsbericht 1947'. Neither the profit & loss account nor the balance sheet for this year are available.
26   'Geschäftsbericht 1948' (Stuttgarter Karosseriewerk Reutter & Co. G.m.b.H., 1949), RECARO Holding GmbH archives.

that some customers had to be turned away. Afterwards, cash became a problem as repairs dried up, evidence of the discontent and anxiety over increasing living costs that quickly replaced the initial euphoria of the post-currency reform consumer boom.[27] The currency reform also required Reutter to grant an extraordinary pay increase of 5%, though in return agreement was reached to extend the standard working week to 45 hours, an early productivity win.[28]

After a period of serious difficulty, though, in which Reutter had to sell off machinery and other equipment to raise cash, the economic clouds seem to have lifted. As for other companies, the currency reform appears to have signalled a revivification of the market, and released new opportunities.[29] New work was won for Opel. Turnover increased by 39% to DM/RM1.16 million. Staff numbers rose to 196 (though difficulty finding skilled workers, especially in sheet-metal work, was again noted). Quickly, however, Reutter's resilience was re-tested: the economic uplift was replaced by a sudden downturn, on this occasion forcing Reutter to begin building small buses. Again, the company rose to the new challenge, exhibiting at trade shows in Reutlingen and Hannover and winning new orders, without which it would have been impossible to retain its workers. But the firm's primary focus was on returning to its traditional business of building car bodies, which it was finally able to do in 1949.[30] It is notable that throughout this difficult period, Reutter did not lower its ambitions or its standards: despite losing its leaders and key customers, it continued to pursue excellence and the surviving members of its owning family remained committed to its long-term success and the retention of skilled staff. The reward for that collective commitment would be Porsche's decision to appoint Reutter as its key partner in the building of its new sports car, the Porsche 356.

Restoration and Growth, 1948 to 1960

In 1949, Reutter was comprehensively audited by the Schwäbische Treuhand, whose activities in this period were concentrated on the valuation of companies following the currency reform.[31] The thoroughness of their report reinforced

27   Christian L. Glossner, *The Making of the German Post-War Economy* (London and New York, 2013), pp. 133–35.
28   Stuttgarter Karosseriewerk Reutter & Co. G.m.b.H., 'Geschäftsbericht 1948'.
29   Glossner chapter 6, especially pp. 138–143.
30   Stuttgarter Karosseriewerk Reutter & Co. G.m.b.H., 'Geschäftsbericht 1948'. The reference in the annual report was presumably to the initial order for the Porsche 356.
31   For the scope of its activities following its foundation in 1919, see Reiner Quick, 'The Formation and Early Development of German Audit Firms', *Accounting, Business & Financial History*, 15.3 (2005), 317–43 (pp. 325–26). In due course it became the foundation of what is now EY Germany. See 'Geschichte' under 'Ernst & Young', Wikipedia (2017)

existing management control measures, while summarising Reutter's problems. It had shrunk to a fraction of its former size during the war.[32] Having been exclusively dedicated to automobile production before the conflict, it found that its major automotive customer, Wanderer, was now in the Soviet occupation zone, and other potential customers now preferred to manufacture their own bodywork. Moreover, the heavy presses previously used to make the most valuable components had been destroyed in the war.[33] Despite these setbacks Reutter had nevertheless begun to find its way forward. In 1948, Dipl.-Ing. Walter Beierbach was recruited as Technical Leader, in due course being granted signatory powers (*Prokura*).[34] Responsible for numerous technical developments which were patented, most significant among them for the company's future a reclining seat mechanism, Beierbach was made co-managing director with Körner in 1950.[35] Like Körner and other recruits, he was connected to the Reutter family through his membership of the Pietist community.[36] He was regarded by Friedrich Greger, a Reutter engineer whose personal record of his time in the business is an invaluable resource for understanding its history, as a "strong man with iron discipline towards himself and his workers, who for all his rigour did have a human side and in principle had very good relationships with his technicians and *Meister*." It was Beierbach who, over the next fifteen years, built the company's capabilities through the development of its machinery and equipment.[37] Supporting him, the company's foremen – its *Meister* – controlled key areas of the business, such as the pre-paint preparation area, the upholstery department and the prototyping shop, with the company's own quality-control systems in all areas being a critical contributor to its success.[38] Their experience and ability was apparently the strategic differentiator which made Porsche choose Reutter as its bodybuilding partner. That decision was not based on the Reutter works' proximity to Porsche's factory in Zuffenhausen, but on the judgement of Professor Ferdinand Porsche, who advised: "You have this offer and you have that offer. Here and there the prices

---

<https://de.wikipedia.org/w/index.php?title=Ernst_%26_Young&oldid=169184426> [accessed 22 October 2017].

32   Schwäbische Treuhand AG, 'Bericht', p. 6.

33   Schwäbische Treuhand AG, 'Bericht', p. 5.

34   A Prokurist's 'powers are for all practical purposes equivalent' to a managing director's, and 'the position of Prokurist carries considerable prestige in Germany': Baker & McKenzie, sec. 3.2.2.

35   Jung and Jung, p. 154.

36   See Chapter 2 on their Pietism.

37   Greger, p. 11.

38   Jung, *Porsche 356 Made by Reutter*, pp. 269, 253, 286.

are a bit more advantageous and so on, but I'll tell you what, go to Reutter. Never mind the money; you see, Reutter has the best foremen."[39]

Beierbach's rigour was complemented by a progressive organisational culture: all employees dined together in the company dining hall, and women workers were paid the same wages as men for the same job from the early 1950s onwards, two decades before the Equal Pay Act was enacted to enforce the same approach in Britain.[40] (At Porsche, too, the owner insisted on identical treatment for all employees, irrespective of their job level or responsibility.)[41] Within the workplace, workers' wellbeing and motivation were maintained by attention to the factory's lighting and to the aesthetics of each machine; the three big presses were painted green and given visible pet names.[42] The appointment of Max Müller-Scholl as managing director (*Geschäftsführer*) in 1953, following the unexpected death of Ernst Körner, reinforced the company's ethos of responsible management. Müller-Scholl's earlier career had given him international commercial experience, but his business acumen was combined with such a commitment to service in social and church offices that the West German Government would eventually confer a national honour on him.[43]

The Porsche 356 contract placed extraordinary demands on Reutter's workforce, requiring them in early 1955, for example, to produce a new model in parallel with very high volumes of the existing product, working excessive overtime in order to meet Porsche's demand for three hundred finished bodies (versus the contractual agreement for 150 per month) in July alone. For the company's owners and directors it was "obvious" in these circumstances that they should "pay the highest amount permitted by law into the staff pension fund."[44] Future managing director Norbert Helmes would later argue that this level of support, within what he called the company's "social enterprise model", would eventually become incompatible with its ability to achieve a satisfactory level of profitability.[45] But while discussion of religious values and social enterprises might give the impression that Reutter lacked hard edges or commercial drive, its performance in the 1950s showed it lacked neither.

Company histories show in detail how Porsche's growth was achieved in a symbiotic relationship with Reutter.[46] Producing at high volumes was, on the face of it, a highly attractive proposition. The cars themselves were sold by

---

39   Richard von Frankenburg, *Porsche, the Man and His Cars*, trans. by Charles Meisl (London, 1961), p. 126.
40   Jung, *Porsche 356 Made by Reutter*, pp. 267, 281.
41   Porsche and Molter, pp. 241–42.
42   Jung, *Porsche 356 Made by Reutter*, p. 271.
43   Jung and Jung, p. 191.
44   Jung, *Porsche 356 Made by Reutter*, pp. 117, 125.
45   Helmes, p. 19.
46   Jung, *Porsche 356 Made by Reutter*, pp. 68–188; Jung and Jung, pp. 167–247.

Porsche in 1950 for DM9950.[47] Reutter sold their finished bodies to Porsche for DM4085 in 1952.[48] The results were attractive. In 1956, its 50th anniversary year, Reutter earned "pleasing profits", investing in new capacity, paying almost DM210,000 into the staff welfare fund, and increasing pension payments for retirees. Helmes's later condemnation of these personnel practices seems misplaced: in a full-employment economy in which high skills were always in short supply, Reutter's generous treatment of its staff was commercially astute as well as socially just. For example, at the same time as they celebrated the anniversary, Reutter's management were having to work out how to increase deliveries of the finished Porsche 356 body from nineteen to twenty-four daily.[49] What Greger calls "the triumphal march" of Porsche required the body works to change and rationalise constantly, ensuring work "was of the highest quality and beauty". But "Porsche needed more, always more", increasing Reutter's revenue but also consuming so much time and resource that its dependency on Porsche grew ineluctably.[50] None of that progress could have happened without the full commitment – in terms of both effort and quality of work – of Reutter's workforce, or the retention of all available skilled staff. Other Mittelstand firms followed a similar approach: dedication from the staff was expected, but rewarded, tying them into the business.[51] As we will see later, Jensen in the UK also needed to meet growing demand, but tried to do so without the same investment of resources or management care for its staff, with predictably less impressive results. Despite its intrinsic attractiveness, though, Porsche's growth engendered a growing fear among Reutter's commercial staff of the risk that any reduction, by accident or intent, in Porsche's purchased volumes would spell disaster for Reutter. They therefore sought a "second leg", but found it increasingly difficult to diversify when all staff were constantly "at the limits of their performance capability" thanks to the pressure of the Porsche programme.[52] These pressures are vividly brought to life in Greger's account and the Jung histories, and illustrate what West Germany's annual increase

47   Porsche and Molter, p. 188.
48   Jung, *Porsche 356 Made by Reutter*, p. 88.
49   Jung, *Porsche 356 Made by Reutter*, pp. 139–41.
50   Greger, p. 17.
51   See, for example, the treatment of employees at Stuttgart engineering company Philipp Müller in this period: 'Payroll 1961–65'; 'Personal Folder of KM, 1955–67' (Firma Philipp Müller Nachf. Eugen Bucher GmbH & Co), WABW B38/ Bü195; 'Personal Folder of HG' (Firma Philipp Müller Nachf. Eugen Bucher GmbH & Co), WABW B38/ Bü190. Names withheld for confidentiality reasons.
52   Greger, p. 18.

in output per worker of 6.40%,[53] within an economy growing by an average of 7.2% annually between 1950 and 1963,[54] felt like to those who delivered it.

In its search for profitable niche products, the board pursued patentable innovation, as Reutter had always done. Reutter's most important achievement was the device patented in 1953 by Beierbach in the firm's name: the reclining seat mechanism, *der Liegesitzbeschlag*. Those already in the market took up too much space or needed the door open to operate. Reutter's was compact, and would fit almost all the car seats currently in use.[55] Requests for licence fee arrangements came from engineers in Munich and Paris, and at the Geneva motor show in 1954 and London motor show in 1956 there were large orders. By July 1957 Reutter had delivered over 500,000 reclining mechanisms. Most car manufacturers in West Germany and abroad were using it, at least in their high-end models. The biggest customer, Mercedes, was taking 3000 sets a month. Reutter's management was never complacent. The *Liegesitzbeschlag* was being constantly modified, creating variants; all were patented, blocking development efforts by Reutter's competitors, who either had to buy from Reutter or apply for a manufacturing licence.[56] This situation led to difficult competitive battles, especially with arch-rival Keiper, and forceful pricing tactics from Reutter's leadership, winning business at Mercedes-Benz and Opel.[57] Their actions and attitudes indicate the degree of competitiveness which drove growth during the *Wirtschaftswunder*.

Though 85% of *Liegesitzbeschlag* capacity was now dedicated to Porsche, making it difficult to serve other customers as quickly and inventively as Reutter would have liked, the seat-mechanism business continued to thrive, and Reutter added work with Volvo in Sweden to its success with Opel. Given the value of the *Liegesitzbeschlag* patents, the board decided to establish a Swiss subsidiary, whose purpose would be to collect licence fees from foreign customers, hold the patents, and invest in potential foreign business opportunities. To avoid concerns over tax avoidance, Müller-Scholl ethically sought the approval of the Economy Ministry. Reutter set up the subsidiary as the worldwide licence-holder, so it paid patent fees but also received royalties. Thus RECARO AG was launched in Switzerland on 9 September 1957.[58] These strategic decisions show again that Reutter's management were commercially astute and forward-thinking, as well as ethical and intent on good governance, as we will see in their management of the company's finances.

53   Eichengreen, p. 88, table 4.1: annual growth per worker 1950–1960. In Britain, it grew at 2.51%.
54   Abelshauser, *Deutsche Wirtschaftsgeschichte*, p. 305, table 15.
55   Jung and Jung, p. 253.
56   Jung and Jung, pp. 254–56.
57   Jung and Jung, p. 256.
58   Jung and Jung, pp. 258–250.

Company Operations and Strategic Change, 1960 to 1963

The West German automotive industry was transformed during the 1950s: its productivity growth averaged 9.37% annually, its share of the national economy rose threefold to 5% between 1952 and 1960, and its employee numbers rose ten-fold to 2.1 million between 1950 and 1962.[59] The number of cars in private ownership grew nine-fold to 4,066,000 between 1950 and 1960, and the car became a quintessential element of the national culture as "motorization became a reality and the car the symbol of a new Germany".[60] The rate of change in the industry was evident at Porsche, which had only started to build its first sports cars in 1950, a modest target of five hundred vehicles reflecting the fact that it had only DM200,000 in capital available. By 1960, Porsche was transformed, its 1250 staff achieving DM108 million in annual sales.[61]

In these circumstances, severe demands were placed on suppliers (and, of course, huge opportunities were presented to them, fuelling the growth of Baden-Württemberg's Mittelstand), and Reutter was forced constantly to adapt and improve, or be left behind. Having managed to do so, it entered the new decade in an apparently strong position.[62] Share capital was increased by DM1 million to DM3 million from its own resources. Although costs had increased, the growth in turnover since the previous year had ensured a "satisfactory result" of almost DM1.1 million of after-tax profit. The remaining reserves were in turn increased by the addition of DM220,000 from 1960's profits. With a wage bill of over DM4.8 million, the directors nevertheless contributed DM100,000 to the employee support fund, plus additional social contributions, expressing appreciation for employees' efforts. Reserves were held as security for obligations under product warranties and pensions payments, as well as for the possible payment of performance-related bonuses. Shareholders received a 6% dividend and 14% special bonus, the two equating to 55% of the earned profit; DM450,000 of the balance was transferred to the company's reserves. Reutter's dividend policy appears reasonable, equivalent to 0.6% of turnover in 1962 and an estimated 1.5% – including the special bonus – of 1961 turnover. In comparison, the Hohner family paid themselves dividends of DM810,000 on DM35 million turnover (2.3%) in 1958 and DM450,00 on sales of DM37 million (1.2%) in 1960 from their musical-instrument manufacturing

59 Abelshauser, *Deutsche Wirtschaftsgeschichte*, p. 416.
60 Harold James, *A German Identity, 1770 to the Present Day* (London, 2000), p. 189.
61 Porsche and Molter, pp. 188, 241, 243.
62 Stuttgarter Karosseriewerk Reutter & Co. G.m.b.H., 'Bericht über das 55. Geschäftsjahr 1961' (Stuttgarter Karosseriewerk Reutter & Co. G.m.b.H., nd), RECARO Holding GmbH archives.

enterprise, also in Baden-Württemberg.[63] In contrast, Jensen's owner Norcros paid itself dividends in 1965 of £122,000, 5% of its turnover and 105% of its £116,000 profit.[64]

Reutter's 1962 results were impressive.[65] Turnover had reached DM39.5 million (double the 1962 sales of DM20 million at its fiercest competitor, Keiper),[66] yielding profit after tax of DM1.59 million, an increase of 49% over the previous year.[67] But while they demonstrated that the company was well run and prudently governed, the financial statements for 1962 also betrayed some potentially worrying signs. At 4.18%, net profit margins were not high (but may have been normal: Volkswagen's after-tax profit margin was 3.8% for the same year).[68] And while Reutter had reserves of DM4.6 million, property and plant worth DM5.9 million, and share capital of DM3 million, over DM3.1 million was owed to financial institutions, suggesting its freedom of movement within the capital-intensive automotive industry was potentially constrained.[69]

However, Reutter's intellectual property, now held by its Swiss subsidiary, was also an important asset in which the company had invested heavily. Of the thirty patents granted to Reutter between 1950 and 1962, eight were published in the 1950s, and nine in 1962 alone.[70] Other German manufacturers invested in the same way. Reutter's customer Porsche, admittedly with a wider range of potentially patentable products, published 757 between 1950 and 1962;[71] the synchromesh gearbox introduced in the Porsche 356 generated seventy patents

63   Hartmut Berghoff, *Zwischen Kleinstadt und Weltmarkt: Hohner und die Harmonika 1857 - 1961 : Unternehmensgeschichte als Gesellschaftsgeschichte* (Paderborn, München: Schöningh, 2006), p. 568, fig 47; p. 574, table 35.

64   Jensen Motors Ltd., 'Jensen Motors Limited: Profit & Loss Account for Seven Years, Ending 31 July 1959 -1965' (Jensen Motors Ltd., 1965), MRC, MSS.215/2/11.

65   Stuttgarter Karosseriewerk Reutter & Co. G.m.b.H., 'Bericht über das 56. Geschäftsjahr 1962'.

66   Putsch and Putsch, p. 149.

67   Jensen Motors Ltd., 'Jensen Motors Limited: Profit & Loss Account for Seven Years, Ended 31 July 1959 -1965'.

68   VW AG, 'Bericht über das Geschäftsjahr 1964' (Volkswagenwerk Aktiengesellschaft, 1965), p. 4 <https://www.volkswagenag.com/presence/konzern/images/teaser/history/chronik/geschaeftsberichte/1964-Geschaeftsbericht.pdf> [accessed 6 November 2018].

69   See Chapter 2 on Bank relations.

70   'Patents List - Stuttgarter Karosseriewerk Reutter 1950–1962', Espacenet (2017) <https://worldwide.espacenet.com/searchResults?submitted=true&locale=en_EP&DB=EPODOC&ST=advanced&TI=&AB=&PN=&AP=&PR=&PD=1950–1962&PA=Reutter&IN=&CPC=&IC=&Submit=Search> [accessed 23 September 2017].

71   'Patents List - Porsche AG 1950–1962', Espacenet (2017) <https://worldwide.espacenet.com/searchResults?submitted=true&locale=en_EP&DB=EPODOC&ST=advanced&TI=&AB=&PN=&AP=&PR=&PD=1950–1962&PA=Porsche&IN=&CPC=&IC=&Submit=Search> [accessed 23 September 2017].

and DM10 million in licence fees alone.[72] Reutter's competitor and future owner Keiper produced thirty during the 1950s and forty-seven in total between 1950 and 1962.[73] In his autobiography, founder Fritz Keiper had emphasised the importance of gaining patent protection, as he did himself for the first and subsequent products he invented; the same need is reiterated by Norbert Helmes five decades later, and was practised by Reutter/RECARO managers throughout the company's history.[74] All these Mittelstand companies, pursuing excellence in their niche markets, demonstrated a greater determination to generate intellectual property and protect it than their British counterpart Jensen Motors Ltd., which published only five patents between 1950 and 1962, and none in the subsequent five years.[75] Reutter's approach was and would remain very different. As we will see below, the eventual sale of a majority of the business to Porsche compelled Reutter to reinvent itself: it did so by publishing thirty-three patents between 1963 and 1968, evidence of its high levels of creativity, and of its continuing strategy of pursuing competitive advantage in niche markets.[76]

1963 to 1965: Acquisition by Porsche and Reinvention

Though 1961's and 1962's results were good, the preceding three years had seen the beginning of a perceptible change in Reutter's relationship with Porsche. In 1958, Reutter had declined Porsche's request to increase its output from twenty-four to thirty-two bodies per day, "which would have required an investment of unbearable scale and bound us even more closely to our principal customer", as Müller-Scholl told the Reutter board. He had discussed the future of Reutter's relationship with Ferry Porsche and agreed to cooperate with a second bodybuilder, Drauz, effectively creating a competitor for himself.[77] In

---

72 Porsche and Molter, p. 236.

73 'Patents List - Fritz Keiper 1950–1962', Espacenet (2017) <https://worldwide.espacenet. com/searchResults?compact=false&page=0&IN=&TI=&locale=en_EP&DB=EPODOC &PN=&ST=advanced&AB=&PR=&PD=1950–1962&IC=&CPC=&Submit=Search& AP=&PA=keiper> [accessed 23 September 2017].

74 Keiper, pp. 91–93; Helmes, pp. 3–5.

75 'Patents List - Jensen Motors Limited 1950–1976', Espacenet (2017) <https://worldwide. espacenet.com/searchResults?submitted=true&locale=en_EP&DB=EPODOC&ST=advan ced&TI=&AB=&PN=&AP=&PR=&PD=1950–1976&PA=Jensen+Motors&IN=&CPC =&IC=&Submit=Search> [accessed 23 September 2017].

76 'Patents List - RECARO AG 1963–1968', Espacenet (2017) <https://worldwide. espacenet.com/searchResults?submitted=true&locale=en_EP&DB=EPODOC&ST=adv anced&TI=&AB=&PN=&AP=&PR=&PD=1963–1968&PA=RECARO&IN=&CPC= &IC=&Submit=Search> [accessed 23 September 2017].

77 Board minutes of 19/2/1958 and 4/6/1958, quoted in Jung and Jung, p. 231; In fact, although Drauz did complete 3514 bodies for the Porsche 356, according to 'Drauz-Werke', Wikipedia

response to the ever-intensifying pressure and growing reliance on its largest
customer, Reutter began talks with a plastics company to develop a plastics
tooling business in order to diversify its risk. The proposed venture came to
nothing, but its initiation highlighted the benefits in German business society
of interlocking responsibilities and relationships: the owner of the plastics
company, B.W. Müller, was also the chairman of Reutter's shareholders'
advisory council.[78] It also highlighted two potential future problems for the
company. First, a concern to avoid a repeat of the excessive dependency on
one market or customer might lead to strategically questionable thinking on
diversification. Second, Müller's willingness to seek what would be a financial
benefit not only for Reutter but also for himself suggested a potential risk of
future governance problems or unethical conduct. Both came to pass.

Reutter was, in fact, now one of a very small number of a dying breed. Being
a coachbuilder had become, in both West Germany and Britain, a precarious
existence since World War Two. At the 1929 Earl's Court Motor Show there had
been fifty-nine British coachbuilders; by 1959 there were thirteen left; by 1967
only one remained independent of mainstream car manufacturers.[79] Likewise,
most of the remaining German specialist firms had been taken over (as Drauz
would be in 1965), gone bankrupt, or were existing only as repairers.[80] For
Reutter, the Porsche relationship had been lucrative but "not at all easy" and
the next logical step, to invest in a deeper collaboration with both Porsche and
the coachbuilder Karmann, required entrepreneurial risk-taking and financial
resources that were not available. Greger notes that the important members
of both the family and the management were now old and risk-averse. Max
Müller-Scholl was already pensionable. The single Reutter family member still
in the business, Fritz, died suddenly at his desk in 1961. The only potential male
family recruit, Welf Koch, was still too young.[81] In the opinion of Jung and Jung,
it now became "all too clear how much over the years the family concern had
missed the driving force that the entrepreneurial vision and leadership of family
members" would have provided, making at this juncture the wartime deaths

---

(2018) <https://de.wikipedia.org/w/index.php?title=Drauz-Werke&oldid=175225324>
[accessed 22 April 2018] their predominant interest was in bus-building, and in 1965 they sold
their car body business to NSU; See also the brief history at 'Karosserien von Gustav Drauz'
<https://stadtarchiv.heilbronn.de/stadtgeschichte/geschichte-a-z/d/drauz-karosseriefabrik.
html> [accessed 22 April 2018].

78   Jung and Jung, p. 232. The engagement and activities of the company's advisory board,
or Aufsichtsrat. a feature of all German companies, do not feature in this account because
there are few mentions of them in the available historical sources. The same is true of the
other German companies reviewed in this book.

79   George Oliver, *Cars and Coachbuilding: One Hundred Years of Road Vehicle
Development* (London, 1981), pp. 212–14.

80   Greger, p. 19.

81   Greger, p. 20. Welf was born in 1942.

of Albert and Otto Reutter and Theodor Koch seem all the more significant.[82] Their argument is understandable in the light not only of Uta Jung's emotional engagement with Reutter's history, but also of the success which Albert Reutter, Ferry Porsche, Wilhelm Putsch and his sons Friedrich-Wilhelm and Ulrich (the son-in-law and grandsons of Fritz Keiper, and the future acquirers of Reutter), and indeed Alan and Richard Jensen, had achieved as leaders of their own family's firms. But the attribution of superior vision and leadership to family membership is not automatically accurate, as the Wandel family were then proving in nearby Reutlingen. Nor, in implicitly denigrating the substantial achievements of Reutter's management, does it explain how a Reutter family member would have devised a more attractive strategy for the coachbuilding side of the business in a period of increasing consolidation in the automotive industry. As Friedrich Greger remarks, Reutter's situation was difficult, but not without prospects: although the coachbuilding part of Reutter was indeed vulnerable, it had been brilliantly managed and was financially lucrative, and the seating-mechanism business was growing, despite tough competition from Keiper.[83] Porsche, though, was alone among German automobile manufacturers in not having its own bodyworks, and no matter what strategy Reutter chose to adopt, the mutual dependency remained. (Jensen was in a similar position: its solvency was almost entirely dependent on Austin wanting it to continue building its sports car bodies.) For Porsche, short of space, expanding rapidly, conscious of its own dependency on Reutter and anxious to be self-sufficient in the future, acquiring Reutter would be a logical and affordable step.[84]

Ferry Porsche sent his comments on a proposed deal in a ten-page personal letter to B.W. Müller.[85] Porsche is cordial, but tough; his brief analysis of the proposed deal highlights his commercial acumen and – even though his company's turnover, output, and staff numbers had grown exponentially in the fifteen years since its foundation – his very personal engagement with every detail.[86] Negotiations moved to a conclusion over succeeding weeks, culminating in a meeting whose conclusions were summarised in a further letter from Ferry Porsche to Müller.[87] The purchase price was set, subject to the agreement of the Baden-Württemberg and German Government Finance

---

82   Jung and Jung, p. 250.
83   Greger, p. 19.
84   Jung and Jung, p. 251.
85   Ferry Porsche, 'Verhandlungen über den Ankauf der Geschäftsanteile der Firma Stuttgarter Karosseriewerk REUTTER & Co. G.m.b.H.', 31 January 1963, RECARO Holding GmbH archives.
86   von Frankenburg, pp. 189, 206.
87   Ferry Porsche, 'Stuttgarter Karosseriewerk REUTTER & Co. G.m.b.H. in Stuttgart', 14 March 1963, RECARO Holding GmbH archives.

Ministries to a special capital allowance.[88] This suggests a willingness on the part of local and national authorities to support entrepreneurs like Porsche, still a relatively young company albeit one whose wartime and pre-war achievements might have resonated with officials.[89] This relationship appears to offer a sharp contrast with contemporary UK policy, where Government attention and support were focused not on helping successful entrepreneurs but on the interests of big business.

The sale contract itself confirmed the deal terms and a commitment to leave, without any changes in their employment status, all those employees who wished to remain in the company: paternalism was maintained.[90] For Reutter's employees the sale – which had been conducted in complete secrecy – of such a successful business was incomprehensible. Greger's response is that none of them could see as clearly as Reutter's leaders "the sword which was hanging over the company" while 85% of its business was dependent on Porsche. It therefore made eminent sense to take "good money" from Porsche, securing a strong starting position for the part of the company which was not being transferred to Porsche. For those in Zuffenhausen, building Porsche bodies for the neighbouring factory, the work would continue just as it was, with only a change of ownership.[91] For the remaining Reutter workers and management, a new start was to be made in the company's long-term headquarters building, in Augustenstrasse in central Stuttgart, which had been left out of the sale. A key element of the sale was that the newly named RECARO (from the initial letters of "Reutter" and "Carosserie") received a contract which would allow RECARO to fulfil Porsche's "total requirement for complete seats and seat reclining mechanisms", an exclusivity which, as RECARO's management quickly reminded their Porsche counterparts, also included newly developed "shell seats".[92]

---

88   Value withheld for confidentiality reasons.

89   Ferry Porsche himself had been an honorary SS officer, which he later described as an unwanted 'honour' which he had been unable to decline, and which briefly caused him some discomfort in his postwar relations with US officials. See Porsche and Molter, pp. 124–25. His father, however, was held as a prisoner by the French after the war ; See Porsche and Molter, chap. XIII; and Ferry Porsche and John Bentley, *We at Porsche: The Autobiography of Dr. Ing. h.c. Ferry Porsche with John Bentley* (Yeovil, 1976), pp. 191–211. Both father and son were, however, recognised as contributors of engineering expertise – for example through the provision of the VW Kübelwagen to the Wehrmacht – and not as Party adherents.

90   'Deed of Sale: "Geschäftsanteilsübertragungen Ella Reutter, Charlotte Reutter, Nachlaß Fritz Reutter und Firma Dr. Ing. h. c. F. Porsche KG. mit dem Sitz in Stuttgart vom 15. Mai 1963"' (1963, RECARO Holding GmbH archives.

91   Greger, p. 22; Greger's account is given credibility by being quoted in full by Jung and Jung, p. 252 and in other places in their history.

92   Letter of 20 December 1963 to Porsche management, reproduced in Frank Jung, *RECARO: Sitzen in Bewegung* (Bielefeld: Delius Klasing, 2016), p. 30.

Although the exclusivity agreement made the new company's finances more secure, the immediate loss of expertise was challenging: of 1250 Reutter staff, 1000 were transferred into Porsche, including Walter Beierbach, Reutter's long-time technical director, whose expertise guaranteed the seamless continuation of production after his transfer (and whose commitment and capabilities had never depended on family membership).[93] His ability was so well respected, in fact, that when Ferry Porsche's son disagreed with the company's chief designer about the design of what became the iconic Porsche 911, Porsche solved the problem by having Beierbach draw it himself.[94] This episode highlights two distinguishing characteristics of German management mentality. It shows that Ferry Porsche was still a hands-on *Mittelständler*, despite his company's size, more concerned by product quality than paternal allegiance (and as engaged in technical detail as he had been in the financial detail of the acquisition); and that senior business leaders like Beierbach remained expert technicians long after they assumed managerial responsibility. Similar technical capabilities existed within senior management at Jensen, where the proficiency of the Jensen brothers and some of their successors enabled the development of innovative models. But none demonstrated an equivalent capacity for operational or personnel management which allowed them to deliver the sustained, long-term, profitable performance of their German counterparts.

While Porsche gained control of its own bodyshop, more land, and the expertise of men like Beierbach, RECARO derived several benefits itself from the transaction. First, some financial security, through the ten-year exclusive seat contract with Porsche, in which supply at current pricing was guaranteed for the first five years and would continue for the second five years provided RECARO's prices were not more than 10% higher than a reputable competitor's.[95] Porsche was growing rapidly. The increase in output from 7055 cars in 1959 to 13,134 cars in 1966 and 16,761 in 1970[96] presented RECARO's staff with considerable logistical challenges in the relatively cramped older premises in Augustenstrasse, but also with constantly growing RECARO revenue.[97] Second, RECARO gained increased freedom of action: there was no longer the monopsonistic relationship with Porsche that had constrained Reutter's strategic options for so long. Their patent-protected seat fittings business had been developing successfully in parallel with the Porsche business, and could now be developed further. RECARO was now free – indeed, if it wished to grow, compelled – to innovate around what had necessarily become "its core

93   Greger, p. 21.
94   Porsche and Molter, pp. 244–46.
95   Greger, p. 23.
96   Porsche and Bentley, p. 256.
97   Greger, p. 24.

competence, seating".[98] Helmes points out that it would do so in a market
which was increasingly safety-conscious and interested in "sports-driving".[99]
Car owners' expectations were transformed during the 1950s and 1960s,
demanding a vehicle that would be safe, stylish, and personalised – on the
face of it, a perfect market for RECARO's innovative new seats and creative
marketing to win drivers over.[100] Consistent with Mittelstand values, RECARO
now had more independence: was secure in its region, had patented, excellent
products, and could look after its remaining staff.

   If the new company seemed to get off to a well-planned start within a viable
long-term strategy, however, an alternative interpretation of its purpose must
be kept in mind. Also consistent with Mittelstand thinking, the real rationale
for the property buy-back and the establishment of RECARO, Greger suggests,
was to give Welf Koch the opportunity, after the completion of his studies and
practical training, to run part of his grandfather's legacy.[101] Was RECARO,
therefore, founded as a viable venture on rational grounds? Or was it a project
of the heart, based for emotional reasons in the space-constrained older
building that Wilhelm and Albert Reutter had occupied (in the same way that
the Wandel cousins insisted on rebuilding their fathers' factory in Reutlingen
city centre) with only limited prospects of long-term success? The answer
may be somewhere between the two. The family could have sold the whole
of the business, or completed the Porsche transaction first and then sold the
remainder. But there was perhaps a sense of a covenant, to honour both the
Reutter legacy and the loyalty and expertise of the remaining staff. There was
too much respect for staff members to retain them as an indulgence which
risked their wellbeing. And for those staff, in a period of full employment,
there must have been a belief in the venture and the family's values, otherwise
they would have found work elsewhere. The realisation of both employee and
family aspirations would, however, depend on the successful leadership of the
business in the time before Welf was able to take over.

1964 to 1969: New Global Brand to the End of Independence

As it turned out, the final few years of the Reutter family's ownership of an
independent business were distinguished by its outstanding inventiveness
and disfigured by its increasing mismanagement. The actions of RECARO's

---

98 Jung, *RECARO*, p. 28.
99 Helmes, p. 3.
100 Norbert Stieniezcka, 'Von fahrbaren Untersatz zur Chromkarosse mit "Innerer
Sicherheit" - der Wandel der Nutzeranforderungen an das Automobil in 50er und 60er
Jahren', in *Geschichte und Zukunft der Deutschen Automobilindustrie: Tagung im Rahmen
der "Chemnitzer Begegnungen" 2000*, ed. by Rudolf Boch (Stuttgart, 2001).
101 Greger, p. 21.

most senior decision-makers demonstrated the concerns over the agency of non-family members alluded to by Jung and Jung. The achievements of RECARO's eventual conqueror, Ulrich Putsch, seemed to prove their point about the desirability of family ownership and leadership. Adopting the formulation of management scholar David Teece and others, Putsch and his brother Friedrich-Wilhelm displayed "dynamic capabilities" during the 1960s, "sensing" new opportunities, "seizing" them, and "transforming" both their business and their industry.[102] Müller-Scholl, in contrast, was clearly capable but no longer dynamic. Norbert Helmes, his replacement, may have been dynamic, but was not evidently capable. And though *Aufsichtsrat* chairman Bernhard Müller was possibly both dynamic and capable, he appears to have used those attributes to promote a cause other than the Reutter family's long-term wellbeing. RECARO's experience did not invalidate Mittelstand values of focused strategies, excellence in niche products, or generational continuity. Instead, it demonstrated that those values were themselves dynamic, as Keiper showed by adapting them so successfully to changing markets and technologies.

The early opportunities facing RECARO were brilliantly managed. Staff realised that to survive they would need to be quicker than the automotive manufacturers' own work in seat development, which was still unsophisticated. They therefore began working with orthopaedic surgeons to review seat design, creating innovative marketing materials that featured surgeons and other relevant professionals.[103] Innovation appears to have been the product of an egalitarian and cooperative working environment: "We had at that time lots of freedom and lots of ideas", the seating department leader recalled fifty years afterwards. In a workplace distinguished by close working together and interaction with colleagues, a contemporary colleague remembered, "We had good people, who from the outset shared responsibility and ideas. The boss was someone you only needed for the trickiest decisions."[104] This suggested an environment that was less hierarchical and more flexible than was common in British business.[105] For the external market, the company launched the RECARO *Sportsitz* (sports seat), which could be retrofitted to a range of cars. One may question whether the two long-retired colleagues quoted here retained an objective memory of their workplace fifty years later (though their recollection of the positive working atmosphere matches Ferry Porsche's recollection of the

102 David J. Teece, 'Dynamic Capabilities: Routines versus Entrepreneurial Action', *Journal of Management Studies*, 49.8 (2012), 1395–1401 <https://doi.org/10.1111/j.1467-6486.2012.01080.x>; David J. Teece, *Dynamic Capabilities and Strategic Management: Organizing for Innovation and Growth* (Oxford, 2009).
103 Jung and Jung, pp. 263–65.
104 Jung, *RECARO*, p. 102.
105 Carl Duerr, *Management Kinetics: Carl Duerr on Communication* (London, 1971), pp. 187–93; Lazonick, p. 20.

Figure 20 Advertisement for RECARO Sports Seats, 1964. Frank Jung, Private Collection.

"enthusiasm with which we all went to work" in the early years of Porsche).[106] But their emphasis on the responsibility devolved to individual technicians to develop complex products suggests a high level of technical competence across the workforce, and by integrating the "traditional" Reutter emphasis on performance and quality into their seating innovations, and producing striking new marketing materials, RECARO was soon able to build a strong brand. The outcome of inclusive innovation was soon plain to see: at the 1965 international IAA motor show in Hannover, RECARO exhibited its new "sports seat" under the slogan, "*Wer gut sitzt – fährt besser*" (whoever sits well drives better). It thereby created for itself not only a new product, but also a new way of thinking about and marketing what had largely been a commodity item within the car until that point. Now, RECARO told the market, anyone who wanted "to drive better had to sit properly". Superb public relations work, later used by American Carl Duerr to good effect at Jensen but decried by his British managers, reinforced their message, as the advertisement in Figure 20 shows.[107]

In parallel with this marketing success, though, came operational and financial pressures. Building seats to meet Porsche's booming requirements was a challenge. The reclining seat mechanism business, which had continued to be a success since the 500,000th system was delivered back in 1957,[108] offered some financial security thanks to what Keiper's Ulrich Putsch acknowledged

106   Porsche and Molter, p. 240.
107   1964 advertisement, image kindly provided by Frank Jung; see also Jung, *RECARO*, pp. 33, 63.
108   Jung and Jung, p. 256.

to be Reutter's "unbreakable" patent,[109] which blocked competitors' development opportunities. But Keiper had achieved equivalent market dominance to Reutter/RECARO with its own, different reclining technology,[110] and Putsch realised that RECARO had become vulnerable. The once-dominant, famous bodybuilder was now a small specialist supplier, for which heavy investment in new seat mechanisms, as well as in the Sports Seats and in production for Porsche, would be difficult.[111] Increasingly onerous demands from customers like Mercedes Benz would just drive RECARO's costs up and allow Mercedes to play one seat mechanism manufacturer off against another, ensuring each made minimum profits.[112] Furthermore, RECARO developed its market knowledge by working with dealers and end-users, which was expensive, and had to outsource some elements of its manufacturing, adding to costs.

In contrast, Keiper had anticipated years previously the move to automotive mass-production, and implemented mass production techniques for their own components. RECARO and Reutter certainly met the rising production demands of Porsche and benefited from judicious intellectual property protection, but their company culture continued to venerate technical excellence and *Handwerk* (craftsmanship). Keiper shared Mittelstand values with RECARO and valued its own technical excellence. But in its own pursuit of excellent niche products it had been working since the early 1950s with process-improvement consultants to achieve its stated company mission "to develop simple, effective and economical constructions which can be produced and marketed in large quantities for the building of new vehicles of all types."[113] And Keiper was not the only threat to RECARO. Greger shows that while management had successfully set up "three legs" on the new company's strategic "stool" – finished-seat design and supply, seat mechanism production, and a new repairs business – Müller-Scholl clearly also recognised "a new direction would require the replacement of older, experienced colleagues by young, dynamic staff."[114] For this he engaged Norbert Helmes in 1964 as assistant to the directors (*Assistent der Geschäftsleitung*).[115]

Helmes's recollections of this period, written in 1977, offer a critical perspective. We have focused on the value RECARO accorded to quality and creativity and its paternalistic ethos, typical Mittelstand values. In his

---

109   Putsch and Putsch, p. 155.
110   Putsch and Putsch, pp. 154–57.
111   Putsch and Putsch, p. 157.
112   Greger, p. 26; see also Gary Herrigel, *Industrial Constructions: The Sources of German Industrial Power*, pp. 153–56 on the evolution of Daimler-Benz's relationships with its suppliers.
113   Putsch and Putsch, pp. 142–43.
114   Greger, p. 24.
115   Jung and Jung, pp. 266–67.

retrospective criticism of RECARO's shortcomings, though, Helmes implicitly identifies the hard edges that also characterised successful Mittelstand businesses, including Keiper, but were missing from RECARO. Thus for Helmes, RECARO in 1963 lacked a "battle-hardened sales force", strong management, and a construction department which was able to analyse its own costs; an R&D department was only set up in 1965.[116] Furthermore, there was no short- or medium-term business plan with alternative options which, with quick decision-making, could have been executed in response to new circumstances. The allocation of overheads was significantly improved in 1964, but the insights that could be gained from this and applied to returning the business to a profitability-mindset were not effected.[117] Helmes's report is a problematic source in several respects, inviting not only the question of why he did not do more himself to solve these problems during his tenure, but also the observation that its real purpose was to exonerate Helmes himself from the Reutter family's criticism of RECARO's eventual sale.[118] The more successful Helmes was in depicting difficult circumstances, the more reasonable his later actions in selling off RECARO would appear.

Nevertheless, the contrasts between RECARO and Keiper in this period actually *were* stark. RECARO had lost some of its best people, transferred to Porsche. Its shareholders were not actively involved in the business, were not competent to shape its strategy, and were emotionally attached to its Reutter history and its increasingly unviable city-centre premises. Its managing director, Max Müller-Scholl, was now in his mid-sixties and represented increasingly old-fashioned, albeit virtuous, values. Greger's own commentary appears more respectful, but his insights reinforce Helmes's criticisms. He cites the "low-key care" taken of business relationships as a frequent cause of abortive negotiations. Generous sales-support programmes were not seen to be necessary: reputation, quality, and principles should suffice. Unfortunately, RECARO "only recognised later that this type of representation did not always suffice" in a world of evolving business morality.[119] The evolving relationship with Porsche can be seen as an indication of the increasingly competitive nature of the automotive industry, in which the principle of "loyalty to the supplier", codified by Daimler-Benz in 1958 and practised by Ferry Porsche in the days of Reutter,[120] was beginning to be superseded by manufacturers' pursuit of dual or multiple sourcing unless a supplier's patent dictated a sole-supplier

---

116   Helmes, p. 7.

117   Helmes, p. 8.

118   Martin Sandberger, 'Letter headed "Verkauf der RECARO im Jahre 1969"', 4 August 1977, RECARO Holding GmbH archives.

119   Greger, pp. 30–31.

120   Stéphanie Tilly and Jean-luc Malvache, 'Des partenaires des grands ? Les relations entre constructeurs automobiles et sous-traitants et leurs conséquences spatiales en Allemagne

relationship.[121] Although the automotive industry was undergoing a change from a "seller's to a buyer's market", only 12–15% of suppliers, by one estimate, depended on one customer for over half their turnover.[122] RECARO's dependency on Porsche was therefore, despite the fears expressed a decade earlier about Porsche's controlling power, still exceptionally high.

Where had this increasingly dangerous competitor come from? Keiper and RECARO had similarly humble origins,[123] but unlike Reutter's luxury products, Fritz Keiper's were innovative but unglamorous metal parts made in high volumes.[124] After the Second World War, Keiper's factories benefited from long-term investments in automation and process improvement under Wilhelm Putsch, who took over from his father-in-law Keiper in 1950 and worked closely with local politicians to expand Keiper's premises and in-house production capabilities.[125] When Wilhelm Putsch suffered a stroke in 1961, his sons Friedrich Wilhelm and Ulrich were forced to assume control. Though still in their twenties – almost forty years younger than RECARO's Max Müller-Scholl – they were well prepared (having trained as an administrator and a machine-design engineer respectively), entrepreneurial, dynamic, and locked into the family firm.[126] One public notice, from 1964, encapsulates their focus on productivity and staff communication, and can be contrasted with RECARO's emphasis on creativity and handcraft skills:

> Our modern card-punch machines in Remscheid have taken over a lot of the work which would have occupied many members of staff ... That means we can save personnel costs, and our staff get time for things which only people can do: planning for the improvement of our products, of production-sequencing, of the organisation, of our social benefits [*soziale Leistungen*] – planning for the future.[127]

It was during this period that Keiper's progress began to threaten a dramatic worsening of RECARO's situation. In 1965, RECARO impressed the motoring world with its brilliant new *Sportsitz*. But in 1966, Keiper patented a highly

---

depuis 1945, Abstract', *Revue du Nord*, 387 (2013), 877–94 (p. 884) <https://www.cairn.info/revue-du-nord-2010-4-page-877.htm>.

121 Tilly and Malvache, pp. 885–86.

122 Stephanie Tilly, 'Das Zulieferproblem aus Institutionenökonomischer Sicht. Die Westdeutsche Automobil-Zulieferindustrie zwischen Produktions- und Marktorientierung (1960–1980)', *Jahrbuch Für Wirtschaftsgeschichte/Economic History Yearbook*, 51.1 (2010), 137–60 (pp. 138, 142).

123 See Chapter 4 on Reutter's and Keiper's origins as *Meister*.

124 Keiper, pp. 125–39.

125 Putsch and Putsch, pp. 140–48.

126 Putsch and Putsch, p. 104.

127 Putsch and Putsch, p. 151.

innovative new seat mechanism which they called the *Taumel*. Over the next decade they were able to take the price down to 25% of the level of predecessor products, with the result that "through this price level there was no car which didn't have adjustable seats within a decade" and Keiper became the world leader in seat mechanisms.[128] Both firms had created the perfect Mittelstand niche product. But while RECARO's was a superbly conceived and crafted, low-volume, automotive luxury, Keiper had created an unglamorous, ubiquitous, world-beating bestseller.

In contrast to Keiper's apparently well-managed, forceful development, company historians Jung and Jung present the performance of RECARO's business and its management in the same period as a series of missteps and inappropriate choices, beginning in 1965.[129] RECARO's disastrous "false move into diversification", buying a graphics company and its factory 70km away at Schwäbisch Hall, "involved lots of cost and delivered big losses" in an industry of which RECARO's managers knew nothing.[130] Their decision can be contrasted with the very different path of Keiper. For Ulrich Putsch, it was exciting to try new products, as he also was conscious of Keiper's dependence on the automotive market, but he was prudent and focused:

> Why should we struggle with things that others might understand more about? In all the areas that we made other things, we were not the number one. But we definitely were with seat mechanisms, and by a distance.[131]

When Ford cancelled a potential seat deal with RECARO in 1967, the unused factory space in Schwäbisch Hall emphasised the wasted expenditure. It came at a bad time. Ford's decision was part of a downturn in the automotive market. Volkswagen's CEO Heinrich Nordhoff told his Board that he saw this as a "turning point" and "the end of an unusually prolonged boom since the end of the war".[132] Abelshauser argues that the rise in unemployment to 2.1 per cent in 1967 persuaded the population that the era of Reconstruction had reached its end, and West Germany's "was now an economy like almost any

---

128   Putsch and Putsch, pp. 159–60.
129   It should be remembered that co-author Uta Jung's brother was the putative future business leader Welf Koch. Both were shareholders in RECARO, their interests managed by company chairman B.W. Müller. See Memorandum of Understanding for the sale of RECARO: 'Vorvertrag zwischen dem Nachlaß Fritz Reutter und Firma Fritz Keiper KG, Remscheid', 1969, p. 1, RECARO Holding GmbH archives.
130   Jung and Jung, p. 269.
131   Putsch and Putsch, p. 105.
132   VW Board minutes, December 1966, quoted in Manfred Grieger, 'Die "geplatzte Wirtschaftswundertüte": Die Krisen 1966/67 und 1973/75 im deutschen Symbolunternehmen Volkswagen', in *Automobilindustrie 1945–2000: eine Schlüsselindustrie zwischen Boom und Krise*, ed. by Stephanie Tilly and Florian Triebel (Munich, 2013), pp. 1–75 (pp. 32–33; 34).

other".[133] To add to the sense of pressure felt by RECARO's management, the friendly personal relationships between each company's older generation of leaders had not continued into the younger generation of Porsche managers.[134] 1968 marked the end of the first five years of the RECARO-Porsche seating contract. Porsche's aggressive management wanted to renege on the 1963 contract, and RECARO demonstrated "an absence of decisive company leadership for the implementation of the contract conditions" by conceding a major price reduction, sacrificing income and re-creating the earlier subservience to Porsche.[135] If Porsche found themselves at this point celebrating the management weakness which Jung and Jung quite appropriately criticise, they must have been further gratified by RECARO chairman B.W. Müller's decision, inexplicable to later observers, to make substantial tax payments to the city of Stuttgart for which Porsche, not RECARO, was liable under the terms of the 1963 sale agreement.[136] To have given two huge concessions when RECARO was about to make a loss for the 1967/8 financial year suggests at best ineffectual management and at worst the possibility that RECARO managers had some ulterior motive.[137] It also suggests that, in due course, Müller would be guilty of establishing a self-fulfilling prophecy by his insistence that the company's relatively weak financial state should be a cause for its sale: he and his decisions were a key element in its weakness.

In April 1969 Helmes became managing director on the retirement of the 70-year old Max Müller-Scholl, who had been in post since 1953. Helmes subsequently gave the following analysis of the company's position at the time.[138] RECARO produced seat structures for the aftermarket and some smaller manufacturers. Series production for the big OEMs (Mercedes-Benz, Opel) was done by competitors, especially Keiper. Keiper's *Taumel* mechanism significantly reduced the chance of RECARO competing with any new, patent-protectable mechanism (at this point and others, Helmes reiterates the need for any competitive product to have its own patent). Though RECARO designs were innovative, OEMs tended to make their own seats and headrests, and the possibility of patenting headrests was limited.[139] Keiper's profitability was significantly higher than RECARO's thanks to its series production, but RECARO

133   Abelshauser, *Deutsche Wirtschaftsgeschichte*, pp. 307–08.
134   This difficulty is also discussed in detail by Greger, p. 32.
135   Jung and Jung, p. 271.
136   Bernhard Müller, 'Teilbericht über die Betriebsprüfung RECARO/REUTTER' (RECARO G.m.b.H. & Co., 1968), p. 15, RECARO Holding GmbH archives.
137   Dr. Franz Lipfert Wirtschaftsprüfungsgesellschaft und Steuerberatungsgesellschaft GmbH, 'Ergänzungsbericht über die Prüfung des Abschlusses für die RECARO G.m.b.H.& Co., Stuttgart, für das Rumpfgeschäftsjahr vom 1. April bis 31. Dezember 1969' (RECARO G.m.b.H. & Co., 1971), RECARO Holding GmbH archives.
138   Helmes, pp. 3–7.
139   Helmes, p. 5.

was unsuitable to be a mass-producer itself and OEMs had not anyway shown any interest in mass-produced seats. Helmes concluded his report with a clear but paradoxical recommendation: "Over a long timeframe, the only market that will remain to RECARO will be the delivery of series-production seats."[140]

Helmes had contradicted himself: his proposed long-term strategy, series-production, was what he had also said was unsuitable for RECARO. His review seems to have been unduly pessimistic, either designed afterwards to fit subsequent events, or reflective of his own entrepreneurial shortcomings. He does not mention the possibility of developing aircraft or train seating or growing exports, let alone launching unpatented but innovative new solutions. Yet he and RECARO's board found there were no opportunities for sales growth. Nor could costs be reduced. At a board meeting in July 1969, Helmes was authorised to approach Keiper regarding a cooperation between the two companies.[141] Jung and Jung argue that this decision was taken because for many company leaders in this period, the way out of any business difficulty was by cooperation, merger, or acquisition: this was the thinking of RECARO's management and they influenced the shareholders (that is, co-author Uta Jung's mother and grandmother) accordingly.[142] They ask "why it was not possible after so many years of the business being led by salaried business leaders to delay the negotiations until Welf Koch, as a member of the shareholding family and joint shareholder, could take his own view of the situation and make his own decision."[143] The company had a business leader and the owners had their Board of Directors. The family had to be able to rely on their competence and integrity. But in rushing the deal through and ignoring Welf, their agents had let the Reutter family down. Despite family misgivings, in October 1969 Keiper's offer for the whole RECARO group was accepted by B.W. Müller under his power of attorney, and the sale agreement was signed on 30 December 1969. The takeover happened on 1 January 1970, affecting 130 staff in Schwäbisch Hall and 250 in Stuttgart. In their objection to the final outcome, Jung and Jung take a classic Mittelstand position. For them, family leadership was the differentiating factor between the two companies. In contrast to the incompetently managed RECARO, Keiper "had under the constant participation of its own family members in management been able to expand even during the sales crisis of the automotive industry".[144] The solution for RECARO should therefore have been clear. No matter that Welf Koch had no experience yet: with the support of the Reutter family shareholders RECARO would have been able

140   Helmes, p. 6.
141   Helmes, p. 11.
142   Jung and Jung, p. 272.
143   Jung and Jung, p. 274.
144   Jung and Jung, p. 273.

to ride out its temporary difficulties, making it possible for a family member to resume control of the company and, by extension, make things right again.

Their assertion was less naïve than it might appear, for as Jung and Jung correctly argue, Müller and Helmes had made an incorrect assessment of the industry. By the time they were practising their arguments for a sale, the industry's recovery was already under way, in most businesses with a dynamism that recalled the results of the *Wirtschaftswunder* years. The predicted "catastrophe" was in practice short-lived. Although there *was* a definite downturn in the automotive market in 1967, it was temporary: as Figure 21 illustrates, car production faltered briefly in 1967 during West Germany's recession, but quickly returned to growth, suggesting that RECARO could have not only seen out the storm but also prospered in ensuing years.[145]

In this ever-growing market, drivers' demands for better comfort and new legal requirements would have given a company like RECARO, which had repeatedly made a mark in the past, good business opportunities.[146]

Jung and Jung end their review of Helmes's perspective with his conclusion that the "continuation of the concept of a 'social undertaking' with special consideration for long-serving workers would not have been compatible with the aim of achieving acceptable profit levels".[147] This can be read as a fair assessment of the changing cost dynamics of a German workplace in which average employee remuneration had increased by 54% since 1965, as Schneider's ultimately fatal experience in Ludwigsburg was now proving.[148] Equally it can be seen as a deliberate disavowal of the model which had served RECARO and its highly skilled, extremely employable but loyal staff well for the previous six decades, by a management team whose strategic errors had proven so costly to the business that its sale had become the only viable rescue plan. When contrasted with the performance of Ulrich Putsch and his brother, the insistence on the need for *family* leadership to guarantee family interests now seemed justified.

Under New Control, 1970 onwards

January 1970 saw the Reutter family leaving the business they had formed sixty-three years earlier. Jung and Jung conclude that, with the sale, Keiper had bought out its strongest competitor and obtained the world-renowned

---

145   Table created by the author, based on Statistisches Bundesamt, 'XII. Industrie und Handwerk', *Statistisches Jahrbuch für die Bundesrepublik Deutschland*, 1974 (1975), p. 236, table 13; and Abelshauser, *Deutsche Wirtschaftsgeschichte*, p. 305, table 15.

146   Jung and Jung, p. 275.

147   Helmes, p. 19; cited at Jung and Jung, p. 275.

148   Kettenacker, p. 279, table 11.

A Verbrauchsgüter: Personenkraftwagen = Consumer Goods: Passenger Vehicles Production. Index: 1962 = 100

	1955	1956	1957	1958	1959	1960	1961	1962	1963	1964	1965	1966	1967	1968	1969	1970	1971	1972	1973
A	15.6	22.8	29.5	42.8	55.1	74.5	84.0	100	121.7	126.6	143.7	148.7	121.5	158.2	194.8	227.5	239.2	232.1	246.7
B		7.2%				5.7%					3.6%					3.8%			

B Average annual growth rate pre economic cycle (%) (1950–1954 = 8.8%)

Figure 21 Passenger Vehicle Production and Annual GDP Growth, West Germany, 1955–73.

"RECARO" name and numerous granted and applied-for patents, totalling altogether some 130 internationally registered product developments. For Keiper and the Putsch family, the acquisition of RECARO was a masterstroke. They had taken their strongest competitor out of the market, got all its patents, secured all the know-how on both types of seating mechanism, and achieved access to a new range of ideas created by RECARO's design staff. They were now also in a significantly stronger position vis-à-vis their larger customers.[149] For RECARO's staff, used to seeing Max Müller-Scholl as managing director until shortly before his 71st birthday, Keiper had a noticeably "modern management team", made up of the Putsch brothers, both in their early thirties, and their similarly young two senior managers.[150] There were no immediate redundancies and the future outlook for individuals and the business looked as though it would be secured by the new owner.[151]

Following the takeover, RECARO's existing managers were initially left in place. Helmes appointed a new, young sales director. He developed the vehicle seating business, launched new advertising and a new logo, and found new markets, while continuing on RECARO's strategic path of "proper seating" (*richtiges Sitzen*).[152] The product range included complete RECARO seats for Porsche and the *Idealsitz* for the aftermarket. The Keiper team, in contrast, remained focused on door handles, gear levers, and window winders. The *Taumel* remained Keiper's most important product: in 1972, 720 came off the line each hour for twenty-four hours a day,[153] an eloquent symbol of their distance from the handcrafted workmanship that had characterised Reutter/RECARO's thinking and was lovingly captured in photographs which adorn its company histories.[154] Keiper has been cited by one scholar as an example of a market-orientated specialist which saw its strengths as solving problems and developing know-how, and thus was able to escape the "supplier problem" of being treated as a servant by its customers.[155] (With its aircraft seating in particular, RECARO would duly find a way to combine its tradition of craftsmanship and innovative design with the cultivation of similar relationships, a combination which distinguishes it still in 2022.) The Mittelstand commitment to remaining independent specialists providing excellent niche products as part of a long-term strategy was maintained in ways which best suited each division's market and provenance.

149 Putsch and Putsch, p. 166; Greger, p. 34.
150 Greger, p. 34.
151 Jung and Jung, p. 276.
152 Jung, *RECARO*, p. 114.
153 Putsch and Putsch, pp. 168–69.
154 See for example the workplace photographs in Jung, *Porsche 356 Made by Reutter*, pp. 224–70.
155 Tilly, p. 158.

But, given Keiper's commitment to mass production, would it not have made more sense now to move away from Mittelstand gradualism and push ahead more aggressively with mass-producing straightforward products? It seems that Putsch saw a better opportunity in taking the best of RECARO's expertise and flair, building on it, then streamlining the manufacture of the resultant products. He began carefully, pragmatically seeking a licensing arrangement with an American aviation seat manufacturer until RECARO had enough expertise to operate autonomously.[156] He then sought leaders with special technical expertise to deliver RECARO's strategy. In 1971 Horst Sommerlatte was appointed chief designer of RECARO's own range of aircraft seats. Aged only 31, Sommerlatte seems to have shared the youthful energy, allied to very high technical competence, of the Putsch brothers. As well as aircraft seats he developed a modular family of seats for cars, trucks, and buses, customised to suit a range of driver types: specialised, niche products again.[157] In support, Friedrich Greger was tasked with transforming RECARO's "artisanal" (*handwerklich orientiert*) approach to manufacturing seats, which contrasted with Keiper's mass production of individual items using process-improvement consultancy REFA's methodologies to maximise productivity.[158] Sommerlatte recalls positive working relations with RECARO's technical team, distinctive designs, and clever marketing, all of which led to new business in all areas of vehicle interiors.[159] In other words, RECARO's practices and values were respected and adapted, not replaced.

Putsch's other notable appointment was Dr.-Ing. Rolf Bahmann who succeeded Helmes in autumn 1972. Bahmann appears from Greger's account to have made an immediate impact, prioritising a new product range and new premises for RECARO.[160] Some detail is warranted. In late 1973 RECARO moved to Kirchheim unter Teck, 40km away from Stuttgart. Many colleagues refused to move. There followed an extended period of "the highest tension" and "a mountain of work" for staff.[161] Within the same period, RECARO won major contracts for headrests with Daimler-Benz and Opel, and launched the entire *Idealsitz-Generation* range. Greger comments that "Tied in with all the problems of the move, this was no easy task for the entire RECARO team."[162]

156 Frank Jung, *RECARO: Seating in Motion* (Bielefeld , 2016), p. 118.

157 'RECARO Seats', Sommerlatte Industrial Design <https://sommerlatte-industrial-design.de/werke/zeitstrahl_recaro_seats.html > [accessed 30 November 2018].

158 Greger, p. 35; Wilhelm Putsch had first begun to use the operations-improvement techniques taught by REFA, which was founded in 1924, at Keiper in the 1950s: 'Home | REFA' <http://www.refa.de/home> [accessed 15 September 2018].

159 'RECARO Seats'.

160 Bahmann died in 1975 of cancer, leaving no papers on which to base a review of his performance (per Frank Jung, meeting of 6 October 2016).

161 Greger, p. 38.

162 Greger, p. 39.

The detail reminds us again that the business achievements which powered the "economic miracle" and the high growth which continued into the 1970s were not in fact "miraculous"; German companies were confronted constantly with logistical challenges, staff shortages, technical innovation opportunities, and the concomitant leadership challenges, just as their counterparts were in the UK and elsewhere. Greger notes, for example, that when RECARO won its first contract for its own aircraft seating at Christmas 1974 with Korean Airlines, it followed "very many setbacks including production, quality control, and material stability which nevertheless were overcome within 1½ years by very energetic efforts."[163] Success appears to have been made possible by the leadership of a focused, technically educated business leader, Baumann, with prior experience in the aviation industry[164] and a Ph.D. in mechanical engineering:[165] patient investment from the company's owners, who waited three years for the first substantial order; and personal commitment from the workforce, who were willing to tolerate considerable personal upheaval. In principle, fixing problems in this way should also have been possible at Jensen, except it lacked leadership of equivalent quality, patient investors, and a workforce who were equally capable and equally well looked after.

Growth was further secured by holding true to Mittelstand values of solidifying regional attachments, looking after staff, and accepting institutional support. For example, Keiper announced investment in RECARO's Schwäbisch Hall factory (still the home of RECARO Aircraft Seating) and changed the company's legal name to "Keiper GmbH & Co., Schwäbisch Hall". At a reception to launch the new company, Ulrich Putsch promised seven hundred new, secure jobs and explained their inclusion of the town's name as an expression of their desire to be considered a native business which would attract new workers. He received a positive response from the mayor, who promised that the town had "patience and optimism and enough energy to do everything necessary to bring success" to Keiper, including investment in new infrastructure. The mayor's speech, and Putsch's, and the presence of "over 80 leading representatives of [Schwäbisch Hall's] authorities, government agencies, chambers, work organisations, political parties, institutions, as well as industry, trade and banks, the mayor and the member of the state parliament (*Landrat*)"[166] reveal the social and commercial systems within which Mittelstand firms could flourish: broad

---

163   Greger, p. 39.
164   Greger, p. 36.
165   'Doctoral Theses Supervised by Professor Lueth, Professor Heinzl, and Professor Unterberger since 1953', Chair of Micro Technology and Medical Device Technology, Technical University of Munich (2018) <https://www.mec.ed.tum.de/en/mimed/structure/doctoral-theses > [accessed 6 December 2018].
166   'Schwäbisch Hall: Geeigneter Wirtschafts- und Lebensraum', *Haller Tagblatt* (Schwäbisch Hall, 6 October 1971), section 'Aus Stadt und Kreis', Frank Jung Archive.

institutional and political support, strong networks, the ambition to create long-term jobs, and a willingness to invest public money in the infrastructure required to support them.[167]

The leadership structure and underpinning values which remained with the larger and growing business are significant. A detailed examination of its evolution, which is of particular interest in relation to aircraft seating (gradually achieving a position of dominance in a world market by 2022, in typical Mittelstand "hidden champion" fashion), is beyond the scope of this chapter and the available archival evidence. The speed and scale of progress following the RECARO acquisition can, however, be estimated from a company brochure produced in 1985. Over fifteen years, the group had grown to approximately 5500 employees and more than DM650 million of annual sales in several countries.[168] Its executive team were non-family members, its president one of the two young men observed by Friedrich Greger in 1970, who had been "grown" from within, showing that the Putsch family were conscious of succession issues. But most strikingly the brochure identified the "Personally liable Partner and Chairman: U. Putsch." At the end of twenty-three years during which he had increased staff numbers eleven-fold and total sales by a factor of thirty-two, developing a substantial international company, Ulrich Putsch clearly still felt that this was his family's company, and would not delegate his personal sense of fiduciary accountability as its *Unternehmer.*[169] In this respect, his conduct and values reinforced the belief of Jung and Jung that family leadership was best able to deliver sustainable competitiveness through Mittelstand precepts. In 2013, RECARO's published *Values* restated the Putsch family's commitment to "Modern entrepreneurship", centred in a "performance-oriented family company ... Our managing partner Martin Putsch [evidence of generational continuity] puts it very clearly: 'With the right team, there's no better type of company. It guarantees a focus that doesn't depend on quarterly figures,

---

167   In contrast, for companies seeking to grow in the West Midlands, an already inconsistent approach to supporting SMEs in Britain was later weakened further by the Thatcher Government's preference for market forces over local institutional commitments. See for example: C.G. Pickvance, 'Introduction: The Institutional Context of Local Economic Development: Central Controls, Spatial Policies and Local Economic Policies', in *Place, Policy, and Politics: Do Localities Matter?*, ed. by Michael Harloe, C.G. Pickvance, and John Urry (London, 1990), pp. 27–28; Dennis Smith, 'Coping with Restructuring: The Case of South-West Birmingham', in *Place, Policy, and Politics: Do Localities Matter?*, ed. by Michael Harloe, C.G. Pickvance, and John Urry (London, 1990), pp. 113–14 explains the particularly inefficient response in the West Midlands.

168   Keiper-Recaro GmbH & Co., 'RECARO Aircraft Seating Division' (1985), RECARO Holding GmbH archives.

169   Putsch and Putsch, p. 149.

as well as financial freedom and the ability to make decisions quickly.'"[170] In reinforcing the value of family ownership over several decades, even as their group developed into a global force, Martin and Ulrich Putsch have exemplified the leadership qualities which propelled the original Reutter business but whose absence from RECARO was lamented by the surviving members of the Reutter family.[171] And they have done so while providing the social benefits that Norbert Helmes had judged to be inimical to company growth and profitability, but which they themselves appear to have found are the best means of aligning the long-term interests of valuable, skilled staff and their employer.[172] Though their companies' size long ago outstripped the conventional criteria for consideration as an SME, the continued engagement in active management of the Putsch family substantiates the IfM's 2019 definition of Mittelstand membership and the continuing strength of Mittelstand values.[173]

170   RECARO Holding GmbH, 'Family Business and Philosophy' (2013) <www.recaro. com/family-company-and-philosophy.html> [accessed 13 October 2013].

171   Jung and Jung, p. 250.

172   Putsch and Putsch, pp. 276–77.

173   'IfM Bonn: Mittelstandsdefinition Des IfM Bonn': see Chapter 1 above.

10

Jensen Motors Ltd., West Bromwich

Almost five decades after its production ceased and its manufacturer went into liquidation, the Jensen Interceptor remains an iconic touring car. For the *New York Times*, even in 2021 the "Jensen Interceptor's very name suggests exceptional power and drama, tugging at the heartstrings of car lovers. The machine in the flesh makes good on the imagery."[1] But despite its appeal today and at the time of its production in the late 1960s and early 1970s, the Interceptor could not save a company which was characterised less by its appealing flagship product than by the mismanagement that made its survival impossible.

Early History to 1945

Brothers Alan and Richard Jensen were Birmingham-born car enthusiasts and motor-trade apprentices. From the moment they hand-crafted their own stylish sports body onto a standard car chassis in 1928, their youthful brilliance earned them orders for custom models and the admiration of vehicle designers. In 1932, both still in their twenties, they were appointed joint managing directors of a truck builder in West Bromwich, quickly accumulating broad experience in bodybuilding. Unlike Wilhelm Reutter and Fritz Keiper, they were not experienced *Meister*. But they were capable. In parallel with trucks they developed stylish custom-built sports cars, most famously for Clark Gable, changing the company name to Jensen Motors Ltd. in 1934 and working with numerous skilled workers who would remain with them for the next thirty years. In a foreshadowing of their future preference for working with American components, they met Edsel Ford and created a number of stylish coupes using handmade Jensen bodies on Ford chassis.[2] Precocious technical acumen was combined with the personal credibility to develop commercial relationships: when the newly launched Jensen S Type was praised by *The Motor* in 1936,

1 Paul Stenquist, 'English Charm, Italian Flair, Global Fans', *New York Times* (New York, 29 January 2021) < https://www.nytimes.com/2021/01/28/business/classic-cars-jensen-interceptor.html > [accessed 3 July 2021].
2 Keith Anderson, *Jensen* (Yeovil, 1989), pp. 7–16.

they were still only thirty and twenty-seven years old. And while their sports cars continued to attract attention, in 1937 they produced the world's first aluminium bodied commercial vehicle, followed by the first Pantechnicon, or high-bodied furniture removal truck.[3] When their factory was compelled to switch to war work, they showed their innovativeness again with the Jen-Tug, a new type of commercial tractor-trailer combination.[4] Wartime production grew Jensen's sales significantly, taking them from £28,800 in 1938 to £384,633 in 1944. However, profitability was apparently poor: having recorded a loss of 9% in 1938, the company reached a high of 3% profit in 1941, thereafter recording none, the brothers complaining bitterly that Excess Profits Tax had consumed it all.[5] Whether that lack of profitability was a reflection of the nature of their war work – K&J's nearby factory was, after all, highly profitable throughout the war – or an early indication of commercial weakness is not clear.

Post-war Developments, 1945 to 1959

Despite the war-work challenges, performance during the immediate post-war years indicated management capability. Though continuing material controls[6] and a rising wage bill[7] initially kept profits low, post-war sales were strong, reaching £345,000 for 1951. And Jensen's performance strengthened through the following decade. Sales doubled from £383,000 to £764,000 over five years to 1955/6,[8] and from 1948, the last loss-making year until 1961, pre-tax profits averaged £48,000, reaching £119,613 in 1958. These increases reflected, and enabled, a substantial increase in machinery investments, taking the value of plant from under £6000 in 1949 to over £176,000 in 1958. As the company outgrew its original factory, the brothers also invested £144,000 in freehold property within West Bromwich. As a consequence of its progress and reinvestment of increasing profits in the business, the value of the balance sheet grew fivefold to £293,559.[9]

---

3   'A Brief History of Jensen' (Jensen Motors Ltd., 1966), MRC, MSS.215/6/2.
4   Anderson, *Jensen*, pp. 35–40; Hans Kamp, 'Jensen Commercial Vehicles', The Jensen Museum (2017) <http://www.jensenmuseum.org/jensen-commercial-vehicles/> [accessed 16 January 2019].
5   'Handwritten Duplicate Book', pp. 4, 18, 22–23, 27.
6   Geoffrey Owen, *From Empire to Europe: The Decline and Revival of British Industry Since the Second World War* (London, 1999), p. 218.
7   'Jensen Motors Limited: Profit and Loss Account Summary, 1946–51' (Blakemore, Elgar & Co., 1951), MRC, MSS.215/2/2.
8   Jensen Motors Ltd., 'Handwritten Profit and Loss Account Summary, 1951/52 to 1955/56' JML date stamped May 1954, suggesting it was updated yearly.
9   'Jensen Motors Limited: Summary of Accounts, 1949–58'.

They remained innovative, pioneering the use of fibreglass for truck cabs and then using it on the 541 and CV-8 car bodies. While the glamour and indisputable technical achievement of their custom-built touring cars attracted acclaim, however, their business model was reliant for its viability on cross-subsidies from less stylish activities, especially their commercial vehicle building. Other notable projects, such as the Mark I Jensen Interceptor in 1948, had been funded by military contracts.[10] By mid-1958 high-volume assembly of cars for other manufacturers was in full swing. Though this made the company less dependent on commercial vehicle sales, an internal summary detailing ten months' profit shows the extent to which sub-contract assembly work supported the production of Jensen's own cars, as Figure 22 shows.[11]

As the analysis suggests, Jensen was potentially vulnerable. Enthusiasm for its own cars was high, but they were made in tiny volumes, averaging less than seven per month, and were less profitable than any other product; this was more of a subsidised enthusiasts' workshop than a serious vehicle manufacturer. More importantly, their construction was apparently only made possible by the subcontract manufacture which provided 90% of revenue and 86% of gross profit: without work from Austin, Jensen could not nearly cover its own overheads.

Nonetheless, Jensen's own cars and reputation as car designers – reinforced by the engagement of the highly esteemed Eric Neale as chief designer in 1946 – were what distinguished them.[12] An undated Jensen press release from the 1950s speaks to the self-conception of the firm and its owners: "A great deal is talked these days about the fine British tradition of skilled and specialised craftsmanship ... this craftsmanship is held, and rightly too, to be one of the old country's chief assets." In a company which was "still owned and directed by them alone ... the Jensen brothers are craftsmen, still more they are artists." They had already "solved a great number" of technical problems as they aimed for "that final effect, for that gasp of admiration as a man first takes the wheel." Such achievements required long-term commitment as well as admirable craft skills, as an "effect such as this can only be produced by years of painstaking and devoted work. It cannot be produced by making quick profits out of short term demands."[13] The Jensen brothers had achieved their success to this point, as had Reutter, by the application of this philosophy, which has remained central to the continued hagiography of Jensen car enthusiasts. The difference

10   Kamp.
11   Jensen Motors Ltd., 'Jensen Motors Limited: Summary of Estimated Profit, Ten Months from 1st August 1957 to 31st May 1958' (Jensen Motors Ltd., 1966), MRC, MSS.215/3/19. Additional analysis and table by author.
12   Anderson, *Jensen*, pp. 51–54.
13   'Craftsmanship. Britain's Great Weapon in the Face of Competition' (Jensen Motors Ltd., 1955), MRC, MSS.215/6/2.

	Quantity	Sales £	Gross Profit £	% GP	Reconciliation	£
Subcontract Assembly						
Austin Healey 100	3,978	1,021,148	146,306	14.3	Estd profit to March	6,813
K.D.	149	30,290	6,456	21.3	Countryman Price Adjustments	29,200
Prototype		1,710	832	48.7	Est profit April	1,984
Sundries		5,240	1,064	20.3	A.H. 100 material handling	
Austin Countryman	1,363	215,515	44,545	20.7	charge to April	20,294
C.K.D.	372	24,180	7,800	32.3	Estd profit May	7,444
Spares/Repairs		83,990	32,578	38.8		65,735
Jensen Cars	46	66,805	8,874	13.3	Deduct	
Car Spares & Repairs		9,821	3,965	40.4	A.H. 100 Retrospective Costing	
Commercial Vehicles	3	5,584	813	14.6	Adjustments	6,605
Spares/Repairs		20,736	5,609	27.0	Jig, Tool, etc	1,735
Articulated Vehicles	4	2,423	455	18.8		57,395
Spares/Repairs		6,294	3,469	55.1		
Hard tops (740) & Misc bodywork		37,291	10,696	28.7	**Author's Analysis (Ignoring Reconcilation Values)**	
Plastics (Sundry)		1,076	553	51.4		
Sale of Petrol, Scrap Metal, etc		4,600	3,183	69.2	Subcontract products as % of all Revenue	89.9
		1,536,703	277,198	18.0	Jensen cars & spares as % of all Revenue	5.0
					Subcontract products as % of all Gross Profit	86.4
Estimated Gross Profit as above			277,198		Jensen cars & spares as % of all Gross Profit	4.6
Overhead expenses			205,650		(All % Calculations by author)	
Jigs, Tools & Development etc			14,153	0.9		
Net			57,395		**Net Profit as % of Sales**	3.7

Figure 22 Jensen Motors Ltd., Key Production Data, 1957–58.

was that Reutter was carrying through the same philosophy with a large team of *Meister* and experienced staff, building market-defining cars for Porsche in increasingly high volumes, after pre-war experience of building in similar volumes for similarly demanding customers.

The Jensens' achievements by the late 1950s were, however, indisputable: starting as very young men, they had built a company in which technical innovation across a range of vehicle types was combined with the ability to carry out subcontract assembly to a satisfactory standard for other British manufacturers, enabling a progressive increase in revenue and profit. But as the preceding analysis shows, Jensen's own cars – though highly regarded by themselves and others – were not particularly profitable and were subsidised by the remainder of the business. Sales were low, just 718 cars between 1936 and 1962.[14] Both brothers were in poor health, which Richard later "ascribed to the effort of running a business in the face of increasingly disruptive labour practices."[15] It may still have been true that, in the words of an undated press release from the late 1950s, the Jensen brothers "[had] the spirit of pioneers" who had never "lacked faith in their abilities, or of the unique products they have designed and build from time to time."[16] But given the growing risk of diminishing returns to their efforts, the brothers now sought outside help. In June 1959, they sold their shareholding to a new financial conglomerate, Norcros, for £712,000: £182,000 in cash and the remainder in Norcros shares.[17]

Norcros had been created in 1956 to acquire and manage, with the former owners' continued engagement, family firms which were threatened by death duties or whose owners felt they lacked the resources for further growth. Its founder, Eton- and Cambridge-educated financier John Sheffield, later viewed as "one of the most innovative financial minds of his generation", looked to build a mini-conglomerate of mostly unrelated businesses. Despite the portfolio companies' dissimilarities, "the method worked, profits soared and many of the early company owners who joined the group became millionaires." The group itself "became a darling of the stock market and was always well-capitalised".[18] On the face of it, the Jensen brothers' action was sensible: they

---

14   Keith Anderson, *Jensen and Jensen-Healey* (Stroud, 1998), Appendix.

15   'Mr Richard Jensen - Obituary', *The Times* (London, England, 14 September 1977), p. 18, The Times Digital Archive; see also 'Two Brothers with Vision - Alan & Richard Jensen', The Jensen Museum (2016) <http://www.jensenmuseum.org/alan-richard-jensen/> [accessed 16 January 2019].

16   'Press Release: "The Faith of the Jensen Brothers"' (Jensen Motors Ltd.), MRC, MSS.215/6/2.

17   'Norcros Acquires Jensen Motors', *The Times* (London, England, 18 June 1959), p. 16, The Times Digital Archive; 'Jensen Motors Bought by Norcros', *The Manchester Guardian* (Manchester, 18 June 1959), p. 12.

18   'John Sheffield', *The Telegraph* (1 July 2008), section News <http://www.telegraph. co.uk/news/obituaries/2230560/John-Sheffield.html> [accessed 17 July 2017].

had taken a pay-out from a reputable business and would remain as Chairmen – each for an alternating year – of the company which would continue to bear their name, designing exciting new cars while a Norcros appointee became managing director and took responsibility for most of the less pleasant tasks. However, they had also taken the first step away from the business model which had brought them to where they were. That model was at this same time working well for Porsche, where the engineer/entrepreneur Ferdinand Porsche remained in complete personal control of a business to which he was passionately committed; and for Reutter, whose long-term business leader and senior advisors were all completely familiar with the industry, knew Porsche and other customers and suppliers, and shared the values of the company's founders. Unlike its German counterparts, Jensen was now in the hands not of serious automotive constructors with long-term strategies and supportive local banks, but of financial engineers with profit-hungry shareholders and no industry knowledge or expertise.

Jensen under Norcros Ownership

Management and Operations

The first accounts Norcros received must have been a gratifying justification for John Sheffield's judgement: sales for 1958/9 were £3.02 million, up £950,000 from the prior year, with net profit of £200,406 paying a special dividend of £200,000.[19] The gratification did not last. By 1960/1, a year in which Jensen had had to lay off 350 men during an industry-wide slump,[20] sales had dropped from £3.4 million to £2.1 million.[21] This was despite revenues being boosted by a contract with Volvo, under which Jensen painted and equipped, in West Bromwich, body shells made in Scotland. The finished body was then shipped to Sweden, where Volvo added the mechanicals. This was the same relationship that Reutter had with Porsche, the difference being that the finished body was shipped 1700km from West Bromwich to Gothenburg rather than 200m between buildings in Zuffenhausen. Following disagreements over poor quality, the contract was terminated after three years.[22] Though Jensen were compen-

---

19   Blakemore, Elgar & Co., 'Jensen Motors Limited: Accounts for the Year Ended 31st July 1959.' (Jensen Motors Ltd., 1959), MRC, MSS.215/2/6/56.

20   Our Own Correspondent, 'Dunlop Introduce Short Time', *The Times* (London, England, 19 November 1960), p. 5, The Times Digital Archive; Our Own Correspondent, 'Recession In Car Industry Feared', *The Times* (London, England, 13 September 1960), p. 3, The Times Digital Archive.

21   Jensen Motors Ltd., 'Analysis of Sales by Products 1958/59 -1964/65' (Jensen Motors Ltd., 1965), MRC, MSS.215/2/11.

22   Anderson, *Jensen*, pp. 117–19.

sated, their complaints about Volvo's excessive quality demands suggest a difference in mentality between themselves, Volvo, and Porsche/Reutter that presaged problems to come.

There were also concerns about management quality. Norcros's first appointed managing director was recruited from an airline company, had no experience of the motor industry, and was replaced within a year.[23] Norcros then appointed Brian Owen as managing director, to run the business jointly with the Jensen brothers. A former Army Lieutenant-Colonel, Owen also had no experience of the motor industry and had a difficult relationship with the Jensens, but remained managing director until January 1968.[24] Owen's experience and knowledge were no match for his direct competitor, Ferry Porsche, but the Jensens did manage to make one significant addition to the management team. Kevin Beattie was recruited in 1960 as deputy chief engineer and would eventually serve as managing director himself.[25] He was innovative and aware. He immediately became involved in the development of the new C-V8, praised by *The Times* as "among the most advanced high-performance cars in the world".[26] Jensen targeted a niche market, pricing the C-V8 at £3860, but managed to sell only 499 units.[27] Beattie and the Jensen brothers then took the revolutionary step of approaching Harry Ferguson Research Ltd. in Coventry, agreeing with Ferguson to jointly develop the world's first four-wheel drive road car. *The Times*, whose correspondent favoured Jensen, reported that "the marque has become synonymous with prestige and performance" after "many years of producing only cars of exceptional quality and revolutionary conception." The new "Ferguson Formula" (FF) car was to be, they expected, the forerunner of a new generation of four-wheel drive cars.[28]

Facing the risk of contract manufacture for Austin and Sunbeam coming to an end, Beattie insisted that Jensen needed a new model by the end of 1966 if it was to survive.[29] He persuaded Owen to make the necessary investment, and delivered two new cars, the FF and the Interceptor, within one year.[30] Beattie was later credited by Richard Graves, Jensen's marketing director, as the company's

23   'Jensen Motors Employees A-Z', The Jensen Museum (2016) <http://www.jensen-museum.org/jensen-motors-employees/> [accessed 16 January 2019].

24   'Jensen Motors Employees A-Z'.

25   Anderson, *Jensen*, pp. 107–8.

26   'Jensen To Produce Car With Four-Wheel-Drive', *The Times* (London, England, 26 October 1964), p. 6, The Times Digital Archive.

27   'Jensen CV8 | From Drawing Board To Reality', The Jensen Museum (2018) <http://www.jensenmuseum.org/jensen-cv8-from-drawing-board-to-reality/> [accessed 16 January 2019].

28   'Jensen To Produce Car With Four-Wheel-Drive'.

29   Anderson, *Jensen and Jensen-Healey*, pp. 93–94.

30   In 'Foreword' to Richard Calver, *A History of Jensen: All the Models* (Melbourne, 2007).

saviour. But he alienated the Jensen brothers and their design chief, Eric Neale, by insisting the new cars' bodies be designed in Italy. Within four weeks, all three had left,[31] removing their design flair, public reputation, and industry credibility. Without them, the business became a different cultural proposition. Employees might have identified with the cars themselves. But no matter whether Norcros turned out to be competent investors, they were not car people, and they were not Jensens.

Despite the preceding internal politics, the new cars themselves actually met with very positive reviews. The FF in particular invited admiration for its technical advancements – Porsche bought one for themselves – and was awarded "Car of the Year" in 1967. But having excited potential buyers, Graves soon ran into problems, as he recalled in a company history, "production was increased substantially to meet demand, but then quality problems arose, customer demand began to decline, dealers became overstocked and cash flow suffered."[32] Another company historian argues that Alan and Richard Jensen had opposed the Italian relationship because they had foreseen the problems that quickly arose. First, Italian quality levels were well below the handcrafted Jensen standards that justified the cars' high prices. Second, cancelling the Italian supply contract enabled the cars to be built in West Bromwich, but Jensen's union job demarcation precluded their efficient assembly. Finally, Jensen had been building fibreglass cars, and therefore did not have staff capable of producing a high-quality steel body shell like the Interceptor's.[33] It is clear that, by this point, the resemblance to Reutter had ceased. No matter what the flair for design and publicity, these failures of operational management now became damaging,

Financial Management
Norcros's relationship with the Jensen factory had already become problematic. The disappointing 1961 group financial results were publicly attributed to unspecified "temporary setbacks" at Jensen.[34] From then onwards, revenues were inconsistent and unreliable. A summary of seven years' results from 1958/9 onwards shows Jensen had delivered £19.3 million in sales revenue. But two of those years had seen drops of over £1 million since the previous year. More worryingly for a company which presented itself as the builder of the world's finest grand touring cars, sales of those cars and spares amounted to less than £1.4 million of total revenue. The company still depended on its subcontract assembly work for 74% of its revenues, hence Beattie's concern. Any deterioration in relationships with Austin and others would be devastating; £1.66

31   Anderson, *Jensen*, pp. 122–23; Anderson, *Jensen and Jensen-Healey*, p. 99.
32   Foreword to Calver, pp. xi–xii.
33   Anderson, *Jensen*, p. 135.
34   'Norcros', *The Economist* (17 February 1962), p. 660.

million of the £19.3 million had already been lost as a result of the terminated Volvo contract.[35] As we have seen, Reutter staff were anxious for years about their dependence on Porsche, but having to rely on the strike-ridden Austin plants for 75% of one's revenue was a much more worrying proposition.

Norcros's 1966 group results actually showed a strong balance sheet, reflecting prudent financial management and recent acquisitions. A slightly increased profit had resulted. The announcement of £1.4 million in group investment in operating assets appeared to indicate their commitment to growth. But it sat uneasily alongside their decision to pay out £535,000 in dividends. Representing 50% of after-tax profit, the pay-out substantiates automotive-industry historian Wayne Lewchuk's criticism of the "industry-wide preference for satisfying the short-run demands of investors rather than the long-run demands of sustained growth."[36] And little of Norcros's capital investment seemed to be coming Jensen's way anyway: while other automotive firms were investing heavily in automation, additions to Jensen's plant were minimal.[37]

Despite the excitement of the Interceptor's reception at the Motor Show, Norcros's worries about Jensen were likely reinforced by Graves' 1967/8 sales forecast. For the brand new Interceptor, "Orders are already being lost due to our inability to provide cars fitted with [power steering] and we are being further embarrassed by the lack of accurate information as to its availability and cost", even though production was to start in four months. FF sales were "dependent on the early receipt" of the remaining bodies and tooling from Italy. Cars for the US would require extensive modifications to a tight deadline, after which Graves hoped to "establish a market capable of absorbing one car per week by the beginning of April 1968." His summary rested on optimism: "Throughout 1968 it is assumed that Production will be able to maintain Sales targets and the problems encountered in 1967 will have been overcome."[38] There is no specification of what those problems were, nor of how they would be overcome; the future was to be based on fragile assumptions, which would in the best case result only in a tiny number of production cars. Following the loud congratulations for the launch of the Interceptor and FF, there is no sense at this point that the company was being managed in such a way that the cars would actually be produced to meet market requirements, or in numbers that would secure the business's future.

35   Jensen Motors Ltd., 'Analysis of Sales by Products 1958/59 -1964/65'.
36   Wayne Lewchuk, *American Technology and the British Vehicle Industry* (Cambridge, 1987), p. 186.
37   Jensen Motors Ltd., 'Jensen Motors Limited: Balance Sheet Summaries 1959 -1965' (Jensen Motors Ltd., 1965), MRC, MSS.215/2/11/2.
38   R.A. Graves, 'Memorandum: Sales Forecast 1967/68' (Jensen Motors Ltd., 1967), MRC, MSS.215/6/7.

This uncertainty was conveyed in Owen's Five Year Budget, created in 1967 after Graves's report. It reinforces the sense of managerial ineptitude. In terms of planning ahead, for example, the "figures in advance of 1969 can at this stage only be considered as tentative because unless the whole economy of the country is changed, it could well be that the present malaise within the car industry could bring about wholesale changes in design and selling patterns." He goes on to review other car projects, including the Austin Healey successor. Amazingly, given the date of his report and the necessary planning and operational organisation required, he concludes: "At this stage, without any concrete projects or contracts, we have only been able to work on a hypothetical basis, as those things which could materialise in 1968 or 1969 are at the moment only in an embryo stage." Two other projects were mentioned, "but insufficient is known about either to take into serious account".[39] This did not look like the focused, long-range strategy of a competent managing director and dynamic leadership team.

Neither Owen's budget nor the business he was running can have inspired Norcros. By now, the Austin and Sunbeam contracts had ended, creating a loss of £43,000 in 1967 after average pre-tax profits of £145,000 over the previous five years.[40] Forecasts were all for pre-tax losses, no matter what the operational scenario. And in this period of dubious managerial competence, Jensen was unfortunately only one of Norcros's challenges. According to *The Economist*, two of its four divisions (printing, consumer products, construction, and industrials) were a "hodgepodge". These included the consumer products group which combined Jensen with Hygena Kitchens (presumably on the basis that individual buyers bought both, not a compelling strategic justification) and two medical companies. Though respected by *The Economist* for its performance relative to other holding companies, there needed to be "some savage sorting out of the group's priorities"; management needed to "cut out, not just unprofitable companies, but those that do not fit into a clear industrial framework."[41] For all the praise heaped on its founder in later years, the vaunted financial conglomerate's variety of capitalism seems in practice to have produced less than the sum of its parts.

---

39   B.C. Owen, 'Five Year Budget' (Jensen Motors Ltd., 1967), MRC, MSS.215/6/7.
40   Jensen Motors Ltd., 'Jensen Motors Limited: Profit & Loss Account for Seven Years, Ended 31 July 1959–1965'.
41   'Holding Companies: Disappearing Breed?', *The Economist* (1 April 1967), p. 63.

Carl Duerr and William Brandt's Sons, 1968 to 1970

In response to Jensen's woes, Norcros appointed management consultants to review their options. The consultants sent American turnaround specialist Carl Duerr to West Bromwich. Duerr reported back in negative terms and was appointed to replace Owen: the company said that "there have had to be some radical changes in thinking and, in particular, management thinking."[42] Duerr recorded his impressions in a subsequent business memoir. He found that Norcros's "disapproving, semi-absentee ownership"[43] had destroyed staff morale, and Jensen "combined all the deficiencies of a big company with all the disadvantages of a small one, and had none of the benefits of either."[44] Six months later, Norcros's decision to divest Jensen was announced.[45] Duerr and Jensen's PR consultant persuaded merchant bank William Brandt's Sons to buy them out, with Duerr and other directors investing, and the bank publicly proclaiming its intention to shake up the industry and add to Jensen by acquisition.[46] The purchase price was less than a third of what Norcros had paid.

Duerr's memoir is valuable not only for its commentary on Jensen and its analysis of the prevailing problems and culture there, but also for his observations on British management. Although he too had not come from an automotive background, he was a University of Pennsylvania-trained graduate engineer who had been in engineering and sales positions in both smaller companies and General Electric. Since the war he had served initially as an economic officer for the US Army in Austria and subsequently as a management consultant in Germany, which he now considered home. His commentary on British approaches therefore benefits from comparison with German and American practices. One German capability he embodied himself, and whose absence he perhaps noted among some of Jensen's managers, was the need to be *kontakfähig*, a concept he explores in his memoir and translates as being "intuitively able to establish unspoken two-way communications with others". In conventional German usage, it may usually be translated as "sociable".[47] In daily management practice, Duerr defined it as "a sympathetic interest in others, a

42 'American to Head Jensen', *The Times* (London, England, 6 January 1968), p. 9, The Times Digital Archive.

43 Duerr, p. 187.

44 Duerr, p. 189.

45 'Not so Much a Luxury', *The Times* (London, England, 12 June 1968), p. 27, The Times Digital Archive.

46 *The Economist* (31 August 1968), p. 63; 'Bankers Take Major Stake in Jensen', *The Times* (London, England, 23 August 1968), p. 17, The Times Digital Archive.

47 'Kontaktfähig', LEO Englisch ⇔ Deutsch Wörterbuch (2022) <https://dict.leo.org/englisch-deutsch/kontaktf%C3%A4hig> [accessed 2 May 2022].

curiosity as to what makes them tick, a desire to influence their thinking."[48] From the appreciations of Duerr expressed by some of his workers (though not, as we will see, by some of his senior managers), it would appear that being *kontaktfähig* was a German way of working and interacting that Duerr aimed to make an important element of Jensen's culture. On his arrival at Jensen, Duerr "had never set foot in a factory where morale was so low." Communication was poor, departments did not work together, productivity was disastrous, and management of the union relationship was poor. In particular, management had ceased to communicate with the staff and keep them aware of Jensen's difficulties. Boosting productivity, improving internal communication, growing sales, and enhancing Jensen's image therefore became his priorities.[49] Being *kontaktfähig* would help him achieve them.

Staff Relations
Duerr attracted very different feelings among Jensen employees. He thought highly of the skills and attitudes of local workers. His evaluation of them is important, both for its general relevance to this chapter and indeed the whole book, but also as a counterpoint to the generally negative perception of unionised British labour in this period. He saw that at Jensen,

> a critical asset was the basic calibre of the workforce. They were Black Countrymen, a breed, with one exception, unique in my experience. That exception is the metal-workers of the Ruhr district in Germany. Like the Ruhr workers, the Black Countrymen are the inheritors of a centuries-old tradition of metal-working craftsmanship. As a result, they have a remarkable degree of technical integrity, and an unparalleled willingness to devote themselves to a product they believe in. Generations of hard work at the forge have made them very, very independent and bloody-minded, suspicious of 'outsiders' such as people from Birmingham seven miles away, given to mischievous behaviour, hard drinking, and hard work. With half a chance, and some leadership, these very qualities produce a rare degree of team effort. Just get that stubborn steadfastness and wonderful sense of humour harnessed and pulling in the right direction, and your company is going to be very hard to stop.[50]

His appreciation seems to have been reciprocated. One assembly worker, who discovered a way to save Jensen money, decided to report his idea to Duerr directly: "I would never have done this with previous managing directors (or even those that came later), but Carl Duerr was approachable. He would often walk along the track early in the morning saying hello to everyone, and

48   Duerr, pp. 18–19.
49   Duerr, pp. 187–93.
50   Duerr, p. 190.

asking how people were doing. All the assembly guys liked him."[51] One visiting journalist found on his factory tour that "Everyone was pleased to see the boss. They were enjoying their work and they had Carl Duerr to thank for the work and for enjoying it."[52] Being *kontaktfähig* was, it seemed, an imported German practice that Duerr used to good effect within Jensen.

Though he discusses at length in his book his frustration with elements of British union conduct and organisation,[53] Duerr's appraisal of relationships at Jensen reflects his generally positive disposition towards "the skilled British worker [who] is first of all a craftsman of above average literacy and outstanding character. It goes against the grain for him to down tools and walk out."[54] In his relations with Jensen's shop stewards, whom he challenged very quickly on the need to improve productivity, "we learned to understand, trust, and respect each other."[55] He was, however, "horrified at the insulation of the offices from the factory" – "not one office worker had ever set foot in the factory"[56] – which he addressed by the introduction of factory tours and encouraging other senior managers to "get out onto the floor."[57]

Duerr was unimpressed with British managers in general, and some of those he found at Jensen in particular. He was sceptical about British ambivalence towards the need to make profit, and scornful about the evolution of various management "types" in Britain, from nepotistic family appointees, to Oxbridge graduates, to the prevailing fashion for "professional management".[58] He gave some credit to degree-trained managers with life experience, and to business-school trained business intellectuals. He was, however, contemptuous of managers who like committees but then "duck into the background when the time comes for the decisions, or the shouldering of responsibility" and he warned British business that moving into the EEC in the future would expose its lack of managerial professionalism compared to German, Dutch or Belgian managers.[59]

Jensen marketing director Richard Graves was personally opposed to Duerr, a large part of whose strategy was the systematic development of Jensen's,

---

51 'Jensen Motors Assembly Line Finisher | Day In The Life', The Jensen Museum (2017) <http://www.jensenmuseum.org/jensen-motors-assembly-line-finisher-day-life/> [accessed 22 July 2017].

52 Geoffrey Howard, 'How to Turn Red Into Black. Jensen and Their Nerve-Centre, Mr. Duerr', *Autocar* (1970) <http://www.jcc.ch/fileadmin/user_upload/Jensen_Firmengeschichte/ Artikel/AC_70_FACT.pdf> [accessed 20 July 2017].

53 Duerr, pp. 92–101, 133–47.

54 Duerr, p. 94.

55 Duerr, p. 192.

56 Duerr, p. 193.

57 Duerr, p. 193.

58 Duerr, p. 35.

59 Duerr, pp. 47; 39–49.

and his own, public profile. For Duerr, the PR strategy was essential to build the company's image and raise staff morale.[60] Communication was clearly a personal mantra, hence the title of his book and its dedication to a long list of journalists "whose sincere and critical interest" helped Jensen. It should be recalled that RECARO's achievements owed a great deal to their own superb PR, by which they created a global seating brand. However, Graves's criticism of Duerr and his obsession with PR was vitriolic: "I'm not sure how good a businessman he was. I don't generally take badly to people, but I couldn't stand him."[61] This view was unhealthy when both were board directors. The roots of his dislike may have been located in Duerr's criticism of the British, and Jensen's, approach to selling, arguing that being a salesman or an engineer in Britain was socially unacceptable, "which is maybe why sales managers all seem to be renaming themselves marketing directors."[62] In Jensen, on "the marketing front the company exhibited a hyper-British syndrome: neither the firm nor its dealers were oriented to sell Jensen cars. They were (sometimes reluctant) order takers." As for the exclusivity of the Jensen product, the cars had always sold themselves "largely because they were in chronically short supply, had been carefully engineered, meticulously built, and often priced below cost."[63] Graves outlasted Duerr and has remained a hero to Jensen aficionados. In his own very negative criticisms of aspects of the company, quoted below, Graves was open and candid. That the cars sold at all must have owed something to his ability. But his insistence that "you have to have customers who want the cars, rather than you wanting the [manufactured but unsold] cars to have customers",[64] indicates a lassitude and lack of growth orientation which added weight to Duerr's insistence that "supine reliance on order taking was no longer enough."[65]

Business Performance Under Duerr

Duerr's intention was to take Jensen public in 1972.[66] In itself, this plan – so alien to the thinking of most Mittelstand businesses, even those which grew very large like Keiper – suggested that the "turnaround man" had adopted a short-term plan for Jensen from which he himself stood to gain as a shareholder. The details of his plan are not known, but it is possible that those critical of his management and his pushing for more output believed that he

60   Duerr, pp. 191, 195.
61   'Jon Pressnell – Richard Graves Interview', *The Jensen Museum*, 2017 <http://www.jensenmuseum.org/jon-pressnell-richard-graves-interview/> [accessed 22 July 2017].
62   Duerr, p. 167.
63   Duerr, p. 188.
64   'Jon Pressnell – Richard Graves Interview'.
65   Duerr, p. 199.
66   Duerr, p. 201.

was pumping the business unnecessarily hard with a view to enhancing its IPO value. This criticism was not apparent in *Autocar's* congratulatory review in January 1970, which pointed out that the firm had taken thirty-three years to build its first 1000 Jensens but thirty-three months to build its first 1000 Interceptors, with a managing director who was popular with the workforce and passionate about the product.[67] The business appeared to be thriving in a way that it had not thrived previously. Five months later, though, Duerr had resigned, sold his 30% holding, and left.[68]

The origins of his departure can be found in a review of the financial results for the thirteen weeks ending 31 January 1970.[69] Though 138 cars had been sold over the quarter, producing revenues of £532,000 in car sales and a further £82,000 of servicing and spare parts, the accounts showed a £28,000 loss. Duerr had cut hundreds of jobs and each car was in itself profitable, but his battle to improve quality was apparently not over. "Rectification costs" totalled £8000. A later statement showed 429 cars under guarantee, costing on average £118 per car each year, a huge potential liability.[70] There was almost £1.1 million of stock and work in progress: in the four weeks to 30 January 1970, 116 cars had been built, but only thirty-nine actually sold, substantiating Graves's complaint about building too many cars, and Duerr's criticism of Graves for failing to sell them. The loss for January alone was nearly £15,000. And with creditors and accrued expenses at £1.2 million as against debtors at £234,000, the business lacked liquidity, not least because it was paying £15,000 in interest and £19,000 in Norcros royalties per quarter.[71]

Duerr's defence was simple: all the development and other charges had been loaded into the costs, they had invested for growth, and were on target for £250,000 profit before the IPO. There were slack sales periods each year, and it was more efficient to run the factory consistently and then push hard to sell the cars produced, than to lay workers off in quiet periods. The bank's chairman demurred, recommending instead that overhead be cut, and – echoing the conservative Graves – "a proven rate of production to match proven sales" implemented. Mirroring Duerr's own experience, the bank appointed former Rolls Royce aviation manager Alfred Vickers to report on Jensen's financial position. His negative report was ill received by Duerr who, in response, looked around for an alternate investor to join him. He found Kjell Qvale, American

67 Howard.
68 Giles Smith, 'Duerr of Jensen Resigns', *The Times* (London, England, 9 May 1970), p. 11, The Times Digital Archive.
69 'Monthly Trading Report, 13 Weeks Ended 30th January 1970' (Jensen Motors Ltd., 1970), MRC, MSS.215/6/9.
70 'Guarantee Costs, 4 Weeks to 26th June 1970' (Jensen Motors Ltd., 1970), MRC, MSS.215/6/9.
71 'Monthly Trading Report, 13 Weeks Ended 30th January 1970'.

distributor of Jensen and other British makes including the Austin Healey, and the latter's designer Donald Healey, who bought out Brandt's shares. But Qvale and Healey then decided to cancel – by telegram – the agreed scheme by which Duerr would return to Germany and set up a Jensen sales franchise, instead appointing Vickers as Jensen's new managing director.[72]

Duerr claimed in his book, published the following year, to have succeeded in his turnaround. He warned that Jensen could be returning to its past problems, again dependent on a single customer – Qvale himself – and on sales in an increasingly competitive American market.[73] He was right. We have no record of the reaction of staff to Duerr's departure, but they now found themselves with new owners for the third time in barely a decade and their third managing director in less than three years.

Labour Relations

As labour problems were said to have contributed to the brothers' decision to sell Jensen, and were frequently mentioned by journalists and Qvale as the business neared its end, it is appropriate at this point to consider how they varied over time within the context of industrial relations difficulties right across the British motor industry.[74] Within it, Wayne Lewchuk argues, "management was being challenged to take direct responsibility for planning, maintenance and the organisation of shop floor activity. It was a challenge for which they were ill prepared."[75] Lewchuk's analysis of the industry between the 1950s and 1980s pays particular attention to the challenge of relating pay to productivity, and productivity to automation, and both to the management of labour relations.[76] Strikes were endemic: there were 401 strikes of more than one hundred days each in British car factories in the period 1960 to 1964. At the Austin plant closest to Jensen, there were 935 internal disputes between 1966 and 1971, in a climate in which labour generally found it effective to launch small stoppages which blocked the increasingly integrated production systems.[77]

Some stoppages were caused by indirect action or impact and must have frustrated even the most pro-union manager. Back in July 1956, for instance, three hundred Jensen workers had refused to work on Austin Healey bodies in

72 Duerr, pp. 204–05.
73 Duerr, p. 206.
74 Geoffrey Owen, pp. 220–21, 231–38; David Kynaston, *Austerity Britain 1945–51* (London: Bloomsbury, 2007), pp. 487–99.
75 Lewchuck, p. 195; other than at Vauxhall, where 'crucially, workers were treated as human beings': Kynaston, p. 489.
76 Lewchuck, pp. 184–225.
77 Lewchuck, p. 203, table 9.8.

sympathy with a strike at British Motor Corporation.[78] In 1957 the National
Union of Vehicle Builders (NUVB) wrote to the Trades Union Congress (TUC)
to advise that the Birmingham and Midland Sheet Metal Workers' Society
(BMSMWS) had withdrawn all their members from Jensen from 14 October,
causing all four hundred members of the NUVB to be suspended from work
themselves. As the BMSMWS had claimed "sole prerogative", NUVB interests
could not be represented, hence the appeal for TUC support. BMSMWS wrote
to the TUC on 5 November reporting: "the Dispute at Jensen Motor Co. Ltd.,
is now settled, and you will be pleased to know that we have received from the
Management everything we asked for."[79] In this case, having lost production
from 14 October to 2 November, the Jensen brothers then had to concede
all that had been demanded.[80] The financial impact on the business of this
particular strike is not known. Later disputes also required workers from an
unaffected union to cease work while a separate disagreement was enacted
between management and the disaffected workers.[81]

Limitations in available source material preclude a detailed examination
of Jensen's personnel-management practices. But the challenge posed by
management–labour relations to productivity, quality, and long-term viability
can be judged from various documents relating to factory wage rates as well
as to the strike actions referenced above. Pay was complicated. Production
wages included elements of basic pay, overtime, incentives, piecework – and,
later, day working – and holiday pay. Additional payments were agreed by
trade and by union, and included both "domestic" and nationally agreed levels.
The craft-demarcated culture made management extraordinarily challenging.
From February 1969, for example, Jensen paid eight different rates to adult
male workers, plus six to workers aged twenty and under according to their
age.[82] Piecework rates, which differed by trade and between the two production
unions, and other supplements added further complexity to the pay scales.
An analysis completed in April 1970 showed changes in Jensen wages from
1961 (when the working week was forty-two hours) to 1965 (when it was
reduced, first to forty-one and then to forty hours), to 1969 and then 1970. The

78   'More Motor Workers Join Strike', *The Times* (London, England, 26 July 1956), p. 8,
The Times Digital Archive.
79   H. Townsend, 'Letter from Birmingham and Midlands Sheet Metal Workers Society to
Sir Vincent Tewson, TUC', 5 November 1957, MRC, MSS.292/251/6; 'Sports Car Production
Halted by Strike', *The Times* (London, England, 19 October 1957), p. 4, The Times Digital
Archive.
80   'Car Factory Strike Ends', *The Times* (London, England, 2 November 1957), p. 4, The
Times Digital Archive.
81   For example, 'Production Halted at Jensen Works', *The Times* (London, England, 5
April 1962), p. 5, The Times Digital Archive.
82   Jensen Motors Ltd., 'Domestic Wages Agreement' (Jensen Motors Ltd., 1969), MRC,
MSS.215/6/11.

combination of decreasing hours and increasing weekly rates meant that on basic wages alone, the company had to bear nominal cost rises of between 36% and 61% for three sample roles over the period. Rates of increase on piecework and other supplements are not recorded. It is not clear how much the price of Jensen cars or of other inputs rose over the same period, so the actual impact on the business cannot easily be determined.[83] But some sympathy must be offered to the workers, who were having to combat soaring living costs: when normalised for inflation, actual increases between 1961 and 1970 for those roles were between -6% and 12% (though a 12% real terms increase is of course highly significant).

Sympathy for the inflationary climate aside, wage demands clearly became untenable and, in hindsight incomprehensible, as Jensen's situation deteriorated. In August 1974, for example, with Jensen in crisis, production was yet again halted. Management agreed to pay demands which would "improve holiday pay and pension benefits, provide better security of earnings, and the employees [sic] general credit worthiness". Basic wages for forty hours would rise and include an irrevocable productivity element, even if productivity was not sustained. Thus a £47.80 per week basic wage would become a £54.00 basic wage plus a £3.75 incentive payment for a worker who did forty-nine "good minutes" work in an hour, i.e., was less than 82% efficient. This plan would apply for the remainder of 1974, then rise again. On top of this 20.8% pay rise, holiday pay would also rise by 5.3%, the whole agreement being backdated to 1 July 1974. The BMSMWS and TGWU signatories "recognised that the Company's financial difficulties prohibit a more generous settlement" but looked forward to the meeting which would review indirect workers' pay the following week.[84] In an environment in which operational incompetence and a rapid recourse to dismissals were both commonplace, it is not surprising that Jensen's unions – emboldened by a national culture of labour militancy – were willing to seek greater security for their members. It is also not surprising that their doing so, even without the use of stoppages to reinforce their demands, had a deleterious effect on the company in which they wanted to continue working.

83 Jensen Motors Ltd., 'Basic Wages 1961–1970' (Jensen Motors Ltd., 1970), MRC, MSS.215/6/11. Calculations by the author.
84 Jensen Motors Ltd., 'Meeting Held in Mr. Beattie's Office on the 16th August 1974' (Jensen Motors Ltd., 1974), MRC, MSS.215/3/JE/1; Jensen Motors Ltd., 'Memorandum of Agreement Between Jensen Motors Limited and The Birmingham and Midlands Sheet Metal Workers Society and the Transport and General Workers Union' (Jensen Motors Ltd., 1974), MRC, MSS.215/3/JE/1.

Where did accountability for these self-induced problems lie? The Trim Shop's Senior Trimmer, Gilbert Hughes, was also the union Works Convener.[85] A colleague who began work in the Press Shop in 1951 and later became its manager, Ron Freckleton, remembered Hughes as one of "the few trade unionists that I ever came across, that understood that companies had to make a profit at the end of the day. He was respected by both the management, as well as those working on the shop floor."[86] Duerr remembered Hughes as "exhibiting a degree of maturity and business insight that would probably surprise the union-knockers."[87] While there were no doubt other union officials involved in organising industrial actions, these impressions of Hughes do not suggest an all-dominating attitude of obstructive militancy. However, neither management nor unions seem to have had the constructive vision of their German counterparts. Whereas staff of both sexes were paid the same rate for the same job at Reutter and Porsche from the early 1950s onwards, establishing an egalitarian culture of equal commitment, all adult women workers at Jensen were paid a flat rate which was 79% of the lowest-paid male labourer's wage. Ferry Porsche went further: though he also suffered strikes and disagreements with his (single) union, he insisted that "workers and staff all be on an equal footing" in his business, an approach as unimaginable in the them-versus-us environment of British motor manufacturing as Porsche's consequent results were.[88]

At Jensen, the available evidence suggests that management did not always manage the wage situation or general operations effectively. Given that first piece rates, then bonuses, relied on the throughput of cars, which in turn depended on accurate planning and reliable material supplies, the onus was on management to plan and execute properly. When they did not, the worker's standard of living would immediately be affected, giving rise to understandable tensions. Lewchuk is generally sympathetic to the labour perspective, but his analysis of the industry's difficulty in moving from piecework pay to managed day rates is persuasive, as is his wider appraisal of work organisation and his conclusion that, in many situations, it was management incompetence rather than labour intransigence that caused line stoppages. The workers' perspective at the Austin plant, for example, was of growing frustration at management's inability to keep the plant running.[89] Similar frustrations were expressed at Jensen. It can be imagined that in the prevailing external industrial climate with constant internal pressure to produce enough cars to keep the business

85   'Jensen Motors Trim Shop Employees A-Z', The Jensen Museum (2016) <http://www.jensenmuseum.org/jensen-motors-trim-shop-employees/> [accessed 22 July 2017].
86   'Jensen Motors' Press Shop Manager | Recollections', The Jensen Museum (2017) <http://www.jensenmuseum.org/jensen-motors-press-shop-manager-recollections/> [accessed 22 July 2017].
87   Duerr, p. 192.
88   Porsche and Molter, p. 242.
89   Lewchuk, p. 208.

viable and the 'track' always moving and provisioned, acting rationally, much less being hard-nosed and holding out against union demands, was easier to contemplate than to achieve. But both Porsche and Reutter did exactly that. Carl Duerr claims in his book to have done the same.

Company Culture

What was the environment in which these problems were played out? A former draughtsman recalled that the original Jensen site, from which the much larger business moved to a purpose-built factory elsewhere in West Bromwich, "was quite a dingy factory … that was true of most factories at that time" (though it was not true of Reutter's works). But he remembered also "the general friendliness of the workers, one to another, and between staff (not necessarily management) and shop floor workers."[90] There was pride in craftsmanship, as Duerr found. Images of Jensen's Trim Shop recall those of Karosserie Reutter, hand-cutting and sewing leather for seats and trim. A report by one visiting car magazine that "six Connolly hides are used to upholster each Jensen, and roof linings are stitched up with notable skill" adds to the impression that here, and elsewhere in the factory, the quality of the work done by Jensen's workers appears to have been superior to the management done by Jensen's managers.[91]

The Trim Shop's leader started at Jensen in the late 1940s or early 1950s and ran the Shop until it closed in 1976. The level of his training and involvement in decision-making are unknown, so it is not possible to draw a parallel between him and his counterpart *Meister* at Reutter. Press shop manager Ron Freckleton's own memories of working in various production-related roles indicate a can-do attitude among shop floor staff and, in his own case, a willingness to promote men from a trade background to increasing levels of responsibility (though it is not clear how, or indeed whether, they were trained to assume it). The assembly line finisher who approached Duerr with his cost-saving idea had begun as an apprentice at Jensen.[92] He appears to have followed a structured programme, including one day a week at West Bromwich College, and is positive about the atmosphere in the factory. Jensen's approach was to offer a general training, however: after completing his studies, he was asked which area of the factory he wanted to work in, rather than having been trained to an advanced level in a specific skill. The Jensen archive contains the report of the Birmingham Productivity Association's visit to West Germany

90 'Recollections of Nick Maltby, Draughtsman, of Jensen Motors | Carter's Green Factory', The Jensen Museum (2016) <http://www.jensenmuseum.org/jensen-motors-carters-green-factory/> [accessed 22 July 2017].

91 'How Jensens Are Made', *Motor Sport Magazine* (1969) <http://www.motorsportmagazine.com/archive/article/february-1969/44/how-jensens-are-made> [accessed 20 July 2017].

92 'Jensen Motors Assembly Line Finisher | Day In The Life'.

in 1955, which comprehensively reviewed apprenticeship provision in general, and within several companies, including Opel. Some attention was also paid in the report to the training of *Meister*.[93] We do not know whether any of its findings were applied within Jensen.

Given the apparent interest in German ways of working and the problems that company had been experiencing for some time, it is surprising to hear Jensen Quality Engineer Paul Turner report that in 1971 "the Quality Department was a new idea at Jensen." There was no formal description of his job, and he soon encountered resistance from the factory's production foremen, Though he gained credibility once it became clear that he was technically proficient himself (he had worked at Rolls Royce after an apprenticeship at Austin), he discovered that "Many of [the] problems had existed for a long time and had become endemic ... many of the difficulties were never solved, just improved a little."[94] The small Quality team faced pressure from management to pass vehicles which were unacceptable, and the general impression is of a quality system which was reluctantly introduced and inadequately supported; Turner's salary was lower than assembly workers' wages. This management mindset can be contrasted with Porsche. After the war, all its factory machines had been lost, and the first Porsches "were therefore mostly made by hand, but were of an outstanding quality which was internationally recognised."[95] Throughout the build programme for the Porsche 356, which had delivered 40,000 cars by 1960, "quality control was systematically improved" with every fifth production worker given a specific control-task and data-collection sheets being completed for the key features of each vehicle.[96]

Criticisms of Jensen's mindset cannot be restricted to staff managers. The foremen, in Turner's account, are equally at fault, apparently just as concerned with impingement on their status as with maintaining impeccable standards. The difference between Porsche/Reutter and Jensen in this instance is instructive. Though they were apprehensive about the operational pressure of growing weekly demands for Porsche 356 bodies and the concomitantly increasing dependence on Porsche, Reutter did whatever was required to meet those demands without sacrificing quality. When Duerr, quite reasonably, requested an increase in output to capitalise on the popularity of the Interceptor and to improve the company's dire financial position, he was condemned by Graves and others. Following Duerr's departure, Vickers' decision to cut production by one third, which produced an improvement in product quality,

---

93   Birmingham Productivity Association.

94   'Jensen Motors Quality Engineer | Recollections', The Jensen Museum (2017) <http://www.jensenmuseum.org/jensen-motors-quality-engineer-recollections/> [accessed 22 July 2017].

95   Porsche and Molter, p. 183.

96   Porsche and Molter, p. 241.

"proved the point" of Duerr's misjudgement.[97] This outcome suggests a sense within Jensen that producing fifteen good cars in a week was somehow an unreasonable demand, as though product quality were a finite resource which could not be stretched across fifteen cars, rather than an irreducible cultural commitment in whose pursuit all necessary efforts should be made. It also implies a feeling that business growth was somehow distasteful and inimical to the Jensen cachet. And it indicates a significant difference in thinking between the managers and *Meister* of Reutter and the managers and foremen of Jensen.

Duerr's description of the office/works divide suggests a them-and-us culture existed. Whether he was as successful as he claimed to be in mitigating it is not clear. If he was, the problems returned after he left. A 1973 memo written by Jack Warren, a manager or supervisor (it is not clear which from the archival record) in the stores/purchasing area, to a director is highly critical of failings in several areas, including his own. He calls for more assertive management and better communication with workers. His conclusion to the five typed pages, which are literate, organised, constructive, and clearly motivated by his commitment to the business rather than by any desire for self-advancement, is: "Too many projects are taken on at once, or if more than one is taken on, they are not placed in priority order and then thoroughly processed. A realistic budget must be drawn up ... A realistic margin of profit must be placed on the car, with due consideration to sales requirements and/or alterations." There is more of the same. All of it is consistent with the evidence of Jensen's conduct and performance. The director's response is to annotate "Bull" in the margin, and instruct his secretary to file it away,[98] suggesting at best an indifference to the positive engagement of one employee, at worst a refusal to acknowledge the problems which would eventually prove to be Jensen's downfall.

Qvale Period, 1970 to 1975

When Qvale took over, Jensen staff, including Graves, "were all thrilled to bits. We thought we had a new lease of life."[99] Qvale was happy to take credit for an upturn. He had appointed Vickers as managing director. Losses had turned by the end of the 1971 financial year to a £102,000 profit and he had increased the labour force from six hundred to one thousand. *The Times* reported that "Jensen's turnaround is almost entirely due to the arrival on the scene a year ago of Mr. Kjell Qvale" whose US dealership network had boosted sales, with

97   Entry for Alfred Vickers, managing director Jensen Motors, in 'Jensen Motors Employees A-Z'.
98   Jack Warren, 'Untitled Memorandum Re: Jensen Internal Problems' (Jensen Motors Ltd., 1973), MRC, MSS.215/3/W/1.
99   'Jon Pressnell – Richard Graves Interview'.

production at West Bromwich increasing and requiring a further four hundred staff in due course.[100] The growth was to come from the launch of the new Jensen Healey, the fruit of Qvale's cooperation with Donald Healey, though Interceptor sales were also at a record high.[101] The new Interceptor III was praised in 1972 as "the kind of car one would dearly love to own."[102] Its key drawback would become significant in 1973: at 15.2mpg fuel consumption, it was about to become prohibitively expensive to run.

The 1972 accounts showed sales of £3.7 million, £1.2 million of them exported, an increase of 30% over the previous year. But soon problems with the new Jensen-Healey became apparent. They were traceable to Qvale's insistence that he would sell two hundred cars per week in America, and therefore needed a manufacturer who would supply two hundred engines per week, plus an additional three hundred Jensen factory staff to cope with demand.[103] He personally agreed terms with Lotus, who would supply their unproven, new engine only without a warranty. Multiple problems with the cars ensued, with no recourse to Lotus. For Graves, whose marketing team "had hardly any input into the car itself ... it was a fait accompli"; the consequence of Qvale's management of the Jensen-Healey development "was a total shambles. It was awful."[104] Even with the increased sales, Jensen could only achieve 1.5% profit.[105] Of more concern, it now also had £494,000 of loan debt and -£8000 of net current assets. For 1973, it seemed in revenue terms that Qvale's push on exports for the Jensen-Healey and the Interceptors had paid off: sales had more than doubled to £8.3 million, £3.7 million in exports. But the increased sales had produced a loss of £123,000, having paid £99,000 interest on what was now £1.1 million of bank debts and overdrafts,[106] all of them secured by a mortgage over the factory.[107] Net current assets were now -£200,000: the company could not readily pay its bills. The 1055 workers were at risk. Qvale disingenuously told *The Times* that Jensen was "not in any serious financial problem" but that

100   Clifford Webb Midland Industrial Correspondent, 'Jensen Ends Year with a Profit: Staff to Be Bigger', *The Times* (London, England, 26 June 1971), p. 16, The Times Digital Archive.
101   Our Midland Industrial Correspondent, 'Jensen to Expand Its Labour Force by 50 Pc', *The Times* (London, England, 11 February 1972), p. 20, The Times Digital Archive.
102   Edward Eves, 'Taking Stock: What It Means to Own a Jensen Interceptor III', *Autocar* (29 June 1972), MRC, MSS.215/6/2.
103   Our Midland Industrial Correspondent.
104   'Jon Pressnell – Richard Graves Interview'.
105   'Jensen Motors Ltd.: Audited Accounts for the Year to 28 April 1972' (1972), Companies House, archive disk 00182205–05.
106   'Jensen Motors Ltd.: Audited Accounts for the Year to 27 April 1973' (1974), Companies House, archive disk 00182205–05.
107   Bank of America National Trust & Savings Association, 'Certificate of Registration of Mortgage over Jensen Motors Ltd.' (1973), Companies House, archive disk 00182205–07.

he had postponed a £650,000 paint shop investment because mostly "external factors" had regularly stopped production.[108]

Acrimony and job losses followed. One hundred staff were made redundant in October 1974, with the remaining 1200 jobs threatened by a cash flow crisis. *The Times* reported that "one of the mysteries of Jensen Motors' recent confrontation with its employees is now cleared up", as Kevin Beattie was replaced as managing director. Described by "close friends" as a "brilliant engineer" who had "never seemed entirely at home as chief executive", Beattie said he was "quite happy to revert to [his] old job".[109] Qvale threatened to close the business, publicly condemning the workers: "Our present problems are quite simply due to an insufficient level of productivity and unless and until the work force are prepared to honour their agreements, and produce the required number of cars in return for their not ungenerous pay, the future of the company cannot be assured." Union leaders met Qvale and "told him quite bluntly that management inefficiency was the trouble, not laziness among his workers. The fact is cars are not being produced because there are recurring shortages of components".[110] Their comments echo Lewchuk's evaluation of problems in other, larger car plants. Though Beattie was respected by the workforce and was considered by his chief engineer to be unusual as an engineer in being both technically capable and good with people, the appointment of a design engineer to run a production business without any prior executive experience or recorded management training, and without much enthusiasm for the job himself, would seem to substantiate union frustrations about poor management.[111]

Within a month of sacking Beattie, Qvale had decided to halve production and make up to four hundred redundancies, owing to "sharply depressed sales" in the US where the automotive industry was in crisis.[112] He also promoted Richard Graves to deputy managing director to run the business while he himself was in America. Qvale was admired by *The Times'* motor correspondent for being "a dynamo of a self-made millionaire [who] would brook no opposition

108   Edward Townsend, 'Car Output Last Week at Best Level for a Month', *The Times* (London, England, 22 March 1974), p. 19, The Times Digital Archive.
109   'Business Diary: Jensen', *The Times* (London, England, 31 October 1974), p. 23, The Times Digital Archive
110   'Cash Crisis Forces Jensen to Cut Staff', *The Times* (London, England, 4 October 1974), p. 19, The Times Digital Archive.
111   'Jensen Motors Chief Engineer | Day In The Life', The Jensen Museum (2016) <http://www.jensenmuseum.org/jensen-motors-chief-designer-day-life/> [accessed 18 January 2019].
112   'Jensen Will Cut Car Production by 50 Pc', *The Times* (London, England, 21 December 1974), p. 15, The Times Digital Archive.

to his way of doing things."[113] Unfortunately his "way of doing things" was inappropriate. When Graves resigned in May 1975 in a disagreement with Qvale over rescue tactics for Jensen, production was down from 130 to 28 cars per week, and five hundred staff had been made redundant. The Jensen Interceptor, priced at £8717 (three times the annual salary of Jensen's planning manager),[114] had turned into a liability for its drivers, who could no longer afford, in the post-oil-crisis world, to put fuel into its seven-litre engine, and for dealers who could not sell the car.[115]

Qvale was a very capable man. He had built a network of one hundred dealerships on the West Coast of the United States, representing thirty-six makers including Porsche and Rolls Royce as well as Jensen. He was a great salesman of cars in America to Americans, as the sales results there proved. But he was neither an engineer nor a production expert, as the ongoing failure with Jensen's cars, starting at the specification stage, also proved. Nor was he a culturally sensitive people-manager, who could have won over the workforce and unions, as Duerr seemed to have done, and either brought out the best in his senior staff or recruited suitably qualified alternatives. He claimed to have invested heavily in Jensen, but the larger financial inputs came from the bank debt with which he burdened the business. He was, in fact, the last in a line of Jensen business leaders – with the possible exception of Duerr – who failed to match the competence and professionalism of Ulrich Putsch, Ferry Porsche, or Reutter's Müller-Scholl.

The End

On Alan Jensen's death in 1994, *The Times* stated that Jensen had been "crushed by financial troubles and labour unrest".[116] The conclusions of the Receiver, appointed on 25 September 1975, substantiated the first part of this statement. In his official report, he noted a total estimated deficiency of £3.77 million, finding the company had failed for three main reasons: a recession for cars, especially in the USA, which had caused sales to be too low to meet overhead and development costs; high engineering costs incurred to meet new emissions and safety regulations; and the effect of a high rate of inflation on all the company's costs.[117] Numerous efforts over succeeding months to find

---

113 'Business Diary: Jensen Collision', *The Times* (London, England, 6 May 1975), p. 19, The Times Digital Archive.
114 Kjell H. Qvale, 'Letter to J.A. Moore Offering Pay Increase', 25 February 1975, MRC, MSS.215/3/JE/1: £2875 with effect from 1/1/75.
115 'Deputy Chief Resigns in Board Split at Jensen', *The Times* (London, England, 6 May 1975), p. 17, The Times Digital Archive.
116 'Motor Pioneer Dies at 87', *The Times* (London, England, 8 February 1994), p. 2, The Times Digital Archive.
117 J.A. Griffiths, 'Letter from Receiver to Registrar of Companies' (7 November 1975), Companies House, archive disk 00182205–03.

a buyer for the company failed.[118] Union representatives went to London to request a loan from the Labour Government of up to £4.5 million.[119] They were declined, as Kevin Beattie's request for export support from their Conservative predecessors had been declined earlier.[120] The final four hundred jobs were lost when the company was wound up in January 1977. *The Times* concluded: "A respected company, and an ideal for which so many people had fought so gallantly for almost half a century, was finally lost for the want of £5m."[121]

As for *The Times's* attribution of blame to "labour unrest", it might reasonably be argued that labour unrest was a consequence of Jensen's problems as much as, if not more than, their cause. Clearly, union disruption was endemic in Britain's automotive and other industries in this period (and elsewhere: for example, 360,000 Baden-Württemberg workers in 530 factories were off work at one point in 1971 as a consequence of an IG Metall strike).[122] But workers whose craft skills were the essence of the Jensen business had been largely treated as commodities by a series of owners and managers who had proved incapable of running the factory efficiently or selling the cars in sufficient volumes, and had felt free to lay off hundreds of workers whenever it suited them. Counterfactuals are probably unhelpful. But accepting the possibility that 1970s British industrial relations might have been too intractable for any putative owner, it is difficult in the context of this comparative study to imagine that Porsche or Reutter or Keiper would not have run Jensen more effectively. They were not financial engineers, as Brandt and Norcros were, nor short-term transients, as other Jensen owners and leaders were, but were automotive manufacturing professionals who were embedded in their regions and their industry and made a long-term commitment to the success of their products and the workers who made them.

---

118   'Buying Interest Shown in Jensen Motors', *The Times* (London, England, 19 September 1975), p. 18, The Times Digital Archive; 'Jensen Bidders Urged to Pool Resources', *The Times* (London, England, 23 February 1976), p. 15, The Times Digital Archive; 'Hope Fades for Survival of Jensen Motors', *The Times* (London, England, 6 April 1976), p. 22, The Times Digital Archive; 'Jensen Motors Reprieved for One More Week', *The Times* (London, England, 12 May 1976), p. 26, The Times Digital Archive; 'Jensen Wound Up', *The Times* (London, England, 18 January 1977), p. 17, The Times Digital Archive.

119   'Jensen Workers Seek State Aid up to £4.5m', *The Times* (London, England, 21 January 1976), p. 25, The Times Digital Archive.

120   'Correspondence between Kevin Beattie (Jensen) and Peter Walker (Secretary of State for Trade & Industry)' (Jensen Motors Ltd., 1973), MRC, MSS.215/3/W/1.

121   'Memories of Jensen', *The Times* (London, England, 26 August 1976), p. 23, The Times Digital Archive.

122   Washington Post Foreign Service, 'German Metal Strike Threatens Auto Firms', *The Washington Post, Times Herald* (1959–1973) (Washington, DC, USA, 27 November 1971), section General <http://search.proquest.com/docview/148016322/abstract/ FF731FC296744BC6PQ/1?> [accessed 7 March 2015].

Conclusion – A Better Way of Doing Business?

Purpose, we are told, must be the guiding light of business for the 2020s. Business leaders must look beyond the short-term, shareholder-obsessed ideology of the past fifty years to "rethink what a business is, how it grows and profits, what its purpose is, and how it drives change in the world."[1] The British Academy and its members urge businesses of all sizes to be guided by their sense of Purpose.[2] Capitalism must be reimagined, with Purpose at the centre of business practice.[3] The leaders of some of America's most dynamic corporations no longer affirm shareholder primacy, but the need to deliver value to customers, invest in employees, deal fairly and ethically with suppliers, and support the communities in which they work.[4] The questions to ask in this Conclusion, therefore, are fourfold. Were fundamental differences evident in post-war business that amounted to two Varieties of Capitalism? Did they arise at the business level alone, or in the intersection between businesses and the external ecosystems in which they operated? Might Purpose, as it is being defined today, have already been evident decades ago in the companies reviewed here? And if it was, do their histories offer any guidance to present-day practice?

First then, did the day-to-day experience of the case-study companies reflect different Varieties of Capitalism? Let us recall Hall and Soskice's five 'spheres' from Chapter 1.[5] They provide a convenient framework to compare and

1 Paul Polman and Andrew Winston, 'The Net Positive Manifesto', *Harvard Business Review*, 99.5 (2021), 124–31.

2 British Academy, *Policy & Practice for Purposeful Business*, Future of the Corporation (London: The British Academy, September 2021) <https://www.thebritishacademy.ac.uk/publications/policy-and-practice-for-purposeful-business/>; Colin Mayer, 'The Future of the Corporation and the Economics of Purpose', *Journal of Management Studies*, 58.3 (2021), 887–901.

3 Rebecca Henderson, *Reimagining Capitalism* (2020), pp. 83–120.

4 Business Roundtable, 'Statement on the Purpose of a Corporation', Business Roundtable (2019) <https://www.businessroundtable.org/business-roundtable-redefines-the-purpose-of-a-corporation-to-promote-an-economy-that-serves-all-americans> [accessed 25 August 2019].

5 Hall and Soskice, 'An Introduction to Varieties of Capitalism', pp. 6–8; see Chapter 1 above.

contrast each company's history, and to understand whether their separate experiences amounted to the fundamentally different approaches to doing business posited in the VoC debate.

Inter-firm Relations

In their relations with other firms Wandel were internationally successful, despite some operational frustrations, exporting their specialised products through their well-managed representative network and maintaining respectful relations with competitors in their region and within their professional institutions. K&J, in contrast, delivered a high level of operational capability from constantly updated equipment, but sold mostly commodity goods. Sales was an area of pre-war brilliance, with consultative selling and impressive product innovations; for much of the post-war period, though, it was a relative failure, with export success coming only in the mid-1970s. The two steel firms' relations with other companies reflected their different operational contexts. Schneider's decades-long relationships with demanding customers like Mercedes-Benz embodied the Mittelstand approach to long-term commitment and impeccable quality. Their public-sector sales flourished in a political environment in which regional reconstruction was prioritised and organised, meaning Schneider could remain locally focused – and unadventurous. Friendly relations with neighbours Mann + Hummel enabled the seamless transition of Schneider's workers at the company's close. Braithwaites, in contrast, sought and achieved growth overseas through the delivery of sometimes brilliant projects. They needed to do so because the infrastructure projects – and the supply of steel – they relied on in Britain were appallingly mismanaged by government and nationalised industries. In the challenging automotive industry, Jensen's relations with other firms were problematic and symptomatic of the sometimes chaotic management which delivered them. The Volvo relationship failed for want of proper quality controls. The Italian body supplier was mismanaged. Qvale's engine deal with Lotus was disastrous. In contrast, Reutter's relationships symbolised the clear-headed, purposeful management which prevailed for almost all of their history. Their relationship with Porsche was challenging but highly successful, and they achieved considerable success selling their patented seat mechanisms to the most demanding automobile manufacturers. Their shrewd management of their intellectual capital allowed them to maintain clever licensing deals with both customers and competitors. Keiper had maintained reciprocally beneficial relations with its own customers, and the new Keiper-RECARO's cooperative relationships with airlines allowed it time to develop the expertise that made the new aircraft seating business so successful.

Industrial Relations

If relations with external organisations were important, those with each company's respective workforce were critical. None of our case-study companies' archives contains extensive detail on the practice of industrial relations. We nevertheless get some sense of their character. At Wandel, we see the difficult period outlined in the consultants' report in 1960 and evidence of occasionally testy relations between Erna Wandel and her workers during the 1960s, but there is little sense of deteriorating relationships over the company's remaining decades. K&J's great interwar success, producing specialised products that were also internationally competitive, had been built on the traditionally paternalistic approach to the 'K&J family'. But that culture declined among contemporary social changes after the war, and its disappearance was hastened by the 1959 printing strike; thereafter, though, relations remained largely positive. Though there is little archival detail on the industrial relations practices of Schneider and Braithwaites, the evidence of each company's leaders working with their unions to manage site closures decently suggests an element of mutual respect within both companies. Within the automotive companies, in contrast, clear distinctions between the two case studies are evident. The industrial relations practices of Reutter (and of Keiper and Porsche) reinforced equitable and positive working relationships with their staff, which apparently resulted in an environment of reciprocal commitment to each company's purpose. As we saw in Greger's history, conditions were often tough, but there is a sense of mutually respectful collaboration reinforced by the active *Meister*. At Jensen, in contrast, managers appeared frequently to have treated their workers as commodities, and Duerr remarked on the low morale and office–factory split that were the consequence of mismanagement. Though it is obviously true that Britain's national industrial relations climate was unhelpful, and having multiple unions on site was difficult, adverse reaction to management failings which affected workers' livelihoods was, in retrospect, understandable.

Employees, their Knowledge and Commitment

To a large extent, the nature of each company's industrial relations reflected its management's innate consideration for their employees. Though the Wandel cousins' management of their workforce was problematic at the time of the 1960 consultants' report, staff and management were sufficiently capable and committed to enable the business to remain internationally competitive over succeeding decades. At K&J too, despite the external social changes which precipitated the decline of the 'K&J Family' spirit, there does seem to have been a sense of respect for accumulated expertise, borne out in the consistently positive messaging in *K&J News*. More noticeable differences are evident between the two steelwork firms. In terms of employees' knowledge and commitment, Schneider's post-war success was made possible by the continued use of *Meister* and the publicly acknowledged honouring of employees' industry and skills in a collaborative environment. Braithwaites' managers were physically distant from the West Bromwich facility, and the profiles of their late-1970s workforce indicate either challenges in recruiting skills or a different view of their importance in the lower levels of their organisation. Again, the greatest difference in perspective was within the automotive firms. Though some of Jensen's workers had exquisite craft skills, they were ill-served by the management of the factory, from foremen to directors, and the rapid recourse to mass dismissals at inconvenient periods in the business cycle seems to indicate a lack of respect for the workers and their capabilities among most managers except Duerr. At Reutter, in contrast, workers' craft skills were venerated – as the plethora of workplace photographs record – and the elevation of *Meister* to operationally critical roles, leading highly skilled teams, was a critical differentiator. Self-sufficient designers and engineers were left alone to do world-leading work that made an early success of RECARO. The reciprocal of management's respect for staff was their ongoing commitment, even in the most exigent circumstances.

Vocational Training

The different value placed on employees and their skills was reflected in the fundamentally different ecosystems surrounding each company, and was most evident in the provision of, and degree of national commitment to, vocational training. Wandel's approach to vocational training reflected their place in a specialist cluster in Reutlingen. They recruited a large number of apprentices throughout their post-war history, were part of an industry-wide talent programme, and remained committed to high skills. K&J's post-war workforce produced more mundane work than its predecessors. Management struggled to recruit technical talent from a diminishing local pool, though they remained committed to apprentice training, even if the training offered was simplified. While there were some developments in skills like lithographic printing, no transformation in technology or approach was enabled to prevent K&J from being bypassed by their competitors. Both Schneider and Braithwaites valued technical training and education. Both worked with technical institutions, though we have frustratingly little evidence on the ways in which relations might have influenced technical know-how. Karl Walz had been rigorously educated, and Rolf went back into technical education as soon as he returned from the Gulag. Their commitment to apprenticeships and to engineers like Hege was evident, and the surrounding infrastructure enabled continued technical recruitment despite the skills shortages during Baden-Württemberg's economic boom. Braithwaites also valued technical knowledge, evidenced in university sponsorships and the qualifications of their senior management. However, they faced limitations on growth imposed by the failure of the British education system to produce enough of the designers and engineers they sought, and by the loss of skilled workers to other companies once their apprenticeships were finished. Jensen's less focused training, restrictive craft practices, and a personnel management style which varied between confrontation and indifference made it impossible to maintain production flows and consistent quality. Their apprentices were less rigorously trained, and their foremen apparently advanced through seniority and expertise in controlling their own turf. Reutter were committed to apprentice training, and to advancing the *Meister* who effectively ran their factories. In response, staff offered unstinting commitment to superb product quality: meeting continuous demands for more Porsche bodies and later launching the aircraft seating business were evidence of it. Keiper followed the same pattern and continued their shared philosophy and practice after the takeover of Reutter – a practice which is still in place fifty years later.[6]

Governance

Differences in governance are apparent. One example of the consequences could be found in the companies' funding. The stable Wandel family as sole owners were clearly trusted by their bankers, members of the same community, whose support enabled them to remain cash-positive even in periods of strained liquidity. K&J, by contrast, experienced a worsening financial position even as their sales grew, as increasingly demanding shareholders caused them to become reliant on bank overdrafts while still paying large dividends. Control was a challenge for both companies. Erna Wandel was determined for reasons of familial obligation to retain her position for over forty years. A more dynamic solution was necessary, but her weaknesses were mitigated by the supportive context in which her company operated. Tom Jefferson was, in contrast, highly dynamic. But when his fellow director, Hugh Jefferson, urged him to adopt a Chandler-esque management structure, employed by K&J's most successful competitors, he did not do so. His early death left a leadership vacuum from which K&J did not recover, in a context which was less supportive than that

---

6   As this advertisement for the next generation of apprentices shows: RECARO Aircraft Seating, 'Auszubildenden Industriemechaniker (m/w/d) - Beginn 2023 - RECARO Aircraft Seating', RECARO (2022) <https://www.recaro-as.de/de/job-karriere/jobs/details/auszu-bildenden-industriemechaniker-m-w-d-beginn-2023–27513.html> [accessed 9 July 2022].

enjoyed by Wandel and by K&J's interwar forebears. In both cases, well-intentioned family-centred governance structures were ultimately injurious to long-term continuity.

In their own differences in governance and approach, Schneider and Braithwaites seemed to exemplify two completely dissimilar conceptions of business. In this case, the advantage accrued to the British company because it was compelled to react to such negative circumstances outside the business. Adopting Schumpeter's formulation, Braithwaites, from its earliest days, exemplified "creative destruction": large-scale operational innovation delivered early international success; a new business model enabled interwar growth.[7] In the 1970s, Tony Humphryes reinvigorated his business by changing its shareholding structure, transforming its international presence, accepting the inevitability of decline within a too-challenging external context, and subsequently moving into completely new industries. While Karl and Rolf Walz exhibited total personal engagement, they exemplified Edith Penrose's claim that "the most effective restriction on the quality of entrepreneurial services is that which stems from a lack of interest in experimenting with new and alien lines of activity, or in moving into new geographical areas."[8] That is not to deny Schneider's success over six decades. But as reconstruction work slowed and new construction materials began to predominate, long-term Mittelstand thinking seems to have been less conducive to survival. In contrast, Braithwaites survived because Humphryes adopted ideas that would have been anathema to Schneider's leaders.

Finally, fundamentally different approaches to corporate structure, governance, and funding separated the automotive firms. The Jensen brothers were successful as technician-entrepreneurs, less so as managers. The takeover by Norcros, greedy for dividends and knowing nothing of the automotive business, marked the beginning of Jensen's decline. Radical innovation failed. Successive ownership by Norcros, a merchant bank, and an American car dealer continued short-term thinking and short-term funding. Reutter's (and Keiper's) experience was very different from Jensen's. Innovations were incremental and brilliantly brought to market. Funding was long-term and operational processes stable. Müller-Scholl and Beierbach showed that combining family management with family ownership was not the sine qua non of Mittelstand success. *Good* management was sufficient, provided it happened within the stable structure made possible by family ownership. It was when lower-quality managers subverted the Reutter family's values – and denied Welf Koch the opportunity to reassert them – that RECARO went wrong. It did not fail as a business; after

---

7 Joseph A. Schumpeter and Joseph E. Stiglitz, *Capitalism, Socialism and Democracy* (Florence, USA, 2010), pp. 71–75.
8 Edith Penrose, *The Theory of the Growth of the Firm*, Third edition (Oxford, 1995), p. 35.

all, its creativity and engineering excellence won it a world-leading position in half a decade in a market that it created itself. Its management team failed it. Keiper, in contrast, was blessed by the duality of stable family ownership and brilliant family management, reinforced by Ulrich Putsch's willingness to bring in highly capable leaders such as Sommerlatte and Bahmann.

The analysis presented thus far substantiates the differences between German and British approaches identified in the Varieties of Capitalism debate. The case-study companies embodied, at the firm level, the two alternative philosophies of conducting business. If the five spheres explain differences at the level of company operations, there remain three more factors to consider: the ethos and capability of business leaders, the value of each company's surrounding ecosystem, and the importance of family ownership.

How Did Managers Manage?

West Germany
The more successful Mittelstand business leaders, at Reutter, Keiper, and Schneider, demonstrated a combination of emotional commitment and technical mastery in the most successful periods of their post-war history. Reutter's and Keiper's managers showed themselves to be capable of conceiving innovative products, which could be patented and fully exploited, and processes which enabled business growth without the loss of quality. At Schneider, Karl Walz demonstrated absolute commitment and engineering expertise. His son Rolf lacked his father's technical skills, but was spiritually devoted to Schneider and willing to take personal investment risks to enhance its capabilities. Hege, though technically proficient, astute, and cognisant of his responsibilities to family and workforce, lacked a similar desire to fight for Schneider's future as he approached retirement age without a successor in place. At Wandel, circumstances were more challenging from the outset, but Erna Wandel nevertheless showed herself for over thirty-five years to be capable of managing an international sales network which reliably sold Wandel's high-value products. In every case, leaders built and maintained strong teams by recruiting apprentices and devolving power to their *Prokuristen* and capable *Meister*. None of them (except the management team at RECARO in 1968 and 1969) looked for shortcuts or easy fixes: company strategies focused on quality and the long-term interests of their businesses. In the cases of Wandel and Schneider, however, the failure to manage succession militated against the continuation of each company in its optimum form.

Britain

Their British counterparts were in some respects no less effective. Though the Braithwaite business model was quite different from that of the Mittelstand family firms, all three generations of the Humphryes family proved themselves to be technically proficient, as formally trained engineers, and entrepreneurially dynamic. They were resilient and flexible, and like their foreign counterparts aimed to produce a high quality solution to demanding technical requirements. They also had a clear strategy of identifying men who were technically and commercially competent and promoting them to senior executive positions. At K&J, the Kenricks and the Jeffersons continued to insist on high quality standards within a patriarchal environment, and made determined efforts to enter new industries or use new technologies as they emerged. But their insistence on maintaining family control contributed to K&J's continual decline after World War Two. The exceptional energy of Tom Jefferson coincided with the appearance of effective senior managers, but K&J's eventual fate was determined by his failure to grant them more autonomy. Management was much less convincing at Jensen, where the departure of the Jensen brothers led to a succession of inappropriate owners and a failure to manage the workforce properly or to determine and execute a viable strategy.

Though the leaders of Mittelstand companies may not have explicitly articulated their purpose, they clearly lived by its principles: offering long-term careers to properly trained employees, retaining a commitment to their communities, and seeing a return on shareholding not as their principal focus but as the natural outcome of the company-wide pursuit of product excellence.

How Much Did External Context Matter?

West Germany

Baden-Württemberg's Mittelstand firms operated in an environment in which it seems that local, regional, and national institutions were all designed to develop competent, qualified people and give them the resources to deliver internationally competitive products. The regional bank network, notably the *Sparkassen*, existed to provide long-term funding and comprehensive support from staff who had industry knowledge and shared entrepreneurs' sense of local accountability. The education system made it possible to recruit apprentices and engineers who had strong technical skills which could then be built on, again with institutional support. It then enabled the more capable workers to study for further qualification as *Meister*, allowing employers to give those individuals significant responsibility and enhanced esteem. Research and development activities were further supported by the network of technical institutions, coordinated by state-sponsored bodies which also facilitated long-term funding for incremental innovation. In general, the context in which Baden-Württemberg's Mittelstand operated was intended to facilitate the long-term growth of its companies.

Britain
The owners and managers of British SMEs shared some of the personal qualities of their Mittelstand counterparts, but none was able to draw on the institutional support they enjoyed. Largely centralised banks did not see themselves as the providers of long-term funding to regional SMEs, and until the late 1970s offered little of the support that Mittelstand firms enjoyed from their house banks. Britain lacked vocational education infrastructure and national standards, and did not build on regional initiatives. Skilled staff were consequently always in short supply: technical training provision, at all levels, was comparatively and absolutely inadequate, and skilled workers offered neither craft flexibility nor the individual ambition to pursue the professional development that made their German *Meister* counterparts so indispensable.[9] The establishment of Anglo-German institutions in the 1970s to research and compare British and German practices represented a tacit recognition that there was much to be learned from the German approach, though little of what was learned was implemented.[10] And while the German model was of considerable interest to some members of the British Conservative Party in the late 1970s, especially in relation to vocational training and a more collaborative relationship with trade unions, this contemporary validation of its potential to transform British business was sadly not realised once Margaret Thatcher became Prime Minister.[11]

How Important Was Family Ownership?

The histories of the six companies reviewed above show that Alfred Chandler's insistence on the shortcomings of personal capitalism is only partly valid. Succession was a concern and some individual managers were weak. But family ownership in both countries was also the driver of long-term commitment and creativity. Most of our companies *did* make the three-pronged investment in management, manufacturing, and marketing, though they may have lacked the wherewithal to invest in all three consistently and simultaneously. All of them

9   In addition to the commentators identified in Part 2 above, the historical origins of this problem were also emphasised in Chandler, *Scale and Scope*, pp. 292–93.
10   Colin Chamberlain, 'British Attitudes to the German Economic Miracle 1948 to circa 1968' (unpublished Ph.D. thesis, University of Cambridge, 2022).
11   Ben Whisker, 'The Conservative Party, Concerted Action and the West German Economic Model 1975–1981', *Contemporary British History*, 35.1 (2021), 125–50.

grew throughout the period of this study, though Jensen (the only one lacking long-term family influence) collapsed before its end and Schneider closed voluntarily. Family control actually allowed firms in both countries to maintain the "sound, long-term perspectives from the decision-makers responsible for the health and growth of their enterprise"[12] which Chandler valued, rather than indulging in the dangerous short-termism of American big business since the 1970s which he seems to have deplored.[13]

Contrary to Chandler's perspective, it seems that the emotional engagement of personal capitalists characterised our German companies more than it did the British ones. Mittelstand owners were committed to a lifetime of service to their business. Critically, though, each family matched this emotional dedication with the intellectual engagement to achieving excellence in niche products through focused, long-term strategies, using their *Meister*, engineers, and others in a coordinated approach. The most successful, Keiper, combined family values with driven, professional management: the decision of the extremely capable Ulrich Putsch to retain personal financial liability but appoint an industry specialist to direct his aircraft-seating business is one example that validates Chandler's argument that the best family firms sought to bolster their management talent.

Their British counterparts were less emotionally engaged. James Hulse Humphryes set up Braithwaites to be a corporate company which his family ran at a physical distance and with emotional detachment. Though the closure of the West Bromwich plant was conducted respectfully and with what appears to have been some financial generosity, the family easily moved on in search of the next opportunity for shareholder value. Having been a patriarchal family-run business that seemed to resemble the "family" that they claimed it to be, K&J lost its way once greater detachment set in. Though Tom Jefferson was conscious of his covenant, the Jefferson and Kenrick extended families pushed to be treated as though they were stockholders in a quoted company, and strategy and product excellence eventually appeared to be less of a priority than satisfying shareholders. The Jensens ran their business as long as it was exciting to them, and others had an emotional commitment to the cars themselves. But the business model became corporate when the brothers chose to leave. Independence was lost, and later company leaders were either not genuinely engaged, or not competent.

Does this mean that a business must be family-owned to enjoy stability and act with purpose? Not necessarily: what is required in a business leader is

12   Chandler, *Scale and Scope*, p. 627.
13   Alfred D. Chandler, 'History and Management Practice and Thought: An Autobiography', ed. by Shawn Carraher, *Journal of Management History*, 15.3 (2009), 236–60 (p. 252). This is my own interpretation of his perspective, not a view explicitly expressed by Chandler himself.

not a genetic connection, but a commitment to valuing workers and the host community, to being a builder motivated to pass something of value to the next generation of builders, rather than being a seeker of short-term personal material gratification. Achieving long-term success in that way is, however, significantly easier within an ecosystem like Germany's that is designed to enable its achievement.

Does the Mittelstand Model Still Matter?

At various points in Germany's economic history, the Mittelstand has been written off. Despite the challenges identified in transitioning to new ways of working,[14] predictions of its demise,[15] and the closure of firms for want of a leadership successor[16] – experienced in reality by Schneider and Wandel – it has proved to be resilient. More than that, it has demonstrated not only its unbroken contribution to Germany's economic prosperity, but also its emerging influence on international discussion of new and better ways to make national business sectors enduringly competitive. Recent scholarship on the present-day Mittelstand addresses its ongoing capacity for innovation, its economic and social value, its resilience in the face of crisis, all substantiating the continuing importance of the Mittelstand traits identified by earlier scholars and demonstrated historically by the individual companies within our review.[17] One article proposes the Mittelstand way of working as a possible template for politicians in other countries, analysing the approach to innovation and demonstrating how others can adopt it, and highlighting its beneficial impact on youth unemployment and the geographic dispersal of wealth.[18] Another analysis compares critical Mittelstand innovations that are primarily "deeptech", hidden within other companies' products and processes, with Silicon

---

14   Berghoff, 'The End of Family Business?'
15   Herrigel and Sabel, 'Craft Production in Crisis'.
16   Lubinski, 'Path Dependency'; Hilger et al, 'Von Generation zu Generation'.
17   Alfredo De Massis et al, 'Innovation with Limited Resources: Management Lessons from the German Mittelstand', *The Journal of Product Innovation Management*, 35.1 (2018), 125–46 (pp. 136–41); Friederike Welter et al, *Der Geschäftliche Beitrag Des Mittelstands: Konzeptielle Überlegungen*, IfM-Materialien (Bonn, 18 August 2020) <https://www.ifm-bonn.org/fileadmin/data/redaktion/publikationen/ifm_materialien/dokumente/IfM-Materialien-283_2020.pdf> [accessed 2 January 2022]; Carsten Rietmann, 'Hidden Champions and Their Integration in Rural Regional Innovation Systems: Insights from Germany', *Zeitschrift Für Wirtschaftsgeographie* (2021); Michael Berlemann, Vera Jahn, and Robert Lehmann, 'Is the German Mittelstand More Resistant to Crises?', *Small Business Economics* (2021).
18   De Massis et al, p. 137.

Valley's more consumer-oriented products.[19] Its authors praise the robustness of the Mittelstand's innovation culture, its wider social contribution and its "pronounced sense of responsibility towards people and places".[20] They call for future research on the culture of the Mittelstand and participants' self-identification with it, and of the context which sustains it.[21]

The case of RECARO, in particular, has demonstrated how a company's international competitiveness in the twenty-first century can be traced through the evolution of foundational values and concomitant practices over a century, maintaining social responsibility while achieving world-market leadership in several related areas. The Mittelstand approach has potential value in any part of the world where dissatisfaction exists with whichever variety of capitalism is being locally applied. Organisation scholars have, for example, recently addressed the prospect of translating Mittelstand practices to Australia, as "the desired characteristics and future of the Australian manufacturing sector very closely reflects the current and well-known characteristics of the Mittelstand."[22] They reason that "the Mittelstand represents a uniquely German story accommodating societal well-being with economic prosperity", ensuring that "human dignity is manifest in business": its principles should therefore be applied to the development of policy and practice in Australia.[23]

These endorsements of the Mittelstand model can be seen as a validation of its continued potential to deliver long-term competitiveness with social responsibility. That does not mean it is a panacea for economic ills. Mittelstand businesses can fail to remain competitive, or fail altogether, as we have seen, if any element of the model is inadequately tended or the need for change is not confronted.[24] But at a time when business leaders are being urged to put purpose ahead of profits and stakeholders ahead of shareholders, the

---

19   André Pahnke and Friederike Welter, 'The German Mittelstand: Antithesis to Silicon Valley Entrepreneurship?', *Small Business Economics* (2018) 1–14 (p. 353).

20   Pahnke and Welter, p. 351.

21   Pahnke and Welter, p. 355.

22   Danielle M. Logue et al, 'Translating Models of Organization: Can the Mittelstand Move from Bavaria to Geelong?', *Journal of Management and Organization; Lyndfield*, 21.1 (2015), 17–36 (p. 28).

23   Logue et al, p. 33.

24   As Wandel and Schneider failed to adapt to new technologies, so the latter-day Mittelstand must confront contemporary changes: PWC, 'Potenzialanalyse: Wie Digital Sind Die Deutschen Mittelständler?' (Pricewaterhouse Coopers LLP, January 2017) <https://www.pwc.de/de/mittelstand/assets/digitalisierungsbefragung-21122016-auskopplung.pdf> [accessed 31 December 2021]; Felix Franz, 'Germany Is Bracing for a Major Electric Vehicle Shock' Wired UK, (14 September 2021) <https://www.wired.co.uk/article/germany-electric-vehicles-europe> [accessed 30 December 2021]; Das Fraunhofer-Institut für Produktionsanlagen und Konstruktionstechnik IPK, 'Jump 4.0: Mobile Jobeinplanungsunterstützung für den Meister in der Produktion', Jump 4.0 (2020) <http://www.jump40.de/> [accessed 14 November 2020].

Mittelstand way of working can inspire policy-makers and business people to create the sustainable, purpose-driven, human-centred enterprises of the future – provided all stakeholders are willing to invest in the ecosystems which sustain them.

Bibliography

Primary Sources

Archives: Britain
Aston University, Birmingham
    David Bramley Archive
University of Birmingham
    Cadbury Research Library
Companies House
    Braithwaite & Co. Engineers Ltd.
    Kenrick & Jefferson Ltd.
    Jensen Motors Ltd.
Coventry History Centre
    Alfred Herbert Ltd. Archive
    Rootes Archive
HSBC Group Archives, London
Lloyds Banking Group Archive, London
Modern Records Centre, University of Warwick (MRC)
    TUC Archive
    A.P. Young Papers
    Jensen Motors Ltd. Archive
Sandwell Archive, West Midlands
    Braithwaite & Co. Engineers Limited
    Kenrick & Jefferson Ltd.
Teesside Archives, Middlesbrough
    Dorman, Long Ltd.

Archives: Germany
Staatsarchiv Baden-Württemberg, Ludwigsburg
    Amstgerichts Ludwigsburg
Stadtarchiv Ludwigsburg
RECARO Holding GmbH Archives
Wirtschaftsarchiv Baden-Württemberg, Hohenheim (WABW)
    Chr. Wandel KG, B79

Industrie- und Handelskammer, A16
J. Schneider & Co. KG, B4
Philipp Müller Nachfolger Eugen Bucher GmbH & Co., B38

Interviews
Ivan Walker, retired factory supervisor, Kenrick & Jefferson Ltd., 6 August
   2013.
Jeremy Plimmer, retired business development manager, Kenrick & Jefferson
   Ltd., 24 November 2014.
John Saynor, retired branch manager, Lloyds Bank, 27 April 2016.
K. Hugh Jefferson, retired Director, Kenrick & Jefferson Ltd., 9 July 2013.

Email Correspondence
Harrow School Archivist to David Paulson, 'Enquiry Re Old Harrovian', 17
   November 2015.
J.S. Ringrose, Hon. Archivist, Pembroke College to David Paulson, Cambridge,
   'J.A. Humphryes', 24 November 2015.

Newspapers, Periodicals, and Trade Press
   Autocar
   Birmingham Post
   Evening Mail, Sandwell
   Evening Standard
   Institution of Mechanical Engineers
   Ludwigsburger Kreiszeitung
   Motor Sport Magazine
   New York Times
   Passauer neue Presse Niederbayerische Zeitung
   Printing Industries
   Reutlinger General-Anzeiger
   Sandwell Evening News
   Schwäbisches Tageblatt
   The Economist
   The Engineer
   The Financial Times
   The Guardian
   The Manchester Guardian
   The Observer
   The Telegraph
   The Times
   The Washington Post, Times Herald
   Wall Street Journal

Patents
<http://worldwide.espacenet.com>
'K&J Patents, 1903–2000', Espacenet (2014).
'Patents List - Cleveland Bridge', Espacenet (2015).
'Patents List - Fritz Keiper 1950–1962', Espacenet (2017).
'Patents List - Fritz Leonhardt', Espacenet (2015).
'Patents List - Jensen Motors Limited 1950–1976', Espacenet (2017).
'Patents List - Porsche AG 1950–1962', Espacenet (2017).
'Patents List - RECARO AG 1963–1968', Espacenet (2017).
'Patents List - Stuttgarter Karosseriewerk Reutter 1950–1962', Espacenet (2017).
'Philipp Müller Nachf. Eugen Bucher GmbH & Co: Patents Granted', Espacenet (2020).
Gibbon, James, 'Method and Means of Feeding Window Envelopes to a Folding Machine', Google Patents (2014).
Gibbon, James, 'Open Window Envelopes', Google Patents (2014).
Humphryes, J., 'A Method of Applying Distinguishing Markings to Metal Articles', Espacenet (1976).
Humphryes, James Anthony, 'Containers', Espacenet (1968).
Humphryes, James Anthony, 'Improvements in and Relating to Load Lowering and Lifting', Espacenet (1958).
Humphryes, James Anthony, 'Improvements in and Relating to the Strengthening, Preservation and Repair of Roofs', Espacenet (1969).
Humphryes, James Anthony, and Alfred William Pond, 'Improvements in and Relating to Grabs', Espacenet (1959).

Published Primary Documents
Bevan, Timothy H., 'British Banks and Small Businesses', in *The Banks and Small Businesses*. Cambridge Seminar 1978 (London: The Institute of Bankers, 1978), pp. 29–52.
Birmingham Productivity Association, 'Gaining Skill: A Report of an Investigation into the Training of Industrial Apprentices in Western Germany' (Birmingham Productivity Association, 1955), MRC, MSS.289/VB/5/3/3.
Bolton, J.E., *Report of the Committee of Enquiry into Small Firms* (London: HMSO, 1971).
———, 'The Financial Needs of the Small Firm', in *The Banks and Small Businesses*, Cambridge Seminar 1978 (London: The Institute of Bankers, 1978), pp. 1–28.
British Road Federation, *Urban Motorways: Report of the Conference Organised by the British Road Federation, 1956* (London: British Road Federation, September 1957).

Cartwright, Walter H., *The House of K&J – a Booklet Issued to Celebrate the 75th Anniversary of Our Foundation in 1878 for Private Circulation Among Our Friends* (West Bromwich: Kenrick & Jefferson, 1953).

Commerzbank AG, 'Geschäftsbericht Für Das Jahr 1964' (Commerzbank AG, 1964) <https://www.commerzbank.com/media/de/konzern_1/geschichte/download_8/geschaeftsbericht_1964.pdf> [accessed 2 February 2019].

Competition Commission, *Norton Opax PLC and McCorquodale PLC A Report on the Proposed Merger* (London: Competition Commission, 24 September 1986) <http://webarchive.nationalarchives.gov.uk/20111203045905/http://www.competition-commission.org.uk//rep_pub/reports/1986/206norton_opax_mccorquodale_plc.htm> [accessed 30 November 2014].

Confederation of British Industry, *Tales of Two Companies : A Comparison of Industrial Performance in the UK and West Germany* (London, 1988).

Department of Scientific and Industrial Research, *Steel Structures Research; Verbatim Proceedings of a Conference Presided over by Sir Clement Hindley, on 16th October, 1930.* (London: H.M. Stationery Office, 1930) <http://babel.hathitrust.org/cgi/pt?id=coo.31924004638007;view=1up;seq=7> [accessed 14 October 2015].

Deutscher Industrie- und Handelskammertag, *IHK- und DIHK-Fortbildungsstatistik 2018* (Berlin: Deutscher Industrie- und Handelskammertag, June 2019) <https://www.dihk.de/de/themen-und-positionen/fachkraefte/aus-und-weiterbildung/weiterbildung/weiterbildungsstatistiken--2742> [accessed 26 May 2020].

European Commission, *The New SME Definition: User Guide and Model Declaration* (European Commission, 2005).

'Examination in Engineering Studies, Michaelmas Term 1951 - Section II', in Cambridge University Reporter (Cambridge: Cambridge University Press, 1951), MMMDCCLX, 218.

Financial Analysis Group Ltd., *The British Printing Industry - a Financial Survey* (Winnersh, October 1974).

First Report from the Select Committee on Science and Technology. Generating Plant Breakdowns: Winter 1969–70 (London: House of Commons, 13 April 1970) <http://gateway.proquest.com/openurl?url_ver=Z39.88-2004&res_dat=xri:hcpp&rft_dat=xri:hcpp:rec:1969-058351> [accessed 9 January 2019].

'Foot Guards', Supplement to the London Gazette (London, England, 7 November 1947), p. 5240 <https://www.thegazette.co.uk/London/issue/38117/supplement/5240/data.pdf> [accessed 1 November 2015].

Heimisch, Gerd, 75 Years of Mann + Hummel / 1941–2016 (Ludwigsburg: Mann + Hummel GmbH, 2015) <https://www.mann-hummel.com/content/dam/mann-hummel-group/communication-media/historical/Chronicle%20MANN+HUMMEL_EN_2015.pdf> [accessed 15 November 2016].

Institution of Mechanical Engineers, 'Institution of Mechanical Engineers - Membership Proposal Forms', Archivecat.Imeche.Org, 2015.

Institution of Welding Engineers, *Tenth Annual Report* (London: Institution of Welding Engineers, 1933), The Welding Institute <https://www.twi-global. com/pdfs/PDFs-Public/IWE-Annual-Report-10-1933.pdf> [accessed 21 November 2015].

Iron and Steel Board, and British Iron and Steel Federation, 'Iron and Steel Monthly Statistics'.

'Meisterprüfungsstatistik - Detailauswertung 2018', *ZDH Statistik-Datenbank* <https://www.zdh-statistik.de/application/stat_det.php?LID=1&ID=MDQ 1OTI=&cID=00787> [accessed 26 May 2020].

Midland Bank PLC Corporate Finance Department, *The Mittelstand. The German Model & the UK* (London: Midland Bank PLC, September 1994).

Report of the Committee of Enquiry into Delays in Commissioning CEGB Power Stations (London: House of Commons, March 1969).

Stadt Reutlingen, *Industriestandort Reutlingen* (Reutlingen: Stadt Reutlingen, 1984), Stadtbibliothek Reutlingen.

Statistisches Bundesamt, 'XII. Industrie und Handwerk', *Statistisches Jahrbuch Für die Bundesrepublik Deutschland, 1974* (1975), 211–13. <http://www. digizeitschriften.de/dms/img/?PID=PPN514402342_1974%7Clog43> [accessed 23 October 2018].

———, 'Publikation - Preise - Preise Und Preisindizes Für Gewerbliche Produkte (Erzeugerpreise) - Statistisches Bundesamt (Destatis)' (2017) <https://www. statistischebibliothek.de/mir/receive/DEHeft_mods_00070482> [accessed 6 August 2022].

———,'Publikation - Preise - Verbraucherpreisindex Für Deutschland - Lange Reihen Ab 1948 - Statistisches Bundesamt (Destatis)' <https:// www.destatis.de/DE/Publikationen/Thematisch/Preise/Verbraucherpreise/ VerbraucherpreisindexLangeReihen.html> [accessed 27 January 2017].

———, 'Baugewerbe', in *Statistisches Jahrbuch Für Die Bundesrepublik Deutschland 1970* (Stuttgart: W. Kohlhammer, 1971), pp. 224–30 <http:// www.digizeitschriften.de/dms/img/?PID=PPN514402342_1970%7Clog48> [accessed 22 December 2016].

Statistisches Bundesamt Wiesbaden, *Berufliche Bildung 1977*, Bildung Und Kultur (Wiesbaden: Statistisches Bundesamt, 1978) <https://www.statistisch-ebibliothek.de/mir/receive/DEHeft_mods_00131152> [accessed 5 August 2022].

Statistisches Landesamt Baden-Württemberg, 'Statistische Bericht B I 3 und 4: die Studierenden an den wissenschaftlichen Hochschulen und Kunsthochschulen im Wintersemester 1956/57 und Sommersemester 1957' (Statistisches Landesamt Baden-Württemberg, 1957) <https://www.destatis. de/GPStatistik/servlets/MCRFileNodeServlet/BWHeft_derivate_00003819/ BIII_j_WS56_57_SS57.pdf> [accessed 24 April 2016].

Technische Hochschule Stuttgart, 'Programm Der Königlich Württembergischen Technischen Hochschule in Stuttgart Für Das Studienjahr 1910–1911' (Stuttgart: J.B. Metzlersche Buchdruckerei, 1910) <https://digibus.ub.uni-stuttgart.de/viewer/image/1530689129952_1910_1/1/ > [accessed 5 August 2022].

——, 'Programm der Technischen Hochschule Stuttgart für das Sommersemester 1948' (Technische Hochschule Stuttgart, 1948) <https://digibus.ub.uni-stuttgart.de/viewer/image/1530689129952_1948_1/1/> [accessed 5 August 2022].

'The Institute of Bankers: Banking Diploma Examination, Part II. "The Practice of Banking", September 17, 1964' (Institute of Bankers, 1964), Private collection, J. Saynor.

The Institution of Civil Engineers, *20 Years of British Motorways. Proceedings of the Conference Held in London 27–28 February, 1980* (London: The Institution of Civil Engineers, 1980).

——, *Motorways in Britain, Today and Tomorrow. Proceedings of the Conference Organized by the Institution of Civil Engineers Held in London 26–28 April 1971* (London: The Institution of Civil Engineers, 1971).

UK Government Debt Management Office, 'UK Government Gilt Returns' <http://www.dmo.gov.uk/rpt_parameters.aspx?rptCode=D4I&page=Annual_Yields> [accessed 7 September 2014; site inactive on 9 August 2022].

VW AG, 'Bericht über das Geschäftsjahr 1964' (Volkswagenwerk Aktiengesellschaft, 1965) <https://www.volkswagenag.com/presence/konzern/images/teaser/history/chronik/geschaeftsberichte/1964-Geschaefts-bericht.pdf> [accessed 2 August 2022].

'Who's Who In Engineering: Name H', Who's Who In Engineering 1939 (1939) <https://www.gracesguide.co.uk/1939_Who%27s_Who_In_Engineering:_Name_H> [accessed 10 January 2019].

Zentralverband des deutschen Handwerks, 'Meisterprüfungsstatistik - Detailauswertung 2019' (Berlin: Zentralverband des deutschen Handwerks, 25 May 2020) <https://www.zdh-statistik.de/application/index.php?mID=3&cID=814> [accessed 26 May 2020].

Secondary Sources

Books and Articles

Abelshauser, Werner, *Deutsche Wirtschaftsgeschichte von 1945 bis zur Gegenwart*, 2nd edn (Munich: C.H. Beck, 2011).

——, 'Kriegswirtschaft Und Wirtschaftswunder. Deutschlands Wirtschaftliche Mobilisierung Für Den Zweiten Weltkrieg Und Die Folgen

Für Die Nachkriegszeit', *Vierteljahrshefte Für Zeitgeschichte*, 47.4 (1999), 503–38.

Ackrill, Margaret, and Leslie Hannah, *Barclays. The Business of Banking 1690–1996* (Cambridge: Cambridge University Press, 2001).

Ahrens, Ralf, *Die Dresdner Bank 1945–1957: Konsequenzen und Kontinuitäten nach dem Ende des NS-Regimes* (Munich: Oldenbourg, 2007).

von Alberti, Günter, *Steinbeis 1971–1991*, 2nd edn (Stuttgart: Steinbeis Edition, 2010).

Allen, Matthew M.C., *The Varieties of Capitalism Paradigm. Explaining Germany's Competitive Advantage?* (Basingstoke: Palgrave Macmillan, 2006).

Anderson, Keith, *Jensen* (Yeovil: Haynes, 1989).

——, *Jensen and Jensen-Healey* (Stroud: Sutton, 1998).

Ansbacher, H.L., 'German Industrial Psychology in the Fifth Year of War', *Psychological Bulletin*, 41.9 (1944), 605–14 https://doi.org/10.1037/h0058291 [accessed 28 August 2018].

Audretsch, David B., and Erik E. Lehmann, 'Small Is Beautiful', in *The Seven Secrets of Germany: Economic Resilience in an Era of Global Turbulence* (Oxford Scholarship Online: Oxford University Press, 2015).

Baker, Mae, and Michael Collins, 'English Commercial Banks and Organizational Inertia: The Financing of SMEs, 1944–1960', *Enterprise and Society*, 11.1 (2010), 65–97.

Bannock, Graham, and E.Victor Morgan, *Banks and Small Business: An International Perspective* (London: Graham Bannock & Partners Ltd., 10 August 1988).

Bargmann, Holger, 'Innovationshemmnis Industriemeister?', *Zeitschrift Für Soziologie*, 13.1 (1984), 45–59.

Barker, Hannah, *Family and Business During the Industrial Revolution* (Oxford University Press, 2017).

Barnes, Victoria, and Lucy Newton, 'Constructing Corporate Identity before the Corporation: Fashioning the Face of the First English Joint Stock Banking Companies through Portraiture', *Enterprise & Society*, 18.3 (2017), 678–720.

Barney, Jay, 'Firm Resources and Sustained Competitive Advantage', *Journal of Management*, 17 (1991), 99–120.

Bennett, R. J, *Local Business Voice: The History of Chambers of Commerce in Britain, Ireland, and Revolutionary America, 1760–2011* (Oxford; New York: Oxford University Press, 2011).

Berghahn, Volker R., *Modern Germany: Society, Economics and Politics in the Twentieth Century*, Second edition (Cambridge: Cambridge University Press, 1987).

Berghoff, Hartmut, 'Public Schools and the Decline of the British Economy 1870–1914', *Past & Present*, 129.1 (1990), 148–67.

————, 'The End of Family Business? The Mittelstand and German Capitalism in Transition, 1949–2000', *Business History Review*, 80 (2006), 263–95.

————, *Zwischen Kleinstadt und Weltmarkt: Hohner und die Harmonika 1857 - 1961 : Unternehmensgeschichte als Gesellschaftsgeschichte* (Paderborn, München: Schöningh, 2006).

Berlemann, Michael, Vera Jahn, and Robert Lehmann, 'Is the German Mittelstand More Resistant to Crises?', *Small Business Economics* (2021) <https://doi.org/10.1007/s11187-021-00573-7>.

Bessel, Richard, *Germany 1945: From War to Peace* (London: Simon & Schuster, 2012).

Best, Michael, and Jane Humphries, 'The City and Industrial Decline', in *The Decline of the British Economy*, ed. by Bernard Elbaum and William Lazonick (Oxford: Clarendon Press, 1986), pp. 222–39.

Biess, Frank, 'Survivors of Totalitarianism: Returning POWs and the Reconstruction of Masculine Citizenship in West Germany, 1945–1955', in *The Miracle Years. A Cultural History of West Germany, 1945–1968*, ed. by Hanna Schissler (Princeton and Oxford: Princeton University Press, 2001), pp. 57–82.

Binks, Martin, and Christine Ennew, 'The Relationship between UK Banks and Their Small Business Customers', *Small Business Economics*, 9.2 (1997), 167–78.

Binks, Martin, Christine Ennew, and Geoffrey Reed, *The Survey By The Forum of Private Business on Banks and Small Firms. Report to the Forum of Private Business* (Nottingham: University of Nottingham, 12 July 1988).

Birkenmaier, Werner, 'Mentalität der Württemberger: Die schwäbische Ehrbarkeit', stuttgarter-zeitung.de (Stuttgart, 17 March 2016), Online edition.

Blackstone, Brian, and Vanessa Fuhrmans, 'The Engines of Growth: Forget the Familiar Big Global Brands. Germany's Economy Is Powered by a Legion of Smaller Companies', *Wall Street Journal*, 27 June (2011).

Boelcke, Willi A., *Wirtschaftsgeschichte Baden-Württembergs von den Römern bis Heute* (Stuttgart: Theiss, 1987).

Boelcke, Willi A., *125 Jahre Baden-Württembergische Bank* (Stuttgart: Kohlhammer, 1996).

Booth, Alan, 'The Manufacturing Failure Hypothesis and the Performance of British Industry during the Long Boom', *Economic History Review*, LVI.1 (2003), 1–33.

Brenke, Karl, Ulf Rinne, and Klaus F Zimmermann, 'Kurzarbeit: Nützlich in der Krise, aber nun den Ausstieg einleiten', *Wochenbericht des DIW Berlin*, 21 (April 2010), 2–13.

British Academy, *Policy & Practice for Purposeful Business*, Future of the Corporation (London: The British Academy, September

2021) <https://www.thebritishacademy.ac.uk/publications/policy-and-practice-for-purposeful-business/>.

Broadberry, S.N., *The Productivity Race: British Manufacturing in International Perspective, 1850–1990* (Cambridge: Cambridge University Press, 1997).

Broadberry, Stephen, 'The Performance of Manufacturing', in *The Cambridge Economic History of Modern Britain, Vol. III, Structural Change and Growth, 1939–2000*, ed. by Roderick Floud and Paul Johnson (Cambridge: Cambridge University Press, 2004).

Broadberry, Stephen, and Nick Crafts, 'UK Productivity Performance from 1950 to 1979: A Restatement of the Broadberry-Crafts View', *Economic History Review*, LVI.4 (2003).

Broadberry, Stephen N., and Karin Wagner, 'Human Capital and Productivity in Manufacturing during the Twentieth Century: Britain, Germany and the United States' in *Quantitative Aspects of Post-War European Economic Growth*, ed. by Bart van Ark and Nicholas Crafts (Cambridge: Cambridge University Press, 1997), pp. 244–70 <https://doi.org/10.1017/CBO9780511599255.007>.

Broadberry, Stephen, and Mary O'Mahony, 'Britain's Productivity Gap with the United States and Europe: A Historical Perspective', *National Institute Economic Review*, 189 (2004).

Brunner, Alex, Jörg Decressin, Daniel Hardy, and Beata Kudela, *Germany's Three-Pillar Banking System: Cross-Country Perspectives in Europe*, Occasional Papers (Washington, DC: International Monetary Fund, 2004).

Bührer, Werner, *Ruhrstahl und Europa: Die Wirtschaftsvereinigung Eisen- und Stahlindustrie und die Anfänge der europäischen Integration 1945–1952* (München: Oldenbourg Wissenschaftsverlag, 2010) <https://doi.org/10.1524/9783486703276>.

Burhop, Carsten, Timothy W. Guinnane, and Richard Tilly, 'The Financial System in Germany, 1800–1914', in *Handbook of Finance and Development*, ed. by Thorsten Beck and Ross Levin (Cheltenham, UK: Edward Elgar Publishing, 2018).

By, Rune Todnem, 'Leadership: In Pursuit of Purpose', *Journal of Change Management*, 21.1 (2021), 30–44.

Calver, Richard, *A History of Jensen: All the Models* (Melbourne: Richard Calver, 2007).

Carlin, Wendy, 'West German Growth and Institutions, 1945–90', in *Economic Growth in Europe since 1945*, ed. by Nicholas Crafts and Gianni Toniolo (Cambridge: Cambridge University Press, 1996), pp. 455–97.

Carnevali, Francesca, *Europe's Advantage: Banks and Small Firms in Britain, France, Germany, and Italy Since 1918* (Oxford: Oxford Scholarship Online, 2005).

Chandler, Alfred D., 'History and Management Practice and Thought: An Autobiography', ed. by Shawn Carraher, *Journal of Management History*, 15.3 (2009), 236–60.

———, 'Managers, Families, and Financiers', in *Development of Managerial Enterprise*, ed. by Kesaji Kobayashi and Hidemasa Morikawa, *The International Library of Critical Writings in Business History* (Tokyo: University of Tokyo Press, 1986), pp. 35–63.

———, *Scale and Scope: The Dynamics of Industrial Capitalism* (Cambridge, MA: Belknap Press of Harvard University Press, 1994).

Chapman, Stanley, *Merchant Enterprise in Britain From the Industrial Revolution to World War 1* (Cambridge: Cambridge University Press, 1992).

Cheffins, Brian R., *Corporate Ownership and Control: British Business Transformed* (Oxford: Oxford University Press, 2008).

Christensen, C. Roland, *Management Succession in Small and Growing Enterprises* (Boston: Harvard Business School, 1953).

Church, R.A., *Kenricks in Hardware – A Family Business 1791–1966* (Newton Abbot: David & Charles, 1969).

Church, Roy, 'Salesmen and the Transformation of Selling in Britain and the US in the Nineteenth and Early Twentieth Centuries', *Economic History Review*, 61 (2008), 695–725.

Clark, C.M., 'West Germany Confronts the Nazi Past: Some Recent Debates on the Early Postwar Era, 1945–1960', *The European Legacy*, 4.1 (1999), 113–30.

Clark, Christopher, *Iron Kingdom* (London: Penguin, 2006).

Colli, Andrea, Paloma Fernandez Perez, and Mary B. Rose, 'National Determinants of Family Firm Development? Family Firms in Britain, Spain, and Italy in the Nineteenth and Twentieth Centuries', *Enterprise & Society*, 4.1 (2003), 28–64.

Colli, Andrea, and Mary B. Rose, 'Families and Firms: The Culture and Evolution of Family Firms in Britain and Italy in the Nineteenth and Twentieth Centuries', *Scandinavian Economic History Review*, 47.1 (1999), 24–47.

Confederation of British Industry, *Tales of Two Companies : A Comparison of Industrial Performance in the UK and West Germany* (London, 1988).

Corbyn, Jeremy, 'Reckless Tories Wandered into Brexit - Now They Are Scurrying Away from the Mess', *LabourList* (2016) <https://labourlist.org/2016/09/jeremy-corbyn-reckless-tories-wandered-into-brexit-now-they-are-scurrying-away-from-the-mess/> [accessed 31 July 2019].

Cordes, Prof. Dr Albrecht, Prof. Dr Heiner Lück, Prof. Dr Dieter Werkmüller, and Professorin Dr Christa Bertelsmeier-Kierst, *Handwörterbuch zur deutschen Rechtsgeschichte (HRG) - gebundene Ausgabe Band II: Geistliche Gerichtsbarkeit - Konfiskation*, 2nd edn (Berlin: Erich Schmidt Verlag GmbH & Co, 2012).

Crafts, Nick, 'Competition Cured the "British Disease"', VoxEU.Org <http://www.voxeu.org/article/competition-cured-british-disease> [accessed 5 February 2015].

Culpepper, Pepper D., and David Finegold, eds, *The German Skills Machine: Sustaining Competitive Advantage in a Global Economy* (New York and Oxford: Berghahn Books, 1999).

Daly, A., D.M.W.N. Hitchens, and K. Wagner, 'Productivity, Machinery and Skills in a Sample of British and German Manufacturing Plants: Results of a Pilot Inquiry', *National Institute Economic Review*, 111 (1985), 48–61.

Danchev, Alex, *Oliver Franks, Founding Father* (Oxford: Clarendon Press, 1993).

Daunton, M.J., 'Inheritance and Succession in the City of London in the Nineteenth Century', *Business History*, 30.3 (1988), 269–86.

Davenport-Hines, R.P.T., 'Introduction to Markets and Bagmen : Studies in the History of Marketing and British Industrial Performance 1830–1939', in *Markets and Bagmen : Studies in the History of Marketing and British Industrial Performance 1830–1939*, ed. by R.P.T. Davenport-Hines (Aldershot: Gower, 1986).

Dawson, Leslie M., 'Toward a New Concept of Sales Management', *Journal of Marketing*, 34.2 (1970), 33–38.

De Massis, Alfredo, David Audretsch, Lorraine Uhlaner, and Nadine Kammerlander, 'Innovation with Limited Resources: Management Lessons from the German Mittelstand', *The Journal of Product Innovation Management*, 35.1 (2018), 125–46.

Dickinson, A.W., *Industrial Relations in Supervisory Management* (London: Nelson, 1967).

Duerr, Carl, *Management Kinetics: Carl Duerr on Communication* (London: McGraw-Hill, 1971).

Dumke, Rolf H., 'Reassessing the Wirtschaftswunder: Reconstruction and Postwar Growth in West Germany in an International Context', *Oxford Bulletin of Economics & Statistics*, 52.4 (1990), 451–92.

Decker, Stephanie, 'The Silence of the Archives: Business History, Post-Colonialism and Archival Ethnography', *Management & Organizational History*, 8 (2013), 155–73.

Deeg, Richard, 'What Makes German Banks Different', *Small Business Economics*, 10 (1998), 93–101.

Deissinger, Thomas, and Philipp Gonon, 'The Development and Cultural Foundations of Dual Apprenticeships – a Comparison of Germany and Switzerland', *Journal of Vocational Education & Training* (2021).

Deissinger, Thomas, and Silke Hellwig, 'Apprenticeships in Germany: Modernising the Dual System', *Education & Training*, 47.4 (2005), 312–24.

Detzer, Daniel, Nina Dodig, Trevor Evans, Eckard Hein, and Hansjörg Herr, *The German Financial System*, Studies in Financial Systems (Leeds:

Financialisation, Economy, Society and Sustainable Development Project, 2013).

Edwards, Jeremy, and Klaus Fischer, *Banks, Finance and Investment in Germany* (Cambridge: Cambridge University Press, 1994).

Eichengreen, Barry, *The European Economy since 1945: Coordinated Capitalism and Beyond* (Princeton and Oxford: Princeton University Press, 2007).

Eloy, Frank, 'Le rôle des banques régionales dans le financement de l'économie allemande', *Réalités Industrielles* (2013), 56–60.

Ensser, Susanne, 'Die Bedeutung der Treuhandanstalt für die Wiederbelebung des industriellen Mittelstandes in den neuen Bundesländern: eine Ordnungspolitische Betrachtung', *Schriften Zur Wirtschafts- und Sozialgeschichte* (Berlin: Duncker und Humblot, 1998), BAND 53, pp. 34–36.

Enssle, Manfred J., 'The Harsh Discipline of Food Scarcity in Postwar Stuttgart, 1945–1948', *German Studies Review*, 10.3 (1987), 481–502.

Ernst, Eugen, 'Der Brückenbau der Deutschen Bundesbahn im Jahre 1950', *Die Bautechnik* (March 1951), 49–53.

Fear, Jeffrey, 'Heinrich Dinkelbach, Organization Man', in *Organizing Control: August Thyssen and the Construction of German Corporate Management, Harvard Studies in Business History, 45* (Cambridge, MA and London: Harvard University Press, 2005), pp. 677–710.

——, 'Straight Outta Oberberg: Transforming Mid-Sized Family Firms Into Global Champions 1970–2010', *Jahrbuch Für Wirtschaftsgeschichte*, 2012.1 (2012), 125–68.

Fear, Jeffrey, and Christopher Kobrak, 'Banks on Board: German and American Corporate Governance, 1870–1914', *The Business History Review*, 84.4 (2010), 703–36.

Finegold, David, 'The Future of the German Skill-Creation System: Conclusions and Policy Options', in *The German Skills Machine: Sustaining Competitive Advantage in a Global Economy*, ed. by Pepper D. Culpepper and David Finegold (New York and Oxford: Berghahn Books, 1999), pp. 403–30.

Finegold, David, and David Soskice, 'The Failure Of Training in Britain: Analysis and Prescription', *Oxford Review of Economic Policy*, 4.3 (1988), 21–53.

Finegold, David, and Karin Wagner, 'The German Skill-Creation System and Team-Based Production: Competitive Asset or Liability?', in *The German Skills Machine: Sustaining Competitive Advantage in a Global Economy*, ed. by Pepper D. Culpepper and David Finegold (New York and Oxford: Berghahn Books, 1999), pp. 115–55.

Finanzgruppe Deutscher Sparkassen- und Giroverband, 'Diagnose Mittelstand - Winter 2018' (Finanzgruppe Deutscher Sparkassen- und Giroverband, 2018) <https://www.dsgv.de/sparkassen-finanzgruppe/publikationen/diagnose-mittelstand.html> [accessed 14 February 2019].

Flinn, Catherine, '"The City of Our Dreams"? The Political and Economic Realities of Rebuilding Britain's Blitzed Cities, 1945–54', *Twentieth Century British History*, 23.2 (2012), 221–45.

Floud, Roderick, 'Technical Education and Economic Performance: Britain, 1850–1914', *Albion: A Quarterly Journal Concerned with British Studies*, 14.2 (1982), 153–71.

———, *The British Machine Tool Industry, 1850–1914*, 1st edition (Cambridge and New York: Cambridge University Press, 1976).

Fox, Alan, 'Industrial Relations in Nineteenth-Century Birmingham', *Oxford Economic Papers*, New Series, 7.1 (1955), 57–70.

von Frankenburg, Richard, 'Porsche, the Man and His Cars', trans. by Charles Meisl (London: G.T. Foulis, 1961).

Frege, Carola, and John Godard, 'Varieties of Capitalism and Job Quality: The Attainment of Civic Principles at Work in the United States and Germany', *American Sociological Review*, 79.5 (2014), 942.

French, Michael, 'On the Road: Travelling Salesmen and Experiences of Mobility in Britain before 1939', *The Journal of Transport History*, 31 (2010), 133–50.

Frey, Dennis, 'Wealth, Consumerism, and Culture among the Artisans of Göppingen: Dynamism and Tradition in an Eighteenth-Century Hometown', *Central European History*, 46 (2013), 741–78.

Friedman, Walter A., *Birth of a Salesman: The Transformation of Selling in America* (Cambridge, MA and London: Harvard University Press, 2004).

Gennard, John, and Peter Bain, *A History of the Society of Graphical and Allied Trades* (London: Routledge, 1995).

Gerwick, Ben, 'FRITZ LEONHARDT 1909–1999', in *Memorial Tributes: National Academy of Engineering, Volume 9* (Washington, DC: National Academy of Engineering of the United States of America, 2001), pp. 199–202 <https://nae.edu/188253/FRITZ-LEONHARDT-19091999> [accessed 12 December 2021].

Giersch, Herbert, Karl-Heinz Paqué, and Holger Schmiedling, *The Fading Miracle: Four Decades of Market Economy in Germany* (Cambridge: Cambridge University Press, 1992).

Gleixner, Ulrike, *Pietismus Und Bürgertum: Eine Historische Anthropologie Der Frömmigkeit Württemberg 17.-19. Jahrhundert* (Göttingen: Vandenhoeck & Ruprecht, 2005).

Glossner, Christian L., *The Making of the German Post-War Economy* (London and New York: I.B. Tauris, 2013).

Green, Edwin, *Debtors to Their Profession: A History of the Institute of Bankers 1879–1979* (London: Routledge, 2012).

Grieger, Manfred, 'Die "geplatzte Wirtschaftswundertüte": die Krisen 1966/67 und 1973/75 im deutschen Symbolunternehmen Volkswagen', in *Automobilindustrie 1945–2000: eine Schlüsselindustrie zwischen Boom und*

Krise, ed. by Stephanie Tilly and Florian Triebel (Munich: Oldenbourg, 2013), pp. 1–75.

Grotz, Reinhold, *Entwicklung, Struktur und Dynamik der Industrie im Wirtschaftsraum Stuttgart - eine industriegeographische Unterstutzung*, Stuttgarter Geographische Studien (Stuttgart: Im Selbstvertrag des Geographischen Instituts der Universität Stuttgart, 1971), LXXXII.

Grotz, Reinhold, and Boris Braun, 'Territorial or Trans-Territorial Networking: Spatial Aspects of Technology-Oriented Co-Operation within the German Mechanical Engineering Industry', *Regional Studies*, 31 (1997), 545–57.

Grünbacher, Armin, '"Honourable Men": West German Industrialists and the Role of Honour and Honour Courts in the Adenauer Era', *Contemporary European History*, 22 (2013), 233–52.

——, *West German Industrialists and the Making of the Economic Miracle: A History of Mentality and Recovery* (London: Bloomsbury Academic, 2017).

Guinnane, Timothy W., 'Cooperatives as Information Machines: German Rural Credit Cooperatives, 1883–1914', *The Journal of Economic History*, 61.2 (2001), 366–89.

——, 'Delegated Monitors, Large and Small: Germany's Banking System, 1800–1914', *Journal of Economic Literature*, 40.1 (2002), 73–124.

Hall, Peter A., and David Soskice, 'An Introduction to Varieties of Capitalism', in *Varieties of Capitalism* (Oxford: Oxford University Press, 2001).

Hancké, Bob, Martin Rhodes, and Mark Thatcher, 'Introduction: Beyond Varieties of Capitalism', in *Beyond Varieties of Capitalism: Conflict, Contradictions, and Complementarities in the European Economy*, ed. by Bob Hancké, Martin Rhodes, and Mark Thatcher (Oxford Scholarship Online: Oxford University Press, 2008).

Hannah, Leslie, 'Scale and Scope: Towards a European Visible Hand?', *Business History*, 33.2 (1991), 297–309.

Hans. Medick, *Weben und Überleben in Laichingen 1650–1900: Lokalgeschichte als allgemeine Geschichte*, Veröffentlichungen des Max-Planck-Instituts für Geschichte ; 126 (Göttingen: Vandenhoeck & Ruprecht, 1996).

Harrison, Leigh Michael, 'Factory Music: How the Industrial Geography and Working-Class Environment of Post-War Birmingham Fostered the Birth of Heavy Metal', *Journal of Social History*, 44.1 (2020) 145–58.

Heidenreich, Martin, 'Beyond Flexible Specialization: The Rearrangement of Regional Production Orders in Emilia-Romagna and Baden-Württemberg', *European Planning Studies*, 4 (1996), 401–19.

Henderson, Rebecca, *Reimagining Capitalism* (London: Portfolio Penguin, 2020).

Hennock, E.P., *Fit and Proper Persons : Ideal and Reality in Nineteenth-Century Urban Government*, Studies in Urban History, 2 (London: Edward Arnold, 1973).

Herrigel, Gary, *Industrial Constructions: The Sources of German Industrial Power* (Cambridge: Cambridge University Press, 1996).

——, 'Large Firms, Small Firms, and the Governance of Flexible Specialization: The Case of Baden-Württemberg and Socialized Risk', in *Country Competitiveness: Technology and the Organizing of Work*, ed. by Bruce Kogut (Oxford; New York: Oxford University Press, 1993), pp. 15–35.

Herrigel, Gary, and Charles F. Sabel, 'Craft Production in Crisis: Industrial Restructuring in Germany during the 1990s', in *The German Skills Machine: Sustaining Competitive Advantage in a Global Economy*, ed. by Pepper D. Culpepper and David Finegold (New York and Oxford: Berghahn Books, 1999), pp. 77–114.

Herrigel, Gary, and Jonathan Zeitlin, 'Alternatives to Varieties of Capitalism', *The Business History Review*, 84.4 (2010), 667–74.

Herrmann, Andrea, 'A Plea for Varieties of Entrepreneurship', *Small Business Economics*, 52.2 (2019), 331–43.

Heseltine, Michael, *No Stone Unturned In Pursuit of Growth* (London: Department for Business, Innovation and Skills, October 2012).

Hidreth, Andrew K.G., 'In Search of Profits: An Investigation Into the Manufacturing Locational Shift From the West Midlands Conurbation 1880–1986' (unpublished Ph.D. thesis, University of Cambridge, 1991).

Hilger, Susanne, Ulrich S. Soénius, Isabell Stamm, Nicole Schmiade, and Martin Kohli, 'Von Generation zu Generation: der Nachfolgerprozess in Familienunternehmen', in *Familienunternehmen im Rheinland im 19. und 20. Jahrhundert: Netzwerke, Nachfolge, soziales Kapital*, Schriften zur rheinisch-westfälischen Wirtschaftsgeschichte, Bd 47 (Köln: Stiftung Rheinisch-Westfälisches Wirtschaftsarchiv, 2009), pp. 177–87.

Hirsch, Bernhard, Christian Nitzl, and Matthias Schoen, 'Interorganizational Trust and Agency Costs in Credit Relationships between Savings Banks and SMEs', *Journal of Banking & Finance*, 97 (2018), 37–50.

Höhner, Heinz, *Kriegsgefangen in Sibirien: Erinnerungen eines deutschen Kriegsgefangenen in Russland* (Aachen: Mainz, 1994).

Holmes, A.R., and Edwin Green, *Midland: 150 Years of Banking Business* (London: Batsford, 1986).

Hommel, Ulrich, and Hilmar Schneider, 'Financing the German Mittelstand', *EIB Papers*, 8.2 (2003), 53–90.

Hoogenboom, Marcel, Christopher Kissane, Maarten Prak, Patrick Wallis, and Chris Minns, 'Guilds in the Transition to Modernity: The Cases of Germany, United Kingdom, and the Netherlands', *Theory and Society*, 47.3 (2018), 255–91.

Howlett, Peter, 'The War-Time Economy, 1939–1945', in *The Cambridge Economic History of Modern Britain*, ed. by Roderick Floud and Paul Johnson (Online edition: Cambridge University Press, 2004), pp. 1–26.

Jackson, Brendan, and Moreen Wilkes, eds, *West Bromwich at War 1939–1945* (West Bromwich: West Bromwich Local History Society, 2016).

James, Harold, *A German Identity, 1770 to the Present Day* (London: Phoenix Press, 2000).

Jeremy, David J., 'Business Structures, Religious Structures, and Business Élites, 1900–1960', in *Capitalists and Christians: Business Leaders and the Churches in Britain 1900–1960*, Online (Oxford: Oxford University Press, 1990).

——, 'Important Questions about Business and Religion in Modern Britain', in *Business and Religion in Britain*, ed. by David J. Jeremy (Aldershot: Gower, 1988), pp. 1–26.

Jung, Frank, *Porsche 356 Made by Reuter* (Bielefeld: Delius Klasing, 2011).

——, *Recaro: Seating in Motion* (Bielefeld: Delius Klasing, 2016).

——, *RECARO: Sitzen in Bewegung* (Bielefeld: Delius Klasing, 2016).

Jung, Martin H., 'The Impact of Pietism on Culture and Society in Germany', in *Religion as an Agent of Change: Crusades – Reformation – Pietism*, ed. by Per Ingesman (Leiden, Boston: BRILL, 2016), pp. 211–30.

Jung, Uta, and Helmut Jung, *Stuttgarter Karosseriewerk Reutter: Von Der Reform-Karosserie Zum Porsche 356* (Bielefeld: Delius Klasing, 2006).

Junger, Gerhard, *Schicksale 1945: Das Ende Des 2. Weltkrieges Im Kreis Reutlingen* (Reutlingen: Oertel + Spörer, 1991).

Keasey, Kevin, and Robert Watson, 'The Bank Financing of Small Firms in UK: Issues and Evidence', *Small Business Economics*, 6 (1994), 349–62.

Keeble, David, *Industrial Location and Planning in the United Kingdom* (London: Methuen, 1976).

Kempster, Steve, and Brad Jackson, 'Leadership for What, Why, for Whom and Where? A Responsibility Perspective', *Journal of Change Management*, 21.1 (2021), 45–65.

Kershaw, Ian, *The End: Germany, 1944–45* (London: Penguin, 2012).

Kettenacker, Lothar, *Germany Since 1945* (Oxford & New York: Oxford University Press, 1997).

Kipping, Matthias, R. Daniel Wadhwani, and Marcelo Bucheli, 'Analyzing and Interpreting Historical Sources: A Basic Methodology', in *Organizations in Time: History, Theory, Methods*, ed. by R. Daniel Wadhwani and Marcelo Bucheli (Oxford: Oxford University Press, 2014), pp. 305–29.

Kitson, Michael, 'Failure Followed by Success or Success Followed by Failure? A Re-Examination of British Economic Growth since 1949', in *The Cambridge Economic History of Modern Britain, Vol. III, Structural Change and Growth, 1939–2000*, ed. by Roderick Floud and Paul Johnson (Cambridge: Cambridge University Press, 2004).

Kitson, Michael, and Jonathan Michie, 'The Deindustrial Revolution: The Rise and Fall of UK Manufacturing, 1870–2010', in *The Cambridge Economic History of Modern Britain: Volume 2*, ed. by Roderick Floud and Paul Johnson (2012) <https://michaelkitson.files.wordpress.com/2013/02/

kitson-and-michie-the-deindustrial-revolution-oct-20121.pdf> [accessed 13 May 2016].

Kocka, Jürgen, *Industrial Culture and Bourgeois Society* (New York and Oxford: Berghahn Books, 1999).

Kramer, Alan, *The West German Economy, 1945–1955* (New York and Oxford: Berg, 1991).

Kynaston, David, *Austerity Britain 1945–51* (London: Bloomsbury, 2007).

Landes, David S., 'Technological Change and Innovation in Western Europe 1750–1914', in *The Industrial Revolution and After: Incomes, Populations and Technological Change (I)*, ed. by H.J. Habbakuk and M.M. Postan, The Cambridge Economic History of Europe (Cambridge: Cambridge University Press, 1965), VI.

Lane, Christel, 'Industrial Change in Europe: The Pursuit of Flexible Specialisation in Britain and West Germany', *Work, Employment and Society*, 2.2 (1988), 141–68.

———, *Management and Labour in Europe: The Industrial Enterprise in Germany, Britain and France* (Aldershot: Edward Elgar, 1989).

———, 'Vocational Training and New Production Concepts in Germany: Some Lessons for Britain', *Industrial Relations Journal*, 21.4 (1990), 247–59.

Lawrence, Peter, *Managers and Management in West Germany* (London: Croom Helm, 1980).

Lazonick, William, 'Varieties of Capitalism and Innovative Enterprise', *Comparative Social Research*, 24 (2007), 21–69.

Lehmann, Hartmut, *Pietismus und Weltliche Ordnung in Württemberg vom 17. bis zum 20. Jahrhundert* (Stuttgart: W. Kohlhammer, 1969).

Leibinger, Berthold, *Wer wollte eine andere Zeit als diese: ein Lebensbericht*, 2. (Hamburg: Murmann Verlag, 2011).

Lescent-Giles, Isabelle, 'Les Elites Industrielles Britanniques: 1880–1970', *Histoire, Économie et Société*, 17.1 (1998), 157–88.

Lewchuck, Wayne, *American Technology and the British Vehicle Industry* (Cambridge: Cambridge University Press, 1987).

Logue, Danielle M., Walter P. Jarvis, Stewart Clegg, and Antoine Hermens, 'Translating Models of Organization: Can the Mittelstand Move from Bavaria to Geelong?', *Journal of Management and Organization; Lyndfield*, 21.1 (2015), 17–36.

Lubinski, Christina, *Familienunternehmen in Westdeutschland. Corporate Governance Und Gesellschafterkultur Seit Den 1960er Jahren* (Munich: C.H. Beck, 2010).

———, 'Path Dependency and Governance in German Family Firms', *Business History Review*, 85 (2011), 699–724.

Marshall, Alfred, *Principles of Economics*, 8th edn (London: Macmillan, 1920).

Mason, Geoff, 'Production Supervisors in Britain, Germany and the United States: Back from the Dead Again?', *Work, Employment & Society*, 14.4 (2000), 625–45.

Mayer, Colin, 'The Future of the Corporation and the Economics of Purpose', *Journal of Management Studies*, 58.3 (2021), 887–901.

McCabe, Steven, 'Exploring the Realities of Manufacturing in Birmingham', Birmingham Post (Birmingham, 3 February 2014), Online edition <https://www.birminghampost.co.uk/business/business-opinion/steven-mccabe-exploring-realities-manufacturing-6663271> [accessed 16 February 2019].

McDonald, Frank, Jurgen Krause, Hans Schmengler, and Heinz-Josef Tüselmann, 'Frank McDonald, Jurgen Krause, Hans Schmengler, Heinz-Josef Tüselmann, "Cautious International Entrepreneurs: The Case of the Mittelstand"', *Journal of International Entrepreneurship*, 1 (2003), 363–81.

McKibbin, Ross, *Classes and Cultures: England 1918–1951* (Oxford: Oxford University Press, 1998).

McKinlay, Alan, and Joseph Melling, 'The Shop Floor Politics of Productivity: Power and Authority Relations in British Engineering, c.1945–1957', in *British Trade Unions and Industrial Politics 1945–1978: Vol. 1, the Post-War Compromise, 1945–1964*, ed. by Alan Campbell, Nina Fishman, and John McIlroy (Aldershot: Ashgate Publishing Limited, 1999).

Melling, Joseph, '"Non-Commissioned Officers": British Employers and Their Supervisory Workers, 1880–1920', *Social History*, 5.2 (1980), 183–221.

Meskill, David, *Optimizing the German Workforce: Labor Administration from Bismarck to the Economic Miracle*, Open access ebook (New York and Oxford: Berghahn Books, 2010).

Millward, Robert, 'Industrial and Commercial Performance since 1950', in *The Economic History of Britain Since 1700. Volume 3: 1939–1992*, ed. by Roderick Floud and Deirdre McCloskey (Cambridge: Cambridge University Press, 1994), pp. 123–67.

Mitchell, F., and S.P. Walker, 'Market Pressures and the Development of Costing Practice: The Emergence of Uniform Costing in the UK Printing Industry', *Management Accounting Research*, 8 (1997), 75–101.

'Models for Apprentices', *The Engineer*, 210.5453 (29 July 1960), 170.

Musgrave, P.W., *Technical Change: The Labour Force and Education* (London: Pergamon, 1967).

Newton, Lucy, 'Trust and Virtue in English Banking: The Assessment of Borrowers by Bank Managements at the Turn of the Nineteenth Century', *Financial History Review*, 7.2 (2000), 177–99.

Nicholas, Tom, 'Clogs to Clogs in Three Generations? Explaining Entrepreneurial Performance in Britain since 1850', *Journal of Economic History*, 59 (1999), 688–713.

Niethammer, Lutz, '"Normalization" in the West: Traces of Memory Leading Back into the 1950s', in *The Miracle Years. A Cultural History of West*

Germany, 1945–1968, ed. by Hanna Schissler (Princeton and Oxford: Princeton University Press, 2001), pp. 237–65.

Oberhauser, Robert, *85 Jahre Chr. Wandel Metalltuch- Und Maschinenfabrik Reutlingen* (Darmstadt: Archiv Für Wirtschaftskunde, 1954).

Porsche, Ferry, and John Bentley, *We at Porsche: The Autobiography of Dr. Ing. h.c. Ferry Porsche with John Bentley* (Yeovil: Haynes, 1976).

Porsche, Ferry, and Günther Molter, *Ferry Porsche: Ein Leben für das Auto, eine Autobiographie* (Stuttgart: Motorbuch Verlag, 1989).

Ogilvie, Sheilagh, 'The Economics of Guilds', *Journal of Economic Perspectives*, 28.4 (2014), 169–92.

Olaf Storbeck Waldachtal, 'Mittelstand Celebrated as Hidden Champions', *The Financial Times* (London, 17 October 2018), p. 13.

Oliver, George, *Cars and Coachbuilding: One Hundred Years of Road Vehicle Development* (London: Sotheby Parke Bernet in association with the Institute of British Carriage and Automobile Manufacturers, 1981).

Oulton, Nicholas, and Hilary Steedman, 'The British System of Youth Training: A Comparison with Germany', in *Training and the Private Sector*, ed. by Lisa M. Lynch, National Bureau of Economic Research Comparative Labor Markets (Chicago: University of Chicago Press, 1994), pp. 61–76.

Ovenden, Keith, *The Politics of Steel, Studies in Policy-Making* (London: Macmillan, 1978).

Overy, Richard, 'The Economy of the Federal Republic Since 1949', in *The Federal Republic of Germany Since 1949: Politics, Society and Economy before and after Unification*, ed. by Klaus Larres and Panayi Panikos (London and New York: Longman, 1996), pp. 3–34.

Owen, Geoffrey, *From Empire to Europe: The Decline and Revival of British Industry Since the Second World War* (London: Harper Collins, 1999).

Pahnke, André, and Friederike Welter, 'The German Mittelstand: Antithesis to Silicon Valley Entrepreneurship?', *Small Business Economics* (2018), 1–14.

Paulson, David, 'The Professionalisation of Selling and the Transformation of a Family Business: Kenrick & Jefferson, 1878–1940', *Business History*, 0.0 (2018), 1–31 <https://doi.org/10.1080/00076791.2018.1426749>.

Paulson, David W., 'British and German SMEs and the Memory of War: A Comparative Approach', *Management & Organizational History*, 13.4 (2018), 404–29.

Penrose, Edith, *The Theory of the Growth of the Firm*, Third edition (Oxford: Oxford University Press, 1995).

Pickvance, C.G., 'Introduction: The Institutional Context of Local Economic Development: Central Controls, Spatial Policies and Local Economic Policies', in *Place, Policy, and Politics: Do Localities Matter?*, ed. by Michael Harloe, C.G. Pickvance, and John Urry (London: Unwin Hyman, 1990).

Piore, Michael J., 'Varieties of Capitalism Theory: Its Considerable Limits', *Politics & Society*, 44.2 (2016), 237–41.

Pohl, Hans, *Die Rheinischen Sparkassen. Entwicklung Und Bedeutung Für Wirtschaft Und Gesellschaft von Den Anfängen Bis 1990* (Stuttgart: Fritz Steiner Verlag GmbH, 2001).

Pohl, Hans, Bernd Rudolph, and Günter Schulz, *Wirtschafts- und Sozialgeschichte der deutschen Sparkassen im 20. Jahrhundert* (Stuttgart: Deutscher Sparkassen Verlag GmbH, 2005).

Polman, Paul, and Andrew Winston, 'The Net Positive Manifesto', *Harvard Business Review*, 99.5 (2021), 124–31.

Porter, Michael, 'Clusters and the New Economics of Competition', *Harvard Business Review* (November–December 1998), 77–90.

Porter, Michael E., *The Competitive Advantage of Nations* (Basingstoke: Macmillan, 1998).

Prais, S.J., *Productivity and Industrial Structure: A Statistical Study of Manufacturing Industry in Britain, Germany and the United States* (Cambridge: Cambridge University Press, 1981).

Prais, S.J., and Karin Wagner, 'Productivity and Management: The Training of Foremen in Britain and Germany', *National Institute Economic Review*, 123.1 (1988), 34–46.

Putsch, Ulrich, and Martin Putsch, eds, *In Bewegung. der Automobilzulieferer Keiper: Geschichte und Geschichten aus den Jahren 1920 Bis 2011* (Kaiserslautern: Ulrich und Martin Putsch, 2011).

Quick, Reiner, 'The Formation and Early Development of German Audit Firms', *Accounting, Business & Financial History*, 15.3 (2005), 317–43.

Reitz, Adolf, *Werke und Köpfe: Aufstieg und Bedeutung der südwestdeutschen Industrie: Leistung und Auftrag* (Reutlingen: Oertel und Spörer, 1959).

Rietmann, Carsten, 'Hidden Champions and Their Integration in Rural Regional Innovation Systems: Insights from Germany', *ZFW – Advances in Economic Geography* (2021), <https://doi.org/10.1515/zfw-2021-0024>.

Roethlisberger, F.J., 'The Foreman: Master and Victim of Double Talk', *Harvard Business Review* (September 1965) <https://hbr.org/1965/09/the-foreman-master-and-victim-of-double-talk> [accessed 9 February 2019].

Roper, Stephen, *Product Innovation and Small Business Growth: A Comparison of the Strategies of German, UK and Irish Companies* (Belfast: Northern Ireland Economic Research Centre, 1996).

Röpke, Wilhelm, *The German Question*, trans. by E.W. Dickes (London: George Allen & Unwin, 1946).

Russell Knight, Jeffrey, ed., *The Stock Exchange Official Year-Book 1975–76* (Croydon: Thomas Skinner & Co. (Publishers) Ltd., 1975).

———, ed., *The Stock Exchange Official Year-Book 1979–80* (East Grinstead: Thomas Skinner & Co. (Publishers) Ltd., 1979).

———, ed., *The Stock Exchange Official Year-Book 1980–81* (London and Basingstoke: Macmillan, 1980).

Sanderson, Michael, *Education and Economic Decline in Britain, 1870 to the 1990s* (Cambridge: Cambridge University Press, 1999).

Sabel, Charles F., and Michael J. Piore, *The Second Industrial Divide - Possibilities for Prosperity* (New York: Basic Books, 1984).

Schell, Sabrina, Miriam Hiepler, and Petra Moog, 'It's All about Who You Know: The Role of Social Networks in Intra-Family Succession in Small and Medium-Sized Firms', *Journal of Family Business Strategy*, 9.4 (2018), 311–25.

Schmidt-Bachem, Heinz, *Aus Papier, eine Kultur- und Wirtschaftsgeschichte der Papier verarbeitenden Industrie in Deutschland* (Berlin, Boston: De Gruyter Saur, 2011).

Schneider, Benjamin, Marco Kayser, Erdem Gelec, and Hartmut Hirsch-Kreinsen, 'Der Meister in Industrie 4.0-Fabriken', in *Die Digitalisierungshürde lässt sich Meister(n): Erfolgsfaktoren, Werkzeuge und Beispiele für den Mittelstand*, ed. by Thomas Knothe, Patrick Gering, Sven O. Rimmelspacher, and Michael Maier (Berlin, Heidelberg: Springer, 2020), pp. 13–40 <https://doi.org/10.1007/978-3-662-60367-3_3>.

Schulze, Rainer, 'Representation of Interests and Recruitment of Elites. The Role of the Industrie- Und Handelskammern in German Politics After the End of the Second World War', *German History*, 7.1 (1989), 71–91.

Schumpeter, Joseph A., and Joseph E. Stiglitz, *Capitalism, Socialism and Democracy* (Florence, USA: Routledge, 2010).

Schwärzel, Renate, 'Die Berliner Elektroindustrie Nach Dem Zweiten Weltkrieg. Eine Bestandsaufnahme', in *Unternehmen zwischen Markt und Macht. Aspekte deutscher Unternehmens- Und Industriegeschichte im 20. Jahrhundert*, ed. by Werner Plumpe and Christian Kleinschmidt, Bochumer Schriften zur Unternehmens- und Industriegeschichte (Essen: Klartext, 1992), I, pp. 167–78.

Scott, Peter, and Lucy Newton, 'Jealous Monopolists? British Banks and Responses to the Macmillan Gap during the 1930s', *Enterprise and Society*, 8.4 (2007), 881–919.

Scranton, Philip, and Patrick Fridenson, *Reimagining Business History* (Baltimore: The Johns Hopkins University Press, 2013).

Simon, Herman, 'You Don't Have To Be German To Be A "Hidden Champion"', *Business Strategy Review*, 7.2 (1996), 1–13 <https://doi.org/10.1111/j.1467-8616.1996.tb00118.x>.

Smith, Chris, John Child, and Michael Rowlinson, *Reshaping Work: The Cadbury Experience* (Cambridge: Cambridge University Press, 1990).

Smith, Dennis, 'Coping with Restructuring: The Case of South-West Birmingham', in *Place, Policy, and Politics: Do Localities Matter?*, ed. by Michael Harloe, C.G. Pickvance, and John Urry (London: Unwin Hyman, 1990).

Soskice, David, 'Reconciling Markets and Institutions: The German Apprenticeship System', in *Training and the Private Sector*, ed. by Lisa M. Lynch, National Bureau of Economic Research Comparative Labor Markets (Chicago: University of Chicago Press, 1994).

Spector, Cyril, *Management in the Printing Industry* (London: Longmans, 1967).

Spicka, Mark E., 'City Policy and Guest Workers in Stuttgart, 1955–1973.', *German History*, 31.3 (2013), 345–65.

——, *Selling the Economic Miracle: Economic Reconstruction and Politics in West Germany, 1949–1957: 18*, Illustrated edition (New York: Berghahn Books, 2007).

Stadt Reutlingen, *Industriestandort Reutlingen* (Reutlingen: Stadt Reutlingen, 1984),

Stieniezcka, Norbert, 'Von fahrbaren Untersatz zur Chromkarosse mit "Innerer Sicherheit" - der Wandel der Nutzeranforderungen an das Automobil in 50er und 60er Jahren', in *Geschichte und Zukunft der Deutschen Automobilindustrie: Tagung im Rahmen der "Chemnitzer Begegnungen" 2000*, ed. by Rudolf Boch (Stuttgart: Franz Steiner Verlag, 2001).

Stokes, Raymond G., 'Technology and the West German Wirtschaftswunder', *Technology and Culture*, 32.1 (1991), 1–22.

Streeck, Wolfgang, 'Successful Adjustment to Turbulent Markets: The Automobile Industry', in *Industry and Politics in West Germany Toward the Third Republic*, ed. by Peter J. Katzenstein (Ithaca: Cornell University Press, 1989), pp. 113–56.

Streeck, Wolfgang, 'Varieties of Varieties: "VoC" and the Growth Models', *Politics & Society*, 44.2 (2016), 243–47.

Swett, Pamela E., *Selling Under the Swastika: Advertising and Commercial Culture in Nazi Germany* (Stanford: Stanford University Press, 2014).

Teece, David J., *Dynamic Capabilities and Strategic Management: Organizing for Innovation and Growth* (Oxford: Oxford University Press, 2009).

——, 'Dynamic Capabilities: Routines versus Entrepreneurial Action', *Journal of Management Studies*, 49.8 (2012), 1395–1401 <https://doi.org/1 0.1111/j.1467-6486.2012.01080.x>.

——, 'The Dynamics of Industrial Capitalism: Perspectives on Alfred Chandler's Scale and Scope', in *Management Innovation: Essays in the Spirit of Alfred D. Chandler Jr*, ed. by William Lazonick and David J. Teece (Oxford: Oxford University Press, 2012).

'The European Convention for Constructional Steelwork: History and Achievements 1955 – 2015' (The European Convention for Constructional Steelwork, 2015).

Thelen, Kathleen, *How Institutions Evolve: The Political Economy of Skills in Germany, Britain, the United States, and Japan* (Cambridge: Cambridge University Press, 2004).

Thurley, Keith, and Hans Wirdenius, *Approaches to Supervisory Development* (London: Institute of Personnel Management, 1973).

——, *Supervision: A Reappraisal* (London: Heinemann in conjunction with The Swedish Council for Personnel Administration, 1973)

Tilly, Stephanie, 'Das Zulieferproblem Aus Institutionenökonomischer Sicht. Die Westdeutsche Automobil-Zulieferindustrie Zwischen Produktions- Und Marktorientierung (1960–1980)', *Jahrbuch Für Wirtschaftsgeschichte/ Economic History Yearbook*, 51.1 (2010), 137–60.

Tilly, Stephanie, and Jean-Luc Malvache, 'Des partenaires des grands ? Les relations entre constructeurs automobiles et sous-traitants et leurs conséquences spatiales en Allemagne depuis 1945', *Revue du Nord*, 387 (2013), 877–94.

Tiratsoo, Nick, 'The Reconstruction of Blitzed British Cities, 1945–55: Myths and Reality', *Contemporary British History*, 14.1 (2000), 27–44.

Tolliday, Steven, 'Enterprise and State in the West German Wirtschaftswunder: Volkswagen and the Automobile Industry, 1939–1962', *The Business History Review*, 69.3 (1995), 273–350.

Tooze, Adam, *The Wages of Destruction: The Making and Breaking of the Nazi Economy* (London: Penguin, 2007).

Trainor, Richard H., *Black Country Elites: The Exercise of Authority in an Industrialized Area 1830–1900* (Oxford: Clarendon Press, 1993).

Van Hook, James C., *Rebuilding Germany: The Creation of the Social Market Economy, 1945–1957* (Cambridge: Cambridge University Press, 2004).

Vik, Pal, '"The Computer Says No": The Demise of the Traditional Bank Manager and the Depersonalisation of British Banking, 1960–2010', *Business History*, 59:1 (2017), 231–49.

Vitols, Sigurt, 'Are German Banks Different?', *Small Business Economics*, 10 (1998), 79–91.

Vogt, Gert, 'Die Kreditanstalt Für Wiederaufbau: Ein Unterenehmensporträt', *Zeitschrift für öffentliche und gemeinwirtschaftliche Unternehmen*, 17.3 (1994), 373–78.

von Frankenburg, Richard, *Porsche, the Man and His Cars*, trans. by Charles Meisl (London: G.T. Foulis, 1961).

Wagner, Karin, 'The German Apprenticeship System Under Strain', in *The German Skills Machine: Sustaining Competitive Advantage in a Global Economy*, ed. by Pepper D. Culpepper and David Finegold (New York and Oxford: Berghahn Books, 1999), pp. 37–76.

Weber, Max, *The Protestant Ethic and the Spirit of Capitalism*, trans. by Talcott Parsons (New York: Charles Scribner's Sons, 1958).

Wehling, Hans-Georg, 'Reutlingen - Kontinuität Und Bruch Nach 1945', in *Die Zeit nach dem Krieg: Städte im Wiederaufbau*, ed. by Karl Moersch and Reinhold Weber (Stuttgart: W. Kohlhammer, 2008), pp. 311–38.

Welter, Friederike, Susanne Schlepphorst, Stefan Schneck, and Michael Holz, *Der geschäftliche Beitrag des Mittelstands: Konzeptielle Überlegungen*, IfM-Materialien (Bonn: Institut Für Mittelstandsforschung, 18 August 2020) <https://www.ifm-bonn.org/fileadmin/data/redaktion/publikationen/ifm_materialien/dokumente/IfM-Materialien-283_2020.pdf> [accessed 2 January 2022].

Whisker, Ben, 'The Conservative Party, Concerted Action and the West German Economic Model 1975–1981', *Contemporary British History*, 35.1 (2021), 125–50.

Wild, Trevor, and Philip Jones, eds, *De-Industrialisation and New Industrialisation in Britain and Germany* (London: Anglo-German Foundation for the Study of Industrial Society, 1991).

Will, Henner, 'Kurzarbeit - makroökonom(etr)ische Erkenntnisse über einen klassischen allrounder' (presented at the *Seventh IWH/IAB-Workshops zur Arbeitsmarktpolitik "Lohnpolitik nach der Krise"*, Halle, 2010), p. 19 <https://www.iwh-halle.de/fileadmin/user_upload/events/workshops/former/20101021/PDF/2/Henner%20Will.pdf>

Willis, Frank Roy, *The French in Germany, 1945–1949* (Stanford University Press, 1962).

Wilson, John F., and Andrew Popp, eds, *Industrial Clusters and Regional Business Networks in England, 1750–1970* (Burlington, VT: Routledge, 2003).

Winkel, Harald, *Geschichte der Württembergischen Industrie- und Handelskammern Heilbronn, Reutlingen, Stuttgart/Mittlerer Neckar und Ulm 1933–1980: Zum 125jährigen Bestehen* (Stuttgart: Kohlhammer, 1980).

Witt, Michael A., and Gregory Jackson, 'Varieties of Capitalism and Institutional Comparative Advantage: A Test and Reinterpretation', *Journal of International Business Studies*, 47.7 (2016), 778.

Wixforth, Harald, 'Das Universalbanksystem – Ein Erfolgsmodell Auf Den Finanzmärkten?', *Jahrbuch Für Wirtschaftsgeschichte / Economic History Yearbook*, 58.2 (2017), 583–612.

Wixforth, Harald, and Dieter Ziegler, 'The Niche in the Universal Banking System: The Role and Significance of Private Bankers within German Industry, 1900–1933', *Financial History Review*, 1.2 (1994), 99–119.

Wood, Stewart, 'Why Brexit Britain Should Embrace a European-Style Economic Model', *New Statesman* (2021) <https://www.newstatesman.com/world/europe/2021/10/why-brexit-britain-should-embrace-a-european-style-economic-model> [accessed 31 December 2021].

Zeitlin, Jonathan, 'Craft Control and the Division of Labour: Engineers and Compositors in Britain 1890–1930', *Cambridge Journal of Economics*, 3.3 (1979), 263–74.

Websites

'About Us - Andrews Sykes' <https://www.andrews-sykes.com/info/about-us/#t1> [accessed 31 January 2019].

Baker & McKenzie, 'Doing Business in Germany' (Baker & McKenzie, 2015) <https://www.bakermckenzie.com/-/media/files/insight/publi-cations/2015/05/doing-business-in-germany/doing_business_in_germany_29april2015.pdf?la=en> [accessed 19 August 2019].

'BKU - Bund Katholischer Unternehmer e.V. - Geschichte -', Bund Katholischer Unternehmer (2018) < https://www.bku.de/historie.aspx> [accessed 2 August 2022].

Burkhardt+Weber, 'Geschichte', BURKHARDT+WEBER (2015) < https://burkhardt-weber.de/unternehmen/geschichte> [accessed 23 February 2017].

Business Roundtable, 'Statement on the Purpose of a Corporation', Business Roundtable (2019) <https://www.businessroundtable.org/business-round-table-redefines-the-purpose-of-a-corporation-to-promote-an-economy-that-serves-all-americans> [accessed 25 August 2019].

Common Register Portal of the German Federal States (2016) <https://www.handelsregister.de/rp_web/welcome.xhtml> [accessed 29 December 2016].

Das Fraunhofer-Institut Für Produktionsanlagen und Konstruktionstechnik IPK, 'Jump 4.0: Mobile Jobeinplanungsunterstützung Für den Meister in der Produktion', Jump 4.0 (2020) <http://www.jump40.de/> [accessed 14 November 2020].

Department of Defense, Office of Military Government for Germany, 'Record of File on Karl Walz' (2016) <https://catalog.archives.gov/id/7569400> [accessed 31 March 2016].

'Descendants of Archibald Kenrick (Nov 1760 – 16 Oct 1835)', http://www.greywall.demon.co.uk/genealogy/wynnhall/archy.html (2014) <http://www.greywall.demon.co.uk/genealogy/wynnhall/archy.html> [accessed 16 January 2014; site inactive on 9 August 2022].

DAfStb - Deutscher Ausschuss für Stahlbeton e. V. – 'Leitbild', <http://www.dafstb.de/leitbild.html> [accessed 2 August 2022].

'Doctoral Theses Supervised by Professor Lueth, Professor Heinzl, and Professor Unterberger since 1953', Chair of Micro Technology and Medical Device Technology, Technical University of Munich, (2018) < https://www.mec.ed.tum.de/en/mimed/structure/doctoral-theses/> [accessed 6 December 2018].

'Drauz-Werke', Wikipedia (2018) <https://de.wikipedia.org/w/index.php?title=Drauz-Werke&oldid=175225324> [accessed 22 April 2018].

'Engineering Employers' Federation - Archives Hub' <https://archiveshub.jisc.ac.uk/data/gb152-eef> [accessed 10 January 2019].

'Ernst & Young', Wikipedia (2017) <https://de.wikipedia.org/w/index.php?title=Ernst_%26_Young&oldid=169184426> [accessed 22 October 2017].

Espacenet, <http://worldwide.espacenet.com>

'Recaro "Pulverized" Previous Revenue Records in 2018', *Aircraft Interiors International* (2019) <https://www.aircraftinteriorsinternational.com/news/industry-news/recaro-pulverized-previous-revenue-records-in-2018.html> [accessed 29 April 2019].

'The German Mittelstand: Facts and Figures about German SMEs', Federal Ministry for Economics Affairs and Energy (2019) <https://www.bmwi.de/Redaktion/EN/Publikationen/wirtschaftsmotor-mittelstand-zahlen-und-fakten-zu-den-deutschen-kmu.pdf?__blob=publicationFile&v=4> [accessed 20 February 2019].

'Fischer Group' (2019) <https://www.fischer.group/de-de> [accessed 16 February 2019].

Franz, Felix, 'Germany Is Bracing for a Major Electric Vehicle Shock', Wired UK (14 September 2021) <https://www.wired.co.uk/article/germany-electric-vehicles-europe> [accessed 30 December 2021].

Fraunhofer-Gesellschaft, 'Profile / Structure', *Fraunhofer-Gesellschaft* (2021) <https://www.fraunhofer.de/en/about-fraunhofer/profile-structure.html> [accessed 29 December 2021].

'Fritz Leonhardt', Wikipedia (2015) <https://en.wikipedia.org/w/index.php?title=Fritz_Leonhardt&oldid=690616734> [accessed 25 November 2015].

German Design Council, 'SLEEPING COMFORT ABOVE THE CLOUDS – Holistic Approach for the Economy Class Long Range: German Design Award Gold 2020', *German Design Award* (2020) <https://www.german-design-award.com/en/the-winners/gallery/detail/27167-sleeping-comfort-above-the-clouds-holistic-approach-for-the-economy-class-long-range.html> [accessed 19 September 2020].

'Guiding Principles of the RECARO Group - RECARO' <https://www.recaro.com/recaro-group/guiding-principles-of-the-recaro-group.html> [accessed 18 December 2021].

Hager & Elsässer, 'About H+E Group', *Hager & Elsässer* (2020) <https://www.he-water.group/en/about-h-e.html> [accessed 28 July 2020].

'Home | REFA' <http://www.refa.de/home> [accessed 15 September 2018].

'Historic Inflation Germany – Historic CPI Inflation Germany' <http://www.inflation.eu/inflation-rates/germany/historic-inflation/cpi-inflation-germany.aspx> [accessed 23 February 2017].

'Historical Exchange Rates from 1953 with Graph and Charts' <http://fxtop.com/en/historical-exchange-rates.php?A=100&C1=DEM&C2=USD&YA=1&DD1=01&MM1=01&YYYY1=1960&B=1&P=&I=1&DD2=01&MM2=01&YYYY2=1975&btnOK=Go%21> [accessed 24 February 2017].

'IfM Bonn: KMU Definition Des IfM Bonn' (Institut fúr Mittelstandsforschung, 2014), <https://www.ifm-bonn.org/definitionen-/kmu-definition-des-ifm-bonn/> [accessed 16 February 2014].

'IfM Bonn: Mittelstandsdefinition Des IfM Bonn' (Institut fúr Mittelstandsforschung, 2019) < https://www.ifm-bonn.org/definitionen/mittelstandsdefinition-des-ifm-bonn/> [accessed 14 February 2019].

'Inflation, Great Britain, 1977', Inflation EU: Worldwide Inflation Data <http://www.inflation.eu/inflation-rates/great-britain/historic-inflation/cpi-inflation-great-britain-1977.aspx> [accessed 15 November 2014].

'Inflation, West Germany, 1977', Inflation EU: Worldwide Inflation Data <http://www.inflation.eu/inflation-rates/germany/historic-inflation/cpi-inflation-germany-1977.aspx> [accessed 15 November 2014].

'Jensen CV8 | From Drawing Board To Reality', The Jensen Museum (2018) <http://www.jensenmuseum.org/jensen-cv8-from-drawing-board-to-reality/> [accessed 16 January 2019].

'Jensen Motors Assembly Line Finisher | Day In The Life', The Jensen Museum (2017) <http://www.jensenmuseum.org/jensen-motors-assembly-line-finisher-day-life/> [accessed 22 July 2017].

'Jensen Motors Chief Engineer | Day In The Life', The Jensen Museum (2016) <http://www.jensenmuseum.org/jensen-motors-chief-designer-day-life/> [accessed 18 January 2019].

'Jensen Motors Employees A-Z', The Jensen Museum (2016) <http://www.jensenmuseum.org/jensen-motors-employees/> [accessed 16 January 2019].

'Jensen Motors' Press Shop Manager | Recollections', The Jensen Museum (2017) <http://www.jensenmuseum.org/jensen-motors-press-shop-manager-recollections/> [accessed 22 July 2017].

'Jensen Motors Quality Engineer | Recollections', The Jensen Museum (2017) <http://www.jensenmuseum.org/jensen-motors-quality-engineer-recollections/> [accessed 22 July 2017].

'Jensen Motors Trim Shop Employees A-Z', The Jensen Museum (2016) <http://www.jensenmuseum.org/jensen-motors-trim-shop-employees/> [accessed 22 July 2017].

'Jon Pressnell – Richard Graves Interview', The Jensen Museum (2017) <http://www.jensenmuseum.org/jon-pressnell-richard-graves-interview/> [accessed 22 July 2017].

Kamp, Hans, 'Jensen Commercial Vehicles', The Jensen Museum (2017) <http://www.jensenmuseum.org/jensen-commercial-vehicles/> [accessed 16 January 2019].

'Karosserien von Gustav Drauz' <https://stadtarchiv.heilbronn.de/stadt-geschichte/geschichte-a-z/d/drauz-karosseriefabrik.html> [accessed 22 April 2018].

'Klaus Scheufelen', Wikipedia (2018) <https://de.wikipedia.org/w/index.php?title=Klaus_Scheufelen&oldid=177045753> [accessed 5 February 2019].

'Kurzarbeit', Wikipedia (2018) <https://de.wikipedia.org/w/index.php?title=Kurzarbeit&oldid=180005144> [accessed 13 January 2019].

'Längenentwicklung der Bundesautobahnen Seit 1950', *Autobahn-Online.de - Autobahnen in Deutschland* (2021) < https://www.autobahn-online.de/laengen.html > [accessed 12 December 2021].

Max-Planck Gesellschaft, 'Short Portrait of the Max Planck Society', *Max-Planck Gesellschaft* (2021) <https://www.mpg.de/short-portrait> [accessed 29 December 2021].

'Meet the Mittelstand: How German Mid-Sized Companies Went Global | All-Party Parliamentary Manufacturing Group' <https://www.policy-connect.org.uk/apmg/events/meet-mittelstand-how-german-mid-sized-companies-went-global> [accessed 16 February 2019; site inactive on 9 August 2022].

PWC, 'Potenzialanalyse: Wie Digital Sind Die Deutschen Mittelständler?' (Pricewaterhouse Coopers LLP, January 2017) <https://www.pwc.de/de/mittelstand/assets/digitalisierungsbefragung-21122016-auskopplung.pdf> [accessed 31 December 2021].

RECARO Aircraft Seating, 'Auszubildenden Industriemechaniker (m/w/d) - Beginn 2023 - RECARO Aircraft Seating', RECARO (2022) <https://www.recaro-as.de/de/job-karriere/jobs/details/auszubildenden-industrie-mechaniker-m-w-d-beginn-2023-27513.html> [accessed 9 July 2022].

RECARO Holding GmbH, 'Family Business and Philosophy' (2013) <www.recaro.com/family-company-and-philosophy.html> [accessed 13 October 2013; site inactive on 9 August 2022].

'Recaro Seats', Sommerlatte Industrial Design < https://sommerlatte-industrial-design.de/ > [accessed 30 November 2018].

'Recollections of Nick Maltby, Draughtsman, of Jensen Motors | Carter's Green Factory', The Jensen Museum (2016) <http://www.jensenmuseum.org/jensen-motors-carters-green-factory/> [accessed 22 July 2017].

Siebfabrik Arthur Maurer GmbH & Co. KG, 'Eine Geschichte Mit Zukunft' <http://www.siebfabrik.de/de/unternehmen/geschichte/> [accessed 23 February 2017].

'Steinbeis-at-a-Glance' (Steinbeis Foundation, 2019) <https://www.steinbeis.de/fileadmin/content/Publikationen/unternehmenspublikationen/Publication_Steinbeis_at_a_Glance.pdf > [accessed 17 February 2019].*The Times* Digital Archive, https://www.gale.com/intl/c/the-times-digital-archive

Thames TV, *British Leyland Cars | British Car Manufacturing | TV Eye | 1980* <https://www.youtube.com/watch?v=SsizoYrceOg> [accessed 18 February 2019].

'Turnover Rises to over 500 Million Euros for the First Time - RECARO Aircraft Seating' (2018) <https://www.recaro-as.com/en/press/press-releases/details/turnover-rises-to-over-500-million-euros-for-the-first-time.html> [accessed 5 December 2018].

'Two Brothers with Vision - Alan & Richard Jensen', The Jensen Museum (2016) <http://www.jensenmuseum.org/alan-richard-jensen/> [accessed 16 January 2019].

'Über Uns - Papierfabrik Scheufelen' <http://www.scheufelen.com/unternehmen/über-uns/> [accessed 5 August 2017].

'Unternehmen | Stahlbau Nägele' <http://stahlbau-nägele.de/unternehmen/> [accessed 31 December 2016].

'Unternehmen - Stahlbau OTT Kirchheim Unter Teck' <http://www.stahlbau-ott.de/unternehmen/> [accessed 31 December 2016].

Unpublished Theses

Chamberlain, Colin, 'British Attitudes to the German Economic Miracle 1948 to circa 1968' (unpublished Ph.D. thesis, University of Cambridge, 2022).

Considine, Marie, 'The Social, Political and Economic Determinants of a Modern Portrait Artist: Bernard Fleetwood-Walker (1893–1965)' (unpublished Ph.D. thesis, University of Birmingham, 2012) <http://etheses.bham.ac.uk/3639/1/Considine12PhD.pdf> [accessed 31 May 2014].

Finn, M.T.F., 'The Political Economy of Higher Education in England, c. 1944–1974' (unpublished Ph.D. thesis, University of Cambridge, 2009).

Index

Apprentices and apprenticeships
  at Braithwaite & Co Engineers Ltd. 78
  at Chr. Wandel KG 72
  at Jensen Motors Ltd. 78, 283–84
  at Keiper 72–73
    Keiper, Fritz, apprenticeship of
      72–73
  at Kenrick & Jefferson Ltd. 78–80
  at Philipp Müller Nachf. Eugen Bucher
    GmbH & Co 73–74
  Declining importance in Britain 76
  Examinations for 69
  in British history 65, 74–75, 77–78
  in German history 67, 70
  in German workplace, as observed
    by Birmingham Productivity
    Association in 1955 76–78
  Lehrvertrag (German apprentice
    contract) 73–74
  of British engineering entrepreneurs
    74–75
  Pay rates, West Germany 74
  Relative importance of, in Britain and
    West Germany 66 fig 1, 66–67,
    69, 72
  Relative strengths of, in Britain and
    West Germany 80
Aston University 94, 98, 210
Automotive industry
  in Britain
    Strikes 279–80
  in West Germany
    Growth and dynamics of 241,
      254–55, 258 fig. 21
    Changing nature of, in 1960s
      252–3
    Supplier relations 252–3

Baden-Württemberg
  Banking within 42–49

Business systems within 8–10, 297–98
Clusters within 28, 29–30
Ministerium für Arbeit, Gesundheit
    Und Sozialordnung (Ministry for
    Work, Health and Social Order)
    138
Postwar economic conditions within
    26–27, 28
Research infrastructure within 105
Support for entrepreneurs 245–46
Training and vocational education
    within 70–71, 83, 88
Universities 98–106
Banks and banking 38–62
  and Braithwaite & Co. Engineers Ltd.
    60–61, 202, 206, 207, 221–22
  and Chr. Wandel KG 45–46
  and Jensen Motors Ltd. 59, 288
  and Julius Schneider 46–47
  and Karosseriewerk Reutter 48–49
  and Kenrick & Jefferson Ltd. 61
  and Philipp Müller Nachf. Eugen
    Bucher GmbH & Co 47–48
  Baden-Württembergische Bank (BWB)
    43–44
  Britain, structure and attitudes of
    banking system within 49–59
  Britain, banks' management in 56–57,
    57–59
  Britain, Institute of Banking and
    training on SMEs 58
  Hausbank (company's house-bank) in
    Germany 39
  Kreditanstalt für Wiederaufbau
    (KfW)(Credit Institute for
    Reconstruction) 44–45
  Lloyds Bank 53–59, 60–61
  Midland Bank 52, 53–55, 56
  Relationships with SMEs in Britain
    38, 49–50, 62

Relationships with SMEs and
Mittelstand in Germany   38–39,
40–41, 42–45, 62
Sparkasse (savings banks)   39
Origins and development   41,
42–43
Support for Mittelstand customers
6, 42–44, 47, 48, 49, 62, 297
Way of working   43
'Three-pillar system' in West Germany
38
'Universal banks' in West Germany   38
Berghoff, Hartmut (German historian)   2,
4–5, 10, 36, 205
Bevan, Timothy (chairman, Barclays Bank)
40, 58
Birmingham University
Science Faculty, growth in teaching staff
numbers   98
Graduates in Engineering   99 fig 4
Career destinations   102, 104 fig 7
Bolton, John   58
Bolton Committee on Small Firms, 1969
52
Braithwaite & Co. Engineers Ltd.
(steelwork fabricators)   113,
199–231
Employees, their Knowledge and
Commitment   293
Engineering ethos   200, 209–11
Engineering and commercial
achievements   201
Finance and company performance
Banks and funding   202, 206, 207,
221–22
Directors' compensation   222, 227,
230
Financial performance   205–06,
208, 226 fig. 19, 219, 229, 230
Shareholders   206, 208, 222, 230,
231
Trading conditions   206–07, 208,
214, 229–30
Government policies and performance,
effects on company   208, 214,
216, 221, 227
Governance
as an example of different Varieties
of Capitalism   295
Directors, appointments and profiles
of   210–11, 223–24, 225

Establishment of Braithwaites as
public company   200
Humphryes family take and retain
control of company   200,
204–05, 223
Humphryes family, social mobility of
203, 205
Humphryes, James Anthony (Tony)
(chairman 1971–83)
Actions in response to problems of
1970s   295
Attitude to closure of West
Bromwich site   229–30, 231
Attitude towards workforce   227,
229, 231
Education, background, personal
qualities   204–05
Engagement in professional and
industry organisations   225
Succeeds father as chairman, 1971
223
Frustrations with external
circumstances   219, 227
Humphryes, James Harvey (chairman
1927–71)
Education, background, personal
qualities   201, 202, 203
Engagement in professional and
industry organisations   202
Prewar and wartime chairman work
201, 203
Humphryes, James Hulse (founder and
chairman 1912–27)   32, 75, 199
Death and estate   200–01
Early career and education
199–200
Industrial relations   292
Innovations within   201, 219–21
Patents   199, 219–20
Inter-firm relations   291
Motorways, British development of and
consequences for company   206,
207, 208, 214–16, 221
Paternalistic culture, concern for staff
211–12, 228–29
Plastic Recycling Ltd. subsidiary,
acquired in 1978   228, 230
Power Generation, British development
of and consequences for
company   206, 207, 208, 216
Professional and industry organisations
199, 202, 210, 225

Sales
  Exports   201, 202, 203, 206, 208,
    227
  Bridges   206, 220–21
  Motorways   206, 207, 208, 216, 228
  Power stations   206, 207, 208, 216
  Pricing   202, 203, 207, 213
  Sales orientation of directors   202,
    206, 214, 222, 223, 227
Steel supply   201–02, 217–19, 218 fig.
    18
Strategy, diversification and acquisitions
    228, 230–31
Trade unions   207, 228
Vocational training   293–94
West Bromwich works
  Closure, 1979   228–29
Workforce and skills
  Apprentices   209, 210
  Graduates, university sponsorships
    209
  Labour relations   207
  Qualifications of management and
    directors   200, 204, 210–11
  Personnel costs, wages   212–13, 213
    fig. 17, 227, 230
  Recruitment and retention
    challenges   206, 209–11
  Redundancies and layoffs   206, 228,
    229
  Skills and skill shortages   206,
    209–11, 212 fig.16, 228, 230
Bruderhaus (Reutlingen metal-cloth
  manufacturer)   120, 139
Burckhardt & Weber (Reutlingen
  machine-tool manufacturer)   120,
  131

Carnevali, Francesca (Italian historian)
    11, 50, 52–53
Chandler, Alfred D.(American historian)
    6–8
  Scale and Scope   6–8
  'Three-pronged investment' in
    manufacturing, marketing and
    management   7, 8, 298
  Views of British 'personal capitalism'
    7, 299
  Views of German approach to business
    7, 299
  Views of technical education   63, 98
Clusters   29–30, 115

Common purpose in German firms   183
Confederation of British Industry (CBI)
    63
Constitution, West German, and property
    laws   35
Context, external, importance of to
    company success
  in Britain   298
  in West Germany   297–98
Coordinated Market Economy   12, 13

Dividends, to company shareholders   146,
    148, 208, 230, 241–42, 269,
Dorman, Long Ltd. (steel producer and
    fabricator)   68, 200, 202–03

Ecosystem   21, 300, 302
Economy, West German   188
  Employment costs within   196
  Growth rates versus Britain   187
  Slowdowns in   188
  Worker shortages within   187
Education and Training
  British views of specialisation versus
    liberal education at university
    98
  Differences between German and
    British workforces   63
  Dual system in West Germany   67, 71,
    75, 106
  Examinations in Germany for
    work-based learning   70–71
  Failures of British system   75–76, 298
  Resistance to, in British firms   68
  Support for, by Kenrick & Jefferson
    68–69
  Vocational   64, 68, 293–4, 298
External context, importance of to
    company success
  in Britain   298
  in West Germany   297–98

Facharbeiter (skilled worker)   86, 86 n 88
Fachgemeinschaft Druck- und
    Papiermaschinen (Industry
    Association for Printing and
    Papermaking Machinery)   121–22,
    129
  Export success of member companies
    122
  Member companies and products
    produced   122–23

Fachhochschulen (technical colleges) 9,
    71, 105
Family, leadership of company by members
    of 245, 256, 262–63, 296
Family ownership of companies,
    importance of 298–300
Fear, Jeffrey (American historian) 5
Fischer Group 6 n.31
Fleiss, see Swabians, industriousness of
Foremen (*see also Meister*)
    at Alfred Herbert Ltd. 91–92
    at Humber Motor Co. 92
    at Jensen Motors Ltd. 92
    at Kenrick & Jefferson Ltd. 92, 93
    Contrasted with German *Meister*
        81–82, 83, 97, 285, 294, 298
    in Britain, qualifications of 81–82,
        93–94
    in Britain, status relative to other
        workers and to management
        89, 90–91
    in Britain, training of 92–93
        at Birmingham Technical College
            94–96
        Reviewed by House of Commons
            Committee of Inquiry, 1954
            96–97
    in West Germany, qualifications of
        81–82
    The 'Foreman problem' 89–90
Franks, Sir Oliver (chairman Lloyds Bank)
    53
Fraunhofer-Gesellschaft 105
French occupying forces in Germany
    117–118
    Dismantling of German assets 117

Gastarbeiter, see Guest Workers
Germany, circumstances following Second
    World War
    Postwar occupation of 23, 117–18
        Removal of assets and intellectual
            property by Allied countries
            117–18
    Postwar economic recovery of 24–25
'Guest workers' (immigrant labour) 135,
    138, 187–88

Herrigel, Gary (American political
    economist) 8–10
    'Autarkic form of industrial order' 8–9

'Decentralized form of industrial order'
    8–9
German business 'system' 9–10
Role of banks in German SME system
    9
Role of supporting regional institutions
    in German SME system 9
Technical education 9, 71–72, 106–07
Hermann, Andrea (German political
    economist) 14
'Hidden Champions' 3, 262, 300 n. 17
Hierarchy, flatness of within German
    companies 184–85
    Importance of *Meister* in enabling
        185
Humphryes, James Anthony, *see under*
    Braithwaite & Co. Engineers Ltd.
Humphryes, James Harvey, *see under*
    Braithwaite & Co. Engineers Ltd.
Humphryes, James Hulse, *see under*
    Braithwaite & Co. Engineers Ltd.

IG Metall (metalwork trade union) 27,
    197, 289
Industrie- und Handelskammer (IHK)
    (Chambers of Industry and
    Commerce) 9, 30–31, 70–71
Inflation
    in Britain 164, 230, 281, 288
    in Germany and West Germany 42,
        129, 164

Jefferson, Edward (K&J managing
    director), *see under* Kenrick &
    Jefferson Ltd.
Jefferson family, *see under* Kenrick &
    Jefferson Ltd.
Jefferson, Frederick (K&J founder, father
    of Fred and Edward), *see under*
    Kenrick & Jefferson Ltd.
Jefferson, Frederick, "Mr. Fred" (K&J
    managing director), *see under*
    Kenrick & Jefferson Ltd.
Jefferson, K. Hugh (K&J director), *see
    under* Kenrick & Jefferson Ltd.
Jefferson, Thomas (Tom) (K&J managing
    director), *see under* Kenrick &
    Jefferson Ltd.
Jensen, Alan, *see under* Jensen Motors Ltd.
Jensen Motors Ltd. (automotive
    manufacturers) 113–14, 264–89

Beattie, Kevin (deputy chief engineer,
    later managing director)
    270–71, 287
Closure of, 1975   288–89
    Government financial support, failed
        attempts to secure   289
Culture   283–85
Duerr, Carl (managing director)
    Appointment as managing director
        274
    Criticisms of British management
        277
    Departure from JML   278–79
    Evaluation of Jensen culture   275
    Evaluation of Jensen workers   275,
        276
    Kontaktfähig (skilled in
        relationships), necessity of
        being in a manager   274–75
    Management Kinetics memoir
        274, 283
    Origins and education   274–5
    Relations with factory workers
        275–76, 282
    Relations with Trade Unions and
        officials   276, 282, 283
Employees, their Knowledge and
    Commitment   293
Financial Performance
    Annual results   265, 271, 278, 285,
        286
    Banks, relationships with   59, 288
    Budgets and budgeting   273
    Capital investments   265, 272, 287
    Profitability   266, 267 fig. 22, 286
    Shareholders and dividends   242,
        272
    Under Norcros ownership   269
    Warranty costs   278
Governance   295
Graves, Richard (marketing director)
    270, 272
    Under Qvale chairmanship
        285–86, 287, 288
    Management of sales   272, 277, 278
    Relations with Carl Duerr   276–77
Industrial relations   279–83, 292
Innovativeness   264, 266
Inter-firm relations   291
Jensen, Alan and Richard (co-founders
    and co-managing directors)
    Achievements evaluated   268

Departure from Jensen   271
Origins and education   264–66
Sale of business to Norcros Ltd.,
    1959   268–69
Technical capabilities of   247, 264,
    266
Jensen FF (car model)   271
Jensen Interceptor (car model)   264,
    270, 286, 288
Jensen Healey (car model)   286–87
Marketing, publicity and public
    relations
    During 1950s and 1960s   266, 271
    Under Carl Duerr   250, 277
Neale, Eric (chief designer)   266, 271
Norcros Ltd. (holding company)
    Acquire Jensen Motors Ltd., 1959
        268
    Different from Reutter and Porsche
        as business owners   269
    Dividend policy   242, 272
    Failings within Norcros Ltd.   273
    Management by Norcros of JML
        269, 270, 272
    Sell JML to William Brandt's Sons
        Ltd. (merchant bank)   274
    Sheffield, John (founder and
        chairman of Norcros)   268,
        269
Owen, Brian (managing director, under
    Norcros)   270, 273
Production and operations   267 fig. 22
    Craftsmanship   266, 275, 283
    Management of   268, 271, 272, 282
    Mismatch with sales   278
    Quality   270, 278, 284–85
    Supplier relations   271, 272
Qvale, Kjell (Norwegian-American car
    dealer and chairman of Jensen
    Motors Ltd.)
    Assumes control of JML   278–79
    Management of JML   285–88
Sales
    Commercial vehicles   264–65
    During postwar period   265–66
    During Second World War   265
    Exports   286, 288
    Forecasts   272
    of Jensen's own designs, 1936–62
        268
    Management of, by Richard Graves
        and others   272, 277, 278

Subcontract assembly for Austin,
Volvo, other manufacturers
266, 267 fig. 22, 269–70,
271–2, 273
Workforce and skills
Apprentices 78, 283–84
Craftsmanship 266, 275, 283
Demarcation 271
Foremen 284–85
Labour-Management relations
279–83, 286–87, 289
Pay and wages 280–81, 282
Management of workforce
286–87, 289
Women workers 282
Trade Unions 268, 271, 276, 280–81,
289
Vickers, Alfred (managing director of
Jensen Motors Ltd.) 279
Vocational training 294
William Brandt's Sons Ltd. (bank,
acquirer of Jensen Motors Ltd.)
274
Jensen, Richard, *see under* Jensen Motors
Ltd.

Keiper, Fritz 34, 72–73
Keiper KG, *see under* RECARO and
Reutter
Kenrick, Archibald & Sons Ltd.,
management changes within
157–58
Kenrick family 32, 146, 156
Kenrick & Jefferson Ltd. (K&J) (printer
and stationery manufacturer) 112,
142–68
as a 'British Mittelstand' company
147, 162
Competitors of 161–62, 164, 166
Culture, changes in so-called 'K&J
Family' 143, 149, 150, 153, 168
Employees, their Knowledge and
Commitment 292–93
Family members' involvement in
management and board of
directors 143–44, 145, 147, 151,
155, 168
Financial performance
Capital investments 149, 150, 154,
166
Improving conditions in 1960s 150,
153–54

Prewar and postwar positive results
146
Problems in late 1950s and early
1960s 147, 154
Results in 1970s 165–66, 167 fig. 10
Governance, structure of and changes
to 156–57, 294–95
Industrial relations 292
Innovation within 149–50, 151, 153,
161–62
Computer industry and technology,
involvement in 161, 166, 168
Patents granted 151, 161–62
Inter-firm relations 291
Jefferson, Edward (K&J director) 143,
147
Jefferson family 146, 156
Jefferson, Frederick (K&J founder,
father of Fred and Edward) 32,
147
Jefferson, Frederick, "Mr. Fred" (K&J
director) 142, 147
Jefferson, K. Hugh (K&J director)
143, 144
Appointment as production director
158
Concerns about elder directors and
future 143–44, 148, 149, 151
Education and training 159
Views on preferred management
structure 160, 163, 294
Views on Tom Jefferson 159, 160,
168
Jefferson, Thomas (Tom) (K&J
managing director)
Accomplishments of 168–69
Acquisitions of companies by 161,
168
Appointment as joint managing
director, aged 32 151
Appointment as sole managing
director, aged 37 158
Character and management style
159, 160–61, 162
Commitment to K&J of 160, 162,
168
Death of 168, 295
Education and training 159
Innovativeness of 161, 166
Leadership of 161, 162, 168, 295
Sales, management of and influence
on 162, 165–66

Technical expertise of   159
Weaknesses and limitations of
    168–69
Kenrick, Peter (K&J director and
    chairman)   93
    Character and style   148–49, 151
    Commitment to K&J's success
        151
    Makes organisational changes and
        investments in mid-1960s
        150–51, 154
Kenrick, Wynn (K&J director and
    chairman)   147, 148, 150
Management structure   160, 163
    Differences of opinion between Tom
        Jefferson and Hugh Jefferson
        regarding   160, 163
Niche products, production by   112,
    162, 165, 166
Non-family managers and directors
    144, 145
    Hodgson, Simon, marketing director
        158
    Need for, within changing printing
        industry   155
    Plimmer, Jeremy (business
        development director and
        former apprentice)   159, 160,
        162, 166, 168
    Rose, Bertie, non-executive
        chairman   158
    Smart, Albert appointed as first
        non-family director   150–51,
        158
    Young, Mark (export sales manager)
        164–65
Paternalistic management style within
    142, 143, 149, 168
Printing industry, K&J compared with
    other companies within in 1970s
    159–60, 162–63, 164
Sales performance and organisation
    145–46
    Exports   149, 153, 164, 166
    Organisational and administrative
        strengths   152
    Prewar strengths of sales team   145,
        163
    Postwar limitations of sales team
        146
    Reorganisation in 1960s, 'Night of
        the Long Knives'   150, 163

Results in 1960s and 1970s   164,
    166, 167 fig. 10
Service longevity of workers and
    directors   143
Shareholders, challenges presented by
    146, 148, 150, 156–57, 166
Succession of directors within   36,
    144, 168
Strategy, weaknesses in   164–65
Trade unions, relations with   147–48
    Multiple unions within K&J   148
    Printing strike, 1959   147
    Union members' views of K&J
        management   155
    Wage agreements   147–48
Workforce and skills
    Apprentices   78–79
    Changing commitment of workforce
        149
    Employee numbers   155
    Skills within K&J   160, 161, 162,
        165
    Training   79, 93, 152
Kommanditgesellschaft (KG), company
    legal form   121, 184
Kreditanstalt für Wiederaufbau (KfW)
    (Credit Institute for Reconstruction)
    44–45

Lane, Christel (German sociologist)
    10–11, 64, 183, 184
Lazonick, William (American political
    economist)   13
Leibinger, Berthold (CEO of
    Trumpf, German machine-tool
    manufacturer)   36, 100, 102
Lewchuk, Wayne (Canadian labour and
    automotive economist)   272, 279,
    282, 287
Liberal Market Economy   12, 13
Lloyds Bank   53–59, 60–61
Lubinski, Christina (German historian)
    35, 119
Ludwigsburg, employment and economy
    within   194

Made in Germany   1, 83
Marshall, Alfred (British economist)   29
Max Planck Institute   105
Meister (see also Foremen)
    at Chr. Wandel   87, 115
    at Julius Schneider   87, 174, 178, 293

at Keiper   87
at Philipp Müller Nachf. Eugen Bucher
   GmbH & Co
at Stuttgarter Karosseriewerk Reutter
   87, 88 fig 3, 233, 268, 293, 294
Continuing importance of to German
   businesses   106–107
Contrasted with British foremen
   81–82, 83, 97, 285, 294, 298
Contrasted with British managers   89
Definition of term   70 n. 26, 82–83,
   177, 185
Disadvantages of, potential   86–87
Impact on West German productivity
   and business structures and
   performance   82, 88–89, 185,
   298
Origins of, in German history   82
Place in West German management
   81, 82
Qualifications of   81–82, 107
Training
   Content of courses   83–86
   Continuing popularity of   97
   Examinations   86, 107
   Postwar development of, by IHK
      70, 83–86
Midland Bank   52, 53–55, 56
Mittelstand
Benefits derived from availability of
   engineers   106
Excessive admiration of, by
   non-German authors   17
Definition   4–5, 6
   by Institute für
      Mittelstandsforschung (IfM)
      6
   by Ludwig Erhard   5
   by *Sparkasse* organisation   6
Importance to German economy   2, 11
Model, continuing value of   300–02
Networks and clusters of   30, 261–62
Niche products, creation by   1, 5, 48,
   49, 88, 98, 106, 112, 115, 122,
   240, 259, 260, 299
Romanticisation of, warnings against
   17
Values   5–6, 198, 249, 260
Views of, outside Germany   2–4
Mittelstandsromantik (romanticising of
   Mittelstand)   17

Motorways, British development of
   214–16
Contrasted with German *Autobahn*
   developments   214, 215

Networks, local, in West Midlands   31–32

Ownership, companies, differences
   between Britain and Germany   35

Patents
   by Jensen   243
   by Keiper   243
   by Porsche   242–43
   by Reutter / RECARO   233, 240,
      242–43, 255
Paternalistic management
   Decline of, in Britain   32
Philipp Müller Nachf. Eugen Bucher
   GmbH & Co.
   Apprentices in   73–74
   Banks and   48
   Financing of   47–48
   Meister in   87–88
   Niche products, production of   48
Pietism   34, 233, 234, 237
Plimmer, Jeremy (K&J manager)   159,
   160–61, 162, 166, 168
Porsche KG, *see also* under Reutter and
   RECARO
   Employment values   238
   Growth of   241, 247
   Industrial relations   292
   Patents and innovation   242–43
   Women workers   238, 282
   Workforce relations   238, 282
Porsche, Ferdinand (Ferry)   243, 245, 246
   n. 89, 247, 249, 252, 270, 282, 288
Porsche, Professor Ferdinand   234, 237
Porter, Michael (American economist)   29
Prais, Sigbert (German-British economist)
   82, 86, 102, 105
Printing industry, British   155–56, 159–60
Prisoners of war in Soviet Union, return
   to West Germany and personal
   consequences   177, 181, 183, 186
Prokurist (director with signatory powers)
   at Chr. Wandel   118, 122, 131, 132
   at Julius Schneider   181
   at Reutter   237
   Definition of term   118 n.18
Purpose, in the conduct of business   290

Common purpose in German firms
    183
Exemplified by Mittelstand company
    leaders   297
Facilitated by the Mittelstand Model
    301–02
Putsch, Friedrich-Wilhelm (managing
    director of Keiper KG)   245
Putsch, Wilhelm (managing director of
    Keiper KG, father of Ulrich and
    Friedrich-Wilhelm)   245, 256
Putsch, Ulrich (managing director of
    Keiper KG)   245, see also under
    RECARO

RECARO GmbH & Co. (automotive
    manufacturers), previously
    Stuttgarter Karosseriewerk Reutter
    232–263
Culture and working environment
    249–50, 254, 260
Employees, their Knowledge and
    Commitment   293
Family ownership   232, 248
    Family's concerns about
        management   248, 249, 252,
        256–57
Greger, Friedrich (engineer and diarist
    of company development)
    260–61, 262
Governance   295–96
Helmes, Norbert (assistant to directors
    1964–69, managing director
    1969)   238, 248, 251–52, 255–56,
    257
History before 1964, see under Reutter,
    Stuttgarter Karosseriewerk
Industrial relations   292
Keiper KG (automotive manufacturer)
    Acquires RECARO   257, 259
    Apprentices   73
    Differences in strategy and approach
        from RECARO   251–52,
        254, 259
    Growth of   262
    Innovativeness of   253–54
    Inter-firm relations   291
    Negotiations with, by Helmes and
        Müller   256
    Strategy   253, 254
        For RECARO following
            acquisition   260–61

Taumel (market-leading seat
    mechanism)   253–54, 255, 259
Innovativeness   249–50
Koch, Welf (grandson of Albert Reutter
    and putative future business
    leader)   244, 248, 256–57
Management failings   252, 254
Marketing and public relations   250
Müller, B.W., (chairman of
    shareholders' council)   249, 255,
    256
Müller-Scholl, Max (managing director
    of Reutter, 1953 to 1963, then of
    RECARO to 1969)   249, 252,
    255, 295
Niche products, production by   249,
    251, 259
Patents   251, 255
Porsche AG, customer of RECARO
    Concessions to, by RECARO
        management   255
    Contract with   246–47, 255
    Changing relations with   252–3,
        254
    Women workers   238, 282
    Workforce relations   238, 282
Production and operations   251–53
Putsch, Martin (owner of RECARO
    Holding GmbH)   262–63
Putsch, Ulrich (Keiper owner and
    managing director and acquirer
    of RECARO)
    Origins and education   253
    Leadership by   257, 262, 296, 298
    Product philosophy   254
    Values of   261, 262–63
Schwäbisch Hall (town in Baden-
    Württemberg, manufacturing
    location of RECARO)   254,
    261–62
Seat-reclining mechanism
    (Liegesitzbeschlag)   250–51
Sportsitz (sports seat) and Idealsitz
    249, 250 fig. 20, 259, 260
Strategy, constraints and options   249,
    251
    Diversification, failings of   254
    Helmes and Müller approaches to
        255–57
    Questioned and condemned by
        Reutter and Koch families
        256–57

Switzerland, RECARO AG subsidiary
business in 240
Values 232, 257, 259
Vocational training 293–94
RECARO Aircraft Seating
Apprentices 294 n. 6
Employment and recruitment practices
107
Establishment and early history
260–63
Innovativeness 232, 259
Sales performance 2018 232
Recession
in Britain and/or British industries
206, 208, 217, 228, 229, 269
in West Germany and/or West German
industries 47, 186–87, 188, 190,
257
Reconstruction after war damage
Railway bridges in Germany 175–76
REFA (German operations-improvement
consultancy and approach) 85, 260
Religion 32, 34, 233, 234, 237
Research approach and methodology
14–17
Choice of Baden-Württemberg and
West Midlands 15
Choice of case-study companies
15–16
Constraints upon 16
Focus of research questions 15
Sources, use of and limitations of
16–17
Reutlingen 33, 115
Metal-cloth industry 115, 120
Postwar recovery of 120–121
Decline of 139, 140
Postwar conditions in 117
Reutter, Stuttgarter Karosseriewerk
(automotive manufacturers)
113–14
Beierbach, Walter (technical leader,
Prokurist, co-managing director)
237, 295
Moves to Porsche following
acquisition 247
Pietist faith and personal values
237
Relations with Meister and workers
237
Technical skills of 247
Culture 233, 235, 238

Customers
Daimler-Benz 10, 233, 252, 260
Opel 240
Porsche, see separate entry below
Wanderer 233, 237
Employees, their Knowledge and
Commitment 293
Families, Reutter and Koch, ownership
by 244–45, 248
Financial Performance
Annual results 236, 239, 241, 242
Currency reform, June 1948, impact
of 236
Financial reserves 235, 241
Postwar conditions 235, 236
Shareholders and dividends 241
Greger, Friedrich (engineer and diarist
of company development) 239,
244, 245, 246, 248
Industrial relations 292
Innovativeness 233
Inter-firm relations 291
Keiper KG, competition with 240, 245
Koch, Theodor (joint managing
director) 234
Killed following air-raid, 1944 234
Koch, Welf (grandson of Albert Reutter
and putative future business
leader) 244, 248
Körner, Ernst (managing director 1944
to 1953) 234
Meister at Reutter
Contribution of 87, 88 fig 3, 237,
268, 292, 293, 294
Decisive factor in appointment by
Porsche 237–38
Müller, B.W., (chairman of
shareholders' council) 244
Müller-Scholl, Max (managing director,
1953 to 1963, then of RECARO
to 1970)
Appointment and early career
experience 238
Management of company 243, 295
Personal values 238
Niche products, production by 240
Patents 233, 240, 242, 243, 247
Porsche KG
Acquisition of Reutter 245–46, 247
Appointment of Reutter as
body-builder for Porsche 356
237–38

Dependency of Reutter on   239–40,
    245, 246
Ferdinand, Professor   237
Ferdinand (Ferry)   243, 245, 247
Reutter begins relationship with in
    1930s   234
Reutter's changing relationship
    with, in 1960s   243, 244
Women workers at   282
Production and operations   233,
    234–35
Porsche 356, demands of
    manufacturing   238–39
Sale of company to Porsche, 1963
    245–47
Seat-reclining mechanism
    (*Liegesitzbeschlag*)   233, 240,
    245, 247
Reutter, Albert (co-owner and joint
    managing director)   233
Killed following air-raid, 1944   234
Reutter, Fritz, death in 1961   244
Reutter, Otto (technical director), killed
    at Stalingrad, 1942   234
Reutter, Wilhelm (founder and
    co-owner)   233
Strategy, constraints and options   240,
    243–45, 247–48
Switzerland, subsidiary business in   240
Values of company and owners   233,
    234
Vocational training   294
Women workers   238, 282
Workforce and skills   233, 235, 236
    Commitment of staff and workers to
        company   239
    Equal treatment of sexes   238
    Welfare of workers   238, 239, 241,
        246
    Women workers   238, 282
Zuffenhausen, factory at   233, 237,
    246

Sales, British weaknesses in   152–53, 164
Sanderson, Michael (British educational
    historian)   64, 75–76
Saynor, John (British bank manager)
    57–59, 61
Schneider, Julius GmbH & Co. KG
    (steelwork fabricators)   112
    Closure of business   195–98
    Competitors   195

Construction industry, changes to
    193–94
Currency reform, 20 June 1948, impact
    of on business   173
Employees, their Knowledge and
    Commitment   293
Fiftieth Anniversary celebrations, 1960
    179–83
    Discussion of company's culture
        and values   179–80
    Duty, of business owner and of staff
        181–82
    Emotional engagement of staff with
        company   182
Financial management and
    performance   170–71, 172, 185
    Bank relationships   46–47, 196–97
    Capital investment   177, 178, 185,
        190
    Costs   186, 190, 191 fig. 13, 192 fig.
        14, 192 fig. 15, 196
Foundation and early growth   169
Governance and legal forms   177,
    183–84, 186–87, 294
Hege, Karl (senior engineer, *Prokurist*,
    managing director)
    Becomes business leader on death of
        Rolf Walz   186
    Decision to close business   193–98
    Concerns over increasing costs to
        business   190
    Personal history of Schneider
        169–98 *passim*
    Praise of Walz family and their
        values   182–83
    Promotion within business   184
Industrial relations   292
Inter-firm relations   291
Ludwigsburg, move to and premises
    in   178
Management and staff structure   174,
    177, 184
Mann + Hummel GmbH, support for
    Schneider during closure period
    195, 197
Material supply problems, postwar
    174–76, 217
Meister, engagement in business   174,
    177, 185
Postwar management and operation
    under American controls
    171–72

Reputation, company's 197
Sales
  Before and during war 172
  Growth in postwar period 172–74,
    180 fig. 11, 185, 190 fig. 12,
    193
  Lossmaking, during final year of
    operations 196
  Major projects delivered 176, 187,
    197
  Succession problems in 36, 186,
    197–98
Trade association, Verband der
  Metallindustrie (Metal Industry
  Association) 197
Trade union, IG Metall 197
Vocational training 293–94
Walz, Karl (business owner)
  Becomes partner and then owner
    169–70
  Character and work values 171,
    174, 176–77, 182, 295
  Illness and death 177
  Wartime work 170–71, 172
Walz, Rolf (business owner)
  Accountability and sense of
    commitment to firm 177,
    178, 184, 295
  as an *Unternehmer* (entrepreneur),
    his values and sense of duty
    181–83
  Death, aged 48 in 1967 186
  Invests in new facilities 178, 185
  Prisoner of war in Soviet Union
    177, 181, 183, 186
  Studies at TH Stuttgart 100, 177
Workforce and skills
  Apprentices 188
  Cost of 190, 196, 198
  Employee numbers 169, 177, 185,
    187, 193
  'Guest workers', employment of
    187–88
  Loss of work and re-engagement
    194, 195–96
  Redundancy, packages for 197, 198
Second World War 21–22
  British difficulties in recovering from
    22
  British workers' attitudes after 32
  German attitudes after 33

Impact on British economy and
  population 21–22
Impact on German economy and
  population 22–23
K&J benefits financially from war work
  143
Surviving German assets after 23
Simon, Hermann 3
Skills 64, 68, 293–94, 297
  at Chr. Wandel 135
  Britain's 'low skills equilibrium' 76,
    80
  in West Germany, examination of
    by Birmingham Productivity
    Association, 1955 76–77
  Shortage of, in Britain 76
  West Germany's 'high skills
    equilibrium' 80
SME (Small and medium-size enterprises)
  British banks and
  British Governmental policy towards
    11
  EU definition 5
  Importance to British economy 11
  Institute for Mittelstand Research
    definition 5
Sparkasse (savings banks), *see under* Banks
Steel
  Supply difficulties in Germany
    174–75, 188, 217
  Supply difficulties in Britain 201–02,
    217–19, 218 fig. 18
Steinbeis Foundation 105
Stunde Null (Zero Hour), 1945 117
Stuttgart
  War damage to 22
  Postwar economy of 27
  Urban motorway in 214
Swabians
  Industriousness of 27, 33, 34, 121, 180
  Self-identity of 34
Succession, in family firms 35–37, 205,
  223

Tax, British inheritance and impact on
  family firms 157
Technical and vocational education 9, 12,
  13, 31, 38, 64, 67–71, 76, 293–94, 298
  Importance to German system
    (Herrigel) 9
Technische Hochschule Karlsruhe 99 fig. 4,
  100, 102

Technische Hochschule Stuttgart   99 fig
   4, 100
   Civil Engineering curriculum, 1910
      100, 101 fig 5
   Mechanical Engineering curriculum,
      1910   100
   Mechanical Engineering curriculum,
      1948   100, 102, 103 fig 6
Technische Hochschule Mannheim   99
   fig 4
Trumpf, machine-tool manufacturer   36,
   100

Universities
   Aston, *see* Aston University
   Birmingham, *see* Birmingham
      University
   Engineering and technical graduates,
      comparisons between Baden-
      Württemberg and Birmingham
      99 fig 4
   Loughborough
   Warwick
Unternehmer (entrepreneur),
   characteristics of   181–83

Varieties of Capitalism debate   11–14,
   290–91
   Hall, Peter and David Soskice   12
   Coordinated Market Economy
      definition   12, 13
   Critics of   12
   Liberal Market Economy definition
      12, 13
   Spheres (industrial relations,
      vocational training and
      education, corporate
      governance, inter-firm
      relationships, employees'
      knowledge and commitment)
      12, 291–96, and under each
      company's index entry
Vocational training, *see* Technical and
   vocational education

Wagner, Karin (German economist)   82,
   106
Walker, Ivan (K&J factory supervisor)
   93, 144, 159
Wandel, Chr. KG (paper-making
   equipment manufacturer)   111,
   115–141

Banks, relations with   45–46, 140
Betriebsrat (works council)   134
Centenary celebrations and celebration
   of achievements, 1969   129
Decline and demise of, 1970 to 1995
   135–41
Employees, their Knowledge and
   Commitment   293
Factory rebuilding   119
   and limitations on business's
      development   119
Foundation and early history of, 1869
   to 1945   115–16
Governance   294
Innovation, Research & Development
   138
Insolvency declared   140–41
Inter-firm relations   291
Machine production   124, 138
Maurer, Arthur, former *Prokurist* and
   subsequent competitor   118,
   132, 133, 140
Meister within   130, 131, 135
Operations and management, 1950 to
   1970   129–35
   Reviewed critically by Schwäbische
      Treuhand management
      consultancy   129–33
Operational weaknesses   128, 133, 140
Paternalistic culture of   118
Personal financial liability of owners
   121
Prokurists within   118, 122, 130, 131,
   132
Sales management and culture at
   122–129, 138–39
   Commissions and incentive
      payments   124–25
   Export success   123–124, 140
   International agents and
      representatives network
      123–24
   Sales performance data   126–27 fig
      8, 128, 135–36, 137 fig 9
   Succession problems in   36, 141
   Vocational training   294
Wandel, Erich (business owner)
   117–118, 122
Wandel, Dr. Erna (business owner)
   Assumption of control of family's
      business   118
   Birthday, 70th   139

Company's insolvency, attitude prior
to 139–40
Covenant, sense of 118, 295
Criticisms of competence by
consultants 130
Leadership weaknesses 130, 131,
132
Management style 124, 134,
140–41
Relations with workforce 134
Wandel, Kurt (business owner)
118–19, 120–23, 130–33, 135
Workforce and skills
Apprentices 116, 118, 120, 121, 139
'Guest workers' (immigrant labour)
at 134, 135, 138
Labour relations 130–31, 134

Recruitment and retention
challenges 123, 134–35, 138
Skills and skill shortages 115, 122,
129, 135
Training 121, 129
West Midlands
Postwar economic conditions 25–26,
28
Wirtschaftswunder (economic miracle)
25, 136, 188, 197, 198
Reality of German businesses'
experience of 176, 178, 239–40,
261
Women workers 73, 147, 138, 238, 282
World War Two, *see* Second World War

Zero Hour, 1945, *see Stunde Null*

PEOPLE, MARKETS, GOODS:
ECONOMIES AND SOCIETIES IN HISTORY

ISSN: 2051-7467

PREVIOUS TITLES

1. *Landlords and Tenants in Britain, 1440–1660:
Tawney's* Agrarian Problem *Revisited*,
edited by Jane Whittle, 2013

2. *Child Workers and Industrial Health in Britain, 1780–1850*,
Peter Kirby, 2013

3. *Publishing Business in Eighteenth-Century England*,
James Raven, 2014

4. *The First Century of Welfare:
Poverty and Poor Relief in Lancashire, 1620–1730*,
Jonathan Healey, 2014

5. *Population, Welfare and Economic Change in Britain 1290–1834*,
edited by Chris Briggs, P.M. Kitson, and S.J. Thompson, 2014

6. *Crises in Economic and Social History: A Comparative Perspective*,
edited by A.T. Brown, Andy Burn, and Rob Doherty, 2015

7. *Slavery Hinterland: Transatlantic Slavery and
Continental Europe, 1680–1850*,
edited by Felix Brahm and Eve Rosenhaft, 2016

8. *Almshouses in Early Modern England:
Charitable Housing in the Mixed Economy of Welfare, 1550–1725*,
Angela Nicholls, 2017

9. *People, Places and Business Cultures:
Essays in Honour of Francesca Carnevali*,
edited by Paolo Di Martino, Andrew Popp, and Peter Scott, 2017

10. *Cameralism in Practice: State Administration
and Economy in Early Modern Europe*,
edited by Marten Seppel and Keith Tribe, 2017

11. *Servants in Rural Europe, 1400–1900,*
edited by Jane Whittle, 2017

12. *The Age of Machinery:
Engineering the Industrial Revolution, 1770–1850,*
Gillian Cookson, 2018

13. *Shoplifting in Eighteenth-Century England,*
Shelley Tickell, 2018

14. *Money and Markets: Essays in Honour of Martin Daunton,*
edited by Julian Hoppit, Duncan Needham, and Adrian Leonard, 2019

15. *Women and the Land, 1500–1900,*
edited by Amanda L. Capern, Briony McDonagh, and Jennifer Aston, 2019

16. *Globalized Peripheries:
Central Europe and the Atlantic World, 1680–1860,*
edited by Jutta Wimmler and Klaus Weber, 2020

17. *Financing Cotton: British Industrial Growth and Decline, 1780–2000,*
Steven Toms, 2020

18. *Quakers in the British Atlantic World, c.1660–1800,*
Esther Sahle, 2021

19. *The Great Famine in Ireland and Britain's Financial Crisis,*
Charles Read, 2022

Printed in the United States
by Baker & Taylor Publisher Services